Translated by : Dr Peter KING
Yvette MEAD

Published by the Press Syndicate of the University of Cambridge
The Pitt Building, Trumpington Street, Cambridge CB2 1RP
32 East 57th Street, New York, NY 10022, USA
10 Stamford Road, Oakleigh, Melbourne 3166, Australia

Originally published as *Les Pays-Bas Bourguignons*
by Mercatorfonds, Antwerp.

Printed in France

Library of Congress catalogue card number : 85-48192

British Library Cataloguing in Publication Data

Prevenier, Walter
  The Burgundian Netherlands.
  1. Netherlands — History — House of Burgundy, 1384-1477
  2. Netherlands — History — House of Habsburg, 1477-1556
  I. Title   II. Blockmans, Wim   III. Les Pays-Bas
  bourguignons. *English*
  949.2'01   DJ152

ISBN 0-521-30611-6

Jacket
Detail of *The Virgin and Child with a Benefactress and Mary Magdalen*, by the Master of the View on St Gudule.

(Liège, Musée Diocésain.)

Frontispiece
Jason and the Argonauts, page from *La fleur des histoires* by Jean Mansel.

(Brussels, Royal Library, Ms. 9231 fol. 109 V.)

THE BURGUNDIAN
NETHERLANDS

Cy comence hystoire de troyes qui aduint
au temps des luges disrael qui fut
chose grandement merueilleuse.

En vne des contrees de grece
auoit vn roy nōme peleus
lequel auoit vn neuueu
nōme Jason qui fu filz du

roy Eson. Et pour ce que Eson estoit
ancien peleus auoit le gouuernemēt
& Jason et du royāme Jason estoit
vaillant et renōme cheualier par
tout le monde Et pour ce que peleus
vey son nepueu Jason monter en si
grant auctorite Il eut doubte en son
ceur que Jason ne le rapport dancire

THE BURGUNDIAN NETHERLANDS

WALTER PREVENIER and WIM BLOCKMANS

Picture Research by AN BLOCKMANS-DELVA
Foreword by RICHARD VAUGHAN

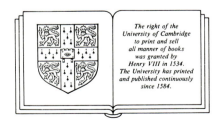

*The right of the
University of Cambridge
to print and sell
all manner of books
was granted by
Henry VIII in 1534.
The University has printed
and published continuously
since 1584.*

CAMBRIDGE UNIVERSITY PRESS
Cambridge   London   New York   New Rochelle
Melbourne   Sydney

Foreword

Here is a book that brings something new.   Even the period which it covers results from new ideas : it ranges over the years 1380 to circa 1530, so that the traditional break, brought about by the death of Charles the Bold in 1477, no longer interrupts the narrative.   The reader will also discern a new point of view, because the starting-point of this book is in no way Burgundian, or even nationalistic (in the sense of French or Dutch for example), but it is firmly based on a single geographic and economic area.   This is well defined in the first chapter.

A cursory glance is sufficient to show that the illustrations are an outstanding feature of this book, but the text is notable too.   This is not only a question of the variety of subject-matter, which ranges from social inequality and the standard of living, family incomes and care for the sick to music and sculpture, miniatures and literature.   What we have here is also a valid and clear reflection of our knowledge in the light of recent research.   It emerges clearly in spite of the varied contents of this book, that there is at present far from enough research being undertaken to solve all the problems so well presented in this book.   Let us hope that it will encourage research on the Burgundian Netherlands.

No one else can have done more in this respect than the authors of this book.   They have devoted all possible time and energy in the course of their active academic careers to research on the Burgundian Nether-lands.   Both have already for years now been authors of excellent books, articles and editions on this subject.   It would hardly be possible to find persons better qualified to write a book like this, than they are.   I am pleased and honoured to present this book to the world.

Prof. Dr. RICHARD VAUGHAN
Rijksuniversiteit Groningen

Introduction

The discussion of the 'Burgundian Netherlands' is based upon a number of choices which require some elucidation. What first comes to mind is of course the rule of the Dukes of Burgundy, descendants of the French royal House of Valois, who between 1384 and 1477, succeeded in uniting an increasing number of principalities in the Netherlands. The importance of the lands thus acquired outweighed from the outset that of the countries of origin, the Duchy of Burgundy with its appendages Charolais and Maconnais. Although extensive and reasonably fertile, not least for wine-growing, these regions were much more sparsely populated and less urbanised than the regions of the Netherlands. The importance of the homelands dwindled with every territorial acquisition made in the Netherlands. According to the ambiguous expression which they themselves used, the Netherlands were increasingly known as the 'landen van herwaerts over', 'the lands hither', (pays de par deça), where the court resided, while the Burgundian lands were regarded as the 'landen van derwaerts over', 'the lands thither', (pays de par-delà). These two ranges of territory were after all separated by an extensive area that did not belong to them. The ultimate result of this shifting of the focal point was that, even after the Duchy of Burgundy had become a French possession in 1477, the Netherlands remained a united territory and even continued to regard itself as 'Burgundian'. The concept Burgundian has come to have a far wider meaning than it had originally when it only had simply territorial and dynastic connotations, referring as it does now to a state structure, an economic and cultural entity, even a common way of life which may well be described as benign. It thus seemed logical to choose the Netherlands – the region of seventeen provinces under the Emperor Charles V – as the geographical area within which the social developments would be studied. Formal dynastic criteria seemed less appropriate than actual political, economic and cultural links. It is for this reason that the prince-bishoprics of Liège, Utrecht and Tournai, although they came under Burgundian rule only briefly or at a later stage, are included in the broad time-span of this book. In the same way, provinces such as Brabant and Holland, which did not come under Burgundian rule until several decades later than Flanders and Artois, have been considered in the context of the nascent unitary state from circa 1380 onwards.

The demise of the male lineage in the ducal dynasty, and the loss of the duchy of Burgundy in 1477, did not result in any serious break in this region. Even without Burgundy and the Burgundians, the Netherlands remained 'Burgundian'. But for how long? According to recent findings, the date 1500 – traditionally the date symbolising the dividing line between the 'Middle Ages' and the modern period – itself a somewhat superficial distinction – has little significance, especially for the Netherlands. Profound structural changes occured in the mid-sixteenth century, when colonial conquests began to have an effect on the world economy. It is difficult and in any case hardly meaningful to attach a precise date to fundamental processes of change. The old disappears gradually and exists for a time alongside the new. Between about 1520 and

1550, a change took place in the main sectors of the society of the Netherlands, which can be seen as signifying the end of the Burgundian structure and culture. So the crucial point is the year 1530. Politically the Netherlands became a peripheral area in the constitutional entity – a world empire – to which they belonged. In that year Charles V accepted his symbolic coronation as Emperor by the Pope in Bologna – the last German emperor to undergo this ritual. This was accompanied by the introduction of new central government structures. Socially and economically 1530 saw the beginning of a series of crises which followed each other in rapid succession and resulted in the so-called pre-revolution. Culturally, the transition from late Gothic to the Renaissance emerged in artistic forms and themes around 1530. Finally this was the period, too, in which religious clashes came to the fore; they highlighted existing antagonisms to such an extent that they became the disintegrating influence which resulted in the break-up of the seventeen provinces in 1585.

The simultaneous occurrence of all these trends is, in our opinion, by no means coincidental. Even in the 150 years from about 1380 to about 1530, which we have defined as 'Burgundian', we can perceive a very close link between the existence of a highly developed urban economy, the changes in the processes of government and the exceptional cultural activity in the Netherlands. The refined artistic taste exhibited by the Burgundian court, which it had inherited from its French background, would never have spread so extensively without a receptive urban culture. Nor would the dukes have been able to display their power to such an extent had they not been able to rely on the wealth of the Netherlands' urbanised regions. The Burgundian State and its culture therefore responded to the pulsation of social and economic developments. These in turn were influenced by the political affiliations.

These are the considerations that have determined where the emphases were to be laid in this study. It does not offer a chronological survey, since it is a thematic treatment which will highlight certain cultural features such as the formation of a state, the secularisation of thoughts and concepts, and laicisation. The economic order and the dynamic within it also features prominently. Everday life with its material concerns as well as their world of ideas are extensively dealt with. In the field of politics, more emphasis is placed upon processes than upon events; in the cultural sphere, artistic creativity is not treated as 'art for arts sake' but in the context of its social functions and inspirations. Should the reader find that Flanders and Brabant figure more prominently than other areas, then this is simply a reflection of their central and dominant position as leaders in every way. They had, moreover, come under Burgundian influence several decades earlier than most other principalities, so that 'Burgundianisation' took root earlier and deeper there.

Finally, the authors and the illustrator would like to pay a warm tribute to Maurits Naessens, without whose enthusiasm and years of perseverance, this book would never have been published.

1. Fifteenth century copy of a missing original illustrating the St Elisabeth flood of 18 th-19 th November 1421 at Dordrecht. The water gushes in (above right) through the Grote Waard dike.

(Amsterdam, Rijksmuseum).

1
The ecological
Situation

THE NETHERLANDS : does the plural form of this name refer to a multitude of components, or perhaps to a weak sense of common identity ? England, France and Germany are denoted in the singular, these Low Country regions are not. For centuries they have been perceived as having a lesser degree of unity. Because of the absence of a national monarchy they were not always immediately recognisable. Those foreigners who did not refer to these provinces by their collective name, called them after a single leading region, generally Flanders or Holland. This nomenclature has indeed stuck to discriminate respectively between the Southern and Northern Netherlands.

Where then is the unity which makes it possible for us to discuss a territory which is actually spread over five states today ? What *did* make it possible for the Dukes of Burgundy and their descendants from the House of Hapsburg to build a unified state here from the late fourteenth century until well into the sixteenth century ? Was their undertaking doomed to failure from the beginning, or was it based securely upon firm principles ? The answer to these questions is primarily related to the nature of the physical environment. Upon this were grafted economic activities and institutions which in their turn determined the development at a later stage.

The heritage : the environment

A GEOPOLITICAL UNITY ? The territory of the Netherlands can be seen as a rough triangle, one side of which is formed by a very long coastline, while along the two remaining sides there are no natural barriers. In the south and west the continuation of the softly undulating fields of grain is interrupted by small rivers. The Aa or the Canche have never restrained the Flemings' expansion aims, so where must they stop ? The Somme which in the Burgundian period too, was the southernmost border ever reached, was understandably regarded by the French as dangerously close to Paris. In other directions too, the game of agressive and defensive powers has determined where, at a particular time, a generally arbitrary border was to be established. Countless attempts by the Burgundians to round off their own territory remained an issue in the different parts of the realm during the fifteenth and sixteenth centuries, and even after this time.

The fact that the dynasty which united most of the Netherlands under its government, originated from Burgundy, created yet another problem. From a geopolitical point of view it was logical to strive for a link between the northern and southern possessions. Even the first descendant of the glorious dynasty, Philip the Bold, had to cope with the duality of his complex territories. By marrying Margaret de Male he acquired the county of Flanders, including Walloon-Flanders, the region of Lille, Douai and Orchies, and the adjacent province of Artois. Bordering the duchy of Burgundy, the county of Burgundy (Franche-Comté), the county of Nevers and the seigniory of Salins belonged to the estate of the daughter of the count of Flanders. (See Appendix : Map A).

In 1430, Philip the Good attempted to conquer Champagne. After the final acquisition of Luxembourg (1451), it seemed particularly worthwhile to attempt to conquer the duchy of Lorraine which lay in between. Charles the Bold succeeded in doing this in November 1475, but barely one year later he found himself having to contend with a revolt there. It could be seen as typical that this enterprising duke not only perished himself at the walls of Nancy at the zenith of his ambition to unite all 'Burgundian' lands, but thereby also lost Lorraine. Moreover, even the Burgundian homelands were finally overrun by French troops several days later. In 1477 it seemed that the dream to unite the 'lands hither' and the 'lands thither' had been in vain. From this point onwards virtually the entire 'Burgundian' territory lay in the Netherlands. The successors of Charles the Bold were always ready to make further territorial gains in this area, but they did not really concern themselves with their lost homelands.

The fact that the principalities of the Netherlands remained relatively small independent units until the fourteenth century, while large monarchies had grown up all around for centuries, requires some consideration. The division, approximately following the course of the river Scheldt, of the territory belonging on one side to the German Empire and on the other to the French Crown (Flanders and Artois), offers only a partial explanation for this, since neither of the major powers apparently succeeded in annexing the peripheral regions. There was, moreover, a reminder of the Middle Kingdom of Lorraine which had been created, after the death of Louis the Pious, between the western and eastern parts of the Empire of Charlemagne. Although this situation was apparently never viable, it was in the mind of Charles the Bold when he united a similar area for one year by conquering the duchy of Lorraine in 1475.

Another possible explanation is that the Netherlands were not only geographically located at the centre of the three great powers of Germany, France and England, but were also situated with their coasts and river-mouths at the junction of the most important connecting waterways. It was therefore in the interest of each of the great powers to ensure that none of the other powers gained control of such a strategic area, and also that a strong autonomous power did not come into existence there.

It is therefore crucial that the period in which the dukes of Burgundy gained the most important principalities of the Netherlands (*i.e.* 1384-1433) coincided with a period of decline in the three powerful neighbours. The German Empire as a whole was no longer capable of carrying through an effective policy. France and England invested their efforts in the Hundred Years War. Moreover, the first Burgundians, Philip the Bold and John the Fearless, held influential positions in the French court and could thus make use of the means available to them to serve their own dynastic interests. When the situation in Paris worsened for Duke John the Fearless, and especially for his son Philip, they chose the side of England. The duel between the giants was evidently advantageous for Burgundy. When the conflict eased towards the middle of the fifteenth century, the Burgundian state was already a *fait accompli.* But even after this time the Netherlands were to benefit from a policy of equilibrium, an opportunistic neutrality or a change of alliance.

POLITICAL BORDERS AND THE LANGUAGE FRONTIER The language frontier which gradually developed during the early Middle Ages after the Germanic invasion, extended from west to east, not least because it followed the principal Roman road between Cologne and

2. *Madonna and child with an anonymous benefactress and St Mary Magdalen.* The background scene is a fine illustration of the wealth of the harbour towns of the Burgundian Netherlands around 1470.

(Liège, Musée Diocésain. Master of the view of St Gudule).

Bavai. The borders of the principalities did not evolve until several centuries later. Broadly speaking they ran from north to south, following the direction of the Maas and Scheldt basins. A this stage these borders seemed to lie perpendicular to the language frontier, and all principalities in the Southern Netherlands were consequently inhabited by both Romance and Germanic-speaking peoples. During the nascent stages of the principalities, this presented no problems at all : the borders were still quite arbitrary ; every prince or nobleman attempted to expand his territory wherever possible and the ruling class of nobles was exceptionally mobile – one might almost be inclined to use the term 'international' – and Latin was the universal administrative language. From the thirteenth century however, a sense of nationalism and of territorial awareness began to prevail. As the vernacular began to penetrate government institutions, so the language problem came into being. This was particularly true of Flanders, where the municipal élite attempted to distinguish themselves from the rest of the populace by using French as their everyday language, thereby also declaring their preference for strong political links with the kingdom of France.

It was the numerical proportions and location of the nucleus within each principality that finally determined the issue. In Flanders only the relatively small areas of Lille, Douai and Orchies were French-speaking. This region had already been separated from Germanic Flanders between 1305 and 1384, and had developed its own independent institutions during this period. Under the dukes of Burgundy it became a separate governorship which only maintained superficial relations with the predominantly Dutch-speaking part of the country.

All the important towns in Brabant were situated in the Dutch-speaking areas, although the small towns of the French-speaking parts in the South regularly took part in representative assemblies. There was therefore within the duchy no segregation of the Walloon minority, which was respected in its own right although it could raise but a weak voice. The few Flemish villages in Hainault presented no more problems than did the Dutch minority in the prince-bishopric of Liège. Here too there was harmony between the recognition of higher authority and the tolerence of minorities. So it was that the Dutch-speaking towns in the prince-bishopric conducted their own separate consultations.

Such differences between the languages as there were on the eve of Burgundian unification, were essentially of a social and not a national nature. The distinction 'French-speaking' was the cause of many conflicts in Flanders during the fourteenth century, signifying as it did both a member of the municipal plutocracy and a link with that oppressive foreign power, France. In other regions, this social differentiation of language did not exist, and as a rule there was considerable tolerence in this area. Contracts between Flemish and Liège artisans during the revolts of the fourteenth century indicate that the conflicts were based upon social and political rather than linguistic differences. Only when the Burgundian administration began paying too little heed to the language of the populace did another conflict arise, which was in fact the expression of their hostility to centralisation.

TRANSPORT AND COMMUNICATION Can we then still speak of an acceptable cohesion between the Low Countries on the sea ? It was in fact precisely the geographical factors which provided a strong bonding element, namely the presence, within a relatively small area, of favourable communications. A predominantly flat relief provides no problems for overland transportation. For a technically unsophisticated society, waterways are by far the most economical means of transporting goods. Consequently both the coastal position of the Netherlands and the many rivers which cross them, were of vital importance. They linked the areas at the lower courses of the rivers with the granaries of Artois and Hainault, with the ore-producing Ardennes, and with the countless natural resources and commercial and artisan centres along the lengthy course of the Rhine.

If the Netherlands was one of the most densely populated areas of Europe in the late Middle Ages, and if trade and industry flourished there for several centuries – albeit with internal shifts – then it was largely a consequence of the exceptionally favourable geographical position, and was determined by the efficient use of a number of international trade routes and the establishment of a large network of ports. These routes were of crucial importance not only for the economy but also for the cultural and artistic commerce and the import and export of works of art, science and technology. The geographical factors can be classified in three groups : the proximity of the sea, the situation along navigable rivers, and the location at the junction of several overland routes which had evolved up to the Roman period.

NAVIGATION Seas obviously offered suitable routes to navigation which until the early sixteenth century hugged the coastlines. The navigational contacts between the coastal areas of the Netherlands and, for instance, the French and English ports were very close indeed. The combination of a long coastline and a tight network of rivers made it possible to achieve a high degree of internal communication and goods transportation. Moreover, they provided

3. Map showing the mouths of the Scheldt and Honte seen from the Flemish bank. Left: the island of Walcheren, right: South-Beveland; below, the numerous inlets and creeks of Flanders with the island of Biervliet in the centre. Natural evolution improved the navigability of the Western Scheldt, which greatly benefitted Antwerp.

(Antwerp, Town Archives. Detail of a map of the Scheldt drawn in 1504 or 1505 after an older map of 1468).

relatively easy links with the surrounding areas, and some that were more distant. The focal points of overseas trade were England, the French Atlantic coast and the Baltic. Coastal ports, especially Bruges with its outer harbours in the Zwin estuary, became involved in this trade. It is as well to remember that Bruges had been unable to receive sea-going vessels since as far back as the twelfth century, although coastal navigation was carried out in small barges. Damme acted as an outer port since its establishment in 1180. The progressive silting of the Zwin affected the small towns more adversely than it affected Bruges, which remained a leading town of importance. Only Sluis survived as a port since it remained accessible for ships of more than 100 tons until the sixteenth century.

Bruges made every attempt to maintain its links with the sea. In 1421 the waterway between Damme and Sluis was deepened. In 1461 a piloting service was introduced. In 1472 a channel was dug which would increase the current into the Zwin from a northerly direction in the proximity of Cadzand. In 1480 this channel was closed again because it appears to have had an adverse effect. In 1501 work was begun on a new canal which was to flow from the north-east. The result of all these efforts was, as is well known, disappointing. Part of the port functions at Bruges were taken over, towards 1400, by the harbours on the Walcheren coast. Middelburg in particular began to function increasingly as an outport where the freight from the sea-going vessels was transferred to smaller vessels, or taken overland to Bruges and beyond. Middelburg took over the previously mentioned trade-routes from Bruges and it also had connections on the one hand with North Germany and the Baltic as far as Russia, and on the other hand with Spain, Italy and the Levant. Her small satellite ports were important for wool (Veere), shipbuilding (Zierikzee), as sheltered winter ports for the German

4. Detail of the coloured map of the Reie at Bruges from the Civic Hall to the Dam Gate. The busy shipping and trading activities at the Dam Gate are shown here in detail.

(Bruges, Municipal Archives).

17

Hanse, and as an outer port (Arnemuiden). Middelburg even managed to take over the English wool trade from Bruges.

From the fifteenth century and into the sixteenth century, this readily adaptable town acted in a similar capacity as a sort of outport for Antwerp. But at the same time Middelburg maintained its trading function in conjunction with Bruges, and the activity in the Walcheren Roads were fairly strictly controlled by Bruges. Via the Zwin and Middelburg, Bruges could easily maintain the routes to Western France and England during the fifteenth century. Even when the port of Antwerp became more important during the fifteenth century, the Walcheren Roads remained an essential port of call for international shipping. Besides, the journey to Antwerp took a day or two longer and the quay at Antwerp provided mooring for only about twelve ships, so that the Scheldt delta can be regarded as a single complex with its various appropriate internal links. Ships of up to 600 tons could moor in the Walcheren Roads, well protected from the westerly winds. The Walcheren ports were therefore essential as trading centres, but this did not alter the fact that 85 % of the turnover came to Antwerp.

During the fifteenth century, still more infrastructural shifts occurred. The most important of these concern Antwerp and the towns of Holland. The traditional account of Antwerp usurping the role of Bruges after 1400, due to the silting of the Zwin, does not explain everything. The infrastructure was indeed a real factor, and it was also true that the floods of 1375-1376 and 1404 meant that sea-going vessels could reach Antwerp directly from the western

5. Miniature showing the inhabited world according to the *Etymologiae* of Isidorus of Seville, an encyclopaedia of the seventh century. The three known continents are, as it were, separated by a T within an O. This miniature comes from Jean Mansel's work *La Fleur des histoires* compiled between 1446 and 1451. This highly traditional image of the world still shows no signs of the rapid advances in geographical knowledge, namely in Portugal and Spain.

(Brussels, Royal Library, ms 9231, fo 281 Vº).

6. Flemish miniature depicting the Earthly Paradise from *Les sept âges du monde*, dating from about 1460.

(Brussels, Royal Library, ms 9047, fo 1 Vº).

branch of the Scheldt. The explanation for the rise of the Brabant ports after 1400 must, however, also take account of a number of other economical and political factors.

It is important to realise, however, that the contrast between Bruges and Antwerp as ports and trading centres in the fifteenth and sixteenth centuries has been overstressed. Both centres dealt in virtually the same range of goods with virtually the same foreign trading nations. Moreover, Bruges, Antwerp and Middelburg were not really hostile to each other ; in fact the Scheldt delta should rather be regarded as an economic and infrastructural whole. It is also important not to lose sight of the fact that the main trading routes to and from Antwerp before 1500 were overland routes, which would account for the fact that the economy of the Scheldt towns remained healthy after the blockade of the sea-route in 1585.

There was also another area in the northern Netherlands which was linked to international trading-routes : the towns situated around the Zuider Zee. This dates back to an old tradition from before 1200, when the overland and river links with North German towns of the Hanseatic League were established. After 1200 a larger type of ship, the *kogge*, was able to use the sea-route to the Hanse towns and even to the Scandinavian centres such as Schonen. Kampen, on the IJssel, became a leading town in this process, and her fleet was larger than that of all the towns of the northern Netherlands combined. This overseas trade which, in addition to the eastern route, included trade with western France and England, was centred mainly in the north – certainly up to 1400, after which it gradually declined in favour of the towns of Holland.

Another region, Holland, had therefore risen to a dominant position. In the thirteenth and fourteenth centuries, Dordrecht had been the only town of trading significance and had functioned as an intermediary port for the international trade between Flanders and the Hanseatic League. From about 1360 onwards, however, we see the gradual rise of merchant shipping in Amsterdam, with its international links with England, France (wine and salt) and in

7. Map of the mouth of the Zwin from the beginning of the sixteenth century showing the large-scale works which the town of Bruges undertook to improve the navigability of the Zwin. The dominant feature of the map is Sluis, surrounded by fortifying walls. To the right (on the north side of the town) is the "great castle", by the entrance to the route to Damme. Philip of Cleves, leader of the resistance against the Roman King Maximilian, remained in hiding in the castle of Sluis from 1488 to 1492. St Anna-ter-Muiden, Knokke, Heist and Blankenberge are shown on either side of the water. The tower of Burgundy rises up from the shores of Muiden. Known as the "small castle", it was built by Philip the Bold for the effective defence of the Zwin.

(Bruges, Municipal Archives).

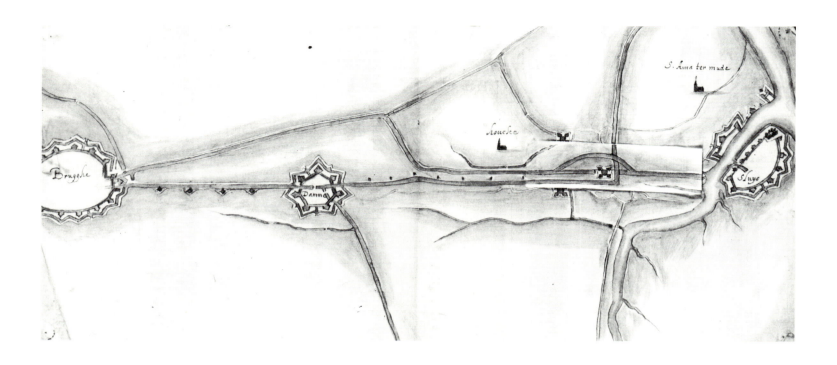

8. Map of the waterways between Bruges, Damme and Sluis during the period 1500-1665.

(Bruges, Municipal Archives).

particular Prussia and Russia, where it was to prove a formidable and undesirable competitor to the Hanse merchants, and resulted in, among other things, a privateers war between Holland and the Wendish towns (Lübeck). The late expansion of the towns of North Holland, in spite of its favourable geographical position, is connected with other environmental factors which will be discussed in the following paragraph. The port of Amsterdam was extremely well situated with its access to northern Germany and Scandinavia, the Zuider Zee (therefore also Deventer and Westphalia), and Brabant and Flanders via the inland waterways. Thanks to its strategic position, Amsterdam became dominant in eastern trade from the fifteenth century onwards, and in the Baltic trade Amsterdam could even be seen to function as Antwerp's outport.

To summarise, therefore, the Netherlands offered transit facilities, a temporary port of call and a destination for Baltic and Mediterranean trade. Originally, the Hanse towns dominated the scene, but from the fourteenth century onwards, the Holland ports became formidable competitors in the North. The Walcheren Roads and the Scheldt marked the northern limit of Mediterranean trade; the Genoese and Venetians traded principally via Sluis/Bruges and Southampton.

When attempting to explain the involvement in European trade of the Hollanders and the Flemings, particularly in the fourteenth and fifteenth centuries, we must not underestimate the language factor. From Boulogne to Novgorod, the merchants spoke or understood a similar language, which was based on Low German. In the Hanse towns this was the language of the dominant classes. The relationship between this and the dialects of the Netherlands was so close that communication problems rarely occurred. Moreover, the élite of the Flemish towns also had at least a passive knowledge of French. The proximity of France and in particular the French-speaking regions of Flanders, Hainault and Artois with whom close relations were maintained, improved the Flemish merchants' knowledge of French. With their knowledge of both Germanic and

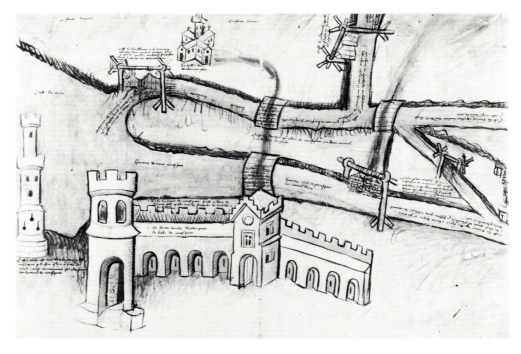

9. The locks at Nieuwpoort as they were in 1416. Nieuwpoort formed the junction of a number of canals linking Ypres with the sea.

(Brussels, State Archives).

10. Hanse cock-boat from the end of the fifteenth century. This type of ship was used for journeys between the Baltic and the North Sea. The capacity of such ships was 200-300 tons.

(Vienna, Graphische Sammlung Albertina).

Romance languages, they could fulfil the role of intermediaries between north-eastern and southern Europe. A similar competence was also present to a certain extent in south-east England–likewise a meeting place for Hanseatic and Mediterreanean merchants – thanks to the combination of French as the official language with the Germanic vernacular.

RIVER ROUTES As briefly mentioned already, the towns of the IJssel which even prior to 1200 had secured a link between northern Europe and the Rhineland, lost the sea routes and fell back on to the inland waterways during the fifteenth century. From about 1450 onwards, the IJssel became gradually less navigable for sea-going vessels, and this together with other factors explains the decline of Kampen in favour of Amsterdam. Kampen and the other IJssel towns such as Zwolle, Deventer, Elburg, Harderwijk and Zutphen, remained, nevertheless, important links in the regional river trading of the northern Netherlands, although this declined during the course of the fifteenth century.

A second important river route is that of the Maas and Rhine. These rivers were particularly suited to the transport of heavy bulk goods (grain, stone, metal, wood). The trade of various towns along the Maas such as Maastricht, Venlo and Roermond, but also Rhine towns such as Nijmegen, was centred on Dordrecht, which from the thirteenth century held a key position close to the river mouths. It lay at the pivot of trade between England, Brabant and Flanders on the one hand, and the central Rhineland and the North (IJssel) on the other. After 1300, Dordrecht successfully expanded into a staple market, expanding still further in 1351-1352 along all the waterways in the area. The river network around Dordrecht was extensively damaged by the flood of 1421, whereas navigability of the Honte and Zwin improved. This sealed the fate of Dordrecht, which declined in favour of Amsterdam and the southern ports.

The other harbours in that delta region, Delft, Schiedam and Rotterdam, were meanwhile only of marginal importance. It is

remarkable that a central position in the network of inland waterways can be an essential precondition for the general revival of a harbour town such as Rotterdam, which expanded demographically as well as economically during the fifteenth century. The town was favourably situated for sea-going routes long before this growth, but lacked a commercially active hinterland. When in 1340 a direct link with the Schie (and thus Delft) was constructed, Rotterdam and Delftshaven became an excellently situated focal point for international overseas trading routes on the one hand, and Dordrecht and the rest of the Netherlands on the other. The inland waterways meant that the town provided a useful link between Amsterdam and Zeeland, Brabant and Flanders.

The Scheldt was also an important trading route, albeit to a lesser extent, not only as a link between Antwerp and Bergen-op-Zoom and the sea, but also as a typical route for the transportation of stone and chalk between Tournai and the Scheldt basins. The many

11. Map of the town of Ghent bearing the date 1534; the foreground shows the abbey of St Bavo with the village of St Bavon at the meeting-point of the rivers Lys and Scheldt. The white dashes on the map represent bleaching fields.

(Ghent, Bijlokemuseum. Anonymous master).

22

12. Miniature by Simon Bening showing a crane in operation at the end of the fifteenth century.

(Munich, Bayerische Staatsbibliothek, Clm. 23638, fo 11 V°).

smaller rivers linked fairly important centres such as Mechelen, Brussels, Leuven, Aarschot and Lier with Antwerp. Towns such as Ypres which did not have such good links with the sea, because of distance or navigability, constructed canals in order to improve their position. The link between Ypres and the IJzer had already been canalised by the mid-thirteenth century, and further work was carried out there during the fourteenth century. The Ieperlee was a second canal, constructed in the fourteenth century, which provided a link between Ypres and Bruges in the polder area. In the beginning of the fifteenth century the inland waterway was constructed between Ypres and the Lys at Waasten, over a distance of 14 km. In 1450 the deepening of the waterway was carried out, and was financed by the levying of a toll. Via this route Bruges was linked, independently of Ghent, to the centres producing light textiles which reached the entire continent by way of the Zwin.

Ghent had constructed a canal, the Lieve, to Damme as early as the thirteenth century. This meant that ships, in particular the smaller ships, no longer needed to take the long route via Antwerp on the Scheldt, and the new canal was free of tolls. The people of Ghent constructed many other small canals in order to facilitate the import of peat from the Four Manors of Axel, Hulst, Assenede and Boechoute. During the fourteenth century, Bruges attempted, by constructing a direct link with the Lys near Deinze, to avoid the control which Ghent exercised over the import of grain from Artois. This 'New Lys' extended as far as Hansbeke, 13km to the west of Ghent. In 1379, however, Ghent permitted the extension of the canal as far as the Lys itself, for fear that its dominant position on the waterways might be challenged.

OVERLAND ROUTES It is important not to lose sight of the fact that the rivers were by no means the only available means of transport in the Netherlands. Iron from Liège and linen from Venlo were transported to Antwerp for export, not by river, but via the network of roads which had been built by the Romans.

The main route from the Rhineland and the annual fairs in Brabant to Flanders was the ancient Cologne-Bruges road via Maastricht, Leuven, Mechelen or Brussels and Ghent. The Hanse merchants laid many of these long-surviving roads in the Netherlands. Apart from those already mentioned, there was also the road from Hamburg to Bruges via Bremen, Deventer, Arnhem, Nijmegen and Antwerp (with a branch to Bergen-op-Zoom in view of the annual fair held there). In the 'Bruges Itinery' which expanded until the late perhaps even the mid-fourteenth century, the trading route runs to Lübeck (and further on to Novgorod and Moscow) via Gelderland or Cologne. There are rarely any indications of wayside churches along the route, and it was obviously therefore purely a trading link. The routes to France have much more to do with pilgrimages.

Heavy goods were transported via the sea-route connecting the Netherlands and France from the end of the thirteenth century when the Genoese galleys were launched. For lighter and more valuable goods, such as silk and spices, the overland routes were as important during the late Middle Ages as they had been before 1300. The English wool staple at Calais was linked to Bruges by a land route running along the dunes. Even the trade between England and Italy passed through several ports in the Netherlands, such as Kampen, Dordrecht and Antwerp, whence the land route over the Alps via Lorraine and Basel was used. The principal route southwards extended from Flanders, via Bapaume, to Paris and beyond. We

23

13. The clearing and laying of a road. Flemish miniature, mid-fifteenth century from the *Chroniques de Hainault.*

(Brussels, Royal Library, ms 9242 fo 270 V°).

may suppose that the people of the Middle Ages could travel an average distance of approximately 56 km per day.

To summarise, we can assume that the focal point of traffic in the west was Bruges and the ports of Flanders, and the focal points of the traffic in the east was Kampen and the IJssel towns. Dordrecht enjoyed a dominant position as a junction between England and the Rhineland. In the fifteenth century a number of routes to the Flemish ports were taken over by Antwerp and Middelburg, and the IJssel towns declined to the advantage of Amsterdam, while Rotterdam took over the position of Dordrecht. In the fifteenth century the most important port on the Anglo-French route was Antwerp, with its access to the Baltic, and Amsterdam was the central port for eastern trade. It is logical to conclude that the maritime situation of the Netherlands predetermined their role as a trading area, which indeed they still fulfil to this day. This was stimulated by a high degree of social interaction, giving an impetus absent from large land-locked areas. Hence a likemindedness developed which formed the basis for real integration. That such a sense of community could grow, was due to self-awareness and the determination to protect selfish interests. Individualism found fertile soil in these dynamic merchant communities which had little concern for the authorities.

THE LANDSCAPE Naturally the network of rivers was not so dense that it covered the whole of the Netherlands at one time, nor was the sea so close that its potential was felt to the same extent throughout the Netherlands. Large areas remained comparatively inaccessible, even during the Burgundian era, due to the absence of good connecting roads and attractive features. Extensive areas of forest remained even after the great period of reclamation lasting from the eleventh to the thirteenth century, as did extensive areas of heath. Forests are obstacles to human contact, the more so since they remain in areas where there are none of the incentives to reclaim that are brought about by the trade routes or expanding regions. The eastern Netherlands were, generally speaking, sparsely populated areas where little or no reclamation had been carried out. In particular the county of Namur, the duchies of Luxembourg and Limburg and parts of Guelders, the Veluwe and Drenthe. The Kempen and Zoniën Forest were extensive natural areas in Brabant; large tracts of heath were to be found in Flanders and also, particularly in the south-west, large woods (*e.g.* Niepe Forest).

The quality of the soil was another significant factor: the loamy soils of Flanders, Brabant, Artois and Hainault were highly suited to the cultivation of wheat, the best cereal crop. These were the areas where reclamation had first been carried out, and which had best been developed for human requirements. On the sandy soils of northern Flanders and Brabant there were more systematically planned villages, housing reclamation workers, where investment was high and the inhabitants had to be content with the cultivation of rye. During the fifteenth century, arable farming in Holland declined as large moorland areas were dug to provide peat. The remaining land was only suitable as meadow.

The soils of Holland were largely unsuitable for the cultivation of the basic bread-grains wheat and rye, due to their heavy and saliferous composition. These soils were better suited to the cultivation of barley and oats, which could be exported to Brabant in not inconsiderable quantities. The early establishment of Holland's brewing industry, which also appears to have achieved large-scale exports, could perhaps be attributed to the surplus of barley in this area. Low-lying areas, moreover, demanded heavy investment in drainage, which continued for longer and on a much larger scale in the north than in Flanders and Brabant. Gradually, therefore, the countryside of Holland became more orientated towards livestock and dairy production than towards the cultivation of grain, and hence also towards more trading. The regular subdivision of plots and the large-scale construction of dikes and irrigation channels, provide further evidence of human intervention. Land reclamation by systematic drainage was carried out to a far greater extent here than in the south, requiring organisation, discipline, and the rational application of resources. It is an intriguing hypothesis to explore

14. Early sixteenth century miniature depicting one of the twelve months from the *Breviarium Mayer van den Bergh.* Typical farming activities are depicted below each month. July: Hay-making with the scythe.

(Antwerp, Mayer van den Bergh Museum).

the connection between the way in which, by centuries of endeavour, large areas of Holland's soil have been wrested from the water, and certain attitudes and conceptions that are even now labelled as typically 'Dutch'. It is, however, certainly true that the natural environment of Holland was less favourable than that of, for example, Flanders or the IJssel region; hence the comparatively late expansion there which could only take hold as a result of laborious reclamation. Once things reached this stage, the relative infertility of the soil drove the agricultural population into the towns. Then the geographical factor, and in particular the position of Amsterdam, began to gain importance, and shipbuilding, fisheries, beer-brewing, and the production of peat, dairy produce and meat were stimulated. The relative decline was thus turned into expansion once the transformation of the landscape had given rise to a population increase of sufficient size to stimulate the growth of the towns.

16. View of part of a town ca 1425. Detail from *Madonna and Child* attributed to the Master of Flémalle.

(London, National Gallery).

15. Allegorical depiction of earthly transience by the northern Dutch master of *Spes Nostra* of about 1500; from the monastery of the Brothers of the common life in Delft.

(Amsterdam, Rijksmuseum).

Human habitation

SETTLEMENT PATTERNS   There is thus a close connection between the physical conditions of a certain region and the nature of its human inhabitants.   The best soils were used for cultivation and these were principally the higher loamy soils.   It was on these soils that the Romans had settled and built their roads.   These early individual reclamations can be recognised in the landscape by blocks of parcelled land usually separated by a natural enclosure.

The lower, marshy soils and also the dry sandy soils were reclaimed later in a more systematic manner from the thirteenth century onwards.   This can be seen in the extremely regular plots, often in the form of strips of land lying perpendicular to a central street or water-course.   Along the coast and rivers, very fertile polderland can be found which, as a consequence of encroachment, breached dikes and the human reactions to these, show mostly an irregular pattern.

The density of the town settlement is also related to the physical environment.   Since towns developed at crossings or junctions almost without exception, there must be a direct link between the density of the river network (including the coast) and the number of town settlements in a certain area.   This accounts for the contrast which has been constant throughout the history of the Netherlands, that is the contrast between the strongly urbanised provinces and the predominantly rural areas.   Flanders, Brabant, Liège (the prince-bishopric which extended for approximately 200 km along the Sambre and Maas), Zeeland, Holland and the IJssel and Zuider Zee regions.   The coasts and rivers have created countless confluences in these areas round which many large towns have developed.   Since rivers mean communication and the transport of people and goods, human interaction, mobility, creativity – these are all to be found pre-eminently in town communities.   Here the tensions are strongest, and the strongest impulses, which are even felt in the more rural areas, come from the towns.

The areas which were seemingly less penetrable in the Burgundian age because the woodlands were too extensive, the terrain too rough and the pace-making centres too far away, must not be regarded as entirely static or cut off.   Although the towns of Walloon-Brabant, Hainault, Artois, Luxembourg and the regions in the north-east usually numbered 1,000-2,000 inhabitants (and in only a single case as many as 10,000), these small towns were nevertheless to be found at fairly regular intervals of twenty to thirty km apart.   These areas also felt the heart-beat of the nearby over-populated areas.   Their economies felt the impact of a large demand for food and building materials, and were thus carried along in the dynamic wake of the urban areas, though often at a lower level of development.

THE WEIGHT OF NUMBERS   In the late Middle Ages the Netherlands, were, along with North Italy the most densely populated areas in the world.   In 1469 around the deltas of a series of rivers from Picardy to Friesland approximately 2,647,500 people were living in a relatively small space. (See Appendix : Table 4).   For certain regions and towns this calculation is not based on the counting of heads of households or tax-payers, but on estimates and extrapolations.   Nevertheless, this figure is more likely to be under than over-estimated.   These 2.6 million inhabitants were unevenly distributed throughout the area, with exceptionally high levels in Flanders,

Brabant and Holland with, respectively, more than 650,000, 400,000 and 250,000 inhabitants. (See Appendix ; Map B).

In order to determine the implications of these demographic figures for the Netherlands as a whole and also for its separate regions, there are a series of strategic variables which must be taken into consideration. The most important are : population density, population size in absolute figures, the degree of urbanisation, the distribution of the towns, and the size of these towns in absolute terms.

Remarkably, the first three of these variables are interdependent, and are in turn also linked to geographic and more specific infrastructural factors. We can distinguish a number of zones within the Netherlands which appear as crude concentric semi-circles, with their centre on the North Sea, showing that the absolute figures and percentages for each of the variables show a decline relative to their distance from the sea.

In the first maritime region with its deltas, dozens of seaports were gateways to world trade and export channels for the flourishing spearhead-industries of their day, which made the area viable for an unusually large number of inhabitants : on the one hand, Flanders with 650,000 inhabitants and on the other, Holland, which reached this level at a later stage. But more especially, it was here that the highest population densities were to be found : 78 inhabitants per km² in Flanders, and at least 66 inhabitants per km² in Holland. These areas were also the most urbanised : in Flanders (and Walloon-Flanders), 36% of the population lived in towns and in southern Holland this figure was as high as 54%. A high population density in rural areas was also connected to urban concentration since, undoubtedly, densely populated towns could not exist without an agrarian hinterland which could answer to the needs of these centres.

The second arc includes regions such as Brabant, Liège, North-Holland and Hainault. The largest of these areas had between

17. The harbour front at Antwerp, as sketched in 1520 by Albrecht Dürer during his tour of the Netherlands.

(Vienna, Graphische Sammlung Albertina).

200,000 (Hainault) and 400,000 (Brabant) inhabitants.   The density of these areas was respectively 40 and 41 inhabitants per km². The degree of urbanisation lay between 28% and 31%.   The relatively high values still shown in these territories was partly due to the ancient trading arteries such as the route via the towns of Brabant and Liège, which linked Bruges, the Flemish trading and finance centre, with Cologne, centre of the wealthy Rhineland.   Moreover, these centres often lay on important and navigable rivers : Liège and Namur on the Maas, other towns on the Sambre, Dijle, Demer, Zenne and Scheldt.   North Holland itself had the sea, the numerous subsidiary rivers and lakes.

The third zone includes Artois, Picardy, Friesland and Guelders.   The largest region (Artois) still had only 180,000 inhabitants.   Population density varied from levels as low as 16-35 habitants per km² (Guelders).   This zone in particular was urbanised to a far lesser extent, namely 21-25%, because apart from an occasional large town (Utrecht, Amiens), only medium-sized towns (i.e. with a maximum of 10,000 inhabitants) and smaller towns were to be found, and the economy was markedly rural.   These areas thus functioned for many centuries as granaries for the most urbanised areas.   There were always agricultural surpluses in these areas, even during difficult harvest years.

The fourth zone includes areas with an urban population of less than 20% which are, then, entirely agricultural : Luxembourg, the duchy of Limburg, the county of Boulogne and problably also Namur and Drenthe.   The population densities in these areas can reach very low levels (as low as the minimum of six per km² in Luxembourg) : elsewhere, according to the nature of the soil, it might be more than thirty : the wooded and variegated terrain of Luxembourg in contrast to the fertile maritime plain of Boulogne.   In this zone, the largest region had only 67,000 inhabitants.   There were, however, several towns in this zone (e.g. Luxembourg had 22), but, with one exception, none had more than 2,000 inhabitants.

THE SCALE OF URBANISATION   The demographic theory of zones distinguished quantitatively and qualitatively as discussed above, must nevertheless be considered with some reservation, at least where the extent and significance of the scale of urbanisation are concerned.

By European standards, the degree of urbanisation in the Netherlands was remarkably high.   For the entire area, the figure was 34% in the fifteenth century, but in certain areas such as Flanders, the figure was as high as 36%, and in South Holland it even reached 54%.   We may suppose that these last figures set the maximum level of urbanisation possible in such an area, since the rural area in the immediate vicinity, which had to supply food to the towns, could not have produced any more.   Agrarian research has shown that the agricultural areas of Flanders and Holland at that time were barely capable of expansion.   This is highlighted by the fact that part of the constant demand for grain in these areas was satisfied by additional grain imports from less-urbanised areas such as Artois (22% urbanised), or even by grain imported from the Baltic.

We must not, therefore, consider the urban percentages of each principality in isolation.   The medieval territories did not exist 'en vase clos', and an area outside the borders of one region could well function as an agricultural hinterland for that region.   In Overijssel for example, there were in 1474, sub-regions such as Salland, with 60% of the population living in towns, and Twente with 31% of the population living in towns.   These improbably high figures are due

18.   Pieter Bladelin, councillor, and treasurer to the Duke from 1444 to 1447, shown as benefactor of the Bladelin tryptich, *The Birth of Christ*, attributed to Rogier van der Weyden.

(Berlin-Dahlem, Staatliche Museen Preussischer Kulturbesitz, Gemäldegalerie. Central Panel).

to the presence of several trading centres such as Kampen, Deventer and Zwolle–all with 5-10,000 inhabitants–which were situated on overland routes and rivers, thereby ensuring excellent links with the trading centres of Holland, Flanders and the Rhineland. The loss of an agricultural base brought about by this urban imbalance was remedied by the import of foodstuffs from other regions in the Netherlands, and even from abroad, from places such as the Lower Rhine, Julich and Berg. It must be remembered, however, that these areas were only small in comparison to the size of Flanders, which as a whole reached a very high average.

The absolute size of the towns is another variable. If the towns are classified in five categories, of respectively : more than 20,000, 10,000, 5,000, 2,000 and less than 2,000, then the highest category will contain those areas where trade and industry predominated. Outstanding examples of such towns would be Ghent and Bruges, with respectively 64,000 and 46,000 inhabitants in the fourteenth century (and possibly slightly less during the fifteenth century). There was only one single town to the north of the Alps which was larger than Ghent, namely Paris. Around 1469 the only other towns that numbered more than 20,000 inhabitants were trading centres such as Amiens, Brussels, Antwerp and Liège. Towns with 10-20,000 inhabitants were, however, much more scattered.

A further interesting observation can be made if we look at a characteristic typology of the regions. In the typically agricultural principalities, the small towns with less than 2,000 inhabitants predominate ; this is the case in Luxembourg, the duchy of Limburg, Namur and Friesland. Of the 22 Hainault towns, twenty have less

19. Interior of a Burgundian chapel, the last remaining part of a fifteenth century patrician's residence in the Lange Nieuwstraat in Antwerp. The chapel was designed by master-builder Herman de Waeghemakere and built after 1493. The decorative paintings were completed in 1497 to mark the occasion of the solemnisation of the marriage of Philip the Fair to Johanna of Castille.

20. Fifteenth century panoramic view of Bruges. Detail from the central panel of the triptych *The Lamentation,* attributed to the master of the St Lucia Legend.

(Minneapolis, The Minneapolis Institute of Arts).

than 2,000 inhabitants. In agricultural areas which are more export-orientated such as Artois and Picardy, there will be just one fairly large town providing a trading centre.

In highly-urbanised Flanders, another phenomenon becomes apparent : two huge towns dominate the scene to such an extent that towns in the category with 10,000-20,000 inhabitants do not exist at all. So Ghent apparently offered no living space for smaller towns. Deinze, at a distance of 12 km, is the exception but it is not only small but being dependent on the Castellany of Courtrai it never developed into an autonomous town. The demands of a major city made it impossible to establish a fully-fledged township within a radius of some 20 km. This kind of domination by the large towns, which smacks of the ambitions of the Italian urban states, did not exist to the same extent in any other region during our period. The four major towns in Brabant, where it might also have been possible, were not quite large enough, and their ascendancy over the middle-sized towns was not sufficient to exert such tendencies. On the contrary, in Brabant we see the most even distribution of towns according to their populations. They hold each other in balance,

33

and even in their relation to rural areas, the balance is not really so one-sided. This balance was also to be seen in Holland and Guelders at the end of the fifteenth century, where towns of every category apart from the largest, had developed. Not until the late sixteenth century did the towns of Holland show such spectacular growth that they began to dominate the hinterland in a similar way.

The last variable is the distribution of the towns over the area in question. We have already seen that for the various economic motives, location along rivers and trading routes was the principal deciding factor. But there is yet another consideration that explains the location of small or very small towns in predominantly agricultural areas. There is always a constant need for centres within a distance of 20-30 km (a day's journey on foot) where a number of community services are available in the way of administration, jurisdiction, the housing of records, local or regional markets, specialised professions and services (*e.g.* financial). The number of inhabitants of such a centre has virtually no bearing upon this. A small town such as Marche in Luxembourg could perform such functions with a mere 450 inhabitants (1495). In Hainault, Leuze and nine other small towns each had approximately 900 inhabitants.

POPULATION DENSITY Why are certain areas generally so much more densely populated than others? The landscape is naturally a determining factor. In Holland and Flanders, with their very flat relief, a higher population density (of up to 78 per km²) is possible than in the wooded region of Luxembourg with its minimum density of six inhabitants per km². The location along good trading routes reinforces this first consideration: the artisans' workshops made it possible for large Flemish towns to develop into industrial and commercial giants. These towns in turn required a densely populated countryside, since their provisioning was determined by high agricultural production and good transport facilities.

Within the various regions, however, there were great variations in density. The significance of soil quality is illustrated by the widely diverging densities in the part of Hainault to the north of the Sambre (where the loamy soils can support 30-35 inhabitants per km²) and much less fertile soil to the south of the river (which barely supports ten inhabitants per km²). Elsewhere, infrastructural factors were dominant. In Artois, the most densely populated subregions (St Omer, Aire and Béthune) had good links with the sea via the Aa and with Flanders via the Lys, with densities of about 40 per km², while the region of St Pol was also linked to the sea via the Canche. In agrarian regions of the south and south-east, where road and waterways were comparatively poor, the population density rarely exceeds twenty inhabitants per km². The same factor accounts for the greater or lesser concentration of people in smaller or larger villages: in north west Artois, villages with more than 100 families were normal; in the south-east they were the exception. (See Appendix: Map B).

THE FAMILY UNIT Generally speaking, rural families were larger than urban families; the average size must have been respectively about 5 and 4.5 during the late Middle Ages. Nevertheless, this is also a variable which depends upon several factors.

There are regional differences: in the villages of Flanders the size of families varied between an average of 3.7 and 5.5 members, in the villages of Brabant the corresponding figure was 4.7, and in the Veluwe 5.8 (with local variations between 5 and 5.6). Crises were

21. Detail from *Rest during the Flight to Egypt* by Joachim Patenier. The painter placed great emphasis on rural life.

(Berlin-Dahlem, Staatliche Museen Preussischer Kulturbesitz, Gemäldegalerie).

a second factor. During times of famine and plague, the figure of 5.5 members per family in rural Flanders (1550-1900) fell to 4.5, reaching 3.7 at the lowest point. The variation in the standard of living was also related to this. This correlation was particularly evident in southern Europe. In the Netherlands, the only example is that of Ypres in 1506, where the average size of families in the richer areas of the town was six, while the corresponding figure among the poorer streets was 3.6.

As a consequence of this, there was also a correlation between the overall social and economic profiles of a town. Since there was a greater proportion of well-to-do families in trading towns such as Bruges, the average size of the family was higher (perhaps as much as five) than in the centres such as Ghent, Ypres and Leiden, where there was an extensive proletarian population and many small or single-person households. In Ypres throughout the fifteenth century, the average figure varied between 3.2 and 4.3. In 1581 the average size of the family in Leiden was 3.8. This correlation with the economic welfare of the town is borne out by the fact that the size of families in Ypres rose from 3.3 to 4.3 between 1412 and 1491, precisely at the time when Ypres' significance as an industrial centre was declining. In a medieval textile centre in prosperous times many new young inhabitants would be attracted from other towns, villages and outlying areas ; financially unable to support a family, they would marry later and there were consequently many single-person households, which in turn kept the average size of the household at a low level. In times of crisis these workers, like the poor who rightly or wrongly expect work and support in the prosperous towns, quickly drift away to other centres, since they are not restricted by strong social or economic ties.

It is difficult to be precise about incomplete families (widows and widowers) and about the number of unmarried adults. The latter category seems to have been large during the fourteenth and fifteenth centuries in the Netherlands. Probably periods of recession led to the conscious postponement of marriage. The purchasing power of the weaker groups in the economy was, during normal times, just sufficient to support an unmarried individual, but not sufficient to allow him to support a family. On the other hand, marriage to a widow from the established world of the professions and trade was a form of upward social mobility for those outside this establishment.

The demographic dynamic

In the course of the thirteenth century Europe recovered rapidly from the demographic blood-letting of the previous century caused by frequent famines, and in turn causing physical vulnerability and high mortality rates. Consequently the population figures for the most advanced economic regions in the Netherlands probably reached their peak around 1300. This at least is the impression to be gained from the large towns of Flanders and Artois. An indication of this was the need, which arose around 1300, to build walls round these towns, which were larger than at any time previously. In Ghent, 644 hectares of land were enclosed, compared with the previous area of 80 hectares, and the corresponding figures for Leuven are 410 hectares against 60 hectares. These walls proved adequate for many centuries, in some cases even seeming too capacious, where the enclosed towns never developed fully. In 1300 it was impossible to foresee that the coming decades would bring no growth, but only decline or stagnation to many regions.

This reversal of fortunes – most heavily felt from the middle of the fourteenth century but noticeable nevertheless from 1315 onwards – was brought about by precipitous growth in the thirteenth century with resultant famine by wars (Hundred Years War), which rendered countless acres of land infertile for decades to come, and also by the emergence of the plague from about 1348, the endemic nature of which slowed the population growth considerably.

Demographic figures relating to the Netherlands in the fifteenth century are, with the exception of a few towns, extremely scarce. So it is a hazardous enterprise to attempt a general survey. The early textile towns of Flanders – the large as well as the smaller towns such as Dendermonde and Aalst, and also centres in Brabant (Leuven) and Holland (Dordrecht) – had already reached their demographic peaks by 1300. The figures then declined from the mid-fourteenth century onwards. A typical example of this is Geraardsbergen, whose population fell from 4,500 to 3,700 between 1338 and 1375, and failed to restore earlier levels throughout the fourteenth and fifteenth centuries. This was also true of Leuven where the level of 20,000 inhabitants in 1300 was never reached again before the eighteenth century. It is not until that time that the newly developing centres of Antwerp, Bergen-op-Zoom, Mechelen and the towns of Holland begin to emerge, doubling their population between the end of the fourteenth and the end of the fifteenth century. The pattern of growth in the towns is therefore not uniform, although the following phase of growth can be distinguished : approximately 1000-1300 in Flanders and northern France ; 1100-1550 in Brabant ; 1200-1650 in Holland.

The situation in the countryside is somewhat better documented at least in Brabant and Hainault in the period 1370-1530/40 and Walloon-Flanders in the period 1450-1550. We may even assume that these trends were fairly representative of the demographic situation in the towns and villages since each expansion of the towns seemed to depend upon an excess of births in the villages. If we compare the two extremes of the period in question (circa 1370 and 1550), the number of inhabitants in the villages appears to be stagnating, or very slightly increasing. This, however, conceals a much more variable trend which remains unseen because the hearth census of the population was not carried out immediately prior to or immediately following periods of crisis.

22. May celebrations in a town.

(Brussels, Royal Library, miniature by Simon Bening (?) from the *Hennesy – Book of Hours of Notre Dame,* ms II 158 fo 5 V°).

During the pre-statistical phase, which extends from the fourteenth century to the eighteenth century in the areas with which we are concerned, individuals were not usually counted since statistically the governments were only concerned to know the number of taxable families. From the latter half of the fourteenth century therefore, in Hainault and Brabant (and later in certain other areas) so-called hearth censuses were carried out *i.e.* the number of families *grosso modo.*

According to the censuses of 1365 and 1424, the decline in the rural population of Hainault, from 150,000 to 100,000 inhabitants, reflects the fact that between 1349 and 1370, the plague struck on three occasions in the space of a single generation. The figure of 150,000 must therefore have been greatly exceeded before 1349, since the census of 1365 took place during a series of crises. After 1424, and possibly even after 1402, the number of inhabitants must have risen yet again to 150,000, and probably even higher (150,000

23. Mid-fifteenth century view of a town in the Southern Netherlands and the surrounding countryside. Detail from the work *The Blessed Virgin with the Carthusian Monk,* by an anonymous master from the Southern Netherlands.

(Berlin-Dahlem, Staatliche Museen Preussischer Kulturbesitz, Gemäldegalerie).

24. View of a town. Detail from *St Luke paints the Madonna,* attributed to Rogier van der Weyden.

(Boston, Museum of Fine Arts).

is the 1365 level, monitored after two plague epidemics), although there are no interim figures with which to support this. When the census of 1440 took place, immediately after the famine and plague of 1438/39, the rural population of Hainault had declined to a lower crisis-level, namely to 135,000. The recovery which apparently followed was interupted by yet another plague epidemic which lasted from 1456 to 1459. Recurrent epidemics of plague, preceded by wars, offer a possible explanation for the low figure of 105,000 in 1479. An indisputable increase in population from 115,000 to 170,000 did not become apparent until the period between the two censuses of 1501 and 1540.

This late expansion also took place in Walloon-Flanders ; between 1498 and 1549 the population increased from 52,000 to 81,750 inhabitants, and the population of Brabant also rose from 225,000 in 1496 to 317,000 in 1526. In the first decades of the sixteenth century, the annual percentage increases were 1.28 in Brabant, 1.19 in Hainault and 1.07 in Walloon-Flanders.

The results of the censuses in Brabant of 1437 and 1464, which revealed a total of 62,000 'hearths' in the villages, conceal the effects of the two epidemics of plague which struck in 1438/39 and 1456-1459. The figures for the interim period must have shown much lower and much higher numbers of families. When a census was carried out in Brabant during later crisis periods, the number of families fell to 56,700 (1473) and further to 54,500 (1480). Between 1464 and 1480 therefore, population had declined in absolute terms by 12%, which gives an annual decrease of 0.75%. Between 1480 and 1490, Brabant felt not only the effects of the plague and hunger, but also the serious effects of external and internal wars. We may suppose, therefore, that a dramatic decline ensued during these years and that the population was reduced to somewhere in the region of 40,000, since in 1496 (six years after the worst troubles), the rural population of Brabant still only amounted to 45,800 'hearths' – 16% less than in 1480, despite six years' recovery.

To summarise – the demographic situation in rural areas, and conceivably also throughout the Netherlands was as follows : stagnation between the fourteenth century and the end of the fifteenth century, with several interim declines brought about by crises and periods of slow recovery. At the beginning of the fourteenth century the population figures, at least those in the southern Netherlands, were considerably higher. In the first half of the sixteenth century there are unmistakable signs of growth. The contrast in the phasing of growth between the old textile centres of Flanders and later-developing towns such as Antwerp and the towns of Holland has already been mentioned above. The powerful expansion which occurred in Flanders until the thirteenth century was to be seen again in Holland and the central and northern parts of Brabant (in the regions of Antwerp and 's Hertogenbosch) from the end of the fourteenth century until the middle of the sixteenth century. There are nevertheless considerable differences between the two phases of growth : in Flanders the process continued uninterupted in the peace of the thirteenth century ; in Brabant and Holland the general rise was not without its setbacks – caused by famine and the epidemics of plague and war. The reintroduction into Europe of the plague virus in 1347 brought about an epidemic of gigantic proportions, which was not merely a consequence of the shortage of food.

PREDOMINANT FACTORS IN DEMOGRAPHIC EVOLUTION The demographic decline in Europe from about 1330-1350 was largely the result of a productivity crisis. The growth of the agricultural economy had been brought about principally by extending the area of land under cultivation ; investment in new techniques was of secondary importance. By the first half of the fourteenth century the amount of land in Flanders which could be transformed into farmland using the available technology, albeit at a high cost, had been exhausted. In certain infertile heath areas, plans for reclamation were even abandoned and less fertile agricultural land was abandoned in the course of the fourteenth century. The decline in population which began after 1350 meant that there was less demographic pressure upon productive resources, hence less of an imbalance. However, there were new factors which disrupted the situation : natural factors and war.

In the fifteenth century there were six long periods during which the price of grain was extremely high ; taken together, these periods spanned eighteen years. Prices were twice and even three times the normal level. Since bread was the cheapest foodstuff and consequently accounted for approximately half the budget of an ordinary worker, this situation led to starvation. The years of consecutive crises were particularly devastating and full recovery was not possible since the grain stored for sowing the following year was gradually consumed. The physical debilitation of the adults also endangered the survival prospects of the children. The generation following a crisis was rarely large, also because of the frequent postponement of marriages. There was, however, less death from starvation and dropsy than during the fourteenth century. Mortality did not strike any less hard, although it did so in a less direct manner. Hunger led to debility and consequently lowered resistance to infection, in particular the plague.

This second natural phenomenon reappeared in Europe after some centuries, in 1347. The mortality rate in one single region varied from 25% to 40%. The impact of the Black Death was felt throughout the Netherlands : in Holland where the fatalities were sometimes as high as four times the normal level, in Utrecht, Guelders, Friesland and Groningen ; perhaps to a lesser extent in Brabant, northern Flanders and Hainault, but higher in the south of these provinces. Further outbreaks of plague occurred virtually every ten years until 1400, and affected two complete generations who were unable to recover. The young were particularly vulnerable to this disease ; this led to a decline in the birth rate, the effects of which were felt demographically for many years to come, in addition to the initial direct mortality.

This was the background to the previously noted population decline in the latter half of the fourteenth century. In the fifteenth century epidemics of plague were less general, since the disease had become endemic. The virus did not usually strike all areas simultaneously, although it did so whenever there was hunger, or troop movements which increased the risk of contagion. The combination of hunger, war and plague in 1436-1439, 1456-1458 and in the 1480s had catastrophic consequences. The population figures showed repeated periods of marked decline, in between which there were repeated periods of slow recovery.

Such far-reaching crises left a profound mark, since everyone, poor

25. The oldest known map of Bruges. Left, the Dam gate complex; slightly to the right the two great sailing ships lying in the so-called Vuil Reitje, and below, an incline along which vessels were dragged on wheeled carriages.

(Bruges, Town Hall. Anonymous master ca 1500).

or rich, young or old, was vulnerable, although the poor and the young were particularly so. Plague of the lungs was, in almost all cases, fatal within three days, while bubonic plague (the form of the disease caused by the bite of an infected flea), caused awful black pustules, and in two-thirds of the cases brought death within ten days. This is the record of the sickness to be found in the chronicles, one of which relates that in 1438,

"There was then in Bruges and other places much death from the epidemic of ulcers and burning fever; these people were one day healthy and the next day dead. And this death lasted from Whitsun until St Martinmass" (1st June until 11th November). The following epitaph of the gentleman from Pittem, placed in the church there, is also enlightening : *Here lies Daniel van Claerhout*
Son of master Daniel
and mistress Jacquemine
van Dovie, daughter of
master Jacob van
Dovie knight, lord of
Nieukercke, Meulebeke,
Who both died, man and
wife from the plague of 1438 which
was so great that year that more
than one third of the people died.

The announcement of the deaths of one third of the population was not totally unrealistic; the death toll did in fact reach these proportions in certain villages. The death toll in Bruges can be estimated at approximately one fifth of the population.

War can also have many different effects upon demography. For example, destruction of the countryside of Flanders, which took place between 1379 and 1385, resulted in a serious deterioration in food supplies. Wars also disrupted the normal trading routes, causing increased migration because of the lack of employment, and eventually also a decline in the number of marriages. Wars had a particularly adverse effect on the economy in the latter half of the fifteenth century. After the end of these upheavals in about 1492, a steady expansion of the population was once more possible.

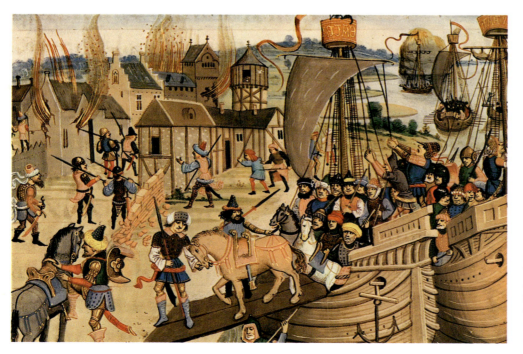

26. Disembarkation of horses and crew. The Burgundian dukes had at their disposal a fleet which was, however, rarely successful. The fleet's greatest worry was defending the coast against pirates. One of their tactics was to burn down the wooden houses.

(Brussels, Royal Library, ms 8, fo 333 V°).

In the earlier discussion there was a brief reference to migration as a demographic factor. The considerable numbers of migrants often moving to the towns indicate that many people (namely of course in the Netherlands, the marginal groups such as unskilled workers, the poor and the single) moved continually between the towns and the countryside, or from one town to another, in accordance with the real or supposed opportunities in these towns and villages. The tendency was for people to leave declining industrial towns such as Ypres and Dixmuide, in favour of towns with a better reputation or wider range of economic activities, such as Nieuwpoort and Bruges. There was also a tendency to move towards rural communities in south-west Flanders or north-east Brabant, where the rural textile industry offered new opportunities. In the late fifteenth century, people flowed into the rapidly developing regions such as Antwerp, Mechelen and 's Hertogenbosch where they expected to find employment and better social facilities (such as poor relief, for example). If this did not work out in practice, the people left again for new lands of promise.

That these 'itinerant peoples' were mainly vagrants and the less educated should not come as a surprise. They had no pressing organic links with the 'establishment' of trades and professions; they were not bound to the town by the ownership of land or property; they were often unmarried and still fairly young. It can be stated with some certainty, however, that a great deal of this migration covers up mere destitution. But the migration was not just an arbitrary to-ing and fro-ing. In the earliest phases of growth, immigration into the towns was principally from the surrounding rural areas.

TOWN AND COUNTRY MIGRATORY DRIFT There is a striking correlation between the demographic evolution of the towns and the countryside. Whenever the population of the towns showed a sudden decline, the gap was quickly filled from surrounding rural areas. Equally, during each starvation crisis or war, we see a retreat to within the safer town walls. In the fairly peaceful years between 1473 and 1480, the rural population of Brabant decreased by 10,500, while the population of the towns increased by about 14,000. Here we can discern an even more remarkable mechanism, namely a variation in the rate of demographic recovery. Between 1480 and 1496 – during the worst crisis of the whole century – the rural population of Brabant declined yet again, this time by 43,000, while the towns lost a mere 1,000 inhabitants. In both cases mortality dealt a hard blow, but in the towns, where concentration increased the risk of infection, the effects were more severe. However, the losses of the towns were quickly compensated by migration from the villages; the marked decline in the population of the villages therefore implies both death in the villages themselves and emigration to the towns. The decline in the urban population must have been considerably higher than 10,800 inhabitants, but was camouflaged by large-scale immigration.

A typical indication of this interpretation of migratory osmosis can be seen in an analysis of the immigration into several towns. In the first half of the fifteenth century, 450 immigrant citizens were registered in Nieuwpoort, which including family members, represents a total of approximately 2,000; however, the population only increased from about 3,200 to about 3,300 during this period. The same indications were to be found in Bruges, though on a larger scale. This was also true of Leiden, where the population increased

by a mere 800 between 1398 and 1418, despite the fact that 260 people immigrated there each year. There must have been therefore, apart from a high mortality rate (and a low birthrate ?) a still higher rate of emigration from the towns. The dubious standards of hygiene in the towns ensured that the mortality rate was generally high, and would have been much higher were it not for the regular burning down of the wooden houses, thereby destroying the focus of infection. The permanent flow of immigrants was therefore the only factor which maintained the population level. Only in a few cases (such as Antwerp and Holland) was the attraction so great and the employment prospects so good that these centres could actually expand.

27. A time calendar dial, ca 1500 which was originally a clock face. Symbolic depictions relating to the hourly and seasonal changes and to the influence of the planets on human lives are placed in concentric circles.

(Leuven, City Museums. Leuven master, ca 1500).

THE SUCCESS AND DECLINE OF THE TOWNS During the fourteenth and fifteenth centuries, the general stability of the towns was in a number of cases positively or negatively affected as a result of some external factor. The most likely cause was economic prosperity and the prospects of employment. At the peak of their economic expansion, a few years before and after 1300, the population of the Flemish towns reached a figure which has never been equalled before the eighteenth century. The towns of Holland such as Haarlem, Delft, Gouda, Amsterdam, Rotterdam and Leiden whose population often more than doubled between 1398 and 1514 equally showed a steady economic expansion. The growth of Antwerp was even more spectacular : from 5,700 inhabitants in 1374 to 15,500 in 1437, 30,000 in 1496 and 39,000 in 1526. Moreover, if those living outside the town walls are taken into account, then the whole agglomeration numbered between 44,000 and 49,000 inhabitants in 1496 and between 57,000 and 63,000 in 1526.

It is also typical that many smaller secondary towns were to be found in the vicinity of the growth centres of Amsterdam and Antwerp : examples of such towns are Bergen-op-Zoom, 's Hertogenbosch, Lier, Mechelen, Herentals and Aarschot, which can be seen as industrial satelites of the Antwerp metropolis.

During the fifteenth century, pessimistic prospects led to the gradual desertion of traditional textile towns such as Ypres and the smaller centre of Dixmuide, and this highlights the correlation between industrial decline and decreasing population.

YPRES

	Year	Total	Year	Total	Year	Total
Inhabitants	1311	20-30,000	1412	10,489	1506	9,563
Cloths	1317	89,500	1356	34,100	–	–
Looms	1311	1,500	–	–	1502	100

The drainage from these outpaced textile centres was to the advantage of those towns with a more diversified structure (such as Bruges and Nieuwpoort), of the new dynamic centres of trade and industry, and of those towns or rural areas which were in the process of industrial reorientation (Leiden, south-west Flanders and Walloon-Flanders). The population of Hondschoote, the most important centre in these areas, increased from 2,300 inhabitants in 1469 to 14,000 in the sixteenth century.

Economic activity also involved increased administration which offered employment prospects. This partly accounts for the quadrupling of the population of The Hague between 1369 and 1477, the doubling of the population of Brussels between 1374 and 1480 (the Burgundian Court was resident there at this time) and the increase of the population of Mons from 6,000 to 15,000 in the period 1300 to 1500. Towns, although economically perfectly viable, can also collapse as a result of unnatural intervention, like the total destruction of Dinant in 1466 and Liège in 1468 by the repressive Duke Charles the Bold.

All things considered, there is no evidence of any long period of recession in the Netherlands during the late Middle Ages, such as is usually attributed to it in European history. Even in Flanders, where the effects of the changing international economy were most keenly felt, there were no deserted villages as there had been in England and Germany, and the declining towns were exceptions.

Unity in diversity

From a geographical, economic and therefore also a social and cultural point of view, there are apparently profound differences between the parts of the whole.   In the mind of the fifteenth century, and even still of the eighteenth century, principality and fatherland were one and the same, rather than the vague and less imbedded notion of the Netherlands.   The political unification achieved by the dukes of Burgundy did not exist long enough for this new concept to take root.   The provincial autonomy continued to answer to the requirements of political, fiscal, economic and also mental reality.   The more rural principalities, such as Luxembourg, were more static and withdrawn.   The urban regions were extrovert and expansion orientated, with many far-reaching links with the outside world.   These regions were therefore abreast of change in production methods, means of government and cultural creativity.   The most urbanised areas enjoyed the highest degree of wealth and the highest average per-capita income.   This does not mean that there were no great differences in income levels.   Within an urban area such as Flanders, the per-capita income level was considerably higher in a prosperous town such as Bruges than in the rest of the province.

In urbanised areas, differentiation, specialisation and trade in agricultural products were on a much larger scale than elsewhere.   On the other hand, however, the many and varied links with foreign countries meant that the towns were inevitably dependent upon events elsewhere, and were therefore highly vulnerable.   For foodstuffs they were dependent upon areas with an arable monoculture (Artois, Picardy) which made their surpluses available.   The central areas are distinguished by their concentration of capital and populations, with their differentiation leading to dynamic expansion and economic predominence over the less developed areas of the Netherlands and elsewhere.   Without the intense if inconsistent exchange between all these areas, the centres would never have developed to such an extent and become so prosperous.   The unity of the Netherlands lies therefore in the high degree of interaction between its various regions.   Hainault gave Flanders and Brabant not only grain and stone, but also Rogier van der Weyden, Guillaume Dufay and Guillaume Pasquier, artists whose birthplaces would never have offered them the opportunities they found in the central areas.

We can speak of a close geographic and social unity in the Netherlands created by the essential flow of goods and people.

28.   Hieronymus Bosch, *The Prodigal Son*.   Detail.

(Rotterdam, Museum Boymans-van Beuningen, ca 1500).

2

The daily Bread

The primacy of agricultural production

In the Burgundian Netherlands, two-thirds of the population made a living from the countryside, and the greater part from agriculture itself. In all other northern European countries apart from northern Italy, the proportion of the population living from the countryside was considerably higher, and the actual density of the population much lower. These two phenomena are closely connected : high population density encourages urbanisation and *vice versa*. A condition for this dialectical development is however, that the ecological balance remains more or less undisturbed. The environment therefore had to yield the increased means of subsistance necessary to support the expanding population in the standard of living considered normal at the time. We shall see below therefore, how it was possible for town dwellers in the Netherlands to be supported by agricultural workers at a rate of two to one while elsewhere an average of twice this number was required.

FARMING ACTIVITIES The reclamation movements of the eleventh and twelfth centuries were headed by large-scale projects. These projects continued the tradition of the ancient feudal structure of domains. However, only wealthy landowners were in a position to provide the considerable capital investment necessary to extend the area of land under cultivation by drainage, deforestation and diking. For this reason the majority of reclamation projects were undertaken by the church, the nobility and also, from the thirteenth century onwards, affluent citizens.

By this time, the traditional domainial method of production had already become outdated, and only continued as an exception in the Netherlands. Serfdom and manorial rights, in so far as they had not fallen into disuse, only survived after being converted into relatively small dues. Large areas of the domains were gradually partitioned. The direct exploitation controlled by the landowner himself, was increasingly replaced by leasing. This led to the estrangement of capital from labour and also increasing organisation of production on a more business-like basis.

The far-reaching demographic crisis of the fourteenth century contributed much towards the decline in large-scale land ownership. For one thing, late attempts at reclamation proved no longer viable due to the poorer quality of the soil. Investment in the reclamation of marginal land no longer yielded the expected returns ; it was no coincidence that these areas had remained undeveloped for so long. The cost of labour also absorbed an increasing share of the returns, for not only was it no longer possible to rely on the cheap labour of loyal serfs, but labour had also become a scarce and therefore expensive resource as a result of the repeated plague epidemics of the latter half of the fourteenth century. Gilles li Muisit, abbot of St Martin's Abbey at Tournai bemoaned the situation in no uncertain terms : "Through the general death in the past year 1349 among men and women, so many wine-growers, workers of the land, workers of handicraft and other trades passed away, that a great shortage of labour came about. So it came to be that many of those surviving were enriched with the possessions of those who had passed away, while the remainder demanded an excessive wage. Thus the land and vineyards in many places were unworked for want of workers."

29. Elderly forester. Early sixteenth century wood sculpture.

(London, Hertford House, The Wallace Collection).

This is an accurate description of the five great epidemics of the plague which raged in the Netherlands between 1349 and 1401 : agricultural production saw a drastic decline (in many regions it fell by as much as half) ; this led to a rise in prices. Wages also increased by leaps and bounds, the largest increase occurring during the very first outbreak of the Black Death. In 1355, agricultural workers in Holland were earning more than twice their earnings before the plague. Although wage increases during successive outbreaks were smaller, they continued nevertheless : they were higher for the skilled workers than the lower paid who could apparently be more easily replaced. Between 1345 and 1401, therefore, the gaps between the wage-groups widened while the cost of all forms of labour increased considerably.

WAGES OF FARM-LABOURERS IN HOLLAND

	peat-digger	reaper	haymaker
1345	10 groats	6	3
1351	12	7	3
1355	22.5	15	7.5
1360	22	10	5
1363	27	15	9
1372	30	18	12.7
1383	33	14	8
1401	44	18	12
ratio 1345-1401	4.4	3	4

Source : D. De Boer, Graaf en Grafiek, Leiden 1978.

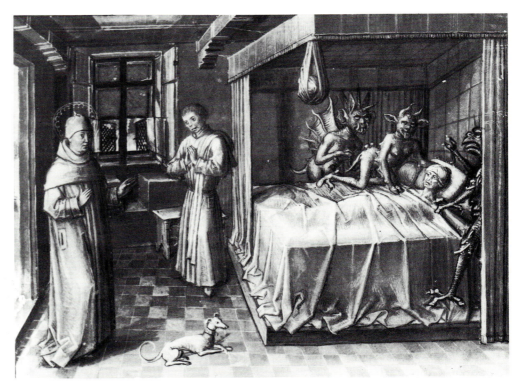

30. A sick man possessed by devils. Miniature from the *Miroir de l'humilité* from the library of Philip of Croy (1461).

(Madrid, Biblioteca Nacional, ms Vit 25-2 fo 52).

It is true to say that both the price of grain and agricultural wages did in fact fall again soon after the epidemics, albeit not to the original level. In the long run, wages showed a strong upward trend, whereas grain prices showed a declining trend from the last quarter of the fourteenth century onwards. The price of rye at Bruges during the twenty-five years after 1390 was generally lower than in the preceding twenty-five years. This development is clearly attributed to the considerable population decline which resulted from the rapid succession of plague epidemics.

This dual trend obviously led to a serious crisis for large agricultural enterprises : they received less money for their grain yet still had to pay considerably higher wages to their workers. The solution was obvious : to employ fewer workers – and in particular, fewer permanent workers. Labour-intensive crops became less profitable and there was consequently a gradual shift towards livestock farming ; this required more land, but since the demand for grain was declining it was now feasible to convert a certain amount of arable land to pasture. In the late fourteenth century and in the fifteenth century there is evidence of an improvement in the quality of demand for agricultural products, with a consequent increase in the consumption of the relatively expensive dairy products (mainly cheese) and meat. The churn, operated by the reciprocal movement of a handle in the lid, typically dates from this period. The shift, too, can also be linked with the general improvement in the standard of living during the second half of the fourteenth century, principally as a result of the heavy decline in the population. Despite a number of short crises, this trend continued until about 1430, and resumed again between about 1440 and 1470.

The development discussed above only affected the smaller holdings to the extent that they employed paid labour. As a rule, the small family holding was able to survive the crises. In areas close to the towns there was even the possibility by working long hours, of taking valuable agricultural products to the market. These were,

31. Miniature from the *Breviarium Mayer van den Bergh*.
April: milk-churning as the sheep and cattle go to pasture.

(Antwerp, Mayer van den Bergh Museum).

50

32. Miniature from the *Breviarium Mayer van den Bergh.*
October: the slaughter of the ox.

(Antwerp, Mayer van den Bergh Museum).

most obviously, various vegetables, but also industrial or trade crops such as madder, woad and weld which were used to produce respectively red, blue and yellow dyes for the textile industry. The demand for flax and hemp-seed also increased considerably in certain areas; namely in the Lys valley, Limburg, northern Hainault, Walloon-Brabant and Namur. During the latter half of the fourteenth century, the cultivation of hops was extended to the Dender region and north Brabant; hops were used to improve the taste and keeping qualities of the native beer. Finally, crops such as rapeseed were grown as fodder and also for oil production. The small concern could therefore, with modest intensification and very hard work, contribute to the existing demand, and was thus able to survive. In Flanders an estimated 40-60% of the farms were no larger than two to three hectares. In Hainault, however, it has been calculated that five hectares was the absolute minimum required to produce the means of subsistance for a single family. In the most urbanised regions, small – even midget enterprises were predominant since it was in these areas that it was still possible for a farming family to make a living from varied, market-orientated production on a small plot of land. If this was unsuccessful for one reason or another, it was still possible for families to supplement their income by temporary work on a large farm or in a trade. The former was, however, very inconvenient since extra labour was elsewhere in demand at precisely the times which were also busiest for the smaller holdings themselves.

Medium-sized farms also experienced difficulties since not only were they dependent upon paid labour, but also had insufficient capital to change to livestock farming. There were two possible solutions to the problem: to split up the land in question or to acquire external capital to enable the conversion to livestock farming. This meant that owners resident in the towns effectively assumed the status of leaseholders. Many citizens invested large or small amounts of capital in land since this was considered to be the most secure

investment. The change in legal status did not result in a new form of feudalism for the farmer, since the relationship was on a purely capitalistic business footing.

This situation spread throughout the Netherlands. The majority of leasehold agreements, with payment made either in cash or kind, were for nine years, sometimes six or twelve years, but in any case traditionally a multiple of three years. The extensive spread of land-leasing meant a considerable investment in the agricultural sector by those living in the towns. Apart from a secure investment, these investors were often looking for a guaranteed supply of food to reduce the risk from periods of inflation. For the farmer, this led to an increased dependence on the urban market economy (that is to say increased dependence on price-fixing which occurred outside the farmer's own village or area), the cultivation of crops in response to market demand, and the incentive to increase yields by intensification and technological innovation.

These factors account for the almost constant emigration of population surpluses to the towns. The farms and villages particularly near urbanised regions could not readily absorb additions to the existing families. Migration was the most obvious solution for young people who found no prospects in the village communities.

INTENSIVE AGRICULTURE The achievement of high yields depended essentially upon intensive cultivation and sufficient fertilisation. In addition to this it was also necessary to ensure the correct crop rotation and seed selection and to choose crops best suited to the soil in question. The Burgundian period saw no spectacular technological innovations in agriculture. These had come during the great period of expansion in the twelfth and thirteenth centuries. From the late fourteenth century until the early sixteenth century, yields were improved by marginal changes, an increase in the variety of crops under cultivation and the general application of more progressive methods. In this area too, the most densely populated areas took the lead.

An example of this is the development of the leasehold agreement. The primitive system of 'half returns' whereby the owner retained half the total yield, was gradually replaced during the fourteenth century by a contract involving a previously agreed rent. This latter arrangement offered the tenant farmer far more attractive prospects of making a profit, and was therefore also an incentive to improving yields. The period of the contract, nine years for example, allowed the tenant farmer reasonable freedom in the management of his business. Throughout the fourteenth century the majority of contracts stipulated the state the farm was to be in when the contract ended; this, in a system of three-year rotation, influenced cultivation during the last three years of the contract term. In the neighbourhood of the large Flemish towns, and also in Brabant, another formula appeared from the beginning of the fifteenth century whereby the final settlement of the contract depended upon the actual condition of the concern at the end of the stipulated term. This system gave the tenant farmer complete freedom in the management of his farm. These developments point to an increasingly business-like approach to social relations : there were no longer any personal obligations, rather a settlement which depended on yields. At the same time, these developments were evidence of an increased confidence in the validity of the applied methods.

These methods tended increasingly to depart from the three-yearly rotation, with one third of the total acreage left fallow each year. In the traditional three-layer system of rotation, this break was to allow the land to regenerate after the cultivation of wheat and/or rye (winter crops) during the first year, and the cultivation of oats and barley (spring crops) during the second year. The land which lay fallow was used for grazing, and natural manuring obviously contributed to the recovery of the soil. The obvious disadvantage of this system was of course that the farmland was not utilised to the fullest possible extent. To achieve this, farmers would have had to breed more livestock, but this was already exerting pressure on arable farming.

Various developments brought solutions to this problem. Firstly, there was an increase in the cultivation of fodder crops such as turnips, spurry and vetch, which had the advantage of adding nitrogen to the soil. Consequently more livestock could be supported, even in stalls. These crops were cultivated partly in the stubble following the harvest of a cereal crop. Sometimes cattle were even put to graze on the turnip or potato tops between the stubble. Mentions of this date from Flanders in the third quarter of the fourteenth century. In other cases fodder crops were planted on fallow; as we know from fifteenth century records in Flanders and Brabant.

Another method of increasing production was to extend the fallow to one year out of every four, five or six years, which was possible with the aid of heavier fertilisation. Apart from animal manure, marl and heath sods were also used. Thus during the original fallow year it was possible to grow cattle-fodder and pulses, which demanded relatively little from the soil.

In Flanders, even before this time, the most intensive form of agriculture then known was being practised – the so-called fallow-grazing. This system involved a regular alternation between arable land and pasture; approximately two-thirds of the acreage was temporarily used for pasture – this made it possible for the farmer to keep much livestock, and to increase the fertilisation of the arable land; in the meantime the quality of the land used as temporary pasture improved. This unique type of intensive cultivation was in full use around Ghent in about 1370.

An essential part of all these improvements was, as we have seen, the increased efforts of the farmer himself, who often had to plough the land as often as four times a year before sowing the winter

35. Miniature from the *Breviarium Mayer van den Bergh.* September: the fields are ploughed.

(Antwerp, Mayer van den Bergh Museum).

54

crops. The smaller farms were probably more labour-intensive, particularly where pulses and other vegetables were cultivated. In these circumstances it is not surprising that in Flanders a lighter type of plough was introduced : the so-called 'eenstart' (single-beam) pulled by a single horse and operated by one man, which was relatively light and easy to manoeuvre. The earliest illustration of such a plough dates from 1430. The scythe was also increasingly used for harvesting in place of the sickle. The latter worked more effectively particularly in straw, but was nevertheless slower. In the illustrations from this period, both implements can be seen in use. These changes were gradual and the sickle remained in use for a long time for wheat, while the lower grade crops were scythed more quickly. The intensification of agriculture demanded not only more labour, but also a great deal more fertiliser. Leasehold contracts are surprisingly specific on this point. When a farm was handed over, not only was the quantity of stored fertiliser investigated, but also the quality of the fertiliser was assessed by the owner himself. Fifteenth century farmers appear to have developed a remarkable talent for this. There was also a considerable trade in natural fertilisers, for which the towns provided large dealers.

UNCERTAIN YIELDS These technical improvements undoubtedly led to increasing yields. However, this can only be said with any certainty of the grain years. There are two very apparent trends here : throughout Europe, yields – measured by the ratio of seed sown to the quantity harvested – increased during the fourteenth and fifteenth centuries. The average yields of winter grain in western Europe were as follows :
1300-1349 1:4.22 ; 1350-1399 1:4.35 ; 1400-1499 1:4.45
This trend of overall increases was also present in the Netherlands. The second general trend was the gradual geographical spread of the high-return ratios from the leading areas which, due to natural and social factors, were persuaded at an early stage to employ the most profitable methods.

There is, moreover, no doubt that grain yields in the Netherlands greatly exceeded the average European yields. Wheat yields in Artois had already reached an average of 1:8.6 by the first half of the fourteenth century, and in the areas surrounding Brussels the ratio had reached an average of 1:13.9 by the latter half of the

36. Miniature from the *Breviarium Mayer van den Bergh*. August : harvesting the grain with a sickle.

(Antwerp, Mayer van den Bergh Museum).

fifteenth century. These results were exceptionally good. A ratio of 1:6 was near the norm, as was noted in the area round Zwolle and Bruges. Yields per hectare varied in the same way : by increasing the amount of seeds sown, it was possible to harvest as much as 180 litres of wheat, though in the vicinity of Bruges at the beginning of the fifteenth century this was rarely exceeded – even in the most favourable conditions.

It is as well to remember that regional variations are also important. Even today, variations in the quality of the soil are still an important factor determining yields. In Flanders and Brabant, rye yields in 1968 were the highest on loamy soils and as much as 8% less on polderland ; 11% less on sandy-loam soils and 17% less on sandy soils. It is easy to see how these differences would have been far more pronounced when agricultural methods were still primitive. Clearly, therefore, the extensive loamy soils of southern Flanders, Artois, Hainault and South Brabant were far more suited to the cultivation of cereal crops than the sandy soils of northern Flanders, Brabant, Limburg and Gelderland. Due to the nature of the soil, wheat was the principal crop on the polders and loamy soils, while rye predominated on sandy soils and in Holland. In the south-east, in the vicinity of Namur for example, spelt was the principal cereal crop. This, then, accounts for the position of Artois and Hainault as the suppliers of grain.

If there were considerable variations between areas, the chronological variations were even greater. There was a gradual increase in productivity throughout the Netherlands, albeit later in the peripheral regions than in the main centres. The chronic declines, which were a result of social unrest or war, were even more remarkable. Those living in the countryside were, unlike the townspeople safe within their walls, exposed to the violence of armies which passed through, or even to the less conventional armed gangs, deserters or thieves. It mattered little, therefore, whether these people were friend or foe, though the regions bordering on France suffered most from the systematic destruction of agriculture during the last quarter of the fifteenth century. However, internal conflicts such as the great Ghent War (1379-1385), the Ghent uprising (1449-1453) and in particular the revolt against Maximilian (1482-1492) also seriously affected agricultural yields. The consequences of this were felt for many years afterwards, particularly where farming capital, such as buildings and livestock, had been destroyed.

37. Miniature from the *Breviarium Mayer van den Bergh*. November: threshing, sifting and spinning.

(Antwerp, Mayer van den Bergh Museum).

56

The short-term fluctuation in yields was also considerable, since harvests varied considerably from year to year as a result of the weather. The winter cereals (wheat and rye), vital for commodities in the form of bread, were particularly vulnerable due to the prolonged growing period; sown in the autumn and not harvested until the following August, these crops were exposed to ten months of changing weather conditions. A damp autumn, a long frost, a dry spring or a wet and stormy summer; any of these factors could have disastrous consequences for the harvest. As a result, corn yields showed considerable divergences; for example, the rye yields from approximately fifteen hectares belonging to the Great Beguinage in Leuven, calculated as a sowing/harvest ratio, averaged 1:6.26 between 1409 and 1494. These yields, however, varied by as much as -40% to $+200\%$; a range of one to five. During the fourteen years following the death of Charles the Bold in 1477 which were beset by various political and economic problems, yields only reached 75% of the average. These were certainly hard times for those tenant farmers bound by long-lasting contracts with a predetermined settlement price.

Agricultural yields in the fifteenth century were considerably lower than those of today. Whereas it is possible today to harvest 4,500 and 4,900 litres of wheat per hectare, then the highest yields under the dukes of Burgundy were no more than 1,800-1,900 litres; that is two and a half times less. To provide the 660,000 inhabitants of the county of Flanders with their daily bread, 2,409,000 hectolitres per year were required – assuming that per capita consumption of grain was one litre per day. This figure accounts for more than a quarter of the total surface area (848,050 hectares) of the Flemish speaking part of Flanders. Also, the many and extensive infertile areas must be excluded from this total : the Maldegemveld (the largest), the Bulskampveld, the Scheldeveld, the large wooded areas in the south, and the Moors. The cultivation of other crops and more particularly livestock farming, took up part of this total area. In Flanders, grassland often accounted for as much as two thirds of the available arable land; this figure increased during the late Middle Ages. All things considered, therefore, we can say that land utilisation was improved to an extremely high level, but not without many risks for both producer and consumer.

It was indeed the tenant farmers who bore the risks in agricultural enterprise. Yields that fluctuated on a scale of one to five, social risks in the form of itinerant military gangs or other criminals, and dangers from the surrounding countryside (wolves, rabbits etc.) ; there were many uncertainties in the lives of those who lived from the land. Misfortune in one form or another reduced many smallholders to the status of tenant farmer, while the rich town-dweller profited by this. The less prosperous had to endure food shortages as a result of these fluctuations, and these shortages appeared to strike hardest just when the limits of demographic growth seemed to have been reached.

39. The weighing of the unleavened bread.

(Liège, University Library. Drawing from the *Tacuinum Sanitatis*, ms 1041, fo 35 V°).

40. The Spooning out butter.

(Liège, University Library. Drawing from the *Tacuinum Sanitatis*, ms 1041, fo 39).

41. Flat cheeses are sold by the cheese farmer.

(Liège, University Library. Drawing from the *Tacuinum Sanitatis*, ms 1041 fo 39 V°).

42. Making of sausages, a typical old-time speciality of Brabant and Liège.

(Liège, University Library. Drawing from the *Tacuinum Sanitatis* ms 1041, fo 48 V°).

The feeding of many mouths

Every European town jealously guarded its food supplies. Limited capacity, slow means of transport and the importance of bread in the staple diet of the majority of the population, meant that the main concern of every town's administration was to ensure a regular, sufficient supply of grain.

THE REGULATED MARKET   In the case of Ghent, this took the form of monopolisation by the Ghent merchants of all the traffic on the Scheldt, the Lys and the Lieve Canal to Bruges.   All grain shipments on these waterways and also shipments purchased by citizens of Ghent for trading purposes, were subjected to the staple regulations – which meant that a proportion of any shipment must be put on the market before a transit permit was granted to proceed further with the remainder of the shipment.   In years of shortage, Ghent demanded that as much as a half of any shipment be sold on the local market, while in normal years this requirement was one-third of a shipment.   This occured in 1409, to the cost of the Bruges owners, and in 1425 Ghent even blockaded all transit trade to Bruges.   Evidence of Ghent's vital role in the grain trade can still be seen today.   The grain shipments were unloaded along the Koornlei and Graslei, where the thirteenth century grain store and Corn measurer's house still stand ; from here five small alleys lead to the spacious Corn Market.

For its supply of home-produced grain from Hainault and Artois, Bruges was dependent both on Ghent – with its control over the Lys and Scheldt and their tributaries – and Ypres, to which Bruges was linked via the Ieperlee, which had been deepened in 1416 with Ypres' co-operation.   For Bruges, the control of grain transport from the hinterland gradually became less important from about 1430 onwards

Butirum.
Natiuꝭ Ꝯ. er. h. melius er eo relacte prouino. Iuuamētū. contra sup flustates pulmonis generacas ꝑꝼrītates er siccitates nocumētū hebrtat stomacil. Remotio nocumētū. Cū rebꝫ ſtipticis.

Caſeus recens.
Natuꝭ. ꝼ. er. h. melius ereo lacte animalis ſanis. Iuuamētum. mollificat corpus er inpinguat nocumētū expullat. Remotio nocumētū. Cū nucabꝫ er amarabꝫ nꝼ melio.

Buseca.
Natuꝭ. ꝼ. er. ꝑ. mꝼ. melius ereo aialum arietum. Iuuamētū quibus abus ſunesſeir instomacho nocumētum. Vanabꝫ. Remotio nocumētū. aum galenga er multo pipere.

59

since its maritime position and evident attractions as a versatile market were having their effect already. The Bruges magistrates did, however, have the power to stop the export of domestic grain from all the ports.

Ypres also found it necessary to implement strict regulations on grain imports since it was situated neither close to the sea nor on a navigable river. At the beginning of the fifteenth century the inhabitants of Ypres constructed a road and a waterway to link their town with the Lys, and they also established a grain staple at Waasten. This was restricted however, under pressure from Ghent, to local consumption. The people of Ghent even installed an officer at Waasten, in whose presence the merchants and shippers were made to swear under oath that no grain or other produce would leave the county. Flanders' third most important town did not therefore succeed, as Ghent and Bruges had, in securing for its own advantage the control of the traffic of one or more products. The less favourable geographical position of Ypres was therefore a factor which contributed to her decline, unlike the two other large towns.

On the subject of the provision of food, the interests of town and countryside were like those of consumer and producer. This was especially true during times of scarcity. During times of inflation, the initial reaction of the towns was to seek the duke's permission to halt the export of domestic grain. Flanders and Brabant resorted to this measure almost simultaneously during fourteen years of the fifteenth century, which almost certainly points to a general shortage. The rural areas continually opposed these restrictions which adversely affected the profit margin of owners and dealers; however, the dukes were apparently more sympathetic to the demands of the towns. Grain shortages could, after all, lead to rioting in the towns. As soon as the prices fell again, the dukes restored the free-trade policy, which also included the export of Flemish grain, and often also the transit of grain from Hainault or Artois. A town such as Aalst, which became involved in the export of grain from Hainault, often came into conflict with its capital, Ghent, which under no circumstances tolerated any intrusions upon its monopoly.

In times of scarcity the large towns were principally concerned for the security of their supplies. In 1410, 1424 and 1447, Tournai incensed the towns of Flanders and Artois when completely in line with other towns it introduced restrictions on grain transit. These restrictions demanded that one twentieth of each grain shipment transported downstream along the Scheldt should be sold in the town itself. Further measures were taken, as the largest cities, organised as the 'Four Members' of Flanders found in 1416/17, 1433 and 1460, against the purchase by merchants of grain which was either just harvested or still standing in the fields. This practice often exploited the farmers' need for liquid funds and was often done for reasons of speculation, since the dealers withheld these stocks from the market for some months, thereby causing an artifical rise in the price. Exorbitant profits could be made in the harvest year from grains which, by dint of early purchase in large quantities, could be acquired from the farmers at an exceptionally low price.

Seldom, however, did magistrates in the towns take measures to combat this extreme form of free-market economics, possibly since this would not have been in the interests of their fellow-citizens. More frequent were the measures to ensure the more or less enforced supply of grain to urban markets. During the two most serious food shortages of the fifteenth century, Ghent and Bruges

45 and 46. Details from a stained glass window of the baker's guild at Diest, showing millers and bakers at work.

(1503, Diest, St Sulpice's Church).

resorted to the purchase of grain with a view both to restricting speculative dealings and to securing supplies. In 1436, twelve official grain-buyers were employed for this purpose in Ghent. In 1438 after a month-long siege, and rendered helpless by the departure of the Hanse merchants, Bruges purchased grain on its own account in Hainault.

During the long crisis of the 1480s, not only was the export of domestic grain forbidden, there were also internal restrictions as when, for example, the district of Veurne attempted to secure all available supplies for its own use. In June 1481, just before the new harvest, Bruges issued maximum prices; Ghent too resorted to this measure in December of that year. The large towns simultaneously attempted to command as large a supply as possible – to the despair of the smaller towns. In April 1482 at Sluis which was, incidentally, under the jurisdiction of Bruges, Ypres had difficulty "in obtaining a quantity of corn sufficient to help the inhabitants in times of need".

From February 1482 until the end of the following harvest year, Bruges, in co-operation with the towns and villages of its quarter, (which then included the whole of western Flanders– urban and rural), stimulated imports by the introduction of subsidies. For each 100 *hoet* (172 hectolitres) of wheat the town paid five pounds of Flemish groats and for each 100 *hoet* of rye half this sum. In terms of prices at that time, these subsidies accounted for 8.33% of the market value of wheat, and 6.25% of the market value of rye. It is remarkable that in these troubled times (during the harvest years of 1481/82 and 1482/83, prices in Flanders and Brabant were the highest in the century), the preference for the more expensive wheat remained. According to figures for the town of Bruges, import subsidies were paid on a total of 47,714 hectolitres of grain in the course of 1482, possibly also including the period up to the spring of 1483. This quantity, and also the cost of subsidies, were most likely distributed throughout Bruges' catchment area according to the distributional code applied for the purpose of taxation. If the total population of this area is taken to be approximately 285,000, each inhabitant, on the basis of the above quotation, would have received 13.728 kg of bread. If, however, only the towns were supplied, and this is more likely, then each of the 150,000 inhabitants would have received 26 kg of bread.

In 1489 Ghent again introduced maximum prices for all grain, and also for beer. In Bruges, import subsisdies were paid out on an astonishing total of 28,390 hectolitres of wheat, and nearly 14,000 hectolitres of other grain. 2,327,980 kg of bread were baked with the wheat alone ; this was sufficient to feed the entire population of Bruges (estimated at 40,000) for almost two months. It is equally possible that these supplies were distributed throughout the Bruges quarter, as they had been in 1482. Such extraordinary purchases made by the town authorities were clearly socially motivated and for the purpose that the "common folk of this town, who were lacking corn, should be better provided with the same" or : "for the refreshment and succour of the poor inhabitants". On the one hand therefore, the measures were clearly intented to supplement existing food supplies, and on the other hand intended to help the poor sections of the population.

All in all these government interventions meant a substantial supplementation of food supplies, from which the poor in particular benefited considerably. The town magistrates could not, or would not, however, sell the grain at a cheaper price – only at a 'reasonable price'. As can be seen from the table below, the highest prices were four or five times higher than the average prices for the 1460s. These were inflationary times and intervention by the towns' magistrates was confined to the provisioning of the market and the restriction of excessive speculation.

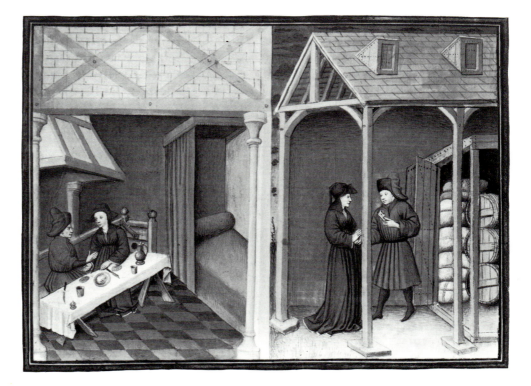

47. View of the warehouse and residence of a Flemish merchant of about 1440.

(Paris, Bibliothèque de l'Arsenal ms 5070, fo 314. Miniature from the French translation of Boccaccio's *Decameron*).

PEAKS IN THE GRAIN PRICES

	Average 1461-1470	Bruges maximum 11th Nov 1482	Ratio	Average 1461-1470	Brussels Maximum 1482-1483	Ratio
Wheat	42.3	180	4.3	97.2	450	4.6
Rye	27.3	143	5.3	69.6	342	4.9
					1491-92	
					369	5.3

The Bruges prices are expressed in Flemish groats per *hoet* (172 litres)
The Brussels prices are expressed in Brabantine groats per *mud* (292.55 litres)

THE EUROPEAN GRAIN MARKET   The purchase of grain in Bruges, the area of the Netherlands about which we are best informed, was undertaken in times of need (such as the crisis periods 1437-1439, 1480-1483 and 1489-1491) by foreign merchants. Grain from Picardy, Normandy or Brittany and even on occasions, grain from Britain was imported into Flanders; this transit could not be described as regular but was rather a matter of convenience, for example as a return cargo. In 1482, Bruges and Ypres bought 1,700 hectolitres of Spanish grain, but there is no further evidence of regular trading. In 1473/74 however, trade took place in the opposite direction when Spain purchased grain supplies from the northern Netherlands, during a period of scarcity. Such movements, however, were the result of exceptional circumstances.

The bulk of foreign corn imports came from Prussia, and by the beginning of the fifteenth century this trade involved regular and considerable shipments. On the Prussian side, this was guaranteed by a more or less constant export productivity and large trading organisations such as the German Hanse, the German Order and other great trading houses. Since dealings between the Hanse and

50. *The Wedding at Cana*, left-hand panel of the triptych *The Miracles of Christ*, by an anonymous Flemish master, ca 1500. Members of the House of Burgundy can be seen among the festively clad guests, who include Philip the Good (?).

(Melbourne, National Gallery of Victoria).

51. A presentation wine-tankard bearing the coat of arms of the city of Ghent, which belonged to the aldermen of the Keure.

(Ghent, Bijlokemuseum. Ypres master, fifteenth century).

52. The serving-up of luxury dishes during a banquet: the fiery head of a wild boar, and a swan.

(Rotterdam, Museum Boymans-van Beuningen. Hieronymus Bosch, *Wedding at Cana*, detail).

the Netherlands (and Flanders in particular) were so intense – one of the four Kontores was set up at Bruges – it was logical that the vital grain surplus from the Baltic countries should also be included in the range of products traded. This grain, however, had the serious disadvantage of being a typical bulk product and consequently had a low value-to-weight ratio, in contrast to products such as pelts and amber, which were exported to Bruges from the same areas. It is not surprising therefore, that a heavier type of ship, the hulk, came into use at the beginning of the fifteenth century. This new ship had a capacity of 200-300 tons (3,000 to 4,000 hectolitres of rye), compared to the capacity of the older cock-boat of 120-240 tons.

There were, however, other restrictions on the Baltic grain trade. The cost of transport between Danzig and Bruges could account for as much as 40% of the market value of the cargo being transported, depending on price fluctuations. The difference between prices in Prussia and the Netherlands had to be considerable if such a journey was to be profitable. In addition to this, the journey via Denmark could take as long as two months. Allowing for the time taken to inform Prussian trading partners of the market situation in the Netherlands, a period of three to four months often elapsed between the placement of an order and possible delivery. Also to be taken into account are the normal maritime risks and the Hanse's opposition to winter journeys–forbidden by regulations but occasionally unofficially condoned.

Regular trade and a good organisation were therefore essential if profits were to be made. The Hanseatic League had the latter without doubt and demand became more constant as the population of Holland increased. This province regularly bought grain from Brabant and Flanders, since its own domestic supplies were insufficient. The people of Holland were therefore the first to be affected by the frequent export restrictions in these areas, and they were consequently forced to find more distant, and more expensive markets along the English, French and Baltic coasts. Prussian grain was to be found on the Amsterdam market for at least another four centuries, despite conflicts between the Hanseatic League and the Hollanders who, with their own ships and knowledge of the Baltic, offered increasing competition to the Hanse. It is therefore no coincidence that in December 1481 ambassadors from Bruges were sent to various towns in Holland to buy up grain stocks which were still at the disposal of the Hanse merchants.

The regular trade between the Netherlands and the Wendish, Prussian and Livonian towns on the one hand, and the permanent demand for grain from Holland on the other, account for the structural development and continued expansion of Baltic grain imports into the Netherlands. This trade however, remained essentially speculative. In order to make large profits, it was necessary for the merchants to withhold their supplies from the market when domestic harvests were abundant; even in times of scarcity, when the producing areas were threatened by trade-blockades or export restrictions, it was in the interests of the merchant to withhold his supplies from the market until the price had risen.

Clearly this dependence on Baltic grain–which was of vital importance in times of crisis–only accentuated the vulnerability of the supply. Apart from meteorological conditions, the trade was dependent on an international chain of diplomatic and commercial circumstances which could be broken by a single weak link. In normal circumstances there was a large degree of homogeneity of markets within the Netherlands. The grain prices in Mol (then a village in the Kempen, 50 km from the nearest important town) for example, fluctuated concurrently with and rarely diverged from those in Brussels and Bruges. Local or regional shortages were quickly made good by imports from other areas, which prevented persistent and considerable price differences.

When domestic harvests failed, all grain stores and borders were, as it were, hermetically sealed; speculation abounded so long as the towns did not demand the surrender of supplies–a demand which foreign merchants, the large-scale speculators, had to respect. The heaviest price rises of the fifteenth century in Flanders and Brabant (1408/09, 1415/16, 1437/38, 1480-1482, 1491-1492) coincided with phases of export restrictions in the Baltic countries; and prices remained high for the duration of the restrictions. It appeared, moreover, that price rises in the Netherlands were almost always

53. Miniature from the *Breviarium Mayer van den Bergh*. December: slaughtering the pig.

(Antwerp, Mayer van den Bergh Museum).

preceded by a decision in the Baltic countries to restrict exports. When these restrictions were lifted, prices immediately fell again; not because the supplies of Baltic grain had arrived in the Netherlands (this still had to undergo two months of transit), but because all domestic grain stocks had been unloaded on to the market in anticipation of the new supplies.

The influence of Baltic grain was not a question of the size of the supplies (even in the sixteenth century, these supplies accounted for no more than 10-15% of the Netherlands' needs), the very withholding or arrival of the supplies was sufficient to bring about large-scale speculation.

The inelasticity of grain consumption thus encouraged the development of a large-scale speculative-capitalist trade which extended along the coasts of northern and western Europe. The Netherlands, with their large population, were the focal point of this trade. Government measures did not provide adequate protection against profiteering wholesale merchants, since there was no effective Burgundian policy to deal with foodstuffs. On only one occasion, in 1473/74 when there was a shortage in Spain, were sufficient measures taken throughout the Netherlands to combat grain speculation; all export was halted, from the Somme to the IJssel. The initiative was taken by the municipalities: the Duke showed his interest merely by granting Genoese merchants, for an appreciable payment, exemption from his recently initiated export blockade, but was then persuaded by the towns (against even larger sums of money?) to adhere to the regulation.

This example illustrates the considerable mobility of grain in fifteenth century Europe which was determined by multinational trading enterprises. Regional and urban governments had little power over the efficient organisation (the German Order established its own postal services and had permanent representatives in western Europe) and the sphere of operation of this continental wholesale trade network. The ineluctable demand for grain disrupted any policy intended to protect the consumer, whenever this was not implemented at the same level as that at which trade was organised. Such a policy was not developed by the central government of the Netherlands until the mid-sixteenth century. The whole Burgundian period was thus a veritable golden age for speculators, who made their profits (from artificial price-rises) not only at the expense of the individual consumer, but also at the expense of the towns who attempted to stave off the worst effects by the use of subsidies–which in turn also found their way into the network of the international wholesale trade.

54. St Joseph depicted as a medieval carpenter in his workshop.

(New York, The Metropolitan Museum of Art, The Cloisters Collection. Detail of the right-hand panel of the retable of the Gospel, attributed to the Master of Flémalle, ca 1425-1428).

3
Urban Economies on the European Scale

Although agriculture in the Netherlands can rightly be called progressive and was fundamental to the survival if not the welfare of the population, and although it provided work for the majority of that population, yet the urban element was the dominant factor in the economy. This is clearly visible in the agricultural economy itself : in urban investment, in farming and the breakthrough of capitalist production methods, which were increasingly market-orientated, rational and profitable. In addition, merchants and entrepreneurs from the towns had almost total control of rural industries. The particular attribute of the Netherlands, their influence throughout Europe, was due to an essentially urban or urban-directed productivity. So it is appropriate to discuss at some length what the towns produced and how they achieved this. Those regions were, after all, in the words of the privilege granted to Flanders by the Duchess Mary of Burgundy in 1477 "... not very fertile but are simply based upon trade, business and privileges".

Industrial production

URBAN PROTECTIONISM From the eleventh century, above all industrial goods were produced in the towns, trading took place there, and other such services as transport, administration and finance provided typical concentrations of non-agrarian productivity. As the influence of the towns grew, so did their attempts to monopolise activities in the secondary and tertiary sectors. This for logistic reasons was easily achieved in the tertiary sector. From the fourteenth century onwards, however, the monopoly of industrial production gradually slipped away from the towns. The reasons for this are clear : in a free market economy, such as prevailed in international trade, each entrepreneur must search for the cheapest factors of production. In the towns – and this is truer of Flanders than of Brabant and of the southern than the northern Netherlands, the growth of corporation placed restrictions on production which led to inflexibility. Moreover, workers' organisations in the towns were able to secure a higher wage than that in the rural areas. Both these factors, in accordance with the logic of the economic system, led to the irreversible shift of mass production to towns where labour was less well organised, mainly in Brabant and Holland, but ultimately, too, to villages as well (mainly in south-west Flanders).

The resistance of the towns, in particular the larger Flemish towns, to the rise of the rural textile industry was both fierce and prolonged, but ultimately fruitless. The growth of a strong state authority under the dukes of Burgundy prevented the towns' imperialistic attempts to impose their laws on the smaller towns and villages by force of arms, as had been their practice during the fourteenth century. The towns did, however, enjoy continued success in their less ambitious attempts to protect their industries. From 1295, the aldermen of Brussels were able to control the production and the sale of beer, and also the taxes levied on that beer in thirteen surrounding villages. The town's income from this source was considerable and, according to Philip the Fair himself, in his decree of 1503, were "... the largest and most profitable of all the receipts and incomes received by this town". It was, therefore, with some dismay that the aldermen saw many brewers setting up just on the edge of town, and the citizens of Brussels enjoying tax-free refreshment after their walks on Sundays and holidays. So the Duke sanctioned the extension of the ban on brewing and drawing of beer to a radius of one mile around the original area. Neither this nor subsequent measures succeeded in changing the pattern of beer consumption, particularly since the environs of the capital appear to have been, and still are, so well endowed with beer-brewing facilities.

This situation was typical of most towns, and was the same for many products. The cloth-guild of Leuven was granted the powers of a special law-court with jurisdiction over the drapery and weaving industry. The guild had the power to trace and seize imitations of Leuven cloth throughout the duchy, and also ensured the enforcement of the ban on cloth production within two miles of Leuven. The guild also intervened in all manner of commercial disputes and even functioned as an authority for appeals in conflicts between the drapery guilds of the smaller towns and villages in the area. The larger towns exercised the right to inspect cloth produced in the smaller towns and villages, to prevent imitations. Ghent tradesmen regularly visited the region to ensure that their monopoly was being respected and that no 'illegal' equipment was in use. The Privilege of Ghent (dating from 1314) included the prohibition of the production of woollen cloth within a radius of 30 km round the town – with the exception of such towns as had been granted a specific privilege by the Duke.

In 1305 Zierikzee had already acquired the monopoly of fulling, weaving, dyeing and shearing in Zeeland east of the Scheldt. Middelburg enjoyed a similar privilege over Walcheren, with the exception of four small towns. Leiden (the most important textile town in Holland) together with Middelburg and Delft, were granted a privilege in 1351 which prohibited the production of cloth within a radius of three miles – (excluding the privileged towns). It was forbidden for parts of the cloth-manufacturing process to be finished

55. Two weavers at their loom ca 1408. (Halle, Basilica of St Martinus. Detail of a stained-glass window belonging to the weavers' guild).

elsewhere.   Urban imperialism over the countryside increased in the course of the fifteenth century.   In 1457 the town of Leiden prohibited all cloth production within its protected area (the *banmijl*), an area of jurisdiction which extended for several miles, such as had already existed in Flanders and Brabant since the fourteenth century.   The sale of appliances or dyestuffs for the textile industry was only permitted within the town.

In 1531 Charles V introduced the 'Decree upon External Trades' at the request of the towns.   This decree prohibited all new rural industrial activities, in particular drapery and the brewing of beer.   The close connection between both these forms of urban protectionism is apparent in the sanction which Leiden introduced in 1451 against the inhabitants within two kilometres of the town, who refused to pay the town's beer taxes : they were forbidden to spin wool and consequently lost a vital source of income.   Inferior or unhealthy activities, or those requiring a particular environment, were occasionally tolerated in the countryside, but always under the control of urban entrepreneurs.   The bleaching of linen, for example, required extremely clean rivers and caused harmful odours.   This activity therefore took place in rural areas such as the area around Haarlem.   Orders from other urban centres were also carried out by the 'Haarlem Bleachers'.   Spinning was also considered to be a menial and unhealthy task and was therefore carried out mainly by the women in rural areas as a secondary occupation.   Wool was spun for the drapers of Leiden in an area extending for several miles all round.   An attempt at the end of the fifteenth century to transfer this work to the many unemployed in the towns, was unsucessful.   The notion of low-grade work which existed at this time between the town and the countryside, can be compared to that which exists today between industrialised and developing countries.

56.   Miniature from the *Breviarium Mayer van den Bergh*.   June: sheep-shearing.

(Antwerp, Mayer van den Bergh Museum).

CORPORATISM AS A TYPE OF MANAGEMENT The protectionism of
the towns was an extension of that of the guilds. It is remarkable
that as the town authorities became more influenced by this in the
course of the fourteenth and fifteenth centuries, corporatism – true
to its economic character – extended its activities beyond the towns
to dealings between the towns themselves. The craft trades had an
enormous influence, formally until the French Revolution but in
reality much longer, so we might well consider their economic
functions.

Corporatism is characterised by the organisation of all categories
of workers within each branch of industry. The young men joined
the craft guild as apprentices and, after completion of the prescribed
apprenticeship, became journeymen. In order to reach the rank of
master craftsman it was not sufficient simply to have worked under
the leadership of such a master for a certain period of time. In
addition to this, the journeyman had first to produce a 'masterpiece'
which showed his craftsmanship, and then to make specified
– sometimes very considerable payments to the guild and its
administration. Most important of all, however, was that the master
insisted on operating his business independently, aided only by a
few journeymen and one or two apprentices. This also meant that
the master had to provide the required means of production, that
is to say, the business premises themselves (which had to include
sleeping facilities for the apprentices), and the necessary tools and
materials. To become a master craftsman therefore, he needed to
have a large, favourably situated house with a workshop which opened
on to the street and quarters sufficient for the master's family and
his apprentices. The access to mastership was thus essentially
financial, and varied according to employment in each branch of
industry.

The master craftsman was therefore the owner of the means of
production, while the journeymen and apprentices were employed
by him. They worked together day after day under a single roof,
and the journeymen were capable of producing work to the same
standard as that of the master ; the title of master craftsman was only
a recognition in the formal sense. Although masters and journeymen belonged to different classes, this was scarcely evident in
practice because of the close personal relations and communal
organisation in a single guild.

The form which corporatism assumed during the Burgundian
period was determined by diverging trends and interests. The guild,
as an organisation of producers, imposed agreements binding on all
those entering a particular trade.

The guild can thus be compared to a modern cartel, which
determines prices, quotas and production. In this way the craftsmen
protected their position against possible competition and divided the
market equally among themselves. The guild had the authority,
within its own sector, to ensure that no unqualified persons (*i.e.*
non-members of the guild) were practising the trade, and secondly,
to ensure that the members of the guild themselves were mindful of
the regulations concerning materials, techniques and working hours.
The guilds acquired these exclusive powers over their trades from the
urban and rural authorities because such organisation also benefited
the consumer, since quality and a reasonable price were guaranteed. It is clear, however, that the elimination of competition and the
strict regulation of production had a debilitating effect in the long
run. This eventually led to the decline of many important crafts since
renewal and innovation had to come from outside the sector.

The branches of industry in which corporatism survived longest were those which operated on a small scale. This was true of both the trades typically involved in local provisioning and certain specialised export industries where production was in the hands of a small number of craftsmen. Local retail trade was well suited to the crafts sector. It is also important to remember that in these small enterprises the production and sale of such goods were combined. The baker, the butcher, the tailor, the cobbler and the candle maker, etc. all sold to the customer what they themselves had produced on their own premises. They knew their clientele personally and were thus closely involved in the established social order. But the gold-and-silver-smith, the leather worker, the carver, the carpet weaver or the metal worker, each of whom used expensive materials and sometimes complicated tools, also operated within this craft-trade sphere. The high business capital required, the great skill involved and the small but scattered market for these expensive goods ensured the continued existence of the small cottage industry, in which the tendency towards heredity was also very much in evidence.

CRAFTSMAN OR CAPITALIST ENTREPRENEUR ? It is self-evident that the organisation of labour in the export-orientated industries would have been different to that in the smaller local artisan industries which were characteristically exclusive. Here there was certainly room for large, financially strong entrepreneurs, firstly to compete with the capital-intensive import of raw materials (wool from England and later from Spain, alum from Italy or Turkey, expensive dyestuffs and preparatory materials) from foreign markets for the production of finished goods for export; and secondly as insurance against the many risks of the geographically dispersed market. The Flemish and Artesian merchants of the thirteenth century fit this description quite well, although by the fifteenth century they no longer had the monopoly of all aspects of production and dealings. By now there were merchants who bought up raw materials abroad and also dealt in the finished cloth, but were not involved with the industrial production process.

In the majority of export industries and in particular the textile industry, which remained dominant in the Netherlands during the Burgundian period, the unit of production was a relatively small or medium-sized workshop belonging to small patrons – namely master weavers. The master weaver owned the most expensive equipment in the whole production process – one or more looms – and was

57. A tailor cuts cloth for clothing to be sewn by his wife and sons or apprentices. (Liège, University Library. Drawing from *Tacuinum Sanitatis* ms 1041, fo 73 V°).

58. Fifteenth-century Gothic chest. (Bruges, Gruuthusemuseum).

consequently the central figure in that process. The looms were worked on the patron's premises (on a small scale, therefore) by apprentices and paid workers. The patron did not, however, organise the many other activities in the production process : spinning (carried out mostly by women), fulling, carding, dyeing, and the more than thirty intermediary activities involved in the production of quality cloth. The patron did, nevertheless, have considerable influence over these activities in so far as he had to decide, given the demand in the market, (but also depending on his own drive and ambition) how much cloth to inject into the production process to be finished, and he must also decide to which fullers and dyers this cloth would be supplied for processing. In a few cases, the better fullers and dyers themselves operated as small entrepreneurs, employing others on piece-wages.

The masters sold their wares on local or regional markets or to a home or foreign merchant who placed orders for cloth for the international export market. The latter was therefore a second key figure in the economic process. The masters of the textile industry were thus intermediaries between the proletariat and the merchants. Production was consequently divided and sub-divided

59. A flemish burgher interior of around 1500.

(Antwerp, Royal Museum of Fine Arts. *The Holy Family*, anonymous master).

among numerous individual producers. Such distribution necessitated the establishment of strict production criteria and standards in order to ensure a uniform, quality product which would be recognised on the international market as totally reliable.

In practice the activities of the masters and merchants showed many traces of capitalism. The master weavers controlled the means of production and the workers sold their labour in return for piece-wages. The merchants, it is true, allowed cottage industry to function, thus maintaining the continued existence of producers who controlled their own means of production, but they then practised forms of trading-capitalism, which will be discussed at greater length below.

In the textile industry and other export industries during the period in question, the emphasis remained strongly on a conglomerate of small producers. This nevertheless created problems. These small producers did not, by and large, have sufficient capital to purchase expensive foreign wool and were thus forced to turn to the middlemen who might even be willing to supply on credit, and in a few cases even supplied looms to the producers. This still cannot be described as industrial concentration of production, but rather as the concentration of capital by way of commercial capitalism. These forms of capitalism and concentration were to be found in varying intensity in the Netherlands between 1300 and 1550. In the fourteenth century there was a clear shift : capital was still supplied by domestic merchants, but from the end of the century the Italians and North Germans became increasingly active in this field. In 1396 a number of weavers from Wervik went to work for the house of Diamonte and Altobianco degli Alberti in Florence. A comparable regulation of production and distribution came into being under the impulse of the somewhat less innovative, indeed conservative German Hanse. In 1417 the merchants of the Hanse at Bruges drew up an agreement with the drapers of Poperinge whereby the latter agreed to produce a particular imitation of St Omer cloth. By the mid-century, this contract took on the form of an exclusive partnership whereby the Hanse undertook to distribute all cloth produced in Poperinge from Spanish wool. In 1512 it appeared that Dendermonde, Aalst, Wervik and Tourcoing had also concluded such a contract. In Hondschoote around 1500, independent weavers increasingly lost control of their means of production and they were consequently forced to hire their weaving looms thereby reducing themselves to the status of wage-labourers where they had previously been masters of their craft. The success of the light textiles (serge), however, continued, and reached a peak between 1565 and 1568. This success was due to the strict organisation of their distribution by exporters from Antwerp, who in a single purchase often bought up a quarter of the cloth production. Hondschoote's decline after 1568 was thus linked to that of Antwerp.

Too often it has been emphasised that the sixteenth century was characterised by forms of capitalism and business concentration that were not known in the fifteenth century. But we have just seen that there were indications of the presence of trading capitalism before 1500. The master weavers of the fourteenth and fifteenth centuries strove on a modest scale to expand their businesses and often succeeded in employing more workers. It is, however, quite clear that there was an increase in both the scale and flow of business between 1500 and 1550, in the sense that it was not only now foreign concerns that were backed by capital, but that large-scale indigenous

60. Penelope at her loom.

(Boston, Museum of Fine Arts. Tournai or Bruges tapestry, ca 1480-1483, fragment from the series of tapestries depicting illustrious women).

industries began to flourish in the Netherlands too – for example the trading entrepreneurs of Antwerp who dealt for instance in the output from Hondschoote, and the powerful Liège dealers in metal and armaments.

This tendency, as we have seen, was already forecast and implicitly evident in the corporatist textile industry, where it first appeared. The trend was also apparent in the fifteenth century in the form of the technological simplification in the production of cheaper (light) textiles, but did not become a conscious aim until the sixteenth century. The trend took a firmer hold in the new industries of the sixteenth century such as silk, sugar and glass industries, and printing, since they were free of the organisational restrictions which were characteristic of the traditional craft trades.

Logically speaking, the concentration of production should have continued in those sectors where technical necessity and a costly infrastructure made this desirable, such as the Liège iron industry, the mines in the duchy of Limburg and the coal industry in Wallonia. Indeed during the fifteenth century, the government transferred the Limburg mines, initially exploited by many small mining concerns, to a number of more capital-intensive groups, though the extent of this concentration was still apparently limited. In 1469, Charles the Bold introduced the calamine monopoly, which replaced free enterprise with the concession of monopolies, hence a form of mercantilism. This process would

61. The two men in this Flemish miniature are busy dipping the white cloth into the dyeing vat.

(London, British Museum, Royal ms 15, E III).

normally have been accelerated by the introduction of new technology and renewal, but the conversion was gradual. It is true that at the end of the fourteenth century, blast furnaces appeared in the Namur and Durbuy areas, but by 1500 there were fewer than there had been at the start. Moreover, the crisis at the end of the sixteenth century led to a sharp decline in the tendency towards concentration and a return to the smaller craft workshop.

It would therefore look as if there was less capital investment in the means of production than in the trading sector during the fifteenth and sixteenth centuries, since fluctuations in the market economy provided greater opportunity for speculation and sudden profits. A second general observation is that capitalism and concentration, even on the modest scale of the lesser master-craftsman, brought about increasing proletarianism between the fourteenth and sixteenth centuries. When around 1510 the production in Hondschoote reached massive proportions, smaller entrepreneurs were put out of business and forced to become wage-earners. Only a small number of luxury-goods manufactures, whose workers had a specialised knowledge of their profession, and the artisan industries producing for local needs, were able to escape this binary trend of capitalist concentration and impoverishment.

THE RANGE OF TEXTILE PRODUCTION   Although neither production nor population statistics from the Middle Ages can be considered accurate, we shall nevertheless attempt an estimate of the annual and per capita cloth production, since this enables us to determine the approximate level at which export was possible

CLOTH PRODUCTION

Town	Date	Total Annual* Production (ells)	Number of Inhabitants	Annual Production (Ell per inhabitant)
Ypres	1317-18	2,076,000	25-30,000	83-69
	1355-56	791,000	c. 20,000	40
Leuven	c. 1350	756,000	18,000	42
	1380	378,000	16,500	23
	1476	26,600	17,700	1.5
	c. 1550	16,000	16,000	1
Mechelen	1322-23	600,000	12,000	50
	1333	720,000	12,000	60
	c. 1550	60-80,000	25-30,000	2-3.5
Leiden	1498	470,000	c. 11,000	42
	1543	256,000	c. 12,000	21
Hondschoote	1561	2,256,104	c. 15,000	197 (serge)

* An ell is with local variations, approximately equal to 0.70-0.80 meter

It can be seen from this table that during the peak production periods of the textile industry (Ypres 1317 or Mechelen 1333), as much as 60 to 80 ells per inhabitant were produced annually, or 240 to 320 ells per family. If production could be calculated on the basis of the active population alone or the number of active textile manufacturers, the figures would be even higher.

In Ypres, for example, where more than half the population were employed in the textile industry, per capita production was noticeably higher than in the towns where only 30-40 % of the population were involved in this sector. Since, in a typical textile town such as Ghent in 1356, 60% of the population earned a living in this sector, we can, assuming 240 ells per family, estimate the maximum production per textile worker at 400 ells. In Ghent 32% of the total population made a living from weaving, this means that each weaver produced 784 ells annually (that is, naturally, with the help of the other workers involved in the process). In Hondschoote in 1580, average annual cloth production was approximately 160 lengths of serge (each of 36 ells ; therefore in total 5,760 ells). The cloth produced here was, however, of a much lower quality.

Taking a different approach we know that the weaving loom could produce three to five ells per day so that in 270 working days (the maximum per year) the ceiling production would have been between 810 and 1,350 ells per loom. It must be remembered, however, that luxury cloth had to be processed as much as thirty times by as many workers.

The maximum amount which could be produced therefore depended on the number of workers involved in one particular process (weaving for example) and their productivity. The maximum production of a single loom (1,350 ells) corresponds with the figure for the production per weaver of 748 ells, which was considered normal for Ghent, since it was necessary for two workers to operate each loom due to the width of cloth.

How much of this cloth was for local consumption ? According to E. Scholliers, a fifteenth century bricklayer's apprentice set aside an estimated 10% maximum of his wage for clothing. With this he could, as head of the household, supply eight ells of cheap cloth or two ells per person. At this time (*i.e.* around 1550) Mechelen was producing at least two to three ells per inhabitant – just enough, therefore, for the town's own consumption. During more prosperous times, production was twenty to thirty times this figure and was therefore mostly destined for export, although domestic demand was also greater during such periods. It must be remembered that the towns mainly produced luxury cloth which was only within financial reach of the wealthy minority, so that this product was very sensitive to economic fluctuations. The production level for the export of normal cloth was thus two to three ells per inhabitant in the towns. Local and home demand for luxury cloth was more elastic, but it certainly cannot have been greater than this.

The methods of production in the Netherlands were based upon a system that derived its essential energy from manual labour with the aid of relatively simple tools such as the loom. This was prompted by the highly specialised techniques involved in the production of fine quality cloths. Yet other techniques would nevertheless have been possible for commoner cloths. The fulling mill, which greatly boosted production, was after all known to be in use in the Netherlands from the thirteenth century, but the urban textile industries of Flanders and Brabant shunned the appliance until about 1540 and its use declined simply as a result of competition from cheap textiles from the rural areas and Liège district, where fulling was indeed done mechanically. In the low-lying, flat areas of Flanders and Brabant, however, the absence of watercourses with sufficient power to drive mills was, to be sure, an adverse factor. It was, moreover, in the interests of the skilled workers to protect their quality products, since these brought higher incomes than mass-

62. A pre-1430 waffle-iron bearing the arms of Philip the Good. The so-called 'lukken', small waffles, were baked with this iron.

(Bruges, Gruuthusemuseum).

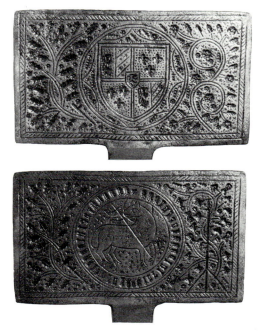

63 and 64. Fifteenth-century jug used during the daily toilet. Such jugs usually stood in a bowl, on a toilet cabinet in the bedroom, as in *The Angel's Message to Mary*, attributed to Rogier van der Weyden. (Paris, Louvre.)

(Rotterdam, Museum Boymans-van Beuningen, Coll. Frederiks, Kb. 44).

produced goods. The social and economic conditions in the older industrial centres were thus not conducive to innovation.

There is a tendency to measure the significance of the production centres in the Netherlands by the wide geographical distribution of their products. Cloth from Flanders and Brabant was to be found throughout the Mediterranean countries, in North West Europe, in eastern Europe – (as far as Russia) – and in England. We should not assume, however, that this expansive market is an indication of the scale of production, but rather an indication of a well–balanced and organised trade network which is needed if a luxury article is to be sold on many different markets in small quantities. To maintain the population of the Netherlands, which was very dense by European standards, it was necessary to produce for export at a level which far exceeded the levels of production in Europe.

RURAL INDUSTRY The distinction between urban and rural areas has traditionally been that the urban areas had a wide range of local craftsmen and a number of basic export industries, while the rural areas were predominantly agricultural with a limited cottage industry producing textiles and trade crafts for local needs (a small brewery, smithy, etc.). This representation is somewhat biassed. In the first place there were the important industrial activities whose location outside the towns was determined by geographical factors : the coal industry in Wallonia, the iron industry, mining in the duchy of Limburg, the quarries and lime-kilns in the duchy of Namur, and peat-cutting in Flanders and Holland. From the fourteenth century, however, this rural industry overtook cottage industry and local production. This development was extremely important for the later industrial development in Europe, since it was accompanied by a move towards technical innovation (fulling mills ; new weaving techniques). This initiative stood the best chance in rural areas,

65. Fifteenth-century bronze ewer.
(Zoutleeuw, St Leonard's Church).

where the restrictive pressures of corporatism and the protection of
the master-weavers were absent. Production in urban and rural
areas was perhaps not so divergent in the thirteenth century unless,
that is, the division of labour was more developed in the towns and
enterprise was also more concentrated there. Domestic wool
production had existed for centuries in the Netherlands with a
national weaving industry as one of its outcomes. Expensive English
wool was also used in the towns, and the cheaper Spanish wool in
the smaller centres. Spanish wool was not, it is true, totally suited
to the carding technique employed in the traditional textile industry;
this wool was combed, and was thus suitable for the production of
a different cloth for which there was increasing demand.

The recession in the latter half of the fourteenth century led to
growing attempts to shift rural production, and this was accompanied
by increasing resistance from the towns. There were two reasons
for this. International merchants (including Hanseatic and Italian
merchants) saw the potential of cheap labour resources (in agriculture
as well as industry) which were not embedded in corporations, where
the monopoly of the master-weavers had not penetrated, and where
there was a desire to use technical equipment, such as the fulling
mill, which along with the lower wages made the end product
cheaper. These factors engendered a flourishing linen industry from
1400 in Flanders, Hainault and North Holland, and so it was
international trade capital that exploited these opportunities. This
was for instance the case with the Grosse Gesellschaft of Ravensburg
which was established around 1380. The scale of agricultural
exploitation in the densely populated rural areas was such that
compensation was necessary to achieve subsistence. We must not
forget that in the fifteenth century there was an endemic poverty level
of some 26% of the rural population. Such people sought refuge
in the linen industry which was responsible for industrialisation of

66. Chain of the Dean of the Skippers' guild in Nijmegen from the second half of the fifteenth century, bearing a ship with Mary and St Olaf.

(Nijmegen, Museum « Commanderie van Sint Jan »).

entire villages from the end of the fourteenth century. Bleaching and spinning were parts of the production process carried out largely by villagers for the entrepreneurs in the towns. In the fifteenth century the rural brewing industry also began to flourish as the cultivation of hops and barley increased. In Liège it was possible for agricultural labourers to earn supplementary wages in the iron industry and nail production. The gradual shift from occasional to full-time wage-labour only began at the end of the fifteenth century, for example in the Limburg mines.

The industrialisation process in rural areas could take hold earlier where its progress was undisturbed and more far-reaching in areas such as the Verviers region, Artois and the duchy of Limburg, which were urbanised to a lesser extent than the highly urbanised Flanders. It was now possible to compete with England where mechanical fulling had been in use for longer. The rural population was, however, used by urban entrepreneurs as a labour reserve ; these people were prepared to do unpleasant and menial tasks often as a secondary activity with less social demands than the urban craftsmen, since they continued to regard agriculture as their main activity.

The absence of social organisations made this source of labour particularly attractive to the entrepreneur : he gave out just as much work as was available, and when there was no work this labour cost nothing. The shift of mass production to the rural areas and the small towns undermined the strong and relatively democratic textile profession in the large towns. The notorious conflict between "the towns and the rural areas" was in reality a struggle between the urban textile workers and their own less costly competitors. The tools which they destroyed during their raids belonged to small-holders who were forced, out of poverty, to do secondary work. The real initiators of the rural industry, the international trading companies who operated in conjunction with the urban patriciate, came off unscathed by such activities. The urban craftsman did not realise that rural industry itself was also in the hands of the very entrepreneurs who could no longer offer any work to the craftsmen themselves.

MINERALS A second export industry, the metal industry, was geographically tied to the ores, fuel (wood) and water-power to be found in Liège and Namur. Prior to the fifteenth century, the emphasis had lain on copper production, and later shifted, particularly after 1500, to the production of iron. The old industry in brass relied principally on supplies of imported copper with tin, zinc and calamine extracted from the mines in the duchy of Limburg where this production in the fifteenth century had progressed beyond the stage of a local industry. The dukes leased the exploitation to entrepreneurs, such as those in Altenburg who then established larger concerns employing some twenty paid workers. The processing into artistic objects and utensils was mainly concentrated in Dinant. Af-

67. The copper mines in the Maas valley showing the exploitation of minerals: on the right the mine-shafts, through which the minerals were pulled to the surface in small baskets. In the centre the lumps of ore are washed and a watermill drives the bellows for the smelting furnace. The finished products are carried away in a cart. On the left: furnace and a smithy. On the far right a drinking place. The artist, Hendrik met de Bles (ca 1510-after 1555), born at Bouvignes near Dinant, was accepted into the Antwerp guild in 1535 and travelled to Italy. This painting was found as early as 1603 in the Tribuna degli Uffizi in Florence.

(Florence, Galleria degli Uffizi).

68. Dutch statuette of St Barbara, made of pipe-clay, with a matching model, from the second quarter of the fifteenth century.

(Utrecht, Central Museum).

ter the total destruction of the town in 1466 by Charles the Bold, the majority of the Dinant specialists moved to Mechelen, where cannon production flourished in the period after 1480, followed by bell-casting and religious artefacts. In the second sector – iron – pig-iron was initially produced by direct firing (catalan kilns). An early technological innovation – the blast furnace – led in the latter half of the fourteenth century to an improvement in the quality of the iron because impurities were extracted by this method. The furnaces were situated mainly in Namur, the Amblève Valley and the areas of Durbuy and Mons. A second innovation, (the so-called Walloon method) known experimentally since the end of the fifteenth century but fully operational after 1550, was mainly dependent on water-energy to provide power for bellows via a water-mill. This industry became concentrated on the Vesdre, Sambre, Ourthe and the Meuse and marked the transition from cast to wrought iron.

The metal industry, the production of salt and beer and domestic heating required increasing supplies of coal, the mining of which expanded considerably between 1512 and 1545, and continued to do so until 1560 particularly in the original mines round Liège but also in the new centre around Mons. The still relatively primitive exploitation from open pits in the fifteenth century made way at the end of that century for deeper shafts, new techniques for the control of underground water and thus for a more capitalistic enterprise with a fair-sized labour force.

SALT The salt industry, equally determined by geographical factors, was concentrated in coastal areas. This industry was particularly successful in those maritime areas, such as Biervliet and the Zeeland

69. An easily manoeuvrable, cast-iron Burgundian cannon of about 1460. Many such cannons were used by the Swiss in 1476. Iron cannon-balls were used as ammunition. It was the artillery which Duke Charles the Bold stringly promoted alongside the already well-equipped archers, heavily armed cavalry and infantry. With these forces he applied modern military techniques and tactics. The Swiss municipal armies, however, armed with long staves, confronted them in closed ranks. The weakness of Charles' army lay in the employment of large corps of mercenaries who proved unreliable when danger threatened.

(La Neuveville, Museum).

coast, where there was salt-retaining peat from which the salt could be extracted by drying and burning in large pans. The salt crystals produced in this way were of a higher quality than the French salt extracted from sea-water. Reimerswaal in Zeeland regularly exported salt to England. Salt production at Biervliet was stimulated by the nearby herring industry which required salt for pickling, and by the butter industry. The production at Biervliet exceeded local and regional demand to such an extent that its salt was exported on a large scale to London, the Baltic, Douai and Lille via the staple markets of Dordrecht, Mechelen and Antwerp. In 1439-1440 Biervliet unsuccessfully attempted to establish a monopoly in salt production, at the expense of other centres such as those in Zeeland. In 1422/23 Biervliet produced 2,900 *hoet* (18-22,000 tons) of salt for local consumption and in addition 38,500 *hoet* for export. The latter figure represents more than half of the quantity exported annually to Rouen at this time; with 90% of these imported supplies Rouen provisioned Nantes, and a large part of France. This clearly shows the European orientation of the small Flemish town. The gradual exhaustion of peat layers provided new opportunities for the competing centres in Zeeland and at Ostend, and forced Biervliet to turn to the refining of crude salt imported from France and Spain. In 1440 the refining of French salt was also carried out in England, having been established there by sixty or so artisans from Holland, Zeeland and Flanders under a royal charter.

FISH The coastal harbours of Flanders, Zeeland and Holland saw the development of a substantial fishing industry during the Burgundian period. The development of a method for preserving herring, when the import of Norwegian fish was blockaded by the Hanse in the 1380s, gave a powerful impulse to the industry. The process of pickling herring consisted in gutting, salting and packing them in barrels. This was often done on board the fishing vessels. In the same way that salt production had been important to Biervliet, so a staple market for pickled herring grew up at Damme. This market supplied not only the inland towns, but also exported to France and England, where it was the only foodstuff which could be freely imported by foreigners, who even received special licences during times of war. The Hanse, which had imported Scandinavian herring into the Netherlands during the fourteenth century, became a regular buyer in the mid-fifteenth century. In the Netherlands themselves it was the Flemish fishermen and merchants who took their catches to the market in towns such as Arras, Cambrai, Tournai, Valenciennes, Douai, and Lille where, naturally, other types of fish were sold. A significant proportion of the distribution in France and England was in the hands of inhabitants of the Netherlands ports. International piracy led, especially where France and England were concerned, to sailing in convoy under escort from armed ships. The size of the fishing industry in the Netherlands at this time is indicated by an incident in the summer of 1468 in which twenty-one boats from Raversijde were escorted to Harfleur. At this time there must have been at least seventy herring boats at Nieuwpoort.

BEER From the thirteenth to the fourteenth century the production of beer in the Netherlands evolved from a cottage industry into a local and then into an export industry. This process evolved first in Haarlem, Gouda, Delft and in Amersfoort near Utrecht, towns in the province of Holland. Prior to 1320, beer was imported into the

70. The salting of fish, an important coastal occupation.

(Liège, University Library. Drawing from the *Tacuinum Sanitatis*, ms 1041 fo 60).

71. Bronze aquamanile of about 1400, showing Aristotle in a humiliating position after his failed attempt to seduce Phyllis, the wife (or lover) of Alexander the Great. The washing of hands before a meal, in water that might or might not be perfumed, was a necessary ritual among the wealthier classes.

(New York, The Metropolitan Museum of Art, The Robert Lehman Collection. Anonymous master from the southern Netherlands).

Netherlands from Germany; after 1320 the production of hop beer in Haarlem increased considerably and was exported primarily to Brabant; hence at Lier in 1408 three quarters of the beer supply was imported – almost exclusively from Haarlem. In Flanders the principal source of supply for beer was Hamburg, which exported 90,000 hectolitres of beer to Sluis in 1411. Beer had therefore become a truly popular drink – far more so than the luxury product wine – as can be clearly seen in the annual consumption per capita figures: 250 litres at Haarlem (1475); 273 litres at Leuven (1524); 369 litres at Antwerp (1526). Although there were already breweries at Liège and Namur in the latter half of the thirteenth century, hop-brewing did not become really significant until the last quarter of the fourteenth century. The level of production at which local demand was satisfied was soon reached at Courtrai, Lille, Lier (where 76% of domestic beer was already being produced by 1474) and elsewhere, and proved effective in preventing Gouda and Delft from dominating the southern Netherlands market with cheaper beer in the period after 1425. There was in any case dissatisfaction there about the quality of the domestic beer, as can be seen in a resolution of the grand council of guild masters and deans in Bruges in 1477 : "That the brewers be made to brew better beer". Large-scale production was only achieved there after 1500 at Lille, in Menen (which was to supply the whole of Flanders) and above all, after 1550, in Brabant (Antwerp) and Haspengouw (Zoutleeuw, Hoegaarden).

ARTS AND CRAFTS The flax industry which flourished in Flanders (Scheldt and Lys, Eekloo) as well as Hainault (Ath), Brabant (Nivelles) and Holland, produced not only ordinary linen but also luxury damask. Another luxury sector, that of carpet weaving, was already in existence in the thirteenth century in Arras, where at least 100 master craftsmen were active between 1420 and 1440. In the fifteenth century, this craft was a suitable alternative to the declining traditional textile industry in Brabant (Brussels, Antwerp, Mechelen), Oudenaarde, Tournai and Lille and also in Holland after 1550. During the fifteenth century, independent guilds of carpet weavers were established in at least ten towns in Flanders and Brabant and membership of these guilds grew rapidly. Around 1500, silk production began in Bruges and Antwerp and replaced the import of silk from Italy and the Rhineland. Diamond-cutting developed in Antwerp after 1478, and sugar-refining from 1500 onwards. Leather and furs were processed in 's Hertogenbosch, Leuven and other centres. Fustian (a mixture of cotton and linen) was produced at Tournai at the end of the fourteenth century. In Bruges, Mons, Brussels and Mechelen weapons were produced, as well as pottery and glasswork.

A considerable range of craft and luxury industries could flourish in Bruges, the wealthy centre of world trade. It is worth noting the fact that there was a series of craft trades in these sectors, ranging from chaplet makers (who used Prussian amber) to milliners, furriers and processors of Spanish leather to gold- and silversmiths and carvers. Jewellery produced in Bruges was frequently to be found

72. Set of four pewter dessert spoons. Knives were also part of cutlery in daily use. Forks were not in general use until the seventeenth century.

(Liège, Musée diocésain. Anonymous master from the southern Netherlands).

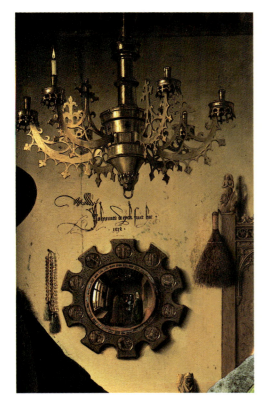

73 and 74. Brass twelve-branch chandelier from Bruges, dating from the second half of the fifteenth century, like the one in, for instance, Jan van Eyck's painting of the Arnolfini.

(Bruges, St John's Hospital).

in English court circles. Hats were also exported in surprising quantities. During the spring and summer of 1450, no less than 71,000 hats produced in the Netherlands were unloaded in London; there were 40,000 straw hats, 27,000 felt hats and several hundred made from wool remnants. 's Hertogenbosch and Antwerp were other important centres for this trade.

At that time less distinction was made between such products of a high standard of craftsmanship and what would now be exclusively regarded as art. Nevertheless the works of artists and in particular wood carvers were valuable exports from the Netherlands just like the rest, and were often taken as return cargoes for the raw materials imported into the Netherlands. Notable examples of this are the retables from Brabant which are still to be seen all over Europe.

75. Fifteenth-century Flemish parade shield. The courtly knight kneels before his lady. On the banner above his head can be seen *Vous ou la mort*.
(London, British Museum).

76. Brooch showing two lovers. A certain Jan van Berchem, active in Bruges in the mid-fifteenth century, improved the technique of cutting precious stones, and this improved their brilliance.

(Vienna, Kunsthistorisches Museum, Weltliche Schatzkammer, Flemish work, ca 1430-1440, triangular diamond and ruby cabochon).

77. One of the twelve medallions in enamelled gold set with pearls and precious stones, linked in more recent times by a double gold chain. The lower, and most beautiful 'margriet' shown here, depicting a girl dressed in white, was said to have belonged to Margaret of Brabant, wife of Louis of Male, count of Flanders, whose daughter married Philip the Bold, duke of Burgundy. All twelve medallions date from around 1400 and were supposedly made in a French workshop.

(Cleveland, The Cleveland Museum of Art, J.H. Wade Fund).

78. Portrait of Margaret of York, sister of king Edward IV of England and third wife of Charles the Bold. The Duchess played a significant role in the politics of the Burgundian lands against king Louis XI of France. She greatly influenced Mary of Burgundy for whom she lovingly acted as a second mother. Through her interest in literature she also stimulated the production of manuscripts as well as the new art-form: that of the printing of books.

(Paris, Louvre Museum. Anonymous Flemish master, ca 1480).

Monoculture : the basis
of economic vulnerability

The industry of most towns and regions in the Netherlands was nevertheless characterised by a high degree of uniform specialisation. The smaller as well as the larger towns of Flanders and Brabant in the fourteenth and fifteenth centuries, and also Leiden and Gouda, were mainly producers of textiles of only one kind, quality cloth. Biervliet made a living exclusively from the exploitation of salt, Dinant from copper, and the other centres round Liège from the iron industry. A true monoculture therefore, as the structure of the professions in the towns reveals. In Ghent between 1356 and 1358, 60% of the total population was employed in one of the textile trades ; this figure represents 67% of the working population. The corresponding figure for Ypres is 48-64% of the total population ; 34% in Leiden ; 40% in Lier and 40% in Dendermonde (each figure is a percentage of the total population). This overspecialisation can in itself be economically advantageous as is shown by the sustained spectacular success of the Flemish and Brabantine centres, and also Leiden.

This monoculture did, however, in retrospect, have disadvantages, as for instance during economic recessions, or whenever shifts in fashion or demand, or economic options or mechanisation were ignored because of conservatism.

Quality textile production was vulnerable in several ways. The industry was dependent upon foreign sources for the supply of raw materials, English and Spanish wool and Turkish or Italian alum. Flemish producers were consequently at the mercy of the political relations between England and Flanders, which was governed largely by French policies. The import of British wool was blockaded in 1270, between 1338 and 1345, from 1379 to 1407 and from 1436 to 1443. Hence the frequent spasmodic attempts on behalf of Flemish commercial and industrial interests to secure an Anglo-Flemish trade agreement which was detached from the political conflict between France and England. Since raw materials were necessarily purchased far from home, production was vulnerable to price fluctuations on these foreign markets, and these could make heavy inroads on the selling price : in Leuven in 1442 the price of wool took 55% of production costs. A second disadvantage was that quality cloth was produced for a small, well-to-do section of the population and consequently demanded a scattered and hence vulnerable European market. Such long-distance trade involved high overheads in terms of insurance, diplomatic protection and organisation. The producer was thus left with a narrow profit margin. In Leiden at the end of the fifteenth century this amounted to 13% of the market value.

The problems of the textile industry in the Netherlands cannot therefore be considered apart from social circumstances. At the slightest hint of misfortune, employment in a monocultural economy was seriously threatened and there was little opportunity for conversion to other sectors. Whenever the traditional textile industry came under pressure, there were always social upheavals in Flanders. In Brabant, where there was less corporatist pressure, the reaction was less violent. A light drapery business had begun in towns such as Brussels in the mid-fourteenth century, and though there was unrest, it was followed by greater tolerance and improved

79. Cloth market at 's Hertogenbosch, about 1530. Painting by an anonymous North-Brabantine master, commissioned by the merchant drapers, whose guild was the most important in the town.

('s Hertogenbosch, Noordbrabants Museum).

regulations and even before 1394 Brussels had a thriving production in serge as an alternative. In Flanders the production of cheap textiles, the so-called 'new drapery' did not develop in the countryside until the fifteenth century; this production was mainly in small towns or villages such as Armentières, Belle, Hondschoote and St Winoksbergen.

STRUCTURAL CHANGE AND MARKET DYNAMICS The relatively general prosperity from 1385 to 1550 gave new life to the economy and thus also to domestic consumption. Even in periods of crisis, producers still concentrated production on the prevailing up-market demand for luxury products which actually expanded during the years of Burgundian prosperity, and in particular between 1400 and 1480. The Burgundian court with its surrounding environment, and also the wealthier inhabitants of the towns, saw an increase in their purchasing power, and therefore could afford more luxury goods. The Flemish centres could also supply this demand since they could draw on the long experience of highly qualified craftsmen. This, however, meant relatively high wages which could only remain at such a level in the luxury sector. The domestic market in the Netherlands, as one of Europe's most densely populated regions, was itself not insignificant and the continued prosperity in the fifteenth century first of Bruges and later of Antwerp as international markets were also permanent factors which ensured the rapid and efficient distribution of their products.

According to various indicators such as the levies on the annual markets at Antwerp, Bergen-op-Zoom, Lille, at the Zwin harbours or on overland routes at, for example, Leuven, the volume of trade in the Netherlands must virtually have doubled between 1400 and about 1480.

The textile centres of Holland also appear to have enjoyed continuous expansion between the fourteenth and sixteenth centuries. In Leiden, production increased from 9,600 lengths of cloth in 1400 to 21,000 lengths in 1476, and to 28,100 lengths in 1502. The population there also showed a corresponding increase, from 5,000 in 1398 to about 11,000 in 1497 and 14,250 in 1514.

Annual cloth production at this time was 470,000 ells, the level which had already been reached by the smaller Flemish centres between 1300 and 1350, but which was considerably lower than the level reached at Bruges during peak production. The explanation for this lies in the fact that the towns of Holland and the towns of the southern Netherlands did not develop simultaneously. The latter had reached their demographic and economic peak around 1300, while the growth in the towns of Holland, which is comparable to the thirteenth-century upsurge in Flanders, took place between 1380 and 1500. A second explanation lies in the fact that the towns of Holland, unlike the Flemish, experimented in the production of luxury cloth from the beginning, albeit using cheap wool, and found a market for this cloth in the Mediterranean.

Since monocultural centres are theoretically vulnerable, towns with a diversified economic structure should logically be less so. Between 1338 and 1340, 38% of the population of Bruges were local traders and craftsmen and 20 % were involved in international trade – apart that is, from the 25% of the population employed in the textile sector. There were no problems here in the fourteenth and fifteenth centuries. Although Bruges had less inhabitants than Ghent, they paid more taxes and Bruges even saw an increase in its share of the general fiscal demands on the county. Bruges no less than Antwerp

80. A watermill seen on Hans Memlinc's painting *The Blessed Virgin and Child worshipped by angels and benefactors.*

(London, National Gallery).

had all the marks of an international market and the prosperity of the town continued undisturbed throughout the greater part of the fifteenth century, and even into the sixteenth century there are signs of a lingering prosperity. The town was sufficiently adaptable in the fifteenth century to accommodate new sectors such as colonial goods, the export of copper to central Europe and the handling of English cloth.

Mechelen is another example of successful adaptation. Here the production of traditional quality textiles fell from 600,000 ells in 1322 to 60-80,000 ells in 1550, while the population continued to increase from 12-15,000 to 25-30,000 in the period between 1370 and 1544. When the textile industry in Brabant was suffering setbacks from 1340 onwards, Mechelen shifted to leather processing and the casting of bells and cannons, and even took over the metal industry of Dinant. In the fifteenth century, furriery was also carried out in Mechelen as well as artistic trades (embroidery) and the dyeing of cloth imported from England. A direct compensation for the declining textile industry was the introduction, during the latter half of the fifteenth century, of the carpet industry. The city further ensured its prosperity by exploiting existing and new trading activities.

As a transit port Mechelen was linked with the Antwerp metropolis and many other towns in Brabant by an extensive network of waterways and overland routes. The main turnover was in beer, wine and grain. Mechelen was a staple market for fish, salt and oats. Finally, the city was also the residence of central institutions such as Parliament and the Central Chamber for Finance in 1473, the Grand Council in 1504, and the Court of Governess Margaret of Austria from 1507 to 1530.

The reverse situation was true of Ypres, where cloth production declined between 1317 and 1356 from 89,000 lengths to 34,100 lengths; the number of looms declined from 1,500 to 100 between 1311 and 1502 and, as can be expected, the population also declined from 20-30,000 in 1311 to 10,489 in 1412 to 7,626 in 1491. The main reason for this economic collapse was undoubtedly the inability of the entrepreneurs and politicians of this town to adapt to the shift in demand from luxury textiles to cheaper products. The social consequences were catastrophic. In 1431, only 21% of the households in one particular area of Ypres were taxable ; the financial capacity of the (comparatively) wealthy was so reduced that many of the remaining 79% indigents could not be supported. Poor-relief was given to a mere 10% of the population, that is, approximately one-eighth of those who were actually destitute.

The situation in Dixmuide in the fifteenth century was not much better. Although it still flourished during the fourteenth century, production (measured in terms of the number of the town's lead seals sown on to lengths of cloth) fell from 10,500 in 1403 to 400 in 1420. Revenue from taxes levied on cloth production also showed this declining trend between 1380 and 1420.

As a result, the number of indigents in the fiscal levies of Dixmuide in the 1440s increased to 40%, and the number of destitute households in the census of 1469 totalled more than 40%, thus revealing the fact that many workers were socially depressed. Here too, monoculture and traditionalism were largely responsible for the recession.

The situation was different again in centres such as Courtrai, Wervik and Poperinghe with their traditional industries. These centres competed strongly with the large towns from the last quarter of the fourteenth century and received large injections of capital through foreign merchants. The towns of Brabant managed to overcome the crisis by themselves actively selling their products at the Brabant and Frankfurt annual fairs, and by going to these fairs, merchants from Mechelen managed to survive the difficult years between 1470 and 1505.

Finally there were the up-and-coming centres in South Flanders such as Hondschoote, Armentières and others. The population of Hondschoote rose from 2,300 to 14,000 between 1469 and the sixteenth century; this was a symptom of prosperity which itself resulted from the exploitation of the European demand for cheaper textiles that could be produced cheaper in Hondschoote than in the old centres. This was therefore a case of monoculture, but a monoculture which had adapted to the new demand and was therefore successful for a time, at least until recession set in after the crisis in the late sixteenth century.

81. The luxurious brocade and woolen cloth are an excellent illustraton of the high quality of the textile industry and refined taste in dress. At this time Flanders set the fashion – even abroad. Fragment from *The Legend of St Eloy* by Petrus Christus. (New York, the Metropolitan Museum of Art, The Robert Lehman collection).

International trade

Despite fluctuations, the international trade of the Burgundian Netherlands was concentrated in the Scheldt delta during the whole period in question. Two complementary centres were connected to the delta : Bruges, the earliest developed and most internationally orientated port, and Antwerp which, along with Bergen-op-Zoom, supplied among others the fairs of Brabant, held four times each year. These markets were particularly important for the whole of the Netherlands, as well as western and southern Germany. Countless small coastal towns were also important as export harbours, and as Amsterdam and Rotterdam expanded, Dordrecht remained as a distribution centre for the Rhine wine and beer, and the towns on the Zuider Zee were also active.

The position of Bruges as a concourse for all European nations was unchallenged throughout the whole of the period in question even when, from the end of the fifteenth century, Antwerp developed considerably and became more internationally orientated. Although the handling of the goods themselves took place at Damme, Sluis or Middelburg, the owners and commissioners continued to meet at Bruges. The headquarters of all international trading companies were established there, where there was also a tradition of brokerage and an established experience in money-trading.

THE HANSE The traditionally most important trading partner was the German Hanse, which had established one of its four *kontore* in Bruges (the others being in London, Bergen and Novgorod). The Hanse office at Bruges controlled not only all other establishments in the Netherlands but also those along the Atlantic coast in Bourgneuf (the centre for salt production near Nantes), La Rochelle, Bordeaux and Lisbon. Bruges thus profited from the extensive export of French and Portuguese salt to the Baltic countries, as well as from more limited trades such as that in wine. The strict regulations included a stipulation that no member of the Hanseatic League could form trading partnerships with foreign merchants or indeed engage in contracts based on credit. All goods purchased in the Netherlands had to be taken to the Bruges *kontor*. The purpose of this was to limit competition from the products of Holland. Naturally, such unpractical regulations were not strictly observed. On the contrary these regulations contributed to the isolation of the Hanse which, due to outdated commercial techniques, made the League less and less competitive towards 1500. The Hanse merchants brought mainly raw materials from the Baltic countries to the Netherlands, while the return cargoes comprised mainly finished industrial products. Apart from the export of grain discussed above, Prussia, Poland, Livland and western Russia also supplied wood, charcoal, tar, furs, wax, honey and amber. Hamburg exported beer which had an excellent reputation in the Netherlands. Their return cargoes consisted principally of textiles, a wide range of craft products with a high unit value, and also transit goods such as wine and salt.

Relations between Flanders and the Hanse were frequently disturbed by reciprocal rumours concerning tolls, hijacking, reprisals and legalities. The Hanse moved its *kontor* on four occasions and blockaded all trade with Flanders in order to obtain satisfaction for its grievances. It is striking that each of these blockades coincided with or were a direct result of uprisings in Flanders that were harmful to trade. In 1436 the Hanse merchants moved to Antwerp, but the Flemish were soon forced by the grain shortage to restore normal relations at the cost of considerable reparation payments. In 1451 the Hanse moved its *kontor* first to Deventer, and when this location proved unsatisfactory, to Utrecht. The use of blockades as a weapon gradually became less effective, due on the one hand to internal division between the Wendish towns (under the leadership of Lübeck) and the Prussian towns, and on the other hand to the duke of Burgundy's increasing sphere of influence. Apart from misgivings about increased levies and privateering, the League demanded that only the Four Members of Flanders, that is Bruges, the castellany of Bruges (the Franc), Ghent and Ypres, should have jurisdiction over them, as had previously been the case. This was such a blatant affront to the superior jurisdiction of the duke that these demands were not met, no matter how far the Hanse compromised. This ineffective blockade was lifted in 1457, under the promise of reparations to be paid over a period of ten years.

We have a typical indication of the relations between the Hanse merchants and the authorities of Bruges when in 1446 the furriers guild complained to the town magistrate that a member of the Hanseatic League had discovered a method of dyeing pelts whereby cheaper pelts could be sold as more expensive ones. The aldermen of Bruges, at the request of the magistrate, asked their suppliers in Prussia, Poland and Russia, to prevent the spread of this fraud. The sample of this forgery, attached to their letter, has, however, kept its colour to this day. Craft conservatism therefore hindered the spread of a new technique which is in general use today.

The departure in the 1480s was of a different nature. In 1484, Maximilian, during his clash with Flanders which refused to recognise him as regent, ordered the trading nations to leave Flanders and establish themselves in Antwerp. At the same time he exerted diplomatic pressure on England to establish an economic blockade of Flanders. In the summer of 1485, and from 1488 to 1493, the Hanse moved to Antwerp since safe trading was no longer possible in the besieged town of Bruges. The Hanse's close association with Bruges can be deduced from the dalliance in the prolonged deliberations about transferring its *kontor* to Antwerp from 1500 onwards. An agreement with the Scheldt town was not drawn up until 1546. Co-operation had been hindered by a conflict of

82. Letter of protest from Hanse merchants in Bruges to their Prussian colleagues about the supply of a dyed pelt. A sample of the pelt in question is attached to the letter.

(Torún, Poland, Municipal Archives).

83. An anonymous sketch of the Hanse office in Bruges in 1602.

(Cologne, Historisches Archiv).

interests, but also by a certain incompatibility in their temperaments. Although in 1468 Antwerp had donated a house on the Corn Market for the use of Hanse merchants during the annual fairs, the latter continued to believe "... that the Brabanters are a rash people, as everyone says".

ENGLAND Trading relations with England were partly in the hands of the Hanse merchants. The wool export was supposed to go via the English staple at Calais, where the monopoly was in the hands of a special company. However, the crown granted export licences on a considerable scale, and these often accounted for a significant proportion of the export via the staple.

Between 1453 and 1467, English traders exported an average of almost 6,000 sacks annually. The distribution of this demand among the various centres of production depended on local regulations and also the position of the market. A large proportion of the supply was bought up by merchants to be sold at the annual fairs at Bruges or Brabant. On the other hand, merchants from Leiden bought approximately 1,000 sacks of the best English wool, which were exclusively for the town's own industry. Merchants from Ypres, Ghent, Amsterdam and Delft were also to be seen at Calais, while some of the merchants from Mechelen specialised in a transit trade in English wool. In the minor centres of production much smaller quantities of English wool were used as it was mixed with other qualities. For this reason they often relied on middlemen for their supplies, which naturally drove up the price. A sack of English wool cost 50% more in Bruges than in England; this was due not only to transport costs and trading profits, but also the royal customs duties at Calais and the ducal toll at Gravelines. It is not surprising therefore, that alternative supply routes increasingly gained favour.

In addition there were the 'Merchant Adventurers'; exporters of cloth who visited the annual fairs of Brabant in groups, and then returned to England. These merchants were not welcome in Flanders because of the embargo on the import of English cloth which had been enforced in order to protect domestic production. This did not, however, prevent the handling of a considerable amount of English cloth at Bruges, not only illegally but principally in transit by the Hanse, the Genoese and even by the inhabitants of Bruges themselves who had consignments sent to Middleburg or Antwerp, thus evading the Flemish import embargo.

Approximately two-thirds of English textile exports were destined for the Netherlands, to be finished there and re-exported. This trade was carried out essentially via the Brabant annual fairs by the Merchant Adventurers, but Hanse merchants also claimed part of the market. At a trading volume of at least 10,000 lengths of cloth (1465-66), manual workers in Brabant earned 10,000 Flemish pounds for dyeing and finishing, and the middleman earned 3,330 pounds. It is therefore understandable that, in these circumstances, other regions were not prepared to support Flanders in its attempts to ban the import of English cloth. There are two explanations for the success of the textile finishing process in Brabant: it was both technically superior and less costly than English methods. The necessary raw materials such as woad, madder, and alum had after all to be imported into England from the Netherlands themselves.

The textile industry in the Netherlands was also quick to respond in other circumstances. In the second quarter of the fifteenth century, England imported 107,000 ells of linen via the ports of

London and Sandwich; 82,000 ells of which came from the Netherlands. Of this amount, 34% was produced in Flanders, 30% in Brabant, 20% in Hainault and 15% in Holland and Zeeland. The cloth imported via Sandwich was principally Flemish. In 1530 the quantity of cloth imported into England from the Netherlands was ten times greater than the figure mentioned above, which gives an indication of the powerful expansion in this sector.

The many disruptions in this Anglo-Flemish trade were partly compensated by the use of another traditional channel – the import of wool via Scottish merchants. In 1387, after the Ghent war, when relations with England were still uncertain, Duke Philip the Bold hastily sought to implement a privilege dating from 1359 which gave protection to the Scots, thereby securing the import of wool from Scotland.

Although the focal point of Scottish trade lay in Flanders, Zeeland, (in particular Middelburg and also Veere after 1444) took this over whenever there was conflict between Scotland and Flanders, as there was in 1466. Middelburg managed to acquire even the Scottish staple between 1478 and 1483, and once again between 1522 and 1526. This staple was, however, never completely exclusive and wherever it was based, the trade in wool and cloth took place via both Flanders and Zeeland.

SOUTHERN EUROPE Although the relations with England and the Baltic countries accounted, quantitatively, for a significant proportion of the volume of trade in the Burgundian Netherlands, the southern countries were essential to the quality trade, particularly in Bruges. Firstly it must be emphasised that Bruges was the principal centre for the various European trading circuits, in particular those of northern and southern Europe. Without categorically stating that these circuits were complementary, there is evidence that there was actually exchange between north and south during certain periods and for certain products. Such transactions were carried out in the majority of cases via brokers from Bruges and other merchants of the Netherlands. These trading circuits overlapped somewhat along the Atlantic coasts, England and the southern Netherlands. The presence of northern Italians in Bruges had obviously been a crucial factor since olden times. They formed independent communities according to their town or country of origin; they enjoyed privileges granted by the count of Flanders, and elected authorities which exercised legal powers over these communities. The leader of a colony also functioned as a diplomatic representative to the duke of Burgundy. Each colony had a residence in the form of either a house, a lodge or a consulate, and worshipped in a specific chapel. The settlements of the Genoese, the Florentines, the Venetians and the Luccans were to be found in close proximity to what is today the Theatre Square. During the Ghent war, the

85. Portrait of a notary (St Ivo) by Quinten Metsys (first half of the sixteenth century). The landscape in the background is particularly well painted.

(Edinburgh, National Gallery of Scotland).

84. A magistrate's deed dated 28th May 1347, attached to the key of the coffer belonging to the 'Easteners', or German Hanse merchants at Bruges.

(Bruges, Municipal Archives).

Genoese, as the Hanse had done, transferred their staple from Bruges – this time to England. They could not be persuaded to return until 1398, and only then on the condition that reparations were made and additional regulations drawn up. The Venetians also moved across to the English ports during the difficult years. There is also evidence from the mid-fifteenth century of a Milanese consulate. Venice had the oldest consulate (established in 1322). The consulate of the Florentines was not established until 1427, possibly because its overseas trade did not become significant until after the capture of Pisa in 1406.

It is a well known fact that roughly once a year, the towns of northern Italy sent a fleet of galleons to the ports of southern England and to Bruges. These giant ships of 750 tons were propelled by oarsmen.

Italy exported its own agricultural products, luxury goods such as silk and velvet, as well as goods from the Levant and the Mediterranean : wines from Cyprus and Greece, oriental textiles, spices and herbs, and also fruits from the Iberian peninsula. The Italians were, above all, versatile wholesale dealers and specialists in money handling. The Medici bank, which had a subsidiary at Bruges from 1439 to 1490, is justly famous and provided invaluable support for the town itself and also for the dukes of Burgundy.

The Iberian 'nations' were also granted privileges in Flanders around 1400. The Catalan 'nation' which everywhere represented the merchants from Barcelona and Valencia belonging to the kingdom of Aragon, had been founded in Flanders since 1330. Philip the Bold renewed the privilege in 1389 during the period of economic recovery which followed the great uprising of 1379-1385. In 1384 the Portuguese also received a promise of safe conduct for their trade with Flanders, and this was extended in 1411 and 1438. The significance of their increasing presence in Bruges – furthered by Duchess Isabella of Portugal, lay in their contacts with new colonial trading routes. Initialy the Portuguese brought their own products such as rice, olives, raisins, figs, dates, pomegranates, oranges and sugar ; these items were, however, delicacies and were only to be found occasionally on the tables of a few families in the Netherlands. Thus in 1482, the town of Bruges offered "pomegranates, Spanish fruit and other delicacies" to the four-year-old hereditary prince Philip.

The importance of the Portuguese nation grew as the exploitation of the West African coast began to yield tropical products. In the latter half of the fifteenth century, the Portuguese exported African ivory to Bruges, and large quantities of sugar from Madeira (one-third of the total production in 1498) were also imported via Bruges as soon as production started on the island. The Portuguese 'factor' at Bruges was one of the most important exporters of European copper, which was used as a return cargo on the colonial trading routes. This arrangement existed in Bruges long before it reached Antwerp ; regularly from 1440 there was a Portuguese agent or representative of the king of Portugal in residence at Bruges. The first agent, Pedro Eanes, came to Flanders as early as 1429-30 in connection with the marriage of Duke Philip the Good to Isabella, a sister of Prince Henry the Navigator. The Duchess indeed frequently acted as patroness to the merchants from her mother-country.

The 'nation' of Castile was granted privileges in 1348, 1367 and 1384 – again shortly after the cessation (for Bruges, at least) of domestic hostilities. Its most important products were wool, (the

86. The forgery of coins and wine.
(Ghent, Cathedral Archives, miniature from ms 162B fo 36).

102

wool staple was officially established at Bruges in 1493), skins and iron ore. The development of new, lighter textiles depended to a large extent on the wool from the Spanish plain. In 1455 Biscay declared itself an independent nation.

Southern Germans, too, came from the south, but from a different direction. Considering the significance of the part they were to play, principally in the sixteenth century, in their connections with Antwerp, it is important to emphasise that the merchants of Nuremberg had also enjoyed a privilege at Bruges since 1362 ; this privilege was later extended and consolidated–no doubt bearing in mind the merchants' connections with England. In the fifteenth century the famous Grosse Ravensburger Handelgesellschaft opened an office in Bruges which dealt in textiles, copper, silver and other metal products from Germany. South German trade, however, continued to be dominated by merchants from the Rhineland for the greater part of the fifteenth century, and these merchants dealt mainly via Antwerp.

FOREIGN AND DOMESTIC TRADE   The relative importance of the various nations is difficult to determine. The extremely limited role of the French is striking ; at this stage they were apparently not in a position to concentrate on commercial expansion. The merchants of La Rochelle and St Jean d'Angély, however, enjoyed a privilege which had been established in 1331 and consolidated in 1387. This privilege was concerned explicitly with the wine staple at Damme.

87. Houses of the Castilian and Genoese merchants in Bruges.

(Engraving from A. Sanderus, *Flandria Illustrata*, 1641).

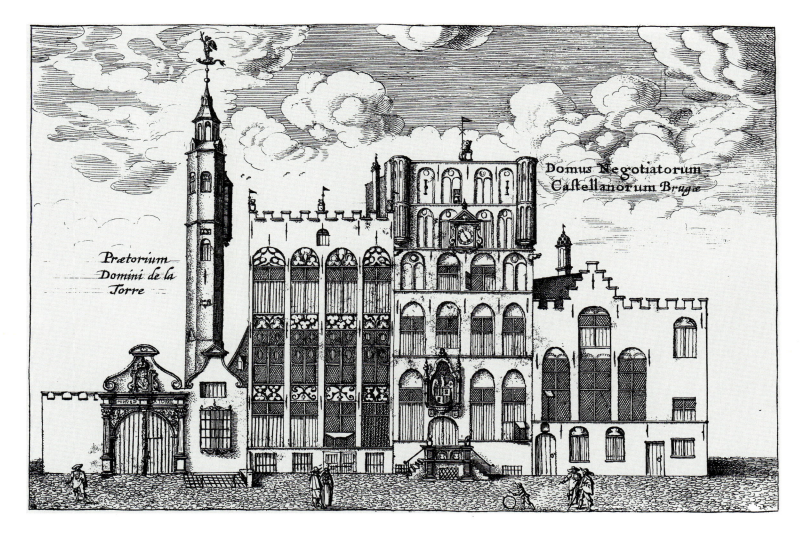

103

During the sixteenth century Antwerp likewise had a brisk trade with La Rochelle and Bordeaux. This by no means excluded the Hanse, the English and the Flemish who took a considerable share of the wine imports. The Bretons' maritime trade increased particularly after the Hundred Years War (1453), when they brought wine and salt to the Netherlands and took herring as a return cargo. Piracy seems to have frequently disturbed the good relations between the various trading partners. However, the French did not develop a permanent trading base at Bruges due to the fact that their trade was only limited and that the merchants involved were only organised on a small scale. Nor had the English had their own trading colony at Bruges since the establishment of a staple on their own territory at Calais. The Merchant Adventurers were, as we have seen, only in the Netherlands for short periods, and the comparatively short distance between the two countries certainly reduced the need for a permanent base. An indication of the numerical strength of these colonies can be obtained by looking at the numbers representing the various nations on ceremonial occasions such as the entry of Philip the Fair to Bruges in December 1440 or the marriage of Charles the Bold to Margaret of York at Damme in July of 1468. The former occasion was attended by : 130 Hansards, 48 Spaniards, 40 Venetians, 40 Milanese, 36 Genoese, 22 Florentines and 12 Luccans. The numbers of those representing Portugal, Catalonia and Scotland were not given.

The web of international trade and the role of Bruges as an international concourse can be gauged from the following. Francesco Datini, the textile dealer from Prato, had agents in Bruges and Spain. This is apparent from his extensive correspondence which has been preserved. In 1387 he was responsible for the loading of 2,000 lengths of cloth (from Wervik, Courtrai and other places along the Lys where 'light textiles' were produced) into Venetian ships at Bruges which were headed for Palermo. A second example : in 1397 Datini loaded 1,740 lengths of cloth of the same origin to supply merchants in Florence and Catalonia and elsewhere. These examples are drawn from a continual flow of textile exports to Barcelona, Valencia and Majorca, where this merchant (whose concern was by no means the largest in Italy) had agents. A similar flow of textile exports went to the Baltic countries which were supplied by the German Hanse. Between 1390 and 1399, 96% of products bought by the agent of the German Knights' Order (which monopolised Prussian trade) consisted of textiles. Most of these were serges, the light fabrics of combed wool, but there were also 11,000 lengths of Flemish cloth and fabrics from smaller centres such as Enghien and Herentals. The question thus arises whether all trade in the Netherlands was in the hands of foreign merchants : Italian, English and Hanse capital, ships, traders and buyers. Had the Netherlands become purely a nation of producers ?

Firstly it is important to note the exceptional nature of Bruges' circumstances. However important the town, it did not shut out other significant markets. The annual fairs in Brabant concentrated on the low Countries, with the English and the Germans as their principal foreign trading partners. There were also annual fairs in the Flemish towns such as Ypres. The drapers of Mechelen, Leuven and Maastricht took the export of their cloth into their own hands when the Merchant Adventurers boycotted the Brabant market from 1464 to 1467, and the merchants from Cologne and the Rhineland also experienced transport difficulties. The drapers of Brabant therefore visited the fairs personally, even those in Frankfurt, and

88. Encounter between fifteenth-century warships. A rowing barque (right) takes a commander on board. In 1460 Anthony, the Great Bastard of Burgundy, set out on a crusade, but got no further than Marseilles.

(Brussels, Royal Library, ms 10777, fo 46. Miniature from *La première guerre punique* of about 1460).

they controlled a significant proportion of the export during the first half of the sixteenth century. At Mechelen this amounted to as much as almost one half during the period 1546-1563.

There were, however, also many examples of entrepreneurial spirit in the Netherlands which were *not* prompted by a disruption of overseas relations. Copper from Dinant was, for example, regularly transported to England and possibly other destinations in Antwerp vessels chartered by two Dinant shippers. Merchants from Holland and Antwerp frequently competed with each other to gain a foothold in the North Sea and the Baltic, which the Hanseatic League regarded as its territory. Several more wealthy Antwerp shippers also exported to the Mediterranean. This even became a fairly regular route during the 40s and 50s. They carried wool from London for Italian shippers.

A close investigation reveals countless examples of Flemish merchants trading along the Atlantic coast and in the Mediterranean. At least five Flemish merchants were resident in Genoa between 1412 and 1437. It was not only Francesco Datini from Prato who was responsible for the export of Flemish cloth; at the end of the fifteenth century, the Grosse Ravensberger Handelsgesellschaft became concerned about a trio of Flemish traders who annually sold 200 lengths of cloth from Menen on the Genoese market, and a further 300 to 400 at Genoa and Naples.

The Scutelare family of Bruges were particularly energetic in reviving trading relations with England after the revolt of 1375-1385. Since the beginning of the fourteenth century this family had played a leading role as wholesale dealers in English wool, and thanks to their exceptional status as 'King's Merchant' enjoyed exemption from tolls. Various members of the family also held positions in local government. Around 1400, Lubrecht Scutelare owned in the street of the same name in Bruges the wool warehouse which was bought by the town from Lubrecht's heirs in 1415. We can catch a glimpse of Lubrecht's trading activities from the occasions on which his goods were confiscated : this happened in 1380 with a large cargo from England valued at 124 Flemish pounds, and also in 1408 at Sluis with a cargo of Scottish goods. In 1402 goods from Seville, belonging to Lievin Scutelare (later to become a burgomaster) were captured by privateers. This family exercised a definite political influence, designed to protect its own trading interests on an urban, national and even international scale.

Accounts of mutual privateering between England and Flanders during the period 1388-1404 mention the following cases which only represent a fraction of the actual Flemish trade. Cargoes mentioned other than wool and cloth comprise salt, fish and wine.

ORIGIN OF SHIPS SUBJECTED TO PRIVATEERING
BETWEEN FLANDERS AND ENGLAND 1388-1404

	Owners of captured Goods	Owners of captured Ships
Bruges	42	–
Sluis	28	42
Nieuwpoort	9	7
Dunkirk	8	–
Other coastal towns	22	10
Other towns	14	–
	123	59

Various Flemish traders sent goods to Spain and Portugal, insured ships and imported goods from Spain in liaison with other foreigners. During the first decade of the fifteenth century conflicts arose over the privateering between Spanish and Flemish traders (from Bruges, Damme and Nieuwpoort) sailing regularly in fleets to La Rochelle and Bourgneuf with wine and salt. When, between 1509 and 1512, Emperor Maximilian closed the Sound to merchants from Holland, Brabant and Flanders at the request of Hamburg and Lübeck, the Wendish towns brought in various ships from the Netherlands, and in particular from Antwerp. So traders and ships from the Netherlands appeared in the Baltic.

It was customary for merchants in overseas trading to share the cargoes and hence the risks. In all these complex transactions brokers played an important part as intermediaries and guarantors. They were associated in a highly respected guild at Bruges and their functions demonstrate their participation in business acumen.

The examples so far given have been concerned with relatively small enterprises ; this does not mean, however, that larger scale concerns did not exist, although not on the scale of those in Italy and southern Germany. The Bruges firm of Despars was particularly dynamic during the fifteenth century ; three of its members held offices in local government at the end of the fifteenth century and another member was a historian in the sixteenth century. The firm was active in many countries, introducing modern methods of payment and affiliation, and working with foreign representatives. Their transactions emanated from the Scheldt and the annual fairs in Brabant, and they had dealings with England, the Baltic countries, Italy, Spain and Portugal. Agents of the Despars Company were involved in the first sugar production on Madeira, where they were among the largest producers. Flanders provided the largest market for sugar, taking one-third of the total production, a proportion of which was, of course, re-exported.

There were undoubtedly countless other examples of hypermodern business enterprises in Bruges in the latter half of the fifteenth century. The Bruges merchant and later burgomaster, Maarten Lem, was associated with the large Genoese firm Lomellini whose monopolies included the grain trade between Andalusia and Genoa. A branch of the Genoese family Adorno from which another Bruges magistrate, Anselmus Adoorne originated, had settled in Flanders during the fourteenth century. In 1472 he took up the office of 'Protector of the privileges of the Scottish Nation', with too small a population to provide a permanent functionary. So the very close relations between the Netherlands and other countries contributed still further to the dynamic attitudes of numerous smaller merchants in the Netherlands.

BRUGES AND ANTWERP   Although the contrast between Bruges and Antwerp can be summarised as stimulating and complementary, and though the shift in emphasis only took place gradually, it was very real for all that.

89. A jeweller, a fishmonger and a pottery merchant stand at their stalls at the town gate to profit from the business there. Miniature ca 1458-1460 from David Aubert's *Les Chroniques et Conquêtes de Charlemagne*.

(Brussels, Royal Library, ms 9066, fo 11).

There are few statistics available showing the volume of trade during the fifteenth century and those which are available are seriously distorted. The difficulty with revenue from tolls is, for instance, that the most important groups of merchants were exempt from them.

The following figures showing the revenues for the toll-rights at the large toll-house at Sluis up to 1464, are very approximate since they are in fact rents. After this date revenues declined and more supervision was introduced. These figures show that a definite collapse came after (and possibly because of) the war with Maximilian.

RENTS FOR THE TOLL AT SLUIS

1384	7,800 pounds parisis	1493	2,800
1423	7,800	1501	3,175
1432	8,400	1511	2,825
1440	8,400	1517	2,600
1464	6,800	1533	2,675
1487	6,100	1540	2,518

The silting up of the Zwin was not an unfamiliar problem and although solutions were found, these proved unsuccessful and the problem became more acute as the traffic and tonnage increased. The heaviest blow came, however, from the war with Maximilian. Apart from the conflict which brought about the civil war between 1483 and 1492, there were repeated uprisings in Bruges. The culmination of this was the imprisonment of Maximilian himself, in Cranenburg House on the Market Place between the end of January and mid-May of 1488. The war proved extremely costly in terms of the disruptions in trade and the loss of cargoes. The leader of the revolt, Philip of Cleves eventually went into hiding at Sluis and blockaded the port until October 1492.

Maximilian, as we have seen, ordered all foreign merchants to leave Bruges in 1484, and he attempted to end the revolt by bringing economic pressure to bear. With or without such an order, the foreign merchants naturally knew that circumstances were not conducive to profitable trading, and they stayed away from Bruges.

For certain nations, such as the Portuguese, the move to Antwerp was intended to be permanent. After all, even after hostilities had ceased, Bruges itself and the whole of Flanders suffered from considerable damage and the crippling reparations which had to be paid. In 1488 and 1490, the municipality of Bruges received a sum of 20,000 Flemish pounds, an amount equivalent to the annual salary of 3,137 bricklayers' apprentices; this sum was provided by the wealthier citizens of Bruges in the form of special taxes and compulsory loans. By confiscating the property of those who had espoused the 'wrong' political cause, the town gained a further 5,500 pounds. Such a climate obviously did not encourage foreign merchants to return to Bruges.

Antwerp, however, enjoyed Maximilian's favour. The town had shown him loyalty, even when other Brabant towns (Brussels and Leuven) had joined the revolt. The social climate in Antwerp was relatively favourable; the guilds enjoyed less autonomy and exercised less political influence than those in the Flemish towns. The hidden advantage of such a climate was the fact that it could easily adapt

90. Fragment of a jeweller's shop contained in the legend of St Eloy by Petrus Christus, pupil of Jan van Eyck.

(New York, The Metropolitan Museum of Art, The Robert Lehman Collection).

to the requirements of the international market : the merchants of Antwerp, unencumbered by the strictures of the staple markets or the regulations of the guilds, could exploit any gap in the market. It is understandable, therefore, that the rapidly growing south German companies preferred to settle in the developing town of Antwerp rather than in the declining backward-looking bastion of their great competitor, the Hanseatic League. The new trendsetters (the Merchant Adventurers, the Portuguese and the south Germans), naturally attracted other interested parties to the area.

The fairs of Brabant were of great importance not only to Antwerp, but also to a large number of surrounding towns. In the weeks during which these were held, Bruges' commerce came to a standstill because a great variety of products and dealers (who enjoyed special legal protection) were to be found in Antwerp or Bergen-op-Zoom. The presence of Rhineland merchants was of great significance, as was the presence, from the mid-fifteenth century onwards, of the south Germans, the Merchant Adventurers, the Hanse merchants, the merchants from the South and, last but not least, the merchants from Brabant itself. Mechelen thus succeeded not only in securing its position at the annual fairs in Frankfurt, but also sold its cloth as far afield as Prussia, Silesia and Norway. Finally, in attempting to explain the shift of trade from Bruges, the effect of the numerous blockades in Flanders must be considered.

Although the Hanse moved to Dordrecht in the fifteenth century, Antwerp was increasingly the destination for other emigrants. It was, however, precisely during these difficult years for Flanders, that Brabant and Holland could begin to show their strength. This was equally true of relations with England. The continued restriction on English cloth imports into Flanders was not implemented in other areas. The serious disruptions of relations in the decade between about 1433 and about 1443 provided a golden opportunity for Brabant and Holland to come into their own, and they were not slow to do so.

The Netherlands : centre of international capitalism and banking

91. Arithmetica with, below, an arithmetic lesson using coins, ca 1500.

(Ghent, Cathedral Archives, miniature from ms 16B, fo 14).

Before 1300, a large part of the financial transactions between merchants (almost all of whom were constantly on the move since they had no other means of communicating) took place at the annual fairs – then the principal means of contact – according to fairly simple methods of payment. Payments were made in cash or on account with a bond. When, after 1300, some trading activities came to be based in certain locations, it was logical for financial transactions also to have a fixed location. This was to be the main factor in the development of banking. One of the European centres in which this system flourished in the fourteenth century was – together with a number of north-Italian towns – Bruges. Bruges, and also London, lay in the most favourable strategic location for contact between the two most important commercial networks in Europe, round the Mediterranean, and the Baltic. The increasing scale of transactions required an infrastructure which provided facilities for exchange and credit. Bruges thus became the centre of banking since it was already the focal point for trade.

Domestic, as well as many foreign bankers, set up in Bruges. It is no coincidence that the Medici family from Florence established one of the main branches of their international banking empire at Bruges. Nor is it a coincidence that the first 'stock exchange' – a fixed location for daily financial transactions – came into being at Bruges. This happened in 1453 long before Antwerp acquired its first stock exchange in 1485. The Bruges stock exchange was situated in a mansion belonging to the Van der Buerse family of brokers, which stood on the present-day Theatre Square, close to the trading houses of the various Italian nations.

In the sixteenth century, Antwerp became a money market on an international scale as the south-German merchants moved to Antwerp to trade with Spain and its colonies, with the English and, finally, also with the Italian concerns which had left Bruges because of the war. Bruges, however, figured more prominently than Antwerp on the international money market during the sixteenth century, since reliable contacts and expertise were vital in such a sector. The specialists who had established themselves in Bruges had built up their commercial network there, and also invested in the town. Certain trading sectors continued to prosper even after 1500, for example in the contact with the Iberian peninsula, formally recognised in the Spanish wool staple. As late as 1552-53 Bruges still took second place to Antwerp, though some way behind it, with 12% of all exports to Spain and 25% of all imports from Spain to the Netherlands. In 1569, when Alva's one-percent tax was levied on all goods, Bruges still took second place in the Netherlands with a revenue of 11,000 guilders, next to Antwerp with 37,000 guilders and far ahead of Tournai, Lille and Brussels where the tax was levied on revenues of less than 7,000 and 5,000 guilders. For many trading financiers there was thus no reason to leave Bruges. Although the contrast between Bruges and Antwerp has long been over-emphasised, and there was structurally not such a great difference between the two, it is nevertheless true to say that after 1500 Antwerp profited from the presence of southern German traders, who were

92. *The money-changer and his Wife* by Quinten Metsys, 1514. The quantity of the various coinages of different weights and content which circulated in the international trading centres such as Bruges and Antwerp meant that continual valuation was necessary. The money-changers became financial experts who also fulfilled banking roles.

(Paris, Louvre Museum).

less evident in Bruges. It was, after all, the Fuggers and the Welsers who dominated the lively Spanish and Portuguese markets and their overseas hinterlands.

There is another striking parallel between the two international money markets. In both cases – as in Lyons and also later in Amsterdam – a flourishing banking sector developed from the trade in commodities. That Antwerp reached its peak as a financial centre later than Bruges was simply due to the fact that transactions in commodities developed later there.

THE STRUCTURAL CHARACTERISTICS OF BANKING Financial transactions and the provision of credit are a part of all trading operations. The mere extension of credit by a merchant to his own clients does not constitute money-trading or banking. It does so, however, as soon as credit is extended or bills of exchange issued to those who are not dealing directly with a merchant. During the period in question in the Netherlands there were traders and trading firms (Medici, Peruzzi, etc.) whose trading activities were combined with various banking functions and even investment in the industrial sector. There were also professional financiers in the Netherlands, who dealt solely with money : from 1230 onwards Lombards, a collective name referring mainly to financiers from northern Italy (Lombardy), although they also originated from other places ; the Cahorsins from the financial centre of Cahors in southern France ;

and the Jews. These professional groups offered facilities for loans and simple currency exchange at money-borrowing tables or banks in various towns from 1280 onwards. Brokers also occasionally engaged in financial activities. This was a logical extension of their role as intermediaries in the commodities trade. Quite a large group of owners of town mansions were active as commodity brokers at Bruges in particular.

In the thirteenth century, banking was still restricted to straight-forward loans, whereby merchants redirected excess capital in the form of loans to other merchants, or simply provided short-term consumer credit. Eventually, following the Italian example, exchange was introduced : the manual exchange of the many foreign currencies which were circulating in the Netherlands, dealings in precious metals, the exchange of coins or the buying up of coins which had been taken out of circulation to be used as metal for melting down (so-called bullion) in the minting workshops. These activities took place at open-air stalls which were to be found mainly in the central streets of the town – in the case of Bruges, close to the Market Place.

The next step was the development of the deposit facility, whereby the banker received and held money for his clients, keeping a current account or 'conto' for each of these clients. This led to a system of transferring money from one account to another at the same bank or at different banks, in the same or different towns, and even abroad without all the risks of transporting ingots. Since in theory not all deposits were ever transferred or withdrawn at any one time, the banker could use these reserves for investment or loans to a third party. The deposit-bankers (so-called 'cambists') were concentrated mainly at Bruges in the Netherlands, where the influence of the Italian financial experts was greatest. The banking activities of figures such as Willem Ruweel and Colaert van Marke in the latter half of the fourteenth century are those with which we are most familiar, since their records happened to be preserved after bankruptcy proceedings. It is known that they had fifteen or so colleagues apart from the agencies of the Italian banks.

Bruges was the most northerly town in which Italian merchant-bankers had agencies. In the northern and eastern countries Hanse merchants engaged in banking activities, albeit in a more primitive manner. They received, for example, the papal revenues which they used as capital to purchase goods to be traded at Bruges. There they transferred the equivalent of the sum received to an Italian firm, which in turn transferred it, by way of a bill of exchange, to the papal court. This again indicates the significance of Bruges as a link between northern and southern Europe.

One of the weaknesses was the lack of systematic agreement between the banks or exchanges, another was the absence of a central bank to which the other banking institutions could themselves turn. Consequently when unexpectedly large withdrawals were made, certain banks did not have sufficient funds and were thus put out of business. Many financiers disappeared from the market in this way during the fourteenth century. There were several solutions to this problem. Although the Bardi and Peruzzi from Florence, with branches in England and Flanders, went out of business in the mid-fourteenth century, this was due to their highly centralised structure which meant that any conflict with the English crown could have disastrous consequences for the entire concern. The success of the Medici family in the fifteenth century was due to the fact that the firm owned the capital of all the branches, but also pursued a policy of decentralisation whereby the central office could not be held legally responsible should one of its branches get into difficulties. In the sixteenth century, protection was provided by the public bank.

THE PROMOTERS OF THE MONEY-TRADE During the Burgundian period the money-trade was in the hands of domestic as well as foreign financiers. Domestic money-changers in Flanders and Brabant operated as bankers from the fourteenth century onwards, and in some towns earlier than that, by accepting deposits, orders for payments and by placing capital investments and municipal loans. Their activities seldom extended further than the borders of their principality. These brokers whose 'float' was initially borrowed from the duke, handled considerable sums of money particularly in connection with public finances.

In addition, the Lombards and Cahorsins had built up powerful corporations in various towns. They paid an annual due to the duke for the right to practice their trade. During the fourteenth and fifteenth centuries their original designations were used at random when more financiers in the home country began to compete. It was thus decreed at Antwerp in 1306 that citizens wishing to extend credit must charge at a rate of interest no higher than that charged by the Lombards. The latter thus enjoyed a reputation for providing loans against collateral or security, although they by no means exercised a monopoly over this market. The secular and clerical authorities profited from this trade in money and so this contravention of canon law was discreetly tolerated. The Jews did not in fact have any great influence in the Netherlands; after the pogroms during the plague epidemic of 1349-50, there was scarcely any evidence of them in Guelders and Brabant, and elsewhere their activities were only modest compared with the Lombards.

The most important group was formed by the large Italian firms which, like the present-day multinationals, spread their agencies throughout Europe and engaged in banking as well as trading activities. At the end of the thirteenth century they poured into the Netherlands from Sienna, Florence and Lucca. It was these concerns which made Bruges into a 'piazza di cambio' on a European scale in the fourteenth and fifteenth centuries, and the amount of money involved in exchanges far exceeded that involved in trading commodities. The first group, to which the Florentine Bardi and Peruzzi concerns belonged were however "giants with clay feet". As well as being active in Flanders, they also financed the English monarchy. When the crown fell into financial difficulties at the beginning of the Hundred Years War, the king shed his own bankruptcy onto the Italian firms that had given credit facilities. At the end of the fourteenth century the Rapondi of Lucca acted as private financiers to the Burgundian crown with more success. Dino Rapondi financed the Franco-Burgundian invasion of England in 1386, and in 1396 he lent 200,000 guilders to Philip the Bold so that the latter could pay the ransom for his son John the Fearless, who had been taken prisoner during the attack on the Ottoman Turks at Nicopolis.

During the fifteenth century banking was dominated by the Medici of Florence who established offices in Paris, Lyons and also Bruges. Their success was mainly due to their innovation of investing not only family capital but also the deposits from a wide range of investors. In this way the Medici developed their business into one of the banchi grossi – large banking houses with an international network.

Tommaso Portinari, who became head of the Bruges branch of the Medici bank after twenty-five years there, was appointed councillor by Charles the Bold. The duke used his contacts with the bank to borrow money for the payment of troops in the Swiss-Burgundian border region during the summer campaign of 1476, and on occasions Portinari also extended credit to Charles himself and his allies. In his turn Portinari profited from the favour of the duke by being appointed leaseholder of the toll at Gravelines and having the monopoly of the import of alum (a fixative in the textile industry) from the papal states. Indeed Portinari became so deeply involved with the financing of the Burgundian wars that Lorenzo il Magnifico, as head of the Medici, broke his contacts with the Bruges branch – possibly also as a result of political pressure from King Louis XI of France.

Northern, central and eastern Europe were not, however, controlled by these Italian concerns. Here, then, there was scope for indigenous financiers – the southern Germans and those from the Hanseatics. It was the southern Germans (of whom the Fuggers are the most well known), active in textiles from 1368, and later also in silk, trade and banking, who built up an international empire in Venice, the Levant, Scandinavia and the Netherlands (particularly in Antwerp) and who were also bankers of the Hapsburg dynasty.

FORMS OF CREDIT Bankers, government institutions and private individuals devised many forms of credit. The oldest form of credit is consumer credit, originally linked to agriculture but necessarily used during the supply crises of the late Middle Ages. A form of social credit would have been a logical development from this. Authors such as Philippe de Mézières in *Le Songe du Vieil Pelerin* (1389) and his predecessors from 1326 onwards, had already proposed the idea of a peoples' credit with low interest rates. This idea was not realised however, until 1428 when the first Refuge of Mercy was

93. Aquarel '*St George's Court*' at Ghent, by Lieven van Schelden, 1584. This well-preserved house belonging to the archers' guild provided the setting for the dramatic assemblies of the States-General in 1477 and 1482.

(Ghent, Bijlokemuseum).

established in Italy under the influence of the Franciscans as an alternative to the lending houses of the Jews and Lombards. In the Netherlands, this example was followed at Ypres, where, in 1534 a 'bursa cambium' was established which granted interest-free loans to the poor. Similar institutions were set up at Antwerp in 1555 and Bruges in 1572.

The normal from of credit was, however, trading credit. In the fourteenth century the system of 'commenda' reached the Netherlands, by which a resident merchant would lend part or all of his capital to a travelling merchant and any profits would be divided as pre-arranged. This form of credit originated principally from Genoa and the Mediterranean, but was also used by the Hanseatic League in the form of 'Sendevegeschaft' or 'Widerlegung'. This formula was incidentally to be the basis for the later marine insurance.

From the fourteenth century the bill of exchange was not only an instrument in international trade whereby capital could be transferred or converted into another currency, but was also used as a short-term form of trading credit. The logic behind this was that a pre-determined period of time should elapse between the issue and maturity of each bill of exchange, allowing for the length of journeys. Between Bruges and Italy, for example a period of two months usually elapsed between issue and maturity (usanza); for London and Barcelona 30 days, and Montpellier 40 days. Whether or not a bill of exchange was encashed, it still entitled the holder to several weeks' or months' credit. The interest on such operations was concealed in the exchange rates – thus skilfully evading the church's ban on usury. The enormous popularity of the bill of exchange can be explained by its simple form : a small note with one or two lines in standard formulae was sufficient.

It was therefore in the interest of the international trader to follow closely the exchange rates of the major European currencies. Consequently from the fourteenth century onwards there emerged a network of European trade correspondents. These correspondents reported several times each week on the general market situation, the climate on the stock exchange, and political and economic circumstances which could influence values and prices ; at the same time noting the fluctuations in prices of certain essential products, such as spices, and also the exchange rates of foreign currencies. Correspondence of this sort has survived from a number of houses, the finest being that of the Datini family from Prato. This correspondence provides highly detailed information concerning the relations between Bruges and Genoa, Paris, Venice, London and Barcelona. During certain periods the head office at Prato was receiving information from four correspondents at Bruges (among whom was Altobianco degli Alberti, the previously-mentioned textile merchant from Wervik). The similarity between the accounts of the various correspondents is striking, which is an indication of the degree of rationalisation and depersonalisation in the international trade of money and commodities.

Finally, there was also credit on real estate whereby profits were made on land which had been leased, or through rents from houses built on such land. In the late Middle Ages, the majority of the town authorities earned considerable sums through the issue of complete and perpetual annuities : in exchange for an initial sum, interest was paid annually for the length of the recipient's life (or in perpetuity). Basically this system meant that the towns covered their expenditure, and often the taxes paid to the prince, by taking up long-term loans. Usually, the interest rate on such loans was 6.25

94 A. Double gold helm bearing the arms of Burgundy and Flanders, minted at Ghent according to the decrees of 1386 and 1388 during the reign of Duke Philip the Bold. The designer was inspired by a French example.

B. Double groat or 'stuiver' with two coats of arms, minted at Ghent according to the decree of 1387.

C. Gold angel holding the Burgundian and Flemish shields. Minted at Ghent according to the decree of 1387. Imitation of a French coin.

D. Gold 'nobel' bearing the crowned figure of Philip the Bold in a ship. The designer of this coin is following an English example. Minted at Ghent according to the decree of 1388.

E. Silver groat with sedent lion, minted according to the decree of 1389. The silver 'groat' of Flanders was the base unit of all currencies in the Netherlands.

F. Gold 'ryder' minted at Ghent according to the decree of Philip the Good anno 1433. A more valuable currency was issued in all provinces after the acquisition of Hainault, Holland, Zeeland and Brabant.

G. Silver double groat, known as the Four-lander, minted according to the decree of 1434. This type of coin was among the first minted for circulation throughout the Burgundian Netherlands.

H. Gold lion of 1454. The first gold coin typical of the Netherlands.

I. The 'mite' of 1451-1458. The mite was worth one twenty-forth of a groat. This small coin contained copper with only very little silver, which made it black. These coins became well-worn due to the lack of attention paid to finishing off (due to their low value) and extensive use.

J. Andries guilder minted during the reign of Duke Charles the Bold between 1468 and 1474, showing the patron saint of the Burgundians, St Andrew.

K. Silver double stuiver minted in Brussels between 1468 and 1474.

L. Silver double stuiver, known as the 'Vuuryser' (fire-iron), dated 1474. Silver coins were dated for the first time during the reign of Duke Charles the Bold.

A, B, C, D, E, J. Bruges, Collection of the European Society of Numismatics.

F, G, H, I, K, L. Bruges, society of Antiquities.

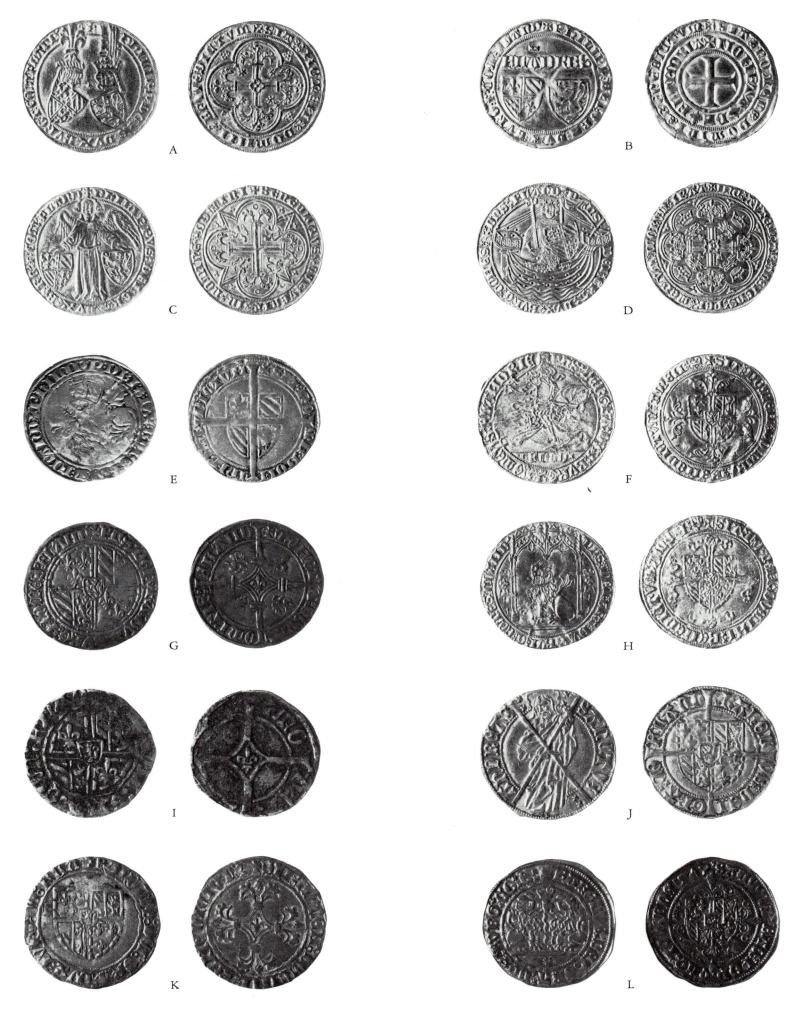

A

B

C

D

E

F

G

H

I

J

K

L

per cent; however, this increased during difficult periods (8.33 per cent in 1488). Since the majority of loans were in the form of annuities which were paid off each year at the current rate of interest, the income for the lender was at best modest – but nevertheless secure. A broad category of small-savers were thus able to invest securely whilst the burden was borne by the whole community. It was also usual for a town taking up a loan to look for money lenders outside its own walls.

The discharge of these debts gradually absorbed a very substantial proportion of the municipal budget. The budget of the city of Ghent thus increased under the pressure of taxes payable to the duke. Although incomes fluctuated during the period 1400 to 1430 between 38,000 and 94,000 pounds groats, they had to be increased to between 170,000 and 355,000 pounds groats during the period 1453-1475. Until 1430 the budget deficit regularly absorbed as much as 20 to 55 per cent of the town's revenue, and this figure would increase to about 100 per cent after a war. Only through loans and increases in consumer tax could the towns meet their increasing financial obligations to the central government. We are in fact concerned here with the phenomenon of the public debt, which was a permanent factor for almost all towns during the fourteenth and fifteenth centuries and grew continually. Well into the sixteenth century this system was adopted on a national scale, resulting in the notorious state bankruptcies in France and Spain (from 1559).

MONEY: 'LA SERVA PADRONA' OF THE ECONOMY   Currency, being the medium for almost all transactions, reflects the economic situation of a particular region. But it also has its own laws and potentiality which can favourably or adversely affect economic activities. There was already around 1400 a considerable knowledge ot the workings of monetary mechanisms in the commercial world of Bruges and other towns. Those involved in central government were, however, less familiar with these mechanisms and frequently sought the advice of experts from the commercial sector, often in the towns. During the Ancien Régime a government could adopt one or two attitudes towards monetary systems. If a government was convinced that a stable currency was beneficial to the wealth of its subjects and consequently also to its own fiscal revenues, then every effort was made to ensure a reasonable rate of exchange which thereby enabled the currency to withstand pressure from abroad. Such pressure could, however, be so strong that adjustments to international exchange rates were inevitable.

Another monetary policy available to the government was to attempt, if driven by an acute monetary shortage, to derive as much profit as possible from its seigniorage. This meant that a government distributed coins whose intrinsic value (i.e. alloy content) was consistently lower than their extrinsic (i.e. market) value. This mechanism was described in a classic manner in 1558 by Thomas Gresham, agent of the English crown in Antwerp, who proclaimed that "Bad money drives out the good". By devaluing its own coinage, a government could pay relatively high prices for minting-metal which was then supplied in abundance to its minting workshops. The devalued currency then flooded the market and the better coins were hoarded or exchanged, but in any case disappeared from circulation.

The rulers of the Burgundian Netherlands employed both forms of monetary policy. For the maintenance of a stable currency they could consistently rely on the sympathy and co-operation of those representing their subjects. A solid and reliable currency was, after all, in the best interest of trade and industry. Well known are the promises made in this connection by Duke John the Fearless in 1410 and 1418, to the effect that he would not alter the value of his money during fifteen years and his lifetime respectively. Philip the Good repeated such a promise in 1433 for a period of 20 years, following a series of devaluations. Although Philip the Fair did not make such a promise – having perhaps seen from his forefathers that such a promise could not be kept – he nevertheless maintained a stable currency from 1496, as did his sister, the Governess Margaret of Austria.

The economic benefits of such a policy were clearly visible during both these periods; good intentions were, however, not always enough.

Duke Philip the Bold found himself obliged to devalue the Flemish currency in 1387 and 1388 by a total of 24 per cent in order to avoid an outflow of precious metals to France, where there had been marked devaluations. The gold price paid by the official mints in

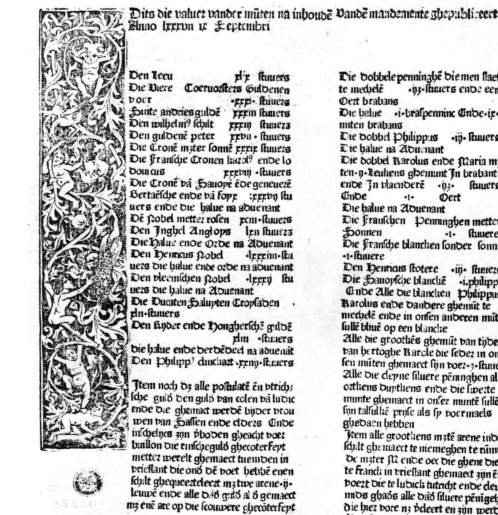

95. A fifteenth-century mint workshop with accompanying text: *This is the value of the coins according to the decree published on 9th September 1487* and published by Louis Ravescot in Leuven. On the right is the smelting oven where the alloy is taken out in a cylinder and cut into discs; next the minting with a hammer and die on the disc, under the arms of the Burgundians. In the centre, the master of the mint selling the new pieces, while in the shop on the left, old coins are being weighed and brought in.

119

Flanders thus rose from approximately 8 pounds per mark (of 244,753 gm) to as much as 13 pounds in 1389. Philip's policy in turn brought about the disruption of the Brabant currency, which was linked to the Flemish currency. From 1389, however, revaluation was possible and devaluations did not occur again until 1416.

We have another instance of inevitable adjustment under external pressure between 1433 and 1466. The avowedly stable gold coin of the recently united provinces of the Netherlands was undergoing increasing competition from the slightly cheaper gold coins minted in Guelders and the Rhineland (Cologne, Trier). The Burgundian mints were frequently having to close their doors because of a gold shortage. The Burgundian gold coin consequently became scarce and even more expensive, and as a result tended to depreciate. The power of the Netherlands market nevertheless still proved sufficient to turn back the ebb of gold – albeit in the form of Rhineland guilders.

In this constant international flow of precious metals and various currencies, we can appreciate the importance of the money-changers' business. Where there was some doubt about the stated weight and content of every gold coin, precise weighing and the verification of the given values was thus essential. Each issue of a new coin had, after all, to bear some form of distinguishing mark. Determination of the alloy content was particularly difficult and only possible by chemical analysis, which involved the destruction of the coin in question. This method could consequently only be used in exceptional circumstances.

96. Fifteenth-century merchants' houses at Damme.

120

Gold coins were so valuable that they were not in everyday use by the populace. A Burgundian gold coin named the 'nobel' was worth 72 silver groats in 1400, when a bricklayer's journeyman was earning 5 groats per day. Obviously he would not have come into contact with many such gold coins during his lifetime. But the intrinsic value (that is to say the value of the metal used to produce the coin) of silver coins was also manipulated, so that each user had to pay constant attention to what he was given. (See appendix : Monetary Systems).

At certain times, rulers with an eye to lucrative gain resorted to the devaluation of their coinage without informing their subjects of the exact extent of the drop in value of their coinage, let alone asking for their compliance. The delayed reactions of the user and his difficulties in trying to discover what had happened to the alloy content of the coins in his possession, were thus exploited and speculated upon. Philip the Good although bound in Flanders by his promise to maintain a stable currency ran into financial difficulties before his conquest of Holland and Hainault and financed this war from 1425 onwards largely from profits derived from the minting of inferior gold coins at Dordrecht and Namur. Despite Flanders' refusal to grant Philip a subsidy for this purpose, it nevertheless found itself contributing to the cause via other channels. From 1426 Philip also issued devalued gold and silver coinage at Ghent, despite protests from the 'Four Members'. Although Philip's income from the issue of coinage before 1425 was negligible, it greatly increased after this time, increasing to as much as 5,459 Flemish pounds, most of which was made at Namur. The effects of this were not restricted to Flanders and Brabant, for where gold was concerned, England was also seriously affected. As the medium of international trade, gold was sensitive to fluctuations in the currencies of any country with which commercial links existed. From 1425 to 1433, devaluations in the Netherlands attracted so much gold from England that the minting of coins there was reduced to a minimum. This is yet another example of the high degree of integration within the European economic system, with the Netherlands at its pivotal point. (See appendix ; fig. G).

This situation naturally led to English counter-measures limiting the export of wool, resulting in tensions which led in turn to unrest among the textile workers of Ghent. In 1433 Philip the Good returned to a monetary policy designed to ensure stability, this time for all the provinces of the Netherlands.

The symbol of this new unity was the 'vierlander' – a silver coin with the value of one stuiver (2 groats) which was to form the basis of the monetary system throughout the Netherlands. Relations with England, however, remained sensitive for many years to come. A second period of lucrative devaluation took place during the reign of Maximilian who, from 1485 to 1489, having been refused a subsidy by his subjects, proceeded to derive his profits from artificially increased mintage. His policy amounted to a tax of 12 per cent on the coinage. Maximilian thus had access, in times of civil war, to pecuniary resources in spite of the fact that these had been denied him by the assemblies of provincial States. The disadvantages of this were of course obvious : galloping inflation during a period also beset by disruptions in trade and harvest failure.

Maximilian's own attempts to return to a strong currency in 1489, during total civil war, only resulted in further chaos. The prescribed revaluation would supposedly reduce all prices, wages and contractual repayments by one-third. But with the war and its scarcities

there was no way this could be achieved. Only after the cessation of hostilities in 1492 was some sort of order gradually re-established in financial matters.

The gradual decline of the Burgundian currency can be seen in the exchange rates recorded in trading correspondence. The strongest currencies in Europe were the Venetian ducat, the Florentine florin and the Genoese guilder. The format, weight, and alloy content of these gold coins remained virtually unaltered for centuries, indicating a solid economic supremacy and a resultant international confidence. The demand for Italian currencies was also considerable at this time, and was reflected in exchange rates which varied according to the direction of transactions; the exchange rate from Venice to Bruges was thus higher than that for the return transaction from Bruges to Venice, with a profit margin of 7.7 to 28.8 per cent for the money-lenders, depending on the ratio of the two exchange rates. By contrast with its relationship to the Venice money market, the Bruges money market was stronger than those of London and Barcelona.

The Netherlands did not have one particular type of gold coin as was the case in the larger Italian towns and in England. The value of a gold coin was in fact based upon its relation to the groat, a silver coin which was the basis of the Flemish coinage and also, from 1433, of the Netherlands' currency. If, as the figures below indicate, the exchange rate of foreign gold coins persistently increased relative to the Burgundian silver coinage, this reflects above all the depreciation of the Flemish groat. (See appendix: fig. 8).

THE EXCHANGE RATE OF FOREIGN GOLD COINS AT BRUGES

	Venetian Ducat		English Nobel
1410	40 groats	1400	72 groats
1458	54 1/2	1447	92
1474	60 1/3	1483	104
		1487	134 1/2

This process is considered by economists today to stimulate economic growth, partly because it benefits producers and traders. This development brought yet more profit, in a system with a double standard – gold and silver – to those holding gold (the capital owners) with respect to the holders of silver. Finally, depreciation of the coinage was a means of increasing the money supply, apart from other methods such as the accretion of deposit money (bank accounts, bills of exchange). So long as the supply of precious metals in Europe remained constant, these were the only means by which the money supply could be increased. Mining produced few precious metals and gold only trickled in from North Africa. It was not until the 1480s that the introduction of new techniques in mining and refining in central Europe and the Hapsburg countries yielded a consistent supply of silver. This ensured the stability of European currencies for several decades to come.

THE CAPITALIST ENTREPRENEURIAL SPIRIT It has been overstated that the church's prohibition on usury placed a considerable restriction on the expansion of trade in the late Middle Ages, although

97. Portrait of Tommaso Portinari (ca 1432-1501), Italian banker and Bruges agent for the Medici bank. He was appointed councillor by Duke Charles the Bold.

(New York, the Metropolitan Museum of Art, Benjamin Altman Bequest. Hans Memlinc).

in practice the edicts were enthusiastically evaded in the most cunning of ways. In his well-known theory of the connection between a capitalist spirit and the Protestant ethic, Max Weber stated that the conditions that promoted the concentration and large scale operation of business in the sixteenth century were not present until the Reformation. The Burgundian Netherlands, however, disproved the exclusive claims of his proposition.

As is often the case, morality lagged far behind well-established custom. The theoretical doctrine was not in fact a great deterrent, although the absence of certain elements in the credit system of the Middle Ages, such as discount, did hinder trade. Even in the Catholic Netherlands, an edict of 1540 lifted the prohibition on usury, admittedly for the purpose of improving control through new legislation. It is nevertheless true to say that the capitalist spirit, the rational pursuit of profit maximisation and accumulation as a goal in itself, clearly dominated international trading during the fourteenth and fifteenth centuries.

Banking is an interesting activity illustrating the rise of capitalist thinking and dealing in the Netherlands. Between 1300 and 1500 we see, in the Low Countries as in Italy (earlier on) and south Germany, the appearance of such signs which gradually gain momentum and scope, finally involving structural changes too.

The accumulation of increasing stocks of capital by a small number of large firms on a European scale and with European ambitions undoubtedly shows a capitalistic tendency. As early as the fourteenth century, the Pazzi of Florence also had such ambitions and had accumulated capital equivalent to the value of 147 kg of fine gold. Increases in the scale are evident from the amount of capital held by the Medici in the mid-fifteenth century (1750 kg) and also from the capital held by the south German Fuggers in 1546 (13,000 kg). The process which was also carried through in the Netherlands, mainly in Bruges and Antwerp where these firms were active, had therefore begun long before 1500.

A second characteristic of capitalism is the concentration within these banking firms. During the thirteenth and fourteenth centuries many individual and locally organised money-changers and banchi were still active; after 1400, however, the money trade came increasingly into the hands of large trading companies with a central office and a network of branches throughout Europe (including the banking town of Bruges). This was the case with the Florentine Medici, and also with the firm of Veckinchusen from the north German trading centre of Lübeck, or the Grosse Ravensburger Gesellschaft at Ravensburg, near Lake Constance. Here we see centralised accumulations of capital with, at the same time, branches of the firms that were able to pursue their own policies in their various locations independent of the central establishment, which in turn was not held legally responsible for financial misfortune or bankruptcy at any of the branches. The growing tendency among firms to plough back profits or to reinvest in other sectors under their control, thereby reducing the risk of bankruptcy in a particular sector, also looks very capitalist.

In the fourteenth century, merchants from the Netherlands were already buying expensive foreign wool for the small textile producers, and even sometimes supplying them with looms and other materials. By doing this the merchants hoped to ensure constant production and secure their right to a part or all of that production in a particular centre. From the end of the fourteenth century onwards, foreign firms also practised this form of trading capitalism. The firms of southern Germany, such as the Fuggers, could attribute their growth from 1368 to investment from their main activity in textiles, in silver mining, in the spice and silk trade with the Levant and in a wide range of banking activities. To a certain extent rural investment by merchants from the towns, which led to the alienation of the farm workers from their patrimony, could equally be seen as a symptom of capitalist aggregation. This argument is even more valid in cases where international merchants provided the financial backing for rural industries. This process was also under way in the Netherlands in the thirteenth century, and became even more evident during the Burgundian period.

The spread of late-medieval capitalism was also evident in the growing impact of banking on the populace. By the third quarter of the fourteenth century, credit and banking had developed in Bruges to such an extent that the banker Ruweel already had 82 deposit accounts on his books. Since there were some fifteen or sixteen money-changers at Bruges at this time, this would imply a total of approximately 1,200 accounts *i.e.* one account for every 38 persons (two out of every seventeen households) at Bruges whose population then numbered approximately 46,000. Even if some citizens of Bruges had accounts with several banks, and clients from outside Bruges dealt with the money-changers, the number of accounts can still be at 1 per 100 inhabitants, or 1 per 20 families.

From the fifteenth century onwards, the banks were less and less inclined to make use of their own capital; not only did they aim to attract the capital of wealthy merchants, they also tried to attract more small deposits from private individuals. Savings institutions underwent, as it were, a process of democratization. This increase in the supply of savings caused interest rates to fall from approximately 20% between 1420 and 1430 to 10% and even 5% thereafter. This decrease meant that the bankers could, in turn, charge less interest on their clients' loans; trading credit, in other words, became cheaper and this also paved the way for the development of capitalist forms of enterprise. Typical of this course of events was the stock exchange at Bruges, which was established in the mid-fifteenth century, originally the place for transactions in goods, loans and dealings in futures, while the stock exchange at Antwerp specialized entirely in finance from 1530 onwards : international loans, wages, and above all debentures.

A further feature of capitalism was the introducing of new and more refined methods of payment, the purpose of which was to facilitate (trading) transactions and to provide better protection against bankruptcy for banking institutions. Throughout the whole of the fourteenth, fifteenth and the first half of the sixteenth century there is a steady development here too, though the financial transactions were regularly restricted by the church's ban on usury. The Italians in Bruges in the fifteenth century and the Germans at Antwerp during the sixteenth century were both forced to take this factor into consideration, though it never entirely paralyzed the banking system. Canonical law could not prevent the spread of devious credit formulae which reached the Netherlands from Italy as early as the fourteenth century. Because of the canonical taboo on the payment of interest, the loan of a capital sum was discreetly concealed in a shipping insurance document in which the loan interest looked like a premium.

Discount and endorsement are formulae which were formerly thought to be innovations of the sixteenth century, but they have recently been traced back as far as 1410. Did the late-medieval system of credit give an essential impetus to the rapid expansion up to 1550 ? The market centres of the fifteenth century, but also those of the sixteenth century, were frequently hidebound by tradition. During both centuries the flow of capital was restricted by the aversion to illicit ursury. The ambitions of figures and groups, such as Jacques Cœur (banker to the king of France), the Italian and south German bankers, and Portinari, bankers to Charles the Bold, were clearly capitalist. However, the economic base and the social structures within which these figures operated had not in many respects advanced to the same degree ; they were too primitive, too corporate, too rigid. Hence the high casualty rate among these early capitalists. Even the Medici ran into serious difficulties between 1468 and 1470, after reaching their peak just before this, and declined steadily from 1484. There seems to be reason to accept Henri Pirenne's thesis concerning the fluctuations in dynasties of businessmen and financiers, which suggests that the descendants of the founders of such firms often had difficulty in adjusting to new economic conditions and did not always inherit the entrepreneurial spirit. Yves Renouard has confirmed this : "L'homme d'affaire dégénère et s'embourgeoise". It would perhaps have been more accurate to say that the third or fourth generation of a trading family aspired to an aristocratic way of life which offered more prestige and less risks. However, during the fourteenth century the Florentines were in the ascendancy, with the Bardi, Peruzzi, Acciaiuoli as were the financiers from Piacenza. At the end of the fourteenth century the Rapondi of Lucca took over in the Netherlands, and later, once again, other Florentines such as the Medici. In England from the end of the fifteenth to the mid-sixteenth century, Tuscan families such as the Frescobaldi and Gualterotti were supreme (as they had been in Flanders), in Antwerp the Ducci and Affaitadi, and in Lyons the Pazzi and Strozzi. During the mid-sixteenth century the south Germans took over, while on the Italian side the Genoese families of Spinola and Grimaldi came to the fore. There was also a continual shifting of merchant interests between successive economic centres. When, during the second half of the fifteenth century, the position of the Levant was threatened by the Turkish expansion, the Italian bankers redirected their interests towards the western Mediterranean, (Spain, Portugal), the Atlantic zone (north-west Europe) and even west Africa. This mobility enabled international capital, which developed into a worldwide system from the fifteenth century, to remain stable. There is no doubt that the Burgundian Netherlands held a key position in this rapidly expanding network.

98. *Duchess Margaret of York performs the seven acts of charity.* Miniature by Dreux Jean from a Brussels manuscript of 1468-1477. An illustration such as this bears witness to the patronage of an art-loving lady, but at the same time conveys the image of the Christian governess.

(Brussels, Royal Library, ms 9296, fo 1).

4

Estates and Class

There have been heated scholarly discussions as to whether late medieval society was divided according to estate or class. The former involves grouping individuals according to their social prestige. This is based upon their lineage and way of life. Awareness of one's own social position and that of others is central to this social concept. The traditional picture of a society divided into three estates of which the first two, the nobility and clergy, were privileged and for the third of which, who were there to maintain the 'leisure class', there was not even a name, was indeed a product of the clerical mind during the High Middle Ages. In their own interest they presented society in such a way that those who fulfilled the most worthy and all-important function of maintaining human relationships with God, were protected by the second estate and supported materially by the third. In order that the nobility could properly devote itself to its role of protector, it had to be free of material concerns.

This theory is a fairly accurate representation of the social situation in western Europe before the year 1000. Although in reality social evolution thereafter followed a different path, the theory of the three estates was still effectively maintained as a justification for the traditional positions of privilege. The clergy still continued to plead fiscal immunity and to emphasise the Christian sovereign's duty to protect the church. At his inauguration each new ruler undertook to maintain the freedoms of the church. During the Burgundian period, however, the nobility also retained its privilege of exemption from taxes. Although the nobles could not refuse to complete their military service, they established various conditions – namely that this service would not exceed forty days nor be beyond the borders of the county where their feudal estates lay; in addition, remuneration for military service was reached by agreement.

An equally hard social reality was the fact that clerics and nobles enjoyed the privilege of only being brought to trial in special courts of law, by members of their own estate and of the same rank. Unlike the present-day territorial principle of justice, the Ancien Régime recognised only the principle of the person; this meant that each individual was bound by the legal provisions specific to his personal legal statute. These every-day realities were not only fundamental to the maintenance of privileges, but also to the perpetuation of class consciousness.

Daily behaviour expressed and symbolised the hierarchical order. The priest presided over the way of life of all those who knelt before him to receive the sacrament. Church dignitaries crowned and anointed kings and emperors. The clergy's way of life and manner of dress in so far as they were applied, contributed to their prestige. The nobility also confirmed its status with armorial bearings, castles, dress, a liveried entourage – and horses which were alone sufficient literally to raise the nobles and the wealthy above all those on foot. Nobles were, depending on their rank, addressed as 'Monseigneur' and Sire or 'mijnheer' and 'heer'. In all western languages these forms of address were democratised during the nineteenth century. But also outside the privileged estates hierarchical relationships became embedded. The urban patriciate imitated

99. *The Haycart.* Centre panel of a triptych by Hieronymus Bosch painted about 1485. This work is an allegory of the social struggle precipitated by greed. The central theme is the ambition of all classes and estates to acquire the hay, the symbol of harvest, wealth, gold. The cart bearing the hay-load is being drawn by monsters, some of which resemble rats, towards Hell, depicted in the right-hand panel, and away from Earthly Paradise, depicted on the left-hand panel. Only a trio of women nursing their babies in the foreground, and four young lovers, surrounded by musicians and angels, appear untouched by the general acquisitiveness. This latter group is, however, sitting directly on top of the source of all the wealth, and it is presumably this which brings them contented peace. The three women are attending to a cooking pot, a pig's head and a fish on a spit, which also appear to interest no-one.

Spiritual and temporal dignitaries follow immediately behind the hay: the Pope and the Emperor, a duke and a bishop, nobles and clerics are in deep conversation or staring intently at the hay-load which is so high that they cannot see where the cart is leading them. There is a fearful commotion alongside the cart: everyone tries with whatever means are available to acquire as much of the hay as possible. Some are trampled in the rush or are in danger of being crushed under the wheels. Fighting and even killing can be seen here and there.

The dentist in the foreground apparently no longer needs to be concerned about money, nor does the plump clergyman who, whilst enjoying a glass of wine, watches the nuns adding to his store of hay.

(Madrid, Prado).

the aristocratic way of life in all respects and were also addressed as 'heer'. The title of 'master' was even used in the trades and professions thus expressing at that level too the tripartite order.

The question thus arises whether in a society which was so deeply engrained with a hierarchy based upon prestige, class-relations should not be dismissed as an anachronistic *Hineininterpretierung* on the part of the historian. The distinctions between the owner of the means of production and the worker were indeed not so sharp in the late Middle Ages as they were in the nineteenth century. If one were to identify a distinct social class as such during the Burgundian period, the dividing line between capitalist and worker ran straight through the trade guilds with the masters on one side and the journeymen and apprentices on the other. In reality, these organisations played such a prominent role in society that to segregate them into class-conscious entities would take us a long way from their experience in reality.

Nevertheless, around 1300 there were numerous testimonies to an awareness of a dual division between rich and poor and between worker and entrepreneur. These references originate from the textile industry, where the scale of production made the workers aware of their common situation. On the other hand, entrepreneurs in various towns came to an agreement to ensure that radical workers expelled from one town would not find work in another. Although in the course of time the political involvement of the guilds smoothed the sharper edges of this class conflict, they were still evident on occasions. For this reason the following discussion of social relations is based as much on the hierarchical order which was so engrained in the social consciousness as on the concept of class struggle which, though only spasmodically expressed as something of which they were aware, was nevertheless a widespread and constant objective reality.

100. The Royal Entry of Jacoba of Bavaria and her actual husband, the Duke of Gloucester, into Hainault.

(Paris, Bibliothèque Nationale, ms fr. 2680 fo 373 V°. Fifteenth century).

101. The tomb of Duke Philip the Bold, by Klaas Sluter and Klaas van de Werve. The alabaster statue lies on a base formed by mourners clad in heavy cloaks. The Duke had commissioned Sluter to build his tomb in 1382, about twenty years before his death. When he died in 1404, 2,000 people followed him to his last resting place.

(Dijon, Musée des Beaux-Arts).

The nobility

The nobility was an estate which distinguished itself from the others by a common lifestyle : they had no profession or trade but devoted themselves to military service, tournaments, hunting, archery, banquets and exuberant dress. It was aware of its own separate identity and also conducted itself as a group.

During the Burgundian period much of the traditional splendour of the nobility had disappeared. Although up to 1300 the nobility in the Netherlands was still the ruling class politically as well as socially and economically, after this time their position was rapidly eroded by other social groups, and in particular by the city burghers. There are many reasons for this. The nobility was supported essentially by the revenue from large-scale land ownership, but the value of this property declined considerably at the end of the thirteenth century due to the decrease in family inheritance and also principally to the debasement of the currency which reduced the value of interest rates and feudal rents whose nominal value had not changed. The purchasing power of the aristocracy consequently fell to a quarter or one fifth of its previous level. The decline of the old families was also due to the many wars between their houses, and the declining birth-rate within this class. This change in the economic status of the nobility also affected its political influence. The rulers of the Middle Ages who, before 1300, were primarily dependent on the nobility in the government of their principalities, opportunistically offered this co-operation to the city burghers. In most parts of the Netherlands in the late Middle Ages,

102. The Prinsenhof in Bruges, the ducal palace no longer in existence, was given a new architectural appearance in 1429 by Philip the Good. It was situated in Noordzandstraat, and its many facilities included a tennis court.

(Engraving from A. Sanderus, *Flandria Illustrata*, 1641).

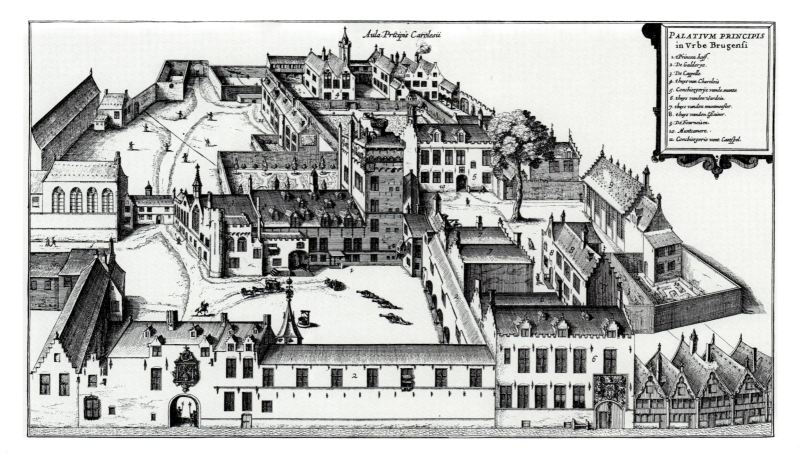

131

– and Flanders is the outstanding example of this – the third estate (the city burghers in fact) provided the only representation of the people vis-à-vis the overlord.   The nobility had become politically ineffective and socially an extremely vulnerable group, whose allegiance the rulers could easily purchase with money, public offices and lands.   In the typically rural areas the nobility retained its political strength.   In 1477-78 in Luxembourg, for example, the nobility opposed the recognition of Mary of Burgundy as duchess for almost a year in favour of the king of Bohemia.

What, then, became of the nobility during the Burgundian period ?   They disappeared into official and military posts.   In administrative offices the nobility were handicapped by a lack of education, particularly during the fourteenth century and part of the fifteenth century, just when the administration was beginning to look for well-educated technocrats.   In the realms of jurisprudence and government, lawyers with a university education were required.   The financial advisers to the ruler were appointed at first from Italian and later domestic specialists trained in the most modern techniques of accounting and financial transactions.   The traditional feudal nobility who had previously held positions in ducal governments and advisory councils had to make way for these new groups in the policy-making process.   Despite these changes, however, the nobility fulfilled several governmental functions during the Burgundian period.   This was possible through the 'back door' of the court offices.   In the ducal household, the international embassies and above all the ducal council, the accent still lay on prestige, etiquette

103.   Detail from a miniature from the *Livre des Tournois*, commissioned by the bibliophile Louis of Gruuthuse of Bruges.   An allusion to this can be found in the inscribed motto: 'Plus est en vous'.

(Paris, Bibliothèque Nationale, ms 7361 fr. 2692 fo 68).

and tradition, as opposed to professionalism. The positions held by the nobles in the court were governed by a strict hierarchy. Uppermost in this hierarchy were the chamberlains, then came the masters of the ducal household (maîtres d'hôtel) followed by those responsible for the various material provisions : the *pannetiers* (who supplied bread) *eschansons* (vintners) ; *escuyer trenchans* (carvers) *escuyers d'escuierie* (marshalls or equeries) and *valets de chambre* (valets). All these lower positions could be held by commoners, such as doctors and artists. Those holding these offices were granted salaries, horses and servants, according to a precise scale.

The embassy staff of the late fourteenth century however, always included a lawyer although other members were, by preference, nobles. On the legal councils (Parliament and the Grand Council of Mechelen, provincial courts) one-third of the seats were reserved for the nobility, who, however, continued to constitute a majority on the privy council. It has been calculated that the ducal court of Charles the Bold must have numbered some 600 nobles. It is, however, true that the new, but also many of the old aristocracy, felt the need for higher education during the course of the fifteenth century. Three sons of Jan II of Glymes, Lord of Bergen-op-Zoom, attended the University of Leuven. These 'intellectual' nobles had no difficulty whatsoever in establishing successful careers. The nobility's chances of success were of course not the same in all professions. Many nobles were governors of a principality or captains of a region or fortified location. It is not surprising to discover that the office of sovereign-bailiff of Flanders was held by Jacob of Lichtervelde, lord of Koolskamp, then by the lord of Steenhuize, the lord of Renescure, and the lords of Peene and

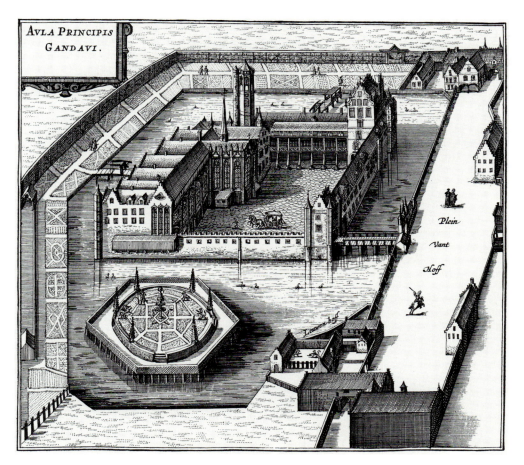

104. The Prinsenhof at Ghent. In the foreground one can see a small menagerie which includes lions as an attraction. Emperor Charles was born in this palace of which only one gate now remains. The dukes had no permanent capital and while in the Netherlands they stayed at their palaces in Lille, Arras, Bruges, Ghent and Brussels.

(Engraving from A. Sanderus, *Flandria Illustrata*, 1641.)

Montigny. The majority of the bailiwicks were entrusted to those with a degree of military experience and ability. The burgraves also came mainly from the lower nobility : many bore the title of squire and were granted a castle in return for proven military service.

At the end of the fifteenth century, and particularly in the early sixteenth century, even legal offices were held by members of the new aristocracy, and also nobles from the old families who had, by studying, adapted to the new demands of the government. As a result of these changes, the distinction between those of noble birthright and the professional aristocracy became less marked.

The fifteenth century aristocracy gave equal evidence of its abilities in the military sector. The military arts had remained an essential part of the young noblemen's education ; the doors of the Burgundian court were open to them. As a rule the young nobleman grew up as a page, and later as a squire for a prominent lord who then became his patron. The knight Jan van Dadizele, who was high-bailiff of Ghent from 1477 until his violent death in 1481, rose to his position in the service of Simon and Josse de Lalaing whom he supported, and sometimes replaced in their respective roles of Grand Master of the Hunt, lord of the castle of Wynendale and supreme bailiff of Flanders. In his *Enseignements paternels* (mid-fifteenth century), Gilbert de Lannoy gave an informative account of the spheres in which nobles of the lineage (the so-called 'noblesse d'épée') were still successful. The nobleman could work upward by engaging in some form of economic activity, although this was forbidden in the eyes of many of his contemporaries. Of central importance were, however, marriage, service to the sovereign and battle. Marriage could improve the financial situation of the impoverished nobles such as Guillaume d'Oiselet, lord of Villeneuve after his betrothal to the daughter of chancellor Rolin, and also Olivier de la Marche who in succession married two daughters from wealthy bourgeois families. Gilbert advises that a nobleman's intrinsic qualities should draw the duke's attention, and that the duke would consequently grant him "so many high offices, which yield such great benefits that you will become rich and powerful". And indeed many noble courtiers benefited from additional royal gifts in return for extra services, or in consequence of marriages and births. Philip the Good was thus responsible for building up the fortune of the Croy family and also that of the chronicler Olivier de la Marche.

The social situation for the majority of the nobility was nevertheless far from glamorous. For those who held office the remuneration was often insufficient, and such people often held more than one office, supplementing their income with remuneration for specific services (such as litigation) or with income from land and property ownership. For those nobles active in the military sector, the regular income was also insufficient and had to be supplemented by holding wealthy prisoners to ransom or by plundering conquered towns, as was the case with the dramatic occupation of Liège by the Burgundians in 1468. The income of those in military service was far below the salary of those holding public offices. There was, however, a considerable class differential between the salary of nobles who were also knights (2,300 écus), and that of the lower nobility who on occasion also claimed to be knights (345 écus), and that of the common soldier (80 écus). Those nobles without a knighthood attempted to prove to the outside world that they were of the same calibre by performing military feats to match those performed by the nobles. The social distinction remained, however, as did the lower remuneration.

105. Sketch portrait of Olivier de la Marche who originally came from Franche-Comté and was captain and master of ceremonies to Duke Charles the Bold (1425/29-1502). La Marche was in fact responsible for Charles' intelligence service. He wrote *Mèmoires*, a court chronicle for the information of his apprentice, Philip the Fair.

(Arras, Bibliothèque Municipale, ms 266. Drawing from the *Recueil d'Arras*).

106. Portrait of Philippe de Croy, Lord of Sempy and Quiévrain, Count of Chimay, sovereign-bailiff of Hainault (1458-1465). In 1473 he was admitted to the Order of the Golden Fleece and in 1474 he was appointed Stadholder of Guelders. Philip was known to be a great bibliophile. The de Croy family of Picardy achieved extensive influence under Philip the Good, which was expressed in offices such as councillor and governor of Luxembourg, Namur, Boulogne (Antoine) and Hainault (John and his son Philip). In 1475 the powerful de Croy family was the cause of a rift between the old Duke and Duchess Isabella, their son Charles the Bold, chancellor Nicolaas Rolin and the chief councillor Jean Chevrot. It is possible that the de Croys conspired with the Dauphin (then resident at the Burgundian Court), just as, in 1435, they were bribed by the King of France to influence Philip.

(Antwerp, Royal Museum of Fine Arts. This portrait is the right-hand panel of a diptych whose left-hand panel shows the Madonna and Child. Attributed to Rogier van der Weyden, ca 1459-1461).

134

This proves that during the fourteenth and fifteenth centuries, certainly in Brabant and probably also throughout the rest of the Netherlands, a new meaning became attached to the concept of knighthood. Knighthood was the title granted to nobles who accomplished a certain number of military feats. The concept was therefore usurped by the nobility, an entire group aspiring to the title without the right to do so. Another form of social mobility which led to the extension of the nobility, was elevation to the peerage and the introduction of patents of nobility, which could be purchased. From 1384 many rose to the ranks of nobility through service to the dukes. Under the Valois dukes of Burgundy, at least a hundred families made use of the patents of nobility. In order to earn the right to such a peerage it was necessary in the eyes of one's contemporaries to own a minimum of real estate, to live nobly – that is to say to perform military services – and not to be engaged in trade or business. Public opinion and members of the old nobility were nevertheless reluctant to acknowledge this new aristocracy.

A third and final form of mobility was the rise of a family in a lesser social category to the top social category. A clear illustration of this were the Croys; a small family from Picardy which grew into one of the most prominent and powerful families of the fifteenth century, thanks to its connections with the Burgundian dynasty.

By way of summary it can be said that birth, elevation, knighthood or the ownership of allodia (goods free of feudal subjection) all provided access to the aristocracy. Included in this was a vague intermediary group of people who legally belonged to the nobility but who were unable to realise this socially, while others behaved as nobles but were not recognised as such. The high nobility distinguished itself by origin and by the extent of their domains and manors which were often scattered. Antoine de Croy left possessions in Brabant, Hainault and Picardy, including Porcien – itself a county of considerable size. The lower nobility, which had to content itself with less income and recognition, and with administrative functions on a local level, maintained a status superior to the commons.

Nobility and the bourgeoisie

During the Burgundian period the barrier between the nobility and the city burghers became extremely flexible. The juridical divide between many noble and commoner families remained, while the lifestyle of these families became very similar. The merchant Michele Arnolfini had his portrait painted by Jan van Eyck who also painted the portrait of Duchess Isabella of Portugal. The equally renowned Rogier van der Weyden immortalised the nobleman Philippe de Croy, and also members of the Brussels patriciate. It is also true to say, however, that where the formal barrier was broken by the elevation of burghers thanks to the patents of nobility, social recognition was not always immediate. Elevation to the peerage was often only an investment in the future. Initially elevation was only recognised on paper; even in the second generation, identification with the established nobility was still not complete, indeed it was not until the third generation that the new aristocracy began to enjoy the benefits of ennoblement – namely various fiscal and legal

107. Oldest known chain of the Golden Fleece. According to tradition it belonged to Duke Philip the Good's senior chamberlain, Antoine de Croy, who was a knight of the Fleece since the establishment of the Order in 1430. According to another tradition, however, Emperor Charles gave this chain to Adrien de Croy in 1547 in recognition of his heroism in the Battle of Mühlberg. The chain is still in the de Croy family. It is said to have been made by Jean Peutin.

(Private collection).

privileges, priority in promotions and the opportunity to enter such prestigious peerages as the Order of the Golden Fleece. A certain period of time thus elapsed before formal elevation was recognised socially.

The social prestige of the nobility as an estate was very great before 1300, but after this time was very seriously affected. Under the Burgundians status recovered again thanks to the prestigious court offices. In the meantime it was just as honourable to belong to one of the great families of the urban patriciate. Up to 1430 such a patrician still referred to himself in the first place as a citizen. After 1430, however, this situation changed in favour of an explicit assimilation into the nobility. Lodewijk Pynnock (c. 1435-1504) belonged to a patrician family in Leuven which had also played a significant role in the fourteenth century. He had a military education at the Burgundian court and at twenty-one years of age became shield-bearer to Philip the Good; this did not prevent him from becoming an alderman in 1458, and burgomaster of his native town in 1460. From 1461 he held the office of high sheriff – that is to say, the duke's foremost legal official. In 1468 he participated in the siege of Liège by Charles the Bold, and consequently received a knighthood. From 1482 he acquired several feudal estates on one of which he built a castle. In the civil war against Archduke Maximilian, Lodewijk supported the latter. His position at Leuven consequently became untenable and his estates around the city suffered at the hands of the citizens. After the submission in 1489 Lodewijk was restored to his office and Philip the Fair made him seneschal. Such a career is typical of the integration of the old patriciate into the Burgundian Netherlands nobility. A further example is that of the Brussels family of Serclaes. Everaart, Lord of Wambeke, became seneschal and counselor to Duke John IV of Brabant; his sister who married Jan van Grimbergen, lord of Asse, became lady-in-waiting to the Duchess Jacqueline of Bavaria.

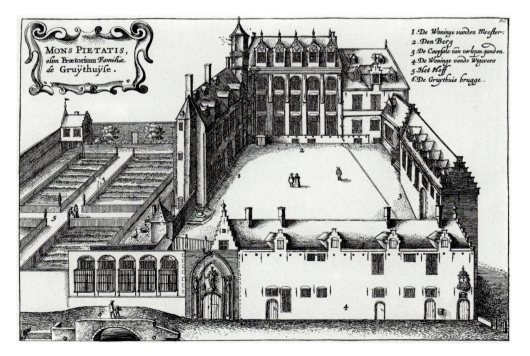

108. The Gruuthusehof at Bruges, one of the few remaining Burgundian palaces.

(Engraving from A. Sanderus, *Flandria Illustrata*, 1641).

What were the burghers' motives for seeking aristocratic status ? Undoubtedly this was in part due to the prosperity of fiscal exemption and other immunities. But this was precisely what did not necessarily come from a patent of nobility; the ducal treasuries and also the local authorities were strongly opposed to this. In 1437 at Dijon the duke's council, in the presence of the chancellor and many other dignitaries, decreed that "Many inhabitants of Dijon declare themselves exempt from the tax of 12 pennies in the pound, under the pretext that they are recognised as nobles by the king or by the duke". The council decided : "That they must henceforth pay these taxes as others did", but promised that the children of these new nobles would enjoy such exemption on the condition that they took up arms when required. Material gain could not therefore have been the deciding factor. It would seem more reasonable to assume that social prestige of the nobility was a prime factor. This would explain why the new nobles attributed their rise to military accomplishments and illustrious ancestry rather than to their personal achievements as office-holders or advisers. Some such as Guyot Duchamps in 1459, did not hesitate to seek patents of nobility on the basis of a forged genealogical dossier with which he attempted to improve his ancestry.

Many anecdotes prove that it was indeed a question of prestige and snobbery. The constable of St Pol opposed the marriage of his daughter to one of the sons of Antoine de Croy, first chamberlain and first councillor of the court (1430-1465) because, as the chronicler Escouchy tells us approvingly, "the young lady concerned came from a lineage as noble as the French royal lily, while Croy was merely one of the gentry." Envy and jealousy lay behind this, since the Croys were a family well respected through their good relations with royalty and princes.

'Vivre noblement' meant to live from the income of one's own domains ; this income was considerable and provided immunity from any fear of scarcity. For centuries to come, land ownership on a large scale, particularly when this included a seigniory – that is to say jurisdiction over the inhabitants – was pre-eminently the basis of social prestige. Every other activity was honourable in origin and retained its ennobling character. In military service nobles were the natural choice as officers and they were also prominent in administrative positions. As the Burgundian court grew in the Netherlands, political offices or mere court sinecures conferred prestige as well as a degree of power that was not to be underestimated. The Burgundians used their many favours to gain the support of the nobility in their new provinces thus consolidating their own position.

The most spectacular expression of this policy was the establishment of the prestigious peerage in 1430 known as the Order of the Golden Fleece, embracing the highest peers of the realm. The Burgundians thus formed a nobility in the Netherlands in the fifteenth century, whose national conscience was strong enough to oppose the influence of the Hapsburg courtiers during the reign of Philip the Fair. The virtual disappearance of the external citizenship of Brabantine cities after 1450, which had been accepted by 147 nobles in Brussels between 1370 and 1430 (*i.e.* approximately 25 per decade) is typical of this course of events. It was only during the insurgent period between 1477 and 1490 that a small group of nobles sought the support of the citizens of Brussels. The integration of the nobility in the Netherlands into the Burgundian court was more successful than the integration of the burghers since the nobility had a universal code of behaviour strongly influenced by the French court, which was just enjoying a 'revival' in the Burgundian court. The city burghers' struggle for power and prestige consequently involved the emulation of the aristocratic way of life which, throughout Europe, still brought the highest prestige and the greatest opportunities.

109. The Arnolfini couple, portrayed on the occasion of their left-handed marriage in 1434, showing Jan van Eyck as a witness in his own painting. The painting possibly shows the marriage of Michele Arnolfini, member of a powerful merchant family from Lucca which operated in Bruges and Paris, with a certain Elisabeth, a lady of lower social standing.

(London, National Gallery).

The clergy as an estate

The clergy in its entirety accounted for approximately one per cent of the population. The senior clergy also became a part of the Burgundian political and social establishment; the politicising and laicisation of much of the clergy came as a result of the increasingly political motivation in the appointment of bishops, abbots, and deans of chapters.

THE CLERGY AS A POLITICAL FORCE It is logical that the views of the bishops who owed their appointment to the Burgundian duke would be determined by Burgundian policy. Jean de Thoisy, appointed bishop of Tournai in 1410, was also councillor to the duke, not as much in church matters as in administrative and even financial matters. Philip the Good was so impressed by the former's accomplishments that he appointed him chancellor in 1419 and allowed him to undertake the successful negotiations to settle the triangular political relationship between France, England and Burgundy, negotiations that led to the treaty of Troyes. A diplomat who was equally active on the duke's behalf, although he was not appointed bishop, was Antoine Haneron, Master of Arts, who was charged by Philip the Good with the education of his son and was also the latter's envoy at the assembly at Chartres concerning the Pragmatic Sanction (1450). This connection between official and clerical promotions is striking: in 1450 Haneron became archdeacon of Cambrai and master of petitions at the duke's court; in 1454 he became a member of the Grand Council and councillor in 1456; then vicar to the bishop of Cambrai, and finally in 1467 dean of the prestigious St Donatus' Chapter at Bruges. The connection could evidently act adversely too: the failure of his diplomatic missions meant that he was passed over for elevation to the episcopate. The clearest example of the connection, however, can be seen in the linking of the bishopric of Tournai to the post of head of the ducal Grand Council, from Bishop Jean de Thoisy (1410) to Ferry de Clugny († 1483). Dismissal from this position meant that in 1460 Jean Chevrot also had to yield his see to the new head; Guillaume Fillastre. A similar case is that of Louis de Luxembourg, bishop of Thérouanne in 1415, who shortly afterwards became the first chairman of the Audit Office in Paris (1418) when he functioned as a pawn for the Burgundians against the Armagnacs.

The role of the bishop in prince-bishoprics such as Liège and Utrecht became entirely political. From 1452 onwards Philip the Good prepared to acquire the principality of Liège by attempting – with encouragement from groups opposed to their official ruler, the bishop John of Heinsberg – to appoint his nephew Louis de Bourbon to the Chapter of St Lambert's in Liège. This attempt was unsuccessful. Three years later, however, when the see became vacant, Philip was more successful and was able to press forward Louis as prince-bishop (1455-1482). This led to an unfortunate clash with the people of Liège. The politicising of the prince of the church was moreover nothing new. In 1390 John of Bavaria became bishop-elect (1390-1418); he was the grandson of the German Emperor and a member of the Wittelsbach family, then a rival of the Burgundian dynasty and closely related to the counts of Hainault and Holland. This prince of the church felt himself so unsuited to the sacred ministry that he saw no call to be ordained priest or consecrated bishop, so that in 1418 he was free to resign his office and – conceivably not only for political reasons – immediately married Elisabeth of Görlitz (niece of the German king), thereby becoming regent of Holland. One of the most brutal rulers of his time – he came to be known as John the Merciless (Jean sans Pitié) – in 1407 he did not even shrink from planning and executing the cold-blooded murder of Louis d'Orleans, his political opponent ; a murder to which he confessed shortly afterwards and the calumny of which he tried to efface by gaining a so-called 'honourable' victory at Othée over the army of his Liège subjects.

In Utrecht, politics came right to the fore in 1423 when the see became vacant and the bishop of Cologne, the count of Holland and the dukes of Cleves and Burgundy each put their own candidates forward as pawns. Zweder van Culemborg was successful for a time as the Burgundian pawn, but was set aside in 1426 in favour of Rudolf van Diepholt, the candidate from Cleves. After his demise political rivalry flared up once again and Guelders' candidate was defeated by Philip the Good's protégé – his illegitimate son David of Burgundy, who was effectively appointed in 1455 after interventions from Rome. Like his colleague John of Bavaria before him, David became known as a hard 'Realpolitiker' and did not hesitate to eliminate the competition from his opponent Gijsbrecht van Brederode by banning him, and poisoning his brother. Gijsbrecht had been the opponent of the previous bishop and was also an outspoken anti-Burgundian politician. The plans of the Burgundians were, however, not always well received, and in 1469 the Bishop of Utrecht saw fit to protect the autonomy of the town of Groningen from Charles the Bold's plans for annexation. Under Maximilian of Austria, however, David was no longer able to pursue this independent course and the bishopric of Utrecht became once again a mindless piece on the Burgundian chessboard.

The above discussion might well give the impression that the bishops of the Burgundian Netherlands concerned themselves solely with politics ; this was indeed of paramount importance, but not to the exclusion of all else. Pierre d'Ailly, bishop of Cambrai between 1397 and 1411, took the 'cura animarum' of his bishopric very seriously and did his utmost to improve the situation of his clergy by the drawing up and distribution of a *Liber Sacramentalis* in which he defined the tasks of pastoral care for the benefit of his young priests. He also built up a library in his bishopric and supported ascetic and spiritual movements (such as the 'Devotio Moderna' and Windesheim). After the reign of Bishop John of Burgundy, which could scarcely be said to have enhanced the reputation of the clergy, Bishop Henri de Berghes of Cambrai (1480-1502) pursued a more chaste course. He closely watched over his clergy to ensure that they adhered to the ecclesiastical code of discipline, and encouraged Master Standonck in his reformation of the abbeys. He sought inspiration in Palestine and Rome and engaged Erasmus as secretary.

The articles concerning the clergy in the privilege granted to Flanders by Mary of Burgundy in 1477 confirm the indications of extensive political activity in church appointments, including those of dignitaries as well as the ordinary clergy. The Duchess undertook henceforth to refrain from such interventions, which were couched in the strictest terms, as is apparent in the text submitted by the clergy itself : "...since on account of the violations by the princes and nobles and the improper appointments of the prelates, a great many famous monasteries and churches have been burdened with lengthy proce-

110. The tree of class struggle. Commoners, clergy and nobility, the three estates into which medieval society was divided, fight within their ranks to reach the top of the tree. Whoever climbs higher up is in a better position to oust his competitors.

(Brussels, Royal Library, ms 9079 fo 10 V°. From H. Bovet, *L'arbre des batailles*, the script by David Aubert and illustrations by a Flemish artist ca 1461).

dures and heavy costs, and because of that have suffered complete and utter privation and poverty, to the great peril and damnation of the souls of the wordly lords and ladies who are guilty of this".

Did the clergy have any political significance as an estate ? This varied from region to region. In Brabant the clergy played no decisive role in the drawing up of the famous 'contracts' between ruler and subjects, known as the 'Charter of Kortenberg' (1312) and 'Blijde Inkomst' (1356). Shortly after the Charter of Kortenberg a separate privilege was drawn up for the abbeys of Brabant guaranteeing the immunity of their churches. But only the secular orders sat on the Council of Kortenberg. From 1383 the clergy participated regularly in the State Assemblies and also in the payment of the taxes approved there. However, only the regulars were

143

111. Miniature from the *Decretum Gratiani*, depicting simony, commissioned by Rafael Mercatellis (1437-1508), abbot of St Bavon's, and illegitimate son of Duke Philip the Good and a 'lady of Belleval'.

(Ghent, University Library, ms 3 Vol II, I, fo 195 V°).

involved in all this, and even then only those of the older monastic orders. The massive ascendancy of the towns is illustrated by the fact that only the towns were represented at 510 of the 850 assemblies of the States of Brabant; while the clergy were invited to be present at only 80 sittings. Not until the Royal Entry of Mary of Burgundy in 1477 was the presence of the clergy at the States of Brabant formally recognised for the first time.

By contrast, the chapters and even the deans were represented in addition to the orders at the States of Hainault. In 1421 in the county of Namur the more important abbeys and chapters were represented at the State Assemblies, although all institutions at this level and also the priories, parish churches and altars, and even churches outside the principality with interests within Namur, were obliged to contribute to the levies. In Holland the abbeys did not begin to represent the clergy as a group until 1455. It is true that the abbot of Middelburg held a seat as member of the representative body, though in his role as lord of a large seigniory. When Burgundians penetrated this area he became instead the representative of the clergy in his province, after the example of the States Assemblies in the more southerly provinces of the Burgundian state.

In Flanders, the payment of taxes did not always guarantee the right of the clergy to participate in the States Assembly. It was not until 1384 that the clergy joined with the second and third estates; the latter had been actively involved in the representative affairs of the Four Members for many years. A more important fact is that from 1384 the clergy had, like the nobility, no real political power in the States of Flanders. They were only 'invited' by the duke or the Members to complete the traditional board of the Four Members, whenever the latter saw an advantage to be gained from their mutual political combat. They, the clergy, were the political football of the effective political powers of the province which maintained the clergy and the nobility in order to gain the favour of public opinion in Flanders for their various ambitions and manœuvres: the attitude towards the Western Schism, neutrality in the Hundred Years War and relations with England. Abbots as well as chapters represented the clergy, and then not necessarily those which were the most powerful; the duke or the Members sometimes gave preference to those which were weaker and thus perhaps more ready to comply with the prescribed scenario. The significance of the clergy in the

112. David of Burgundy, illegitimate son of Duke Philip the Good, was appointed Bishop of Utrecht (1456-1496) through the latter's influence on the Pope. In this way the Burgundians strove to gain influence in the neighbouring bishoprics which also exercised considerable legal and spiritual power in addition to their territorial dominion.

(Amsterdam, Rijksmuseum. Left-hand internal panel of the triptych of David of Burgundy. Anonymous master from the northern Netherlands, ca 1490).

Flemish States was so minimal that by no means all the Flemish delegations at the States General from 1431 included members of the clergy : this was, however, the case for the States of Brabant, Artois, Utrecht, Hainault and Namur.

THE CLERGY AS A PART OF BURGUNDIAN HIGH SOCIETY The majority of bishops and abbots led anything but the lives of custodians of souls, as hermits or in the pious security of closed or isolated monastries, as exemplified in the Observants or the Brethren of the Common Life. The most blatant imitation of the way of the secular élite was to be found among members of the Burgundian dynasty who had been promoted to bishop and who were not motivated by any awareness of a spiritual vocation, but rather by political ambition and a greed for money and splendour. A prime example of this is John of Burgundy, bishop of Cambrai from 1439 to 1479, who was the illegitimate son of John the Fearless and Agnes de Croy. The Pope's conscientious objection to this appointment on the grounds of his illegitimacy was 'bought off' by the duke for a sum of 12,000 ducats. Even at that time the top of the clerical hierarchy was not unimpeachable. At the time of his appointment, John had still not received either ordination or consecration. He was seldom active in his own see, where he was rarely in residence, but carried out his affairs in more wordly centres such as Brussels and Mechelen, where he died. His thirty-six illegitimate children and grandchildren were present at the mass held at Cambrai in 1480 on the occasion of his death. Bishop John of Heinsberg of Liège (1419-1455) was no better. He had become bishop because, as the descendent of an impoverished but noble line, he had to be found some reasonable position. He was therefore less interested in his pastoral duties than in political liaisons and the entertaining of concubines, who naturally bore him children – this was extremely costly and consequently increased the burden on the tax-paying populace.

The bishops and other prelates also imitated Burgundian ducal and urban high society in the cultural sphere. Like Philip the Good, Bishop John of Bavaria had painters, minstrels and other artists at his court. The bishop of Utrecht, not to be outdone by his colleague in Liège, commissioned numerous works of art by renowned masters.

Many worldly priests appear in the *Cent nouvelles nouvelles*, a collection of sarcastic tales comparable to the *Canterbury Tales* and the *Decameron*, which appeared around 1456 in ducal circles, presumably written with a view to amusing the old Duke Philip the Good with salacious stories. For our purposes this is, as it were, a secret keyhole which allows us a privileged view behind the scenes of contemporary decorum. The ninety-second 'nouvelle' relates the tale of a canon and two women of pleasure. The next tale in the series tells of a 'gente femme mariée' who led her husband to believe that she was going on a pilgrimage while she was, in fact, with a galant priest from their native town of Hainault. The Rabelaisian tale of the poor Carmelite who came to Lillers to earn two sous by preaching, but was forced to excess at a 'grande bouffe' given by the local Lady, shows that monks were suspected of a not inconsiderable gluttony, such as this : "bon moyne, qui n'avoit appetit nesqu'un chien". And so it was with many in the collection of tales : the Franciscan Friars – desired by rich bourgeois wives ; the Cordelier more highly thought of than the legal spouse, and for whom the choicest pieces of eel were kept ; the chaplain of a Burgundian nobleman who immediately became enamoured of his master's spouse : "une donzelle belle et

113. Portrait of Isabella of Portugal, third wife of Duke Philip the Good and mother of Charles the Bold. On their wedding day on 7th January 1430 Philip the Good instituted the Order of the Golden Fleece.

(Paris, Louvre Museum. Anonymous Flemish master, ca 1430).

gente, plus fine que moutarde" but who, at the high point of pleasure in the marital bed, was set upon by the husband – who was supposedly sleeping – in a manner which proved extremely painful. Also, "au gentil pays de Brabant", the geographical proximity of "ung monastère de blancs moynes lez ung aultre de nonnains" was clearly disastrous for the young clergymen "qui devient amoureux, si fort que s'estoit rage, d'une nonain sa voisine".

Does this literary image correspond with contemporary reality? An argument supporting this is that such irony was apparently recognised by the people of the time, since the volume was certainly successful, and the stories are only possible in the mental environment of the fifteenth century, although deviations from the moral and social norms were probably emphasized for sensational effect. A second argument is provided by the legal records. In the 'registres

114. The Persian Sibylle or Isabella of Portugal in her middle-age. The unusual power of expression in this portrait clearly brings out the Duchess' tough character. On many occasions she performed the duties of a negotiator and exercised an unmistakable political influence.

(Malibu, California, J. Paul Getty Museum. Copy of the original supposedly painted by Rogier van der Weyden about 1455).

146

115. A woman is caught by her husband committing adultery. She is, however, acquitted. Two Flemish miniatures illustrating the story of Philostrates, from the French translation of Boccaccio's *Decameron*, illustrated by a Flemish miniaturist.

(Paris, Bibl. de l'Arsenal, ms 5070).

de l'audience' which set out the conditions for ducal pardons, the court officials, in hearing the plaintiffs and defendants, take statements from the same sort of people appearing as characters in the *Cent Nouvelles*. The records show the legitimation of the bastard son of Velicq Munier, the pastor at Anthet. According to the registers of the bishop of Tournais'court in 1461-62, several priests had to pay fines, including a priest from Wervik who had deflowered a girl ; a monk from St Amand who had fathered an illegitimate child ; and a priest from the church of St Saviour at Bruges who had supported Margaret of Brussels as his concubine ; and many others like them.

Further proof is to be found in the reports of the ducal commissions of enquiry, such as those instigated by John the Fearless in 1417 to restore order in the abbey of Cysoing ; not only did the monks, driven by greed for money, sell their library, their plate and their land, but they also grossly neglected the organisation of liturgical services in order to live "en concubinage, honteusement et deshonnete-ment". The abbot and several monks were imprisoned and the abbey came under the control of the ducal Audit Office. In 1429, much to his dismay, Philip the Good was forced to admit that the abbot, who had been restored to his post, was continuing to entertain married women, visit taverns, and gamble, and had installed in one of his priories a certain Mathieu Hore, who supported a concubine and several children there, just as his patron had done.

A fourth source of information comes from the internal clerical reports. In the report of the vicar-general of Liège, Pierre de Cortembach, dating from 1516, it would appear that immorality was most rife among the collegiate canons : "il y en a bien peu qui, au su de tous, ne vivent avec leurs concubines dans les demeures claustrales elles-mêmes". The public were therefore, according to this pronouncement, well aware of the 'scandal'. In 1517 the bishop complained that the chapters were only clinging so stubbornly onto their exemption because this enabled them freely to support women and bring up their natural children in security. Nevertheless, we are given the impression that contemporaries were amused by these renegade clerics, but were not excessively shocked. What, then, did a member of high society who himself treated conjugal fidelity lightly and had few scruples with regard to political hypocrisy, political ferocity against opponents and social malice against subordinates, the poor and the outcasts, expect from 'his' clergy? Not very much, nor too many moralizing sermons. The Breton Carmelite Thomas Conecte went to Flanders in 1428 to shower abuse upon the clerics "qui publiquement tenoient femmes en leur compagnie et enfraignoient le vœu de chasteté" and also upon "les femmes de noble ligniée... portant sur leurs testes haulx atours ou autres habillement de parrage"; ladies whose extravagant hats were pulled from their heads by urchins at the order of the Carmelite. But such outbursts remained an exception. The majority of preachers did not adopt such an attitude. This was therefore a reassuring 'nihil obstat' for the merry-making establishment. The infringement of moral and clerical norms by the clergy relieved many laymen of any scruples remaining with regard to their own extravagances. It did not, however, lead to forceful criticism or apostasy; this reaction was not to follow until the Reformation. Meanwhile only moralists and one or two chroniclers, such as the Artesian Jacques du Clercq, bemoaned this moral decline: "c'estoit grande pitié que le pechié de luxure regnoit moult fort...; et mesme regnoit encoires plus icelluy pechié... es prelats de l'eglise et toutes gens d'eglise."

THE BEHAVIOUR OF THE CLERGY WITHIN THE CHURCH The political and social ambitions of the majority of the higher and lower clergy meant that their own functions within the church itself were greatly neglected. Chastellain complained that Jean Chevrot, the bishop of Tournai – also chief of the ducal council – who had grown old, corpulent and powerless, rarely appeared at his court, but was peacefully vegetating at Lille: "sy en estoit le conseil desgarny de chief". But the prelates certainly did not become so impotent that they could not exert themselves outside their bishoprics in search of enchanting mistresses or vacant benefices (stipends). The actual administration of the bishopric was delegated to the auxilliary bishops and vicars-general. Absenteeism among the bishops was mirrored no less clearly at the parochial level: in three deaconries in the bishopric of Liège in 1501, 72 priests (from 241 registered parishes) were not resident in their own parishes and this figure had risen to as many as 95 in 1523 – thus from one quarter to one third. By contrast, the situation in Flanders improved between 1455 and 1527, at least in the 43 parishes of the deaconry of Oudenburg, where the number of resident pastors increased from 12 (i.e. more than two-thirds absentees) to 31.

Members of the more important chapters were equally conspicuous by their absence since it was normal to attempt to become a member of more than one chapter – undoubtedly for the honour, but still more for the prebends (regular incomes). The career of two prominent clerics clearly illustrates the situation of many church dignitaries.

Rudolf de Meyere (c. 1360-1437) was one of the noble De Fressencourt line from Artois that was related to families in Cambrésis and Picardy; he was himself lord of Wailly-lez-Arras en Lannay (at Cobrieux). Two of his brothers, one of whom was also canon at Tournai, were canons at Bruges. Rudolf studied Roman and canon law at the University of Orléans. He did not become a deacon until his fifty-seventh year, and had been ordained into the priesthood by the time of his death. These late recognitions did

116. Flemish (?) Majolica altar vase from the second half of the fifteenth century. Between 1425 and 1475, Spanish majolica was imported and, from 1450-1475, was produced in Flanders itself, and used principally for altar vases.

(Bruges, Gruuthusemuseum).

not prevent De Meyere from acquiring, in 1386, a canonical prebend at Tournai, another at Cambrai (1409) and one in the chapter of St Piat at Seclin. In 1411 he was appointed dean of the chapter of St Donatus' at Bruges; the hereditary chancellorship of Flanders accompanied this office; and it was for this reason that John the Fearless was present at the installation, particularly since De Meyere had been master of petitions and councillor to the duke since 1406. In this capacity he completed many diplomatic missions for the duke; mainly in France and England. In due course De Meyere sat on the privy council, and in 1424 he was a member of the regency council for Flanders during the duke's absence. From 1427 the influence of the chancellor of Flanders waned in favour of the chancellor of Burgundy, Nicolas Rolin. In the meantime De Meyere had managed to acquire still more ecclesiastical prebends : that of the canon – and later dean – of St Aimé at Douai and archdeacon of Boulogne, which he visited by proxy. When he resigned the deanery of St Donatus' at Bruges shortly before his death, he retained an annual pension of 400 pounds; as councillor to the duke he received a yearly salary of 300 francs (33 groats). Added to the five or six other prebends and his manorial entitlements, this provided a not inconsiderable income for this distinguished jurist and diplomat. For him, clerical titles could have meant little more than influence and income.

The second profile is that of Roland Scrivers (c. 1400 – c. 1477), himself an illegitimate child (legitimated by the duke in 1460) and father of numerous illegitimate offspring, four of whom were legitimated by Philip the Good. Scrivers studied medicine at Paris, and was professor there until 1437; with a papal dispensation for his illegitimate birthright, he was able to become sub-deacon in 1431, and in 1442 he was ordained into the priesthood. King Charles VI of France had already nominated him for benefices in 1422, and after repeated papal interventions he acquired the canon-prebends in the Sainte Chapelle at Paris and in St Saviour's chapter at Harelbeke and the rectory of the parish church at Sesme (see of Tournai) in 1427. In 1428 he accepted a prebend in St Donatus' chapter at Bruges of which he became dean in 1439 on the recommendation of Philip the Good, despite opposition from the chapter which resented his continued absence and lack of religious motivation. This conflict even led to the confiscation of the dean's possessions, whereupon the dean had the appurtenances of St Donatus' church seized. Finally in 1476 he had to cede the deanery and be content with the office of pastor at Sluis. Scrivers had also enjoyed prebends from 1439 to 1475 as canon and archdeacon of Arras. All these church benefices, however, only fulfilled a secondary role in his successful career as a man of medicine. He was the author of three scientific treatises. In 1438 he became physician and councillor to the Dukes Philip the Good and Charles the Bold and to the Duchess Isabella. Through their influence, that of his previous royal patron in France, and not least through countless intercessions by two successive popes, this man of medicine found himself holding many and various clerical offices, for the sake of the incomes attached to these positions, for which he seemingly had neither aptitude nor interest.

The political influence upon clerical appointments, but also the deliberate connivance of the papacy, were responsible for this secularization. Such cases do not apply to every member of the clergy, but certainly apply to a large proportion of the upper hierarchy, which attracted attention and encouraged imitation. Is

117. The Pope grants privileges to St Peter's Abbey in Ghent. This Benedictine abbey was among the oldest and most wealthy in the Netherlands, and consequently also among those with the greatest fiscal and political power.

(Ghent, State Archives. Bisdom. B2956 fo 1).

it reasonable to expect that the situation in the training and motivation of the lower clergy would be better than that of their superiors ? In the latter half of the fifteenth century, St John's Hospital at Bruges experienced great difficulties with its pastors due to negligence, greed and drunkenness. There are thus indications that the situation among the lower ranks of the clergy was also far from satisfactory.

The immoral behaviour of those given pastoral cures was not in the least compensated by the commercial inclinations implied by the granting of indulgences. Many such indulgences were a logical reward from the official established church for those who had devoted themselves to the restoration of church buildings. They were also granted during the so-called 'jubilee' years of 1390, 1450 and 1500, in which the faithful who were unable to undertake the journey to Rome were given the opportunity of obtaining their indulgences by paying a sum equivalent to the cost of the journey. Popes and distinguished cardinals such as Nicholas of Cusa, devoted themselves to this policy of indulgences. The Duke of Burgundy also did so – but not without an ulterior motive, since the revenue from 1450 onwards was divided between the pope and the duke, who was to use his share for the restoration of the ducal chapel in The Hague. In the church itself, a veritable trade grew up in this area whereby indulgences were exchanged for various devotional acts, and traders in indulgences, who were authorised by the church and carried relics on their travels, made much money from promises of healing to credulous and superstitious Christians.

Another abuse was the deviation from the vow of poverty. In 1401 the abbot of St Truiden deviated from this rule by granting his monks an income of their own for purposes of sustenance. There was, nevertheless, opposition to this policy from within the church. The abbot of Park Abbey, Diederik van Thuldel (1462-1494), made a stand for a purge and, with the support of the States of Brabant and the prince, was able to bring the pope to issue several Bulls against the 'commenda'; a system whereby non-regulars were placed at the head of abbeys (particularly after 1430) – often under the pressure of the duke of Burgundy – and from which they derived various material benefits. In 1475 Van Thuldel persuaded the pope to abolish the pension of the papal nuncio Lucas de Tolentis, which was proving too great a burden to the abbey of Tongerlo. But the opposition fought back strongly. In 1477 the nuncio used the occasion of Charles the Bold's death to have himself forthwith appointed commendatory abbot of St Michael's at Antwerp, and after a campaign of denigration in Rome he lost no time in excommunicating Van Thuldel, the preacher of purity.

118. The seven acts of charity and the seven deadly sins were often depicted. They attempted to influence the social behaviour of the people of the Middle Ages. Fragments from the *Last Judgment* by an Antwerp master, ca 1485.

(Antwerp, O.C.M.W.).

152

119. Scenes from the life of St Bertin with (left) Guillaume Fillastre in prayer. Fillastre, Bishop of Tournai and head of the Grand Council was also abbot of St Bertin's Abbey, whose buildings are shown in the painting.

(Berlin-Dahlem, Staatliche Museen Preussischer Kulturbesitz, Gemäldegalerie. Left-hand panel of the St Omer's retable by Simon Marmion).

REACTIONS AGAINST THE BEHAVIOUR OF THE CLERGY The persistent absenteeism, the wave of immorality and the pursuit of material gain inevitably provoked strong reactions. Apart from those already discussed, reactions were also evident in mysticism and in theological literature. In the work of Ruusbroec both developments came together, though in the fifteenth century they took distinctly separate courses.

The most noted reaction was that of the Devotio Moderna, which emphasised the practice of asceticism. The literature of Jan van Schoonhoven and Geert Groote did, it is true, retain something of the mysticism of Ruusbroec although this is principally directed towards practical ethics. The revival had to come through the restoration of moral values and improved discipline in the churches and monasteries. These new ideas were spread via confessional books, penitential sermons, treatises and letters – all of which extolled the practice of Christian virtue. In the second generation of the Devotio Moderna, and in particular in the work of Gerlach Peters of Windesheim, the emphasis was once again placed on mysticism as it had been in the work of Ruusbroec. During the fifteenth century therefore, a vast number of works came into being which, in a didactic manner, advocated greater purity of worship and doctrine; Thomas a Kempis' *Imitatio Christi* was the indisputable epitomy of this development. The distribution of this pious literature was promoted in the second half of the fifteenth century by the art of printing. The senior clerics were not disposed to react against the abuse in view of their own way of life. In the cases where such clerics were prepared to do so, such as the bishop of Liège Evrard de la Mark (1505-1538), they were often powerless since they possessed no visitor's powers over the apostate canons of Liège. De la Mark did, however, have more power over the parochial clergy, and in 1508 he ordered the arrest of all those priests of St Truiden who did not conform to his code of morals. In 1526 he also issued a decree to suppress all forms of heresy and moral deviation in his bishopric, since until this time all too many priests had not heeded his summons to this effect and, on the contrary, had even bribed the members of the hierarchy in order to give free rein to their pleasurable way of life.

As a compensation for the decline in clerical morals and religious piety in the fifteenth century there was a considerable grass-roots upsurge of devotional practices among the faithful. These developed essentially in two directions. On the one hand there was a striking growth in chantries and foundations – that is to say establishments which regularly celebrated mass for the souls of the deceased and for other pious intentions. This eucharistic interest manifested itself in the popularising of pilgrimages and processions, instituted around more or less prestigious relics such as the Holy Blood at Bruges. On the other hand there was a striking increase in the worship of the Virgin Mary in the Netherlands during the late Middle Ages. This is evident from the establishment of numerous communities which were established around two aspects of this cult : on the one hand the theme of Mary's suffering, on the other, the more optimistic consideration of the joyous mysteries of Mary. The first concept, which developed in the beginning of the fifteenth century, led to the formation of the Communities of Our Lady of the Seven Sorrows, from the mid-century onwards, culminating around 1480. The second concept – the joyous mysteries – expressed itself in the Communities of Our Lady of the Rosary after 1470.

The above representation of the clerical hierarchy brings into question the role of the church as the bearer of a religious message. Conspicuous absenteeism, pecuniary greed, pluralism,

120. Schoolmaster with his pupils. The master appears to be pulling the ear of the pupil kneeling before him.

(Bruges, St Saviour's Cathedral. Misericord, fifteenth century).

154

politicising, disregard for regulations and behavioural norms, dubious morals and – with the exception of a small number of dignitaries – a poor education and an extremely limited knowledge of doctrine : all these things not only damaged the prestige of the clergy as an estate, but were also detrimental to the credibility of its message. Just at a time when repeated crises in the form of famine, epidemics and wars brought the need for spiritual sanctuary among the populace, the church proved unable to meet such a need in many places. The consequences of this are self-evident : a rapid increase in popular devotion ; attempts from within to achieve greater spiritual purity and – if this did not meet with a sufficient response within the church – schismatic tensions.

The behaviour of the clergy as discussed above is all the more striking since it was in such contrast to the content of their doctrines. But in effect, the religious functions and values of the clergy were eclipsed by their worldly orientation. They also easily adopted the behavioural pattern of the worldly élite : clergy and laity, church and state, were so closely interlocked that the synchronisation of both ways of life appeared to be the next logical development. The work of many members of the church hierarchy, appointed by the Burgundian court, often inadequately educated and hardly motivated for pastoral work or the monastic life, was often no different from that done by courtiers or officials. The average man, however, demanded less devotion of such people than was demanded of the clergy. The close integration of church and state resulted in the religious Reformation movement of the sixteenth century being seen as a threat to the state and as such it was opposed by the secular arm as a rebellion. It is no exaggeration to say that the Burgundian unitary state in the Netherlands was eventually torn asunder by this tension.

The third estate

Within the third estate – by far the largest, comprising approximately 98% of the population – there were also considerable differences in legal constitution and social status. The distinction between rural and town dwellers was fundamental. In the predominantly agricultural areas, feudal serfdom was still evident. In the Nivelles region (belonging to the duchy of Brabant) the receivers of the ducal domains still occasionally collected the proceeds from the sale of property of deceased serfs, even when they were living in Hainault. Their statute was hereditary within the female lineage. In his domain in Hainault, in about 1400, the count still received mortmain from an average of seven serfs annually, about 1450 still from four serfs per year and in 1500 from one every three years. In Flanders, the count also levied mortmain, although it had been reduced – in contrast to Walloon-Brabant – to a modest sum of money. It is possible that mortmain continued to fall on a far greater proportion of those living on the manorial estates of the minor lay lords.

Even in areas where the economic consequences of serfdom had been converted into small financial obligations, or had been completely bought out, the burden of legal seigniory still fell on those in rural areas. Even in the villages, or prescribed areas where a discretionary charter existed, the nobles remained the judges, unlike the towns where members of the judicial administration were themselves townspeople. Those living in rural areas were generally less well organised and protected than town dwellers, consequently lower wages and heavier taxes could be more easily imposed in rural areas, which became subject to the economic hegemony of the towns. Clear evidence of this can be seen alongside the forms of market regulations discussed above, in the endeavour of town-dwellers to conclude all their contracts with the rural inhabitants in front of their own aldermen, even when this involved land and possessions in the country. Whatever consultation there was with the rural inhabitants on financial and other matters, it was at best only with the vassals (*i.e.* fief-holders) and leading land-owners in the village. Larger leaseholders came into this latter category, provided they had sufficient land in use. In the eighteenth century the minimum requirement in West Flanders was 50 measures (approx. 50 acres) of land. Social discrimination was therefore determined more by the size of the farm than by the distinction between owner and leaseholder.

THE CITY BURGHERS The same variations in population density and the degree of urbanisation, which was adduced to account for the continued existence of statute duty, were also evident in the towns. Archaic social structures were to be found in the smaller towns, in areas which had developed later, and in all areas where population density was comparatively low. The urban élite, for example, known as the patriciate, lost its exclusive position in Flanders about 1302. This did not, of course, mean that members of the old lineage had no political or economic part to play. On the contrary; some of the older families such as Borluut, Sersanders and Vaernewijc provided some of Ghent's most active politicians during the sixteenth century. The vast fortunes also remained largely intact. Nevertheless, in Flanders, the patriciate's exclusive hold on economic and political life weakened : they were forced to make room for the smaller entrepreneurs and the guilds.

In Brabant, on the other hand, the patriciate steadfastly maintained their position during the fourteenth and fifteenth centuries. In Brussels, all the aldermen's offices and the position of burgomaster remained in the control of seven families. It was only the result of clashes within rival factions within the patriciate between 1420 and 1423 and during the 1460s that concessions had to be made to the guilds, who were nevertheless unable to maintain a leading position as their Flemish counterparts had done during the previous century. In Leuven too, the patrician families maintained a formally recorded position as one of the four sections of the town's council for external affairs which presided only over fiscal matters. The trade guilds constituted one further section of this council opposite

121. Detail from the central section of the *Deer hunting* tapestry. Dogs feast on the intestines and blood of the deer.

(London, Victoria and Albert Museum. Produced in a workshop in Tournai or Arras during the second quarter of the fifteenth century).

the guild of merchant drapers and the actual magistrature, in which the patriciate and burghers obviously still retained control. This situation can be regarded as typical for Brabant.

In the Walloon provinces the patriciate generally retained its hereditary prerogatives in urban government. In Liège, however, all seats on the town council, and a proportion of those on the council of Huy, had passed into the hands of tradesmen; but in Dinant, for example, nine out of the thirty offices were still retained by patricians. At Tournai – which did not come under the rule of Charles V until 1521, but remained economically orientated towards the Netherlands, the monopoly of power of the patriciate remained until 1423. Until the patriciate was economically motivated to

122. Left- and right-hand panels of the *Baptism of Christ in the Jordan* by Gerard David. The donors of this triptych, Jan des Trompes and his first wife Elizabeth van der Meersch, are shown here with their respective saints and their children.
In 1499 and 1501 Jan des Trompes was deacon of the soapboilers' guild and during this period was often a member of the Council of Bruges.

(Bruges, Groeningemuseum).

123. The brick-makers. Water pipes were laid in order to guarantee efficient fire protection in the towns and all new houses were required to be built in brick.

(Vienna, Österreichische Nationalbibliothek. Cod. 2771, fo 49 V°. Miniature from a Holland bible of about 1470).

support the duke of Burgundy, the king of France granted more consultation to the guilds, without thereby excluding the patriciate. In the small town of Namur the patriciate retained the monopoly of all public offices throughout the Burgundian period. It remained a closed caste based upon consanguinity; its members were, however, still active in trade and finance.

In the towns of Holland throughout the fourteenth century there was a fusion of some members of the impoverished nobility who could no longer survive on the land, and the existing mercantile élite of the towns. The product of this union was the 'vroedschap', a corporation of forty or so city fathers, co-opted for life, whose common aim was to close their ranks against newcomers from lower social classes. These organisations exercised great political influence which was only shared with the guilds to any significant degree in one or two towns (Utrecht and Dordrecht). All in all the dukes of Burgundy found a clearly prevalent aristocracy in most of the towns in the Netherlands, with whom they could make considerable headway due to their concordant life styles and ambitions. The growth in the Burgundian unification of the Netherlands brought considerable opportunity to those who were prepared to collaborate.

MANUAL WORKERS The problem of the organisation and mobilisation of manual workers will be discussed from the point of view of five internal antitheses.

The first general distinction among the manual workers was that which separated members of an organisation from those who were not members. Corporatism was largely an achievement by manual workers who saw it as a means by which their interests could be furthered. Other groups – namely traders, authorities and consumers

– also benefitted from such organisation. The guilds were not, however, universal throughout the Netherlands : they were urban, not national, more deeply rooted in the south than in the north ; within the towns not all manual workers were organised into craft guilds, and there was no autonomous organisation to represent each occupation. The guilds therefore represented those occupations for which a certain amount of training was required – that is to say skilled labour. The entire institution was attuned to the acquisition of the required skills. As a matter of course therefore, unskilled tasks remained outside this system. Consequently, the craft trade offered the greatest advantages to the most able of artisans and embraced the largest groups of those who were concentrated in the most important sectors. The small groups were, however, excluded ; those who were isolated (i.e. those in the rural areas) and the floating population who could be engaged in all types of employment for which no special qualifications or skills were required.

A second obvious distinction among manual workers lay in the employment sector, with the market as a criterion. Wherever groups of people were concentrated in large numbers, there were a number of functions to be fulfilled in connection with the basic necessities of life : food, clothing and the home. It was therefore usual to find guilds of bakers, butchers, brewers, fishmongers, candlemakers, greengrocers, bricklayers, carpenters, cabinet-makers, tailors, shoe-makers etc. Noteworthy variants which were fairly common included buyers of old clothes and cobblers ; at the other extreme there were specialists such as milliners, glove-makers, purse-makers, leather-workers, who were to be found particularly in towns such as Bruges and 's Hertogenbosch.

On the other hand, many towns in the Netherlands also had their own export industries, which employed a large proportion of the working population – as many as 60%. Large-scale enterprises dominated these sectors, particularly in the textile industry but also in the copper and metal industries, brewing etc. ; the scale of these industries was not only large in terms of the numbers of people

124. Reconstruction of part of a town which has been destroyed.

(Brussels, Royal Library. Miniature from the *Chroniques de Hainault*, ms 9242, fo 232).

160

125. St Barbara, the patron saint of builders.

(Antwerp, Royal Museum of Fine Arts. Drawing by Jan van Eyck).

sharing the same conditions, but also in terms of the supply of raw materials and distribution. While the supply for local markets could usually rely upon a constant demand, export industries were often confronted with problems concerning competition and the disruption of international political or commercial relations. The producers in the export sector were therefore, in comparison with those producing for local consumption, more vulnerable to all manner of factors of which they had little foreknowledge and upon which they had even less influence. Because of the scale of these concerns and their concentration in certain streets or in a whole area of a town (at Ypres, for example, the areas were called 'fullers', 'weavers', 'common trades', 'burghers') this economic vulnerability could lead to conflict, mobilisation, and revolt. The butcher or the baker who, together with an apprentice or servant, sold their daily produce to a familiar clientèle, were more easily satisfied with the existing social order.

This distinction is not unrelated to a third distinction, which separated the owner of the workshop from his labourers. The guilds were vertical organisations, that is to say their members came from both the higher and lower social ranks, according to their profession. In Ghent, for example, there were 53 recognised guilds in 1361. The master, who owned his house with its shop and workshop, his tools and raw materials, was a small entrepreneur who employed several paid workers (two or three journeymen and an apprentice). The traditional division within the social classes not only ran across the guilds, which embraced all ranks of the social hierarchy, but also through every place of work where the entrepreneur worked daily in close co-operation with his journeymen and apprentices to produce the same product. In the sector producing for local consumption where small-scale business units were the norm, personal relations must surely have dissolved the traditional class distinctions. As soon as production began to take place on a larger scale and was destined for distant and unknown markets, relations became less personal and, consequently, objective class distinctions became increasingly evident.

Pursuing this train of thought, it would seem logical that strike actions occurred largely in the textile sector, often in the form of an 'exodus' whereby the workers left the town in order to lend force to their demands. Between 1372 and 1478, the fullers of Leiden resorted to such methods on eight occasions, the weavers on two occasions and the dyers on one occasion. Since they felt that their dependent position in the process was exploited by the weavers, who were both more numerous and more strategically placed within the production process, the fullers of Ghent left their town in 1423 and those from The Hague left their town in 1452 and 1478.

This leads to the fourth distinction : that between the organised professional groups, particularly when different groups were involved in the same production process. In the case of the fullers just mentioned, both masters *and* journeymen turned against the drapers and weavers. Trade against trade, therefore. Did this signal a shift in class conflict ? This was so to a certain extent since drapers and weavers themselves became employers, by passing on their basic product to other groups for further processing. The large groups of fullers nevertheless set aside the class conflict with their own masters. In general it is true to say that the vertical organisation of workers according to their trade drew more attention to competition with other guilds than to simple class conflict. In the construction sector there was competition between tilers and

162

126. The slaughter of a pig and jointing of the meat.

(Liège, University Library. Drawing from the *Tacuinum Sanitatis*, ms 1041, fo 44 V°).

thatchers ; the latter were gradually permitted to lay roofing tiles due to the risk of fire in the towns. The carpenters succeeded, after a bitter struggle, in excluding the cabinet-makers from new building – including the furnishing of interiors with large pieces. There were thus continual struggles between the guilds ; the stakes being the dominance of the relevant market and the appropriation of as much profit as possible. This struggle also took place between guilds of different towns, since each town was characterised by protectionism.

A LABOUR ARISTOCRACY WITHIN THE GUILDS The fifth distinction concerns admission to the guilds and employment prospects. These were essentially dependent upon the position of a particular trade in the market : the demand for some goods was declining or stagnant, while for others it was increasing. In the first case, the reaction of the guilds was conservative ; they attempted to preserve as much employment as possible for their own members – possibly to the detriment of other trades and artisans elsewhere. A further reaction was the growing resistance to the admission of new members from outside the principality or the town, by increasing the entry fees, particularly to outsiders.

During the fifteenth century the enrolment fees into the barbers' guild of Leuven doubled ; those of the blacksmith's guild quadrupled, and those of the merchants rose to seven times their previous level. Resident masters also protected their position for the benefit of their successors by ensuring that the conditions of entry to the guilds and of the qualifications for mastership remained in their favour. This evolution began during the fourteenth century : in order to become a master cabinet-maker at Bruges a foreigner was obliged to pay fees for administration and entry to the guild which were twenty-one times as much as those paid by the son of a master. The subscription paid by a Fleming was fourteen times as much, and that paid by an inhabitant of Bruges itself was only eleven times as much. During the course of the fifteenth century the gap grew wider : in 1479 the son of a master, working as a carpenter's journeyman, could earn sufficient for the purchase of a mastership in four or five working days. An outsider from Flanders, however, had to pay the equivalent of 180 working days, while a foreigner paid the equivalent of 244 working days or a full year's salary.

The wall which sheltered these privileges was therefore extremely high, particularly when the other material conditions connected to a mastership are taken into consideration. Even in the smaller enterprises the essentials for a family business – house, tools, raw materials – demanded a very large starting-capital in the fifteenth century. The price of a simple house in Ghent was the equivalent of two years wages of a skilled worker, and five of an unskilled worker. During crisis years these thresholds were higher ; but these workers were obviously unable to set aside their entire wages. Taking into account deductions of essential living expenses, so little remained that even a skilled worker would have to save for twenty-five years in order to be able to afford such a house, and only then if during this period he was never unemployed, or incurred extraordinary expenses due to economic crises or illness. The purchase of a trading house or industrial workshop, which both cost more than twice as much as the house described above, was consequently almost impossible within the lifetime of a single tradesman.

Inheritance was the most common means by which business capital could be acquired. A further possibility was some form of mortgage loan : the vast majority of houses were entailed with rents which

127. Carpenters and bricklayers at work.
(Brussels, Royal Library. Miniature from
J. de Guise's *Chroniques de Hainault,* ms 6419,
fo 106).

usually camouflaged repayments with interest rates. The risk of
becoming incapacitated or crisis situations often prevented many
workers from resorting to such a solution. Finally, there was always
the possibility of renting a business house. This was the case, even
in extremely expensive property, in a shopping quarter such as the
Friday Market in Ghent and the adjacent Langemunt.

The actual result in many trades was in fact the inheritance of the
mastership. This can easily be seen in the case of the brewers of
Ghent :

Period	Number of new Masters	Number of Masters' Sons
1420 – 1449	280	213
1450 – 1479	264	249
1510 – 1539	225	225

These figures clearly show the connection between declining
employment, which decreased by one-fifth over a period of 120 years,
with increasing exclusivity. A similar trend was apparent, again at
Ghent, among blacksmiths, carpenters, bricklayers and white-leather
workers. A formally constituted heritage of masterships in the
butchers' and fishmongers' trades was common from the fourteenth
century onwards in numerous towns of Flanders, Brabant, Liège and
Utrecht. This unusual situation arose partly from the need to
monitor the trade closely in these highly perishable foodstuffs. It

was for this reason that special vending halls were set up ; the number of stalls in these halls was carefully regulated, thereby controlling the number of masters in the relevant trades and preserving the number of profitable posts.

However, the differentiated conditions of admission to the guilds did not always exclude outsiders. The cooperage trade at Bruges, which supplied a large part of the packaging required for European commerce, remained remarkably attractive throughout the fifteenth century. Between 1375 and 1500, 668 new masters were admitted to the trade, and the sons of masters accounted for 21% of this figure. Despite the fact that those who were not citizens of Bruges had to pay twenty times as much to be admitted to the guilds, apprentices nevertheless came from far and wide. Mobility remained high in those sectors where employment and wages were high. There was also a large demand for carpet-weavers, which is reflected in the following figures for admission to the guilds.

THE RECRUITMENT OF CARPET WEAVERS

		Masters	Journeymen	Apprentices
Brussels	1417 – 1431	20	27	81
Brussels	1432 – 1446	15	100	148
Ghent	1467 – 1496	112	28	37

Under Philip the Good, the bricklayers' and stonemasons' guild received more new members than previously. This was also true of expanding regions such as Antwerp and its suburbs, and the towns of Holland, where the pressure of corporatism was not so great.

In the typical export industries (such as Antwerp's silk industry) the tendency towards capitalist entrepreneurship was very pronounced. The milliners of Ghent and Tournai, on the other hand, were allowed to use in their workshops the services of a single apprentice and of their own children ; from the fourteenth century onwards, the number of journeymen was also restricted to avoid the concentration of production in the hands of a few powerful master-craftsmen. In the building trades at Bruges, strong concentration was evident as early as about 1400. A small group of master-craftsmen could acquire virtually all the contracts for public works, since they were the very people who were also deacons and jurymen of their guilds, suppliers of raw materials, and even aldermen or councillors representing the building trade. The tenure of numerous influential offices was the most effective means by which tradesmen could strengthen their position. Although corporate organisation was respected formally, it was in fact reduced to cartels of capitalist entrepreneurs who were actually elected by their less successful colleagues.

Pronounced capitalist concentration was also evident among metal workers in Brussels, particularly the armourers who profited from the demand of the Burgundian court. These occupations required a considerable starting-capital in order to purchase tools and raw materials, and equip a workshop. During the fifteenth century, an élite group of some twenty-three masters won all the important contracts from the municipal authorities, a situation undoubtedly aided by the fact that these masters, as in Bruges, held public offices such as municipal locksmith. These master-craftsmen acquired a

128. Detail of a stained glass window from the north front of Tournai Cathedral, depicting a magistrate taking the oath, ca 1500. The municipal authorities of the Burgundian Netherlands were replaced each year according to various procedures, whereby, over the course of time, the influence of the guilds declined and that of the ruler increased.

considerable amount of property and some even managed in the later fifteenth century to penetrate that most patrician of all organisations, the drapers' guild.

The differences between members of one particular trade and craftsmen in other trades were exacerbated by continual inheritance in some sectors and by capitalist tendencies in others. The textile sector became extremely proletarian although a few master-weavers managed to work themselves up to the rank of small entrepreneurs. So the per capita tax burden on the drapers was considerable. In the latter half of the fifteenth century, the drapers of Leiden

166

and Leuven and elsewhere too, collected together several different processes in their workshops. It is thus easy to understand why journeymen in several trades attempted to form an independent association in order to protect their own interests. Because of opposition from the masters and the town magistrates, this had to be done in the majority of cases under the guise of a charitable organisation. In a few cases these journeymen's associations nevertheless acquired formal status. The most obvious example is that of the 'bonded shippers' of Ghent who sought to protect their interests against the heredity which had entered the 'free' shipping profession as early as the latter half of the fourteenth century. Around the middle of the fifteenth century the shoemakers' journeymen of Antwerp, Brussels, Bruges and Ghent formed separate associations, as did the dyers' journeymen in Brussels and the bricklayers' journeymen in Bruges and Ghent. In 1453 the dyers' journeymen formed an international association with members in forty-two towns.

THOSE ON THE FRINGE OF SOCIETY 'Fringers' are people who live on the edge of society; minorities pushed out by the majority. Groups and occupations which were considered dishonourable because they involved dishonourable tasks (involving for example, blood, as with executioners or slaughterers), because they involved profit-making usury condemned by the church (money dealers), or because they sold themselves (prostitutes). Such occupations were by turns oppressed, rehabilitated, isolated, integrated, and legalised, according to circumstances. Nevertheless, these occupations and

129. Jan Sanders van Hemessen, a busy brothel in Antwerp (?) ca 1540. Homespun subjects were preferred by this artist.

(Berlin-Dahlem, Staatliche Museen Preussischer Kulturbesitz, Gemäldegalerie).

those engaged in them retained a permanent stigma. Fringe existence may reflect socio-economic relations – the poor and the unemployed – and also social and cultural values and circumstances ; prostitutes, witches, gypsies, goliards (non-conformist intellectuals). These many forms of poverty and fringe existence were part of the social structure since they were the outcome of elements such as capitalist organisation, the attitude of the Church, and the interests of a state which wanted to maintain law and order. Both wealth and ideological norms were the prerogative of a small minority.

According to the church, the following were qualified as poor : the sick, widows, the elderly and orphans. But in a broader social context the poor are needy people who are permanently or temporarily vulnerable ; those below or just at subsistence level as a result of famines or epidemics, or as a result of loss of work in a declining industrial or trade sector as in several decaying textile towns of the Netherlands such as Ypres, Dixmude, Geraardsbergen during the fifteenth century or Mechelen and Leiden in the first half of the sixteenth century. Many of those in need were ashamed of their circumstances because of the tension created by the church's narrow definition of poverty and social reality, and they were reluctant to let themselves be recognised as such within the community. Consequently, particularly in rural areas, the poor took to begging outside their own villages. It was said for instance of Comines in 1505, "que par honnesteté les aucuns font leur queste en villes voisines", clearly indicating the fringes to which the poor were reduced.

During the fifteenth century, contemporaries recognised not only those who were supported by public institutions as being poor, but also those who received no support, but who were nevertheless fringers since their livelihood depended on manual labour, small leaseholders with few possessions who were overburdened with taxes, interest-rates and rents. In rural areas, those farming less than an acre were on the poverty line. In the small towns of Flanders during the fifteenth century, 26% of the population were definitely receiving poor relief, and this figure lay between 25% and 30% in the rural

130. A badge of poverty of 1523 showing the maid of Ghent. Such a badge was necessary for the needy to get aid from the Tables of the Holy Spirit.

(Ghent, Bijlokemuseum).

131. The Hôtel-Dieu at Beaune was founded by chancellor Nicolas Rolin.

168

areas of Flanders and Brabant. These percentages are closely linked to the wealth of these regions. In the commercially flourishing town of Antwerp, where the population was increasing, the number of poor supported by the town decreased markedly during the fifteenth century. However, a decrease in the number of those registered as poor is not always an indication of economic growth. During the periods of recession, the absolute figures of those actually registered as poor decreased since the financial capacity of the remainder of the population was reduced and the relief fund was exhausted. So this does not mean that the number of poor decreased; in fact quite the contrary is true.

It is reasonable to suppose that poor relief was not so much determined by actual necessity as by other considerations. That is not to say that for a few well-meaning citizens Christian 'caritas' was not of prime importance but it is noticeable that many social institutions appeared in times of temporary economic depression and large-scale unemployment–but with the prospect of recovery. It would thus seem that the aim of certain large-scale initiatives was to consolidate and safeguard the social order. For this reason, decisions as to which of the poor should receive relief was left to the parochial clergy since they were able to recognise social undesirables and exclude them from assistance.

The bourgeois policy of repressive tolerance was particularly evident in periods of recession when the available means were inadequate. We see how the municipal magistrates then strictly limited poor relief to the needy within their own towns, giving preference to those who were both poor and sick, rather than those who were poor and unemployed, since such people were assumed to be unwilling to work. In the measures taken against begging between 1459 and 1461, when the country was plagued by marauding

132. Visiting the sick in a medieval hospital. Nursing was carried out in large rooms, sometimes with several patients to one bed. During epidemics, admission to such a hospital often increased the risk of death.

(Enschede, State Museum Twenthe. Anonymous master, detail from the *Seven Acts of Charity* of about 1510).

gangs of discharged soldiers, beggars and the poor were treated as vandals. Able-bodied men who did not look for and find work within a period of three days were threatened with forced labour in the galleys. Distinctive badges were distributed to the registered paupers which only served to stigmatize them further. As far as other fringe groups were concerned, the fourteenth and fifteenth centuries saw increasing state intervention which led to their exclusion in isolation or repression, and sometimes to integration. The most dramatic example of this was the treatment of the insane. The therapy for insanity was either medical, or by folk medicine, or religious (i.e. exorcism). The last of these was based upon the conviction that the subject was possessed of the devil, and that the devil could be driven out. The family was considered primarily responsible for the care of such people according to a tradition that persisted particularly at Geel. The towns organised the so-called madhouses. To gain admittance to such an institution, the subject was required either to bring the basic provisions (such as sheets etc.) or to pay. The treatment, such as the incarceration in a metal cage above a small watercourse at the Sint-Jans-ten-Dullen at Ghent was cruel. At first these institutions were also open to the public, though in the fifteenth century healthy passers-by were virtually excluded. A special form of treatment was known as hagiotherapy whereby a cure was attempted using the relics of a saint, like those of St Hermes at Ronse.

Jews were forced to wear a special badge, a stigma. The Jews were made the scapegoat for all misfortunes, particularly during crisis situations such as the plagues of 1347-1350 and 1400. They were relegated to Jewish ghettoes in many towns and were hence forced to specialise in finance. In the Burgundian Netherlands, the Jews were not yet a significant factor in this field.

The peak of the persecution of witches, often linked with various heresies, was reached in the fifteenth century, although the papal and episcopal Inquisition in this activity dates further back. A famous instance is the witch-hunt in the region of Arras, the so-called Vauderie which was associated with the Waldensian heresy from the twelfth century. The bishop of Arras eventually opposed the indiscriminate repression and harsh methods of the Inquisition.

Prostitution was either concentrated in more or less official houses or in unobtrusive areas, but they were generally connected to the bath-houses, and were mostly located outside the respectable areas of the town. Within the old precincts, the women of pleasure were prohibited from soliciting custom on pain of losing an ear. The 'houses of ill-repute' were supposed to be outside the town walls. This was, however, not the case in reality. In 1477 the authorities of Bruges designated a place where the 'vraukins van levene' could live together in what was tantamount to an 'eros community'. These hypocritical gentlemen gave this as their motive : "in order that the virtuous ladies and the virtuous maidens of the city should not be scandalised by them". Most prostitutes left their profession at the age of thirty, either to become an 'abbess' (the 'madam' of other prostitutes) or to be admitted to religious institutions, the so-called houses of the Magdalen Sisters or Maison de Filles de Dieu.

133. Miniature of ca 1500 depicting Fortuna and a young nobleman.

(Ghent, Cathedral Archives, ms 26A fo 30).

Social inequality and the standard of living

134. A so-called 'trippe', worn underneath pointed leather shoes to protect them against the cold and dampness from the ground.

(Schönenwerd, Bally-Schuhmuseum. Wood and leather).

135. Pointed leather shoe. The point is approximately 10 cm long.

(Schönenwerd, Bally-Schuhmuseum).

136. Late Gothic shoe fashioned into a drinking vessel. A shoe used as a drinking vessel was the symbol of the shoemakers' guild. Also, to drink from the shoe of one's lover was a symbol of love, and to do so was to plight one's troth to a chosen one.

(Schönenwerd, Bally-Schuhmuseum. Leather and gilded silver with small bells. Late fifteenth century).

137. A man's silk frock-coat consisting of eleven pieces, from the Burgundian loot plundered by the Swiss in 1476.

(Berne, Historisches Museum. Height: 108 cm).

The social inequality which manifested itself in the legal statutes and regulations was also obvious in the distribution of wealth. The hierarchy within the privileged classes of the clergy and the nobility was also reflected in the income levels, creating enormous differences between, for instance, the financial status of a bishop or abbot and that of a village priest. The clergy and the nobility nevertheless enjoyed secure and regular incomes which were fairly high, accruing mostly from the ownership of land. Interest and rents, generally paid partly in kind, assured the owner of all the necessary provisions, thereby making him independent of fluctuations in market prices. The ownership of a sizable store of grain was one form of wealth in a society confronted every six years by a steep increase in the price of bread.

TYPES AND LEVELS OF INCOME   In order to enjoy a stable income, starting-capital was normally required. Those lacking this were forced to make a living as a leaseholder or paid worker, and were consequently faced with very unpredictable factors affecting the price of foodstuffs, fluctuations in purchasing power brought about by currency manipulation, uncertain employment prospects in the towns, and the threat of disasters in rural areas (the weather, vandals). Within the category of waged labour there were still wage differentials based not so much upon professional qualifications as on legal status. A master-carpenter from Bruges earned, in a working day, 30 percent more than his colleagues in the surrounding villages, and twice as much as the journeymen in his own guild. An apprentice, the only one to have a lower professional qualification, earned at most half as much as a journeyman... Unskilled navvies earned on average 20 per cent less than journeymen in organised trades. Daily wage rates were much the same in all the trade guilds, but outdoor work was always subject to the vicissitudes of the weather.

There was a considerable difference between those masters who could work themselves up to becoming entrepreneurs, and the ordinary fellow-craftsmen. There is evidence of an aristocracy of the artisans engaged in exclusive professions, such as the twenty-three leading metal workers in Brussels (particularly those involved in the making of arms and armour), some building contractors in Bruges, a number of grocers, mercery tradesmen, and craftsmen working in costly materials (fur, Spanish leather, jewels). In such cases income was no longer an earned wage, but rather profit on invested capital. It was this situation which brought about the differentials in the distribution of wealth, as can be seen from per-capita taxes in the towns which, in the case of the Netherlands, were exceptional. Taxes paid by the wealthiest 20 per cent of the population accounted for between 48 per cent and 85 per cent of total tax revenue. In Bruges around 1390, the richest 10 per cent of the population contributed more than 40 per cent of the total tax revenue, and more than 38 per cent in Namur in 1431. At the other extreme, in Leiden for example, 29 per cent were indigent and a further 33 per cent of the town's population contributed no more then 3 per cent of the total tax revenue. Statistics for rural areas are still scarcer, but from the few which are available it can be seen that the distribution of wealth was extremely uneven. In Courtrai at the end of the fourteenth century, out of a total of 1,250 leaseholders, 1,000 had less than 12 acres of land to work ; this was in effect the minimum size of farm to support a family. The linen industry that spread into this area often therefore provided a supplementary source of income for those whose farm earnings were inadequate. Taxation data from Walloon Flanders between 1432 and 1549 show that the number of paupers in the villages there accounted for as much as one half to two thirds of the inhabitants. In the village of Lécluse in 1498 an official recorded 96 families, of which 20 to 24 lived as farmers (owners and leaseholders) ; 69 to 74 as 'manouvriers [wage-earners] vivans du mieux qu'ilz pevent', and two or three lived by begging.

The largest fortunes were shared between town and country. Noble families had both a country castle and a town residence ; the Croy, d'Auxy, Ravenstein, Bergen and Nassau families all had their palaces at Brussels, while the Hoogstratens had their palace in Antwerp and the Gruuthuses theirs in Bruges. The more wealthy town dwellers also had their country seats. Filips Wielant (1441-1520), an outstanding representative of the 'tabard-nobility' (noblesse de robe)

139. Portrait of John III van den Bergh, Lord of Glimes (1452-1531). The Lords of Bergen-op-Zoom belonged to the most important families of nobles in Brabant. He was initially Archduke Philip the Fair's chamberlain, envoy to Emperor Charles and an ardent defender of the Unity of the Netherlands.

(Bergen-op-Zoom. Town hall. Old copy after an anonymous master).

140. Portrait of Adolf of Cleves, Lord of Ravenstein (1425-1492). This grandson of Duke John the Fearless was one of the most important Burgundian councillors and diplomats.

(Berlin-Dahlem, Staatliche Museen Preussischer Kulturbesitz, Gemäldegalerie. Attributed to Jan Mostaert ca 1500).

141. Portrait of Engelbert, Count of Vianen and Nassau, Lord of Breda. From 1473 he was a knight of the Golden Fleece and stadholder in Brabant; under Philip the Fair he became stadholder-general of the Netherlands.

(Amsterdam, Rijksmuseum. Attributed to the Master of the Royal Portraits, ca 1487).

138. Portrait of Filip Wielant (1441/1442-1520), Ghent's illustrious lawyer, from the triptych *Presentation in the Temple*. In 1473 he joined the new Parliament of Mechelen as a councillor. He undertook diplomatic missions and was several times burgomaster of the Franc de Bruges. He drew up a number of practical treatises concerning civil, criminal and feudal law, which were very influential throughout Europe.

(Bruges, Museum of St Saviour's Cathedral. A. Isenbrandt, late fifteenth century).

who had risen through holding ducal offices, owned the old Ser Braemsteen in the Onderstraat at Ghent as well as houses at Bruges, Mechelen, a large farmstead in the vicinity of Nieuwpoort and the extensive estates of Landergem and Eversbeke. Members of the artisan aristocracy also owned land. In 1472 the wife of Roland van de Schuren, a blacksmith from Bruges, bequeathed lands, lakes and a wood situated at Ruddervoorde and Oostkamp.

FISCAL POLICY AND SOCIAL INEQUALITY   Since taxes were never levied on a greater than local level, countless wealthy landowners pleaded citizenship of the towns in order to obtain immunity from taxes levied on their estates. It was not only the real town-dwellers who benefitted from this regulation; people from the country did so too. Whenever they were effectively staying in the town, residents paid indirect taxes via their consumption. The towns usually leased out the collection of these taxes whereby a financially strong group could increase its wealth at the expense of the community. Consumption taxes primarily affected essential items, so that the fiscal policies of the towns therefore exacerbated the existing social inequality.

Landowners who did not take up residence in the towns, but had assumed the extra-mural status of 'country citizen', paid the town and its court-official for this status at the time of enrolment a single payment of 16 Brabant groats at Antwerp in 1463, a slightly smaller sum at Brussels, and an annual sum of five shillings at Antwerp and eight and a quarter at Brussels. These modest sums far from compensated for the fiscal value of the estates which had gained tax immunity. Consequently the tax burden was particularly heavy for the small landowners and tenants remaining in the countryside. In the Walloon village of Wavrin, 1,400 acres of land were owned by the nobility, religious institutions and city inhabitants, none of whom contributed to the local taxes. Only 200 acres belonged to the inhabitants who were liable for taxation. In 1469 in the small seigniory of Coudenburg, in the region of Waas, 60 percent of the land belonged to non-residents who did not contribute towards a single tax levied in the locality. As a result, the tax burden increased considerably and the wealthiest farmers – those who were still able to afford such a move, left the area. Eventually only thirty families remained including just six impoverished tenants living on their farms ; the remainder were paid workers with no property or paupers existing primarily on social welfare. It is then scarcely surprising that there was a revolt among the farmers around Kassel in 1432. But even in the towns too, the populace were sometimes aware that country citizenship was an excessive privilege for the protection of the most wealthy. It was for this reason that in 1432, the insurgent tradesmen of Ghent demanded that the country citizens should immediately enter the town and report.

Fiscal policy weighed heavier on the rural areas than on the towns in yet another way : the national subsidies payable to the duke were determined according to a regional scale. The larger towns had the last word in the negotiations concerning the amount and the conditions of payment. On these occasions the towns tried to have their share reduced while the rural areas almost always paid the full amount. According to the theoretical distribution of the payments in 1517, the rural areas of Flanders were supposed to pay 51.5% of all subsidies, but they actually contributed between 70 and 80% between 1515 and 1550. The Four Members profited from substantial reductions which reduced the share paid by Ghent and Bruges to almost one-third ; that of Ypres to less than one-seventh, and that of the Franc de Bruges (the castellany of Bruges) to three-quarters ; in such cases political power was clearly being wielded in order to protect existing privileges.

142. Detail from a Flemish miniature of 1415, depicting Moses pacifying two fighting opponents.

(Brussels, Royal Library, ms 11041 fo 81 V°).

THE URBAN ELITE In as far as it has been possible to identify individuals from the scarce documents relating to direct taxation, the profiles of those taxed most heavily were fairly constant. It must be remembered, however, that the nobility and the clergy fell outside this category, as did all types of property owned by citizens but located outside the town. The duke's officials and functionaries, although they were often excluded from such taxation lists, were definitely among the most wealthy. This category also included : wholesale traders (in wine, cloth, and also other products, according to circumstances), brokers and also certain members of the artisan aristocracy who had worked themselves up to the status of small entrepreneurs, or worked with costly materials : brewers, drapers, tanners and furriers. Bruges as a trading centre took its lead from money-dealers, brokers and wholesale traders. In the textile town of Leiden in 1498, the 175 drapers (6 per cent of the taxable population) only contributed one quarter of the total tax revenue.

The urban élite was usually organised in one or more exclusive associations. In Brabant the textile guilds provided the nucleus of the urban élite, particularly when representatives of other professions began to be admitted. In addition, these gentlemen met in the quasi-religious archery guilds, chambers of rhetoric or communities such as the Fellowship of Our Lady at 's Hertogenbosch which regularly distributed food and clothing to the poor thanks to the bequests of deceased fellows. During their lives, these members had devoted their attention mainly to banqueting, the costs of which in the sixteenth century rose much more rapidly than their alms. The maintenance of social contacts in a genial atmosphere was essential for the formation of a homogenious urban élite which would embrace all professional groups. In order to gain some idea of the wealth of the Bruges élite we must look at the per capita sums lent to the town by its wealthier citizens. After the end of the revolt against Maximilian and after nine years of economic crisis, 995 heads of households – possibly one-tenth of the total population – saw their way clear to advancing sums varying from 160 to 65,440 groats or, respectively, the equivalent of 40 to 16,360 daily wages paid to an unskilled labourer, and this last figure represented 68 years' wages. The largest group comprising 240 members, (or one quarter of those lending money) paid 360 groats or the equivalent of 90 days' unskilled wages, 136 heads of households (comprising 14 per cent of the lenders) paid 4,000 groats or more – the equivalent of at least 4 years' and 2 months' wages, and a further 43 persons lent sums which were double this amount. There may have been considerable differences within the wealthy bourgeoisie, but the real gulf was between them and the working class. The house contents of Jan van Melle, who was executed in April 1477 during the Ghent uprising, gives some idea of the personal property of a wealthy citizen. As the member of a prominent magistrate's family, Van Melle had openly supported Charles the Bold during and after earlier uprisings in his native town. In 1469 he consequently became one of the most important aldermen, following the centralisation of the urban authorities, and after that became the town's chief tax-collector. The sum raised from the public sale of Van Melle's house contents in 1477 was equivalent to 23 years' wages of a skilled worker (journeyman). This fortune was comprised as follows :

143. Members of the Grand Crossbow guild at Mechelen depicted as benefactors with their patron, St George, and two other saints.

(Antwerp, Royal Museum of Fine Arts. Master of the St George guild of Mechelen, ca 1495).

144. St Ivo (?) champion of the oppressed, reads a request for his help.

(London, National Gallery. Attributed to Rogier van der Weyden).

145. Old and new fashions. Left : a group in 'Burgundian' and mid-fifteenth century costume ; right : a number of persons dressed in the fashions of ca 1500.

(Ghent, Cathedral Archives. Miniature from ms 16, *Biblia Figurata* A, fo 42 r°, draw, for abbot Rafael de Mercatellis).

146. Vanity as depicted by Hans Memlinc. Small breasts and broad hips were the ideal for a woman of the late Middle Ages.

(Strasburg, Musée des Beaux-Arts).

PERSONAL EFFECTS OF JAN VAN MELLE, CHIEF TAX-COLLECTOR OF GHENT, AT THE PUBLIC SALE IN 1477

Item	Value Groats	Percentage of total wealth
Jewellery	11,069	30
Household goods (Silver & Gold)	6,457	17
Cloth	5,834	16
Furniture	4,324	12
Carpets	3,377	9
Household goods	3,312	9
Clothing (of the deceased)	2,660	7
	37,033	100

What is striking about this apart from the substantial value of precious metals (47%), is the quantity of the various cloths, curtains, cushions, counterpanes, and also the 386 ells of linen – which does not even include the bedding for 13 beds. These products were a sign of luxury in towns producing expensive textiles. The difference in

value of the five cloaks which were sold is also striking, two of which (made from fur and velvet) together were worth a sum equivalent to a journeyman's yearly wage. Jan van Melle's house also contained 13 chairs or armchairs, 17 benches, 8 chests, 7 tables, a sideboard, a book shelf, a show-case, a wardrobe, weaponry, a weaving loom, a chess set, three lances, three clocks etc. The kitchen equipment was extensive, and provided for roasting huge joints and also for preparing fish dishes; the eating vessels and cutlery which were in daily use were made of pewter (valued at 620 groats), 12 silver spoons and a single iron spoon were recorded (but no knives or forks); also 23 plates, 21 dishes, 12 sauce-boats, 11 pans, a waffle-iron, several lights etc. There were also barrels for containing oats, meat, herring and butter, and silver ewers, cups and goblets from which to drink wine. All in all this interior seems very similar to those recorded by the Van Eycks and Memlinc.

It is interesting that the most wealthy, as well as holding public office in the towns, were also engaged in professional and/or commercial activities. A wealthy brewer, for example, would find it profitable to collect beer taxes in the town. The starting-capital required for such an undertaking – the tax-collector was required to pay the town a deposit equal to a proportion of the projected revenue – was recovered after one year, often at a considerable profit. The Van den Dale family of Courtrai, who owned one of the town's three breweries, purchased the right to collect beer taxes sixteen times between 1452 and 1480, and wine taxes on a further four occasions. Agreements made between interested parties can be clearly seen in the frequent alterations in the names of those listed as guarantors. As was the case with the master-builders of Bruges or the master-locksmiths of Brussels, the combination of starting-capital and the holding of government office and the rights to collect consumption taxes was extremely profitable. One could even go as far as to say that the increasing disparity among master-craftsmen, some of whom managed to accumulate a considerable amount of

147. Bronze fist of 1551. Instead of suffering corporal punishment for grievous bodily harm, the accused could buy off his punishment with a bronze fist which, together with a text describing the sentence, would be publicly exhibited.

(Veurne, Town Hall Museum).

148. Bronze judicial ransom mask of a certain Pieter de Beert, of which the ring through the mouth has disappeared. In this instance the accused had threatened to throw the jurors out of the window. Instead of being subjected to corporal punishment a bronze mask of the convict was made, which was put on public display along with the terms of his sentence, dated 1499.

(Veurne, Town Hall Museum).

capital, was itself one of the factors that encouraged the industrial expansion of the sixteenth century.

THE AVERAGE, AND THE LARGER FAMILY BUDGET Various researchers, after examining statistics relating to France, Germany, England and the Netherlands, have been able to establish that irrespective of time and place, the proportion of the family budget devoted to food increased as income levels fell. Moreover, their diet would tend to be more unbalanced with a preference for the cheapest available foodstuffs. And in north-west Europe that was bread, right up to the mid-eighteenth century.

For a small price, it was possible for everyone to appease their hunger with bread, whereas vegetables, meat, fruit and dairy products remained far more expensive when compared with their food value. There are several reasons for this : meat and dairy products are essentially second-degree foodstuffs, that is to say the animals which provide them must first extract nourishment from the land before producing food for humans. This double biological cycle uses far more energy than the direct production of grain. Labour intensity and the limited storage capacity of butter, cheese and also vegetables, drove up the prices of these products.

This implies that the demand for cheaper products increases during periods of scarcity, while in times of plenty the consumption – and consequently also the price – of the more expensive items increases. This mechanism can be applied over a period of time in order to trace the evolution of living standards, and also with a view to examining social stratification. In this way we can draw general conclusions from the following results of research relating to Antwerp in the sixteenth century. A typical Antwerp family, composed of a married couple with three young children and receiving one yearly salary of a bricklayers' apprentice (who is typical of the category of skilled workers at the level of a professional journeyman) disposed of their income as follows :

        food 70-80%, of which 45-50% on bread
        rent 5-15%
        heat & light 5-10%
        clothing & other 5-10%.

A budget such as this can be seen as typical of the many skilled

149. Fifteenth-century silver judicial bust. The purpose of this is uncertain since the accompanying text is missing ; it possibly symbolises redemption from execution by beheading.

(Bruges, Gruuthusemuseum).

150. View of the Baliënhof in Brussels, drawn on the occasion of an execution. The so-called Baliënhof, an enclosed square surrounded by a stone balustrade with open Gothic tracery and designed by Anton I and Anton II Keldermans (architects from Mechelen), lay in front of the ducal palace on the Koudenberg. Brass statues of the dukes and duchesses stood on high pillars and the smaller pillars were decorated with statues of birds and other animals.

(Copenhagen, State Archives. Portfolio *Spanske Nederlande*, pen sketch on paper by an anonymous Brussels master).

workers, and was less restricted than that of the unskilled workers or those not belonging to an organisation. The leeway within these budgets reflects individual variations and price fluctuations. It must be emphasised, however, that this income was insufficient during times of crisis when workers were therefore forced to accept poor relief or to suffer shortage. The prices of small houses in Ghent at the end of the fifteenth century varied between 1,000 to 3,000 groats. Approximately one-third of all houses fell within this price-range. In order to accumulate such an amount, a bricklayer's apprentice had to save for a period of 20-25 years. Small wonder that in the St Jacob's district of Ghent – which contained expensive shopping streets as well as poverty-stricken areas, no more than 30% of the houses were occupied by their owners, and 3.5% were inhabited by more than one family.

The worker's diet was extremely monotonous; rye-bread and domestic beer being the main constituents. Mead was also a common drink, a weak brew made by the fermentation of honey. The better quality hop-beer was imported largely from Hamburg (by about 1400, however, beer brewed in Holland had also secured a place in the market) albeit reserved for the wealthy by virtue of its

151. Allegory of a struggle between poverty and wealth. There was a large gulf between the poor and the wealthy and the vicissitudes of life often reduced half the population to poverty.

(Berlin, Library, Printroom. Late fifteenth century engraving by an anonymous master from the Netherlands).

price ; the taxes levied on imported beers were twice as heavy as those levied on home-brewed beer. The wealthy also ate finely milled white bread, more meat and fish coated with seasoned sauces, vegetables and fruit ; the consumption of French and Rhenish wines (considering the absence of alternatives) was also relatively high in this class. Returning to the lot of the ordinary man, the importance of fish consumption should not be overlooked. The high price of meat and the many church festivals meant that herring and dried cod were in high demand even far inland. The wider availability of pickled herring met a demand which was all the greater because its protein content, and provided a welcome supplement to the monotonous diet composed largely of starch.

The budget outlined above was subject to marked fluctuations and changes from time to time. Through the weather and other circumstances, yields varied considerably from year to year by

anything up to 25%, with a consequent ratio of 5 :1 between the highest and the lowest price. In practice there were years when the average worker ate wheat-bread and butter with meat, while the next year that same worker might quite possibly be unable to afford even rye-bread, and would have to content himself with mixtures using barley as a base. This meant that the level of beer production could not be maintained, and the poorer people started drinking water, which because of the lack of hygiene, was likely to be contaminated. This probably explains the outbreak during the fifteenth century of many contagious intestinal diseases which were rife after famines.

Another variable in expenditure patterns was due to the so-called life-cycle. We shall again work on the basis of a family of five, but this time following a typical life-cycle. From birth the child sooner or later found itself, according to its place in the family, fulfilling a particular role. For the first fifteen years, however, each child only represented outgoings for the family that were not offset by any extra income. On the contrary, the responsibility of children prevented the mother working to supplement the income. It is no coincidence that large families were frequently found in the lists of poor who received alms : the more children, the more each member of the family could earn from begging. The situation only improved for such when the children, one by one, reached fifteen years of age and were then able to learn a trade, which meant that they were accommodated in the master's house. The young apprentice himself earned very little, but was well provided for. When his apprenticeship (between one and four years) had been completed, he could earn a wage as a journeyman – this was more than sufficient, provided he remained single. If he married, and his wife had no income from wages or

153. Distributing bread to the poor, one of the acts of charity. In times of shortage the towns closed their gates to the needy who had come there from the countryside.

(Amsterdam, Rijksmuseum. Master of Alkmaar, first half of the sixteenth century).

154. 'It is hard going for a cripple'. Due to insufficient medical treatment, physical injuries did not heal properly. They often caused the sufferer to be unfit for employment and thus led to poverty.

(Diest, Jan Borremans or Nicolaas de Bruyn (?), misericord in St Sulpice's Church, 1480-1490).

155. Reaping of the harvest with a sickle alongside a river, with two workers asking the farmer's wife for food in the foreground. Although the scythe was a popular tool, the most valuable crops were reaped with the sickle in order to maximise yield.

(Brussels, Royal Library. Miniature from the *Hennesy-Book of Hours* from the first half of the sixteenth century, ms II 158, fo 8 V°).

cottage industry, then his financial status declined. Each child was a drain on the means for each member of the family until it in its turn could take up an apprenticeship. Only then – given good health and employment – could our worker begin to enjoy a relatively comfortable lifestyle again. The greatest problems confronting him then would be the maintenance of his work and health ; should either one fail, difficult times would return and he would have to look for support from charity, or even resort to other means.

POOR RELIEF : A DOUBLE EDGED SWORD Right from the start, the towns had various institutions with religious and charitable aims. The guilty conscience of merchants who had made their fortunes in a manner which was not in keeping with the doctrine of the church, drove many of them to make substantial donations late in their lives, in order to relieve the plight of the sick and poor. Church institutions were usually among the beneficiaries because of their centuries-old tradition of donating a proportion of their income to poor relief. In the same spirit, one of the earliest activities of the corporate organisations was the mutual support of their sick and impecunious members.

This explains why poor relief in the Burgundian Netherlands was provided by countless diverse institutions, even in the villages. All such institutions were set up with pious ambitions which were, however, seldom realised. During the fourteenth and fifteenth centuries, countless transactions between private individuals and religious institutions involved, albeit in the guise of a pious donation, the transfer of estates in exchange for an annuity for the donor. Both parties benefitted from such transactions : the institutions increased their holdings and their long-term income,

156. A pickpocket steals from a spectator during a magician's performance.

(Saint-Germain-en-Laye, Musée Municipal. Hieronymus Bosch, *The Magician,* ca 1475-1480).

while the recipient of the annuity secured a form of life-insurance (possibly for his children's benefit too) which would acquire its maximum value during the many periods of fatal epidemics. It was also usual for the receiving institutions to say masses for the soul of the 'donor', for whom the poor were thus the means by which the highest good in the hereafter could be attained.

There was another kind of institution not altogether devoid of vested interest that is worth mentioning. At Ypres, several large entrepreneurs in the textile industry surprisingly started founding hospitals between 1270 and 1280. During this time there was considerable unemployment due to the disruption of English wool imports. It is evident that the Christian love of one's neighbour was not the only motive, but also a shrewd appreciation of their own interests supporting the workers whose labour would very likely be required again.

During the fifteenth century poor relief posed more and more obviously the dilemma : pure religious motivation or also concern for the maintenance of the existing social order. It is not clear which criteria were used by the charitable institutions outside the guilds in order to decide which of the poor would be helped. It is, however, evident that religious ceremony provided the context for the distributions. Parish priests usually controlled the 'Tables of the Holy Spirit', and the abbeys and other institutions also distributed regularly at the church door, usually at church festivals and funerals. Christian love of one's neighbour was scarcely evident in the government policy concerning such matters. In periods of famine, country dwellers sought refuge in the towns, in the hope of finding either work or alms. The town authorities reacted against this by limiting relief to their own subjects since they feared that the influx of applicants for poor relief would accelerate the exhaustion of available funds. Beggars who had not got a token from a 'Table of the Holy Spirit' – the only institution for poor relief controlled by the town authorities – or beggars from elsewhere, were constantly turned away. Brotherly love was thus confined to fellow citizens, and can consequently be seen as concern for social order. Such restrictions, it is true, could not be effectively enforced – that they had to be reiterated shows that they were rarely observed – but the stigmatizing and rejection of those genuinely in need was nonetheless real.

Between 1459-1461 the three densely populated areas, Brabant, Flanders and Holland, decided simultaneously upon analogous measures to combat what was in fact considered to be vandalism, and the tone then became more formal and more repressive : begging was only condoned among those who were unfit for work. All other healthy men were compellled to search for work under threat of forced labour in the galleys. This repressive policy, although leniently applied, had the effect of depressing the wages of unskilled workers, particularly in rural areas. Existing institutions such as the Tables of the Holy Spirit at Ghent reduced their distributions around 1458. This was precisely the time when growing towns such as Antwerp, Mechelen and 's Hertogenbosch were increasing their provision. The Brussels guild of bricklayers and stonemasons similarly set up a support fund for those of its members who were in need. Much therefore depended on the prospects for the future : the more favourable the economic outlook, the greater the willingness to provide relief.

It has thus been calculated that the Tables of the Holy Spirit in Leuven, Mechelen and 's Hertogenbosch (all towns with approximately 25,000 inhabitants about 1500) each distributed, on a regular basis, bread, shoes, meat, herring, linen (and sometimes also other provisons or money) to between 500 and 1,000 people. The rations were, however, even at best insufficient for one adult, but did nevertheless provide an effective supplement. Nine to eighteen per

157. Public announcement of a tax-levy which provokes immediate commentary from the onlookers. From about 1460 the tax burden in the Burgundian Netherlands increased considerably.

(Brussels, Royal Library, ms 9242 fo 274 Vᵒ ; Jacques de Guise, *Chroniques de Hainault* ; translated by Jean Wauquelin).

158. St Jerome in his study. The interior is that of an academic physician of the fifteenth century. In addition to the many books and writing materials there is an hourglass, an astrolabium, a urine glass (?) and a pot of Theriaca, a pain-killer which was in general use during the Middle ages.

(Detroit, The Detroit Institute of Arts. Anonymous Flemish master).

cent of the population, including their families, could benefit from such distributions. From fiscal records it appears that at Leuven in 1480, 18% of families were registered as poor; this figure had increased to 22% in 1526, and the figure for 's Hertogenbosch in that year was 14%.

If fiscal statistics provide reliable figures for those receiving relief, then the situation was much worse in towns whose economies were in decline and where large numbers of paupers could consequently be expected. In Ypres, in the district known as the 'Gemene Neringen' (the small trades) 79% of inhabitants were poor in 1431 according to fiscal statistics, of whom only 13% received poor relief. The situation in Ghent was even less cheerful after the revolt against Maximilian in 1492 : 49% of the inhabitants of the parish of St Jacob were not able to pay the equivalent of an unskilled worker's daily wage in taxes, and 53% were unable to meet a further levy; "because they were very poor or lived from the Holy Spirit". The latter category, however, comprised no more than 17% of the district's inhabitants, and then not even the poorest.

The exceedingly long and serious crisis period between 1482 and 1492 brought almost all welfare institutions into grave difficulties. While the number of those in need increased due to the catastrophically high food prices and the war, these circumstances in turn made it impossible for the institutions to maintain the usual level of distribution. Even in 's Hertogenbosch, where distribution had been relatively generous, bread rations decreased by half and, until 1511, remained below the level of the 1470s. The Table did not receive its normal incomes for a period of twenty years, and consequently accrued a debt equivalent to a whole year's revenue. So during the periods of greatest need, the majority of Tables were underfunded and until well into the second decade of the sixteenth century, they lacked the reserves to survive further periods of difficulty.

After the famines of 1527 to 1532 the need for the reformation of the poor relief system was universally felt. These initiatives were characterised by the amalgamation, rationalisation and stricter control of all forms of relief. In addition to the prohibition on begging and the traditional obligation of those who were able-bodied to search for employment, the behaviour and religious orthodoxy of those receiving relief came under stricter social control for the first time. One of the typical policies which was retained was that by which the needy were pressurised into accepting employment with lower wages. This meant that the rations too became less and less, and in any case far too little to live on. The withdrawal of this relief hung like a sword of Damocles over the heads of the needy. And this sword cut both ways : to maintain the social order and to ensure the salvation of the donors.

ASTROLOGY AND URINALYSIS IN MEDICAL CARE Hospitals were originally closely connected to the institutions for poor relief. Since illness and poverty were often related in their causes, the functions of both institutions continued to overlap partially. Individual cases of illness were often helped by the Tables of the Holy Spirit, which gave weekly donations to the anchorites or Black Sisters for the care of the mentally ill. In the hospitals themselves, however, poor patients were increasingly threatened by the practice of the wealthy, who secured a form of health insurance by purchasing a prebend, thereby bequeathing a share of their property to the institution on their admission or death. They consequently ensured that the autumn of their lives would be comfortably spent in the institution of their choice, where they would be well looked after. The hospitals saw the advantages of such arrangements, but as a result became more élitist. They continued to distribute fixed rations at their doors, but on a reduced scale.

There were, generally speaking, two types of hospital institution. There were those consisting of separate houses grouped around a central courtyard with communal areas designated for treatment and care, for worship and for management. This is where

159. A blood-letter of the beginning of the sixteenth century. Blood-letting was prescribed both as a preventative and a cure, providing that the patient was strong enough.

(Venice, Biblioteca Nazionale Marciana, detail of a miniature from the *Breviarium Grimani,* fo 10 r°).

the benefactors were accommodated. Secondly there were the larger, older hospitals where the sick were nursed in large wards by a religious order. At St John's hospital at Bruges, one hundred or so beds stood in rows, and a maximum of 150 patients could be admitted. There was no privacy for the sick, who lay naked, except in the 'doothouc' or terminal room. Patients were only isolated in exceptional cases since immunology was almost unheard of.

The disease most feared by people in the Middle Ages was leprosy, although this was not very contagious. Those with this disease had been accommodated in special hospitals on the edge of town since the twelfth century. They were dressed in conspicuous clothing and provided with a rattle or clapper so that healthy people would keep their distance. From the twelfth century to the fourteenth century, every town had such a lazaret ; these, however, became largely vacant during the fifteenth century when the disease was brought under control, and the incidence was reduced to one case per thousand inhabitants. Moreover, uncertain diagnosis resulted in other diseases being diagnosed as leprosy. From the fifteenth century onwards, the authorities found it necessary to install control points in the four main towns of Brabant and the three principal towns of the Franc de Bruges in Flanders. The purpose was to check for the disease but also to ensure that beggars did not pass through in the guise of lepers and thus benefit from a prebend. It was not until the seventeenth century, however, that the plague, a far worse contagious disease, could be controlled by systematic isolation. The amount of attention paid to bodily hygiene increased towards the end of the Middle Ages, conceivably under the influence of Arabic medicine. Baths were given in hospitals and bath-tubs were occasionally depicted in illustrations of the more affluent homes. The remarkable combination in the Netherlands of public baths and brothels could possibly have originated in Arabia, where it was customary to bathe prior to and following coitus.

It is very likely that during and after the fifteenth century what was thought to be leprosy or plague was in fact ergotism, that is : poisoning caused by the consumption of bread made from flour contaminated with ergot, a rye parasite. The main symptoms were vomiting, diarrhoea, stomach cramps and atrophy of the extremities. Although lethal when consumed in large doses, lighter doses caused contraction of the womb and thus prevented conception. There are even hypotheses concerning a possible connection between the ingestion of alkaloids present in ergot and the appearance of mass hysteria such as occurred in witch-hunting. There is in fact a correlation between heavy rainfall in the spring (which promotes the growth of the parasite) and the years of mass-psychosis. Moreover, such phenomena were significantly more frequent in areas where rye was the principal crop, while wheat districts appear to have been spared.

Until the middle of the sixteenth century, medical theory and practice were regarded as quite separate and distinct. Physicians studied the writings of Greek, Roman and Arab scholars, but received no practical training. This lack of practical experience gave rise to the most fantastic delusions.

Medical theory attached great importance to astrology, which was thought to control physical symptoms ; consequently, surgery and treatment could only be carried out on 'propitious' days. A second element of academic medicine was the Greek theory of the humours ; the four bodily fluids which had to remain in a state of perfect harmony. Learned medical scholars also occupied themselves with

160. An enema is given with a syringe.

(Bruges, Gruuthusemuseum. Anonymous master. Woodcarving of the fifteenth century).

the most futile issues: why hair does not grow on the nose; why the stomach is not positioned closer to the mouth, etc. They would quote Hippocrates, Galeir and some of the Arab scholars quite uncritically. Their therapies consisted of enemas, blood-letting, enforced vomiting and sweating, and the insertion of various preparations in the bodily orifices. The taking of the pulse and the examination of urine were the methods of diagnosis, performed by the physician himself – preferably in his own house since he eschewed direct contact with the patient. It is thus typical that St John's hospital in Bruges did not have the services of a regular physician, although it did have its surgeons, barbers and priests. Urine samples were taken by the hospital staff to the physician house, where he made liberal use of herbal remedies in his prescriptions. The herbary of St John's hospital incidentally covered an area of more than 3,200 square metres.

However, not all aspects of a physicians' activities were entirely futile. Why else would towns give financial assistance to their inhabitants in order that they might obtain a doctor's diploma at the famous medical faculties of Paris, Montpellier or Bologna? At Bologna large anatomical theatres had even been built so that surgery could be taught more effectively. Those graduating from these progressive centres brought back notes which formed the basis of compendia, medical anthologies and herbals, which, thanks to the development of printing, could be distributed on a large scale from 1478 onwards. Although there was often considerable confusion in these texts they nevertheless stimulated the flow of old and new theories and the exchange of opinion among practitioners.

Surgeons and barbers were normally general practitioners, with midwives looking after obstetrics. Their professional training was empirical and their acquired skills included such surgical operations as blood-letting and the treatment of ulcers and injuries.

St John's hospital at Bruges certainly did employ such people, with brothers and sisters of the religious orders responsible for the day-to-day care of the patients. Texts written in the vernacular by two southern surgeons in the early 1300s became famous, and their approach was even more critical than that of Guy de Chauliac, the renowned personal physician to the papacy in Avignon. The solid tradition of empirical medicine established by the likes of Jan Yperman and Thomas Scellinck, continued until it was finally broken by the work of Vesalius in the mid-sixteenth century.

Recent research into the medical treatment of women has shown that surgical, gynaecological and obstetrical operations were all performed by midwives who had no academic education, only practical experience. The non-academic practical knowledge and experience acquired by the midwives and their male colleagues, surgeons, brought them to a closer understanding of the sick and their ailments than the theoretical training of the physician. In Bruges around 1450 an illustrated handbook was published in the vernacular, containing advice on pregnancy, childbirth and women's illnesses. This was obviously written by someone working in midwifery circles. The authorities of Brussels had drawn up legislation relating to the midwifery profession as early as 1424, and consequently appointed five senior midwifes to train and examine all those wishing to enter the profession. During the course of the

161. An anatomical diagram of a man of 1505 with the various organs depicted in a rudimentary fashion.

(Ghent, University Library, ms 7 fo 237 r°).

162. Mechanical apparatus for the extraction of arrows according to Jan Yperman, a fourteenth-century surgeon. Surgeons were craftsmanly trained master healers who, amongst other things, had to accompany the municipal militia. The physician on the other hand, was an academic who reached a diagnosis and recommended a treatment only by feeling the pulse and analysing the urine.

(Ghent, University Library, ms 1273, fo 34).

163. A tampon made from a cotton pouch with a cord which could be filled with dried herbs and other medicines, and a vaginal flask for introducing herbal smoke or fumigation to the womb.

(Bruges, City Library, *Liber Trotula*, ms 593, fo 4).

164. A woman takes a herbal bath to relieve a gynaecological complaint. Illustration from a West-Flemish textbook for and by midwives, dating from the mid-fifteenth century.

(Bruges, City Library, *Liber Trotula*, ms 593, fo 5 V°).

165 and 166. Toothed forceps (for the extraction of dead foetusses) and speculum (for internal examinations). Two instruments which midwives were able to use.

(Hamburg, Stabi. *Chirurgie Albucasis*, Cod. med. 798 U III p. 247 and 248).

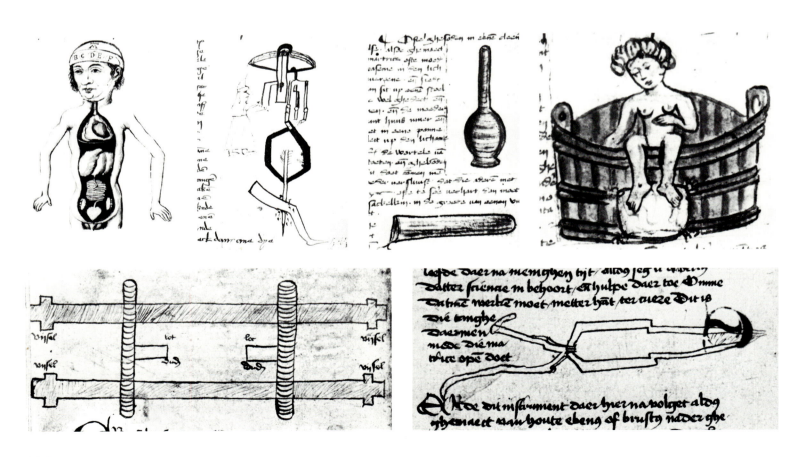

190

167. Less flattering sculpture of, possibly, Philip the Good, with a pox-scarred face. During the last years of his life his health failed and in 1465 he consequently handed over government to his only legitimate son. He died of pneumonia in 1467.

(Dijon, Musée des Beaux-Arts. Anonymous artist. Alabaster bust, ca 1500).

fifteenth century, midwives were officially appointed in all the larger southern towns.

It is difficult to assess the effectiveness of medical treatment at this time. Statistics from St John's hospital showing the number of deaths occurring during and prior to admission only cover the years 1509-1549 (male deaths) and 1543-1549 (female deaths). Twice as many men as women died after admission or on arrival; the average figures for concurrent years were respectively 79 and 42 per year. This implies that women died at home far more frequently than men : discrimination, even in death. The death-rate among males was abnormally high during periods of famine, i.e. the years 1522, 1531-1533, 1540-1541, 1545-1547, when by far the highest number of deaths were recorded during the months of March, April and May. The abnormally high death-rate during crisis years is also recorded at the Bijloke hospital at Ghent : "In the five years of war – 1488, 89, 90, 91 and 92 – we were so overwhelmed by the sick that two or three of them always had to lie together in one bed and within these five years more than 2,000 people died in the above-mentioned hospital". Overcrowding in the hospitals may have precipitated the death of many patients, bearing in mind the fact that there were also outbreaks of plague at this time. Such situations only emphasise how much was still to be achieved in the field of medicine.

THE LAND OF PROMISE ? Philippe de Commynes (1447-1511) was a member of the old Ypres lineage of Van der Clyte, which produced two sovereign-bailiffs of Flanders (1424-1454). De Commynes was a celebrated diplomat and chronicler, and was initially councillor to Charles the Bold, although he shifted allegiance in 1472 and went over to the side of Charles' arch-enemy Louis XI. In 1489, however, he also fell out of favour with the French court. This schemer both as a diplomat and as a historian of his times visited many European countries in his time, particularly Italy. He could therefore draw comparisons, and although he was not strictly a contemporary of Philip the Good he could be kept reliably informed via family connections of what went on in the Netherlands under the 'Grand Duc du Ponant'. De Commynes describes the last 25 years of Philip's reign (1440-1465) as a veritable golden age, perhaps with the intention of highlighting the contrast between Philip and his former employer, Charles. The following comment of his is a useful guide to the standard of living during the Burgundian period : "The subjects of the House of Burgundy lived in great wealth at this time because of peace and the goodness of their prince, who did not burden them with heavy taxes, it would therefore seem to me that his lands more than any other on this earth could be called 'lands of promise'. They were steeped in riches and lived in great quietude, such as they have not known. It is some 23 years ago (writes De Commynes in 1465) that this situation began. Expenditure was great, the clothing of men and women was luxurious ; the meals and banquets grander and more abundant than in any place I know."

How realistic were these statements ? The splendour of the Burgundian court is well-known, but De Commynes extends this to the entire population. It is true that peace prevailed in the Netherlands – except for internal uprisings – and Philip taxed his subjects rather less heavily than Charles. But do all these things constitute national wealth ? Although De Commynes only takes us back as far as the peace treaty with England (1443) we will extend our enquiry to cover the period 1380-1530.

191

There are several indicators which can help us in our investigation. It was stated in the previous chapter that the volume of trade in the Netherlands doubled between about 1400 and 1475. Merchants therefore made considerable profits and employment prospects in export industries and the service sector were healthy. Assuming that a stable currency is an indication of (and a factor contributing to) a healthy economy, then this was especially true of the years 1434-1474 and 1496-1548, and to a lesser extent from 1390-1416. The periods of devaluation (1416-1433 and 1474-1496) were particularly unfavourable for the economy. Other countries, and for that matter the Netherlands too, lost confidence in the currency which consequently decreased in value. International payments were disrupted as a result but more importantly, domestic purchasing-power was affected by the growing gap between prices (which immediately rose) and wages, which did not rise in proportion. Devaluation meant, in effect, that the prince was creaming off the whole economy of his countries, which the subjects were powerless to resist. However, the maintenance of a stable currency during most of the Burgundian period greatly contributed to the wealth of the Netherlands, and was enjoyed by all sections of the population.

De Commynes states that the subjects of Philip the Good were not heavily taxed. We can only verify this in the county of Flanders. It is certainly true when compared with the period 1472-1494 which is when the author was writing his account, when taxes were three times what they had been in the period 1456-1471 and four times as much as in the period 1439-1452. De Commynes' observations are clearly retrospective, for during the last ten years of Philip's reign the fiscal burden increased by 30% in relation to the previous thirteen years of the period which he was discussing ; and this quite apart from the enormous tax penalties imposed by the duke after the uprisings in Ghent (1453) and Bruges (1438). The increase in taxation under Philip did not necessarily have disastrous consequences ; it was met by a possibly even greater increase – certainly in the towns – in what is known today as the gross national product. Similar trends were also apparent in the sixteenth century : the tax burden in Flanders during Margaret of Austria's second period of government (1515-1530) was 134 per cent greater than under Philip the Fair (1493-1506) and 36 per cent greater than during the crisis years between 1484 and 1494. This increase was due to a larger money supply (thanks to the Hapsburg silver) and an absolute increase in the gross national product.

AVERAGE ANNUAL TAXATION IN FLANDERS
(expressed in Pounds Parisis)

1384-1399 :	95,112	1456-1471 :	147,337
1400-1414 :	33,333	1472-1482 :	448,999
1415-1429 :	93,247	1484-1494 :	461,784
1430-1438 :	16,670	1495-1506 :	267,850
1439-1452 :	113,657	1515-1530 :	626,363

Taxation was therefore moderate until about 1450, (and during certain periods could even be described as light) thereafter increasing by 30 per cent, only to treble under Charles the Bold and Maximilian. Under Philip the Fair taxation was once again moderate, despite the increase in the nominal level which was partly inflationary. Although this is largely true for the period 1515-1530, a gradual – but nevertheless real – increase in taxation in 1521 and 1522 could not be avoided : this increase exceeded one million pounds parisis in Flanders. If these figures are representative of the Netherlands as a whole, (and this is unlikely between 1430 and 1438) we can deduce from this analysis and our previous findings that favourable economic cycles prevailed during the first decade of the fifteenth century, and also during the periods 1439-1472, and 1495-1530.

Harvest yields were important for the entire population, but particularly for the farmers who made a living from the sale of their harvest and also for the manual workers who spent half their income on foodstuffs. The distribution of cyclical increases in grain prices is therefore also a relevant indicator to look at. Grain prices appear to have been higher than at any other time during the periods 1408 to 1438 and 1477 to 1492. During the sixteenth century prices remained generally low except during 1521 and 1522, despite gradual increases. Crisis periods occurred more frequently from 1531-32 onwards. We can therefore assume that the first decade of the fifteenth century, the period about 1440-1475 and the years after 1492 were reasonably prosperous, except for incidental crises such as those occurring in 1408, 1458 and 1521.

How did these trends affect the purchasing-power of the average artisan ? The demand for craft products was also adversely affected by a crisis in the grain market. When bread prices doubled or more than doubled, demand shifted since the average worker was forced to buy cheaper bread (for example, rye instead of wheat, barley instead of rye) in order to appease his hunger, and all expensive or unnecessary purchases were postponed until better times. Cheese, butter, meat and vegetables disappeared from the table, clothing was not regularly replaced and workers had to economise on heat and light. Since a large proportion of the budget was spent on food, and in particular on bread, the demand for craft products declined, which in turn affected employment and incomes in this sector, and this aggravated the situation.

Before discussing trends in real wages, it is important to remember that both grain prices and income were sensitive to large demographic movements. Fluctuations in wages and the price of grain will be particularly clear indicators of high death rates, though less accurately in the case of wages. Population statistics are thus central to such a discussion since the size of population determined both the demand for grain and the supply of labour. (See Appendix : figs 2-7).

The second half of the fourteenth century, until about 1401, was generally characterised by demographic decline. This led to a decrease in grain prices, while labour became scarce and wages rose. Real wages and therefore the standard of living improved due to the period of high mortality : it would thus appear that the Netherlands were overpopulated before the outbreak of the plague. The period between 1385 and 1415 would have been economically prosperous were it not for the fact that Flanders was still devoting much energy to repairing the damage incurred during the 1379-1385 war. Grain prices began to rise again shortly after 1400 due partly to the crisis of 1408, while the price of cheese and butter did not increase until after 1410. The worker benefitted from this time lapse since it meant that during the first decade of the fifteenth century, he could allow himself foodstuffs which were later to become rare luxuries. After the plague epidemic of 1400-1401, the population of the Netherlands was not faced with another crisis until 1437-1439, and all evidence points to the fact that the population increased considerably during the intervening period : grain prices remained high while wages remained stable. The fact that wages did not decrease could be attributed to the fact that employment prospects remained favourable thanks to economic expansion during this period. Nevertheless this period must be seen as one in which actual purchasing power decreased as a result of various currency devaluations (and still more damaging revaluations) and the serious disruption of economic relations with England and the Hanse, mainly between 1415 and 1439.

The phenomenal wave of deaths between 1437 and 1439 made life easier for those remaining : between about 1440 and 1470 the price of grain, butter and cheese tended to fall ; wages not only remained constant, but even underwent an annual increase of almost 14 per cent between 1440 and 1450 as a result of higher wage-rates introduced during summer months. The years between 1440 and 1470 thus appear to have been particularly prosperous, judging by all the indications : trading relations were prospering (although the blockade by the Hanse between 1451 and 1457 cannot really be dismissed) ; the currency was stable ; taxation was moderate ; the price of foodstuffs remained low and wages were increasing. Even the sharp increase in the price of grain and the plague epidemics between 1456 and 1459 were of mild proportions. If one follows De Commynes to the letter, then he was indeed justified in describing this period as particularly prosperous.

Population generally increased during periods of prosperity ; however, the danger of a further crisis arose after a period of some thirty years, by which time the second new generation had reached working age. Between 1477 and 1492 food prices increased to unparallelled levels, while wages failed to adjust accordingly. On the contrary, employment prospects were threatened by disruptions in trade, rural areas suffered heavily due to the movement of troops, the country reeled under a crushing fiscal policy and the currency was seriously affected. The fifteen years of war which followed the death of Charles the Bold were anxious times for the Netherlands and were disastrous for certain regions. The southern region was invaded by France and elsewhere there were uprisings in Flanders, central Brabant and Holland. Several decades were to pass before the Netherlands recovered from these events.

The period between about 1490 and 1530 can nevertheless be described as generally prosperous. Food prices returned to a normal level although they began to rise again shortly after 1500. Commercial expansion in Brabant and Holland was spectacular and brought an increase in real wages. This unusually powerful expansion was aided by a stable currency which was even slightly inflated. From 1530 onwards, however, a series of renewed crises followed each other in quick succession. The trend in living standards can thus be outlined as follows :

About 1385-1415 : recovery and growth
1416-1439 : decreasing purchasing power
1440-1474 : boom
1475-1490 : deep crisis
1490-1530 : recovery and powerful growth

Periods of decreasing purchasing power mainly affected craft journeymen and unskilled workers. Strong fluctuations in food prices and shifts in employment came all the harder since they were

170. Pillary at Braine-le-Château, 1521.

unprotected and had no savings in reserve. At Bruges during the 60 years between 1383 and 1443, these groups had twenty-seven years of serious hardship – almost one in two years. The years between 1443 and 1476 were kinder, with only four crisis years out of thirty-three. Thereafter, however, impoverishment was universal. The bricklayers of Mechelen had nine lean years between 1501 and 1530, unskilled navvies had twelve, despite the fact that this period was one of economic growth and Mechelen was an expanding area.

We have already mentioned the fact that 53 per cent of the population of Ghent were paupers in 1492, but the textile industry in a number of towns in Holland – Leiden, The Hague and Naarden – was also in a state of crisis. The breweries of Gouda and Delft were only operating at one quarter of their full capacity.

When discussing the seemingly indisputable wealth of the Burgundian Netherlands, it is important not to lose sight of the following constraints :

1. The periods of expansion which continued for approximately 30 years, were interrupted by two crisis periods which, in total, spanned 20 years.
2. Even during prosperous years the lower working classes still experienced hardship every two or three years, which made recovery impossible. The only exception to this was the prosperous period between 1440 and 1470.
3. Certain regions and sectors experienced structural economic difficulties which caused local, long-term hardship and affected as much as half the population.
4. Even in Brabant, which was expanding and flourishing, structural poverty affected one quarter of the population in the beginning of the sixteenth century. In Antwerp, where the situation was least serious, this figure amounted to 10.5% (1480), which other evidence shows to be on the low side.

If the period between 1440 and 1470 is compared with previous and subsequent periods, and also with other countries, then the Netherlands was indeed a land of promise, as De Commynes claimed. On the other hand the Netherlands, as a highly urbanised society, was prone to strong fluctuations and social inequality.

171. The storming of the City of Jerusalem; a realistic representation of the siege tactics used to subject Holland and Luxembourg and other municipal uprisings during the reign of Philip the Good. The theme of this manuscript was also apt in view of the fear in the Christian Western world of the Turkish advance in Asia Minor, which gave rise to the crusading ideal.

(Vienna, Österreichische Nationalbibliothek, ms 2583. Miniature from the *Chronique de Jerusalem,* produced ca 1450 by master Girart de Roussillon for Philip the Good).

5

The State and Society

The development of
a Burgundian consciousness

NATIONAL SOVEREIGNS? Jules Michelet, the French romantic historian, wrote of the first of the great Burgundian dukes, Philip the Bold : "Nulle part, pas même en Bourgogne, le duc n'était vraiment le seigneur naturel".

Chroniclers of the fifteenth century such as Jan and Olivier van Dixmuide also stressed that Philip was only prince by virtue of his wife, Margaret de Male, daughter of the 'real' Flemish prince. In the anonymous work *Die Wonderlycke Oorloghen van Keyser Maximilian*, the first part of which was undoubtedly written before March 1482, and which was completed between 1519 and 1531, the Burgundian dynasty is depicted in a different light. In the first part of this work, which was a contemporary account, Mary of Burgundy is said to have moved representatives of the States-General to tears at Ghent on the 26th January 1477 when she voiced fears of annexation by France and asked for support. The ambassadors of Brabant are said to have replied : "O worthy princess, be not afeared, we, the States of Brabant, hold you as our natural lady and princess of all the lands, and shall remain loyal to you until death". The Flemings and the representatives of Hainault and all the other regions reacted similarly. The same author later records the wave of popular goodwill which surrounded the birth of Mary's child on June 8th 1478. In order to continue the Burgundian dynasty, it was necessary for Mary to give birth to a son. The fact that Mary had actually given birth to a son was doubted by some who were 'goet Fransoys' and supported the French king. After the christening in the court at Bruges a murmur ran through the crowd and Mary was forced to show "the young prince Philip all naked" whereupon Mary took "his little testicles in her hand". Those present, "seeing that it was a son, were extremely glad".

The obviously subjective impressions of a chronicler are borne out by other contemporaries, although not everyone was so favourably disposed towards the Burgundian dynasty. In 1384 Duke Philip was still clearly considered a foreigner, although his successors Mary and her son Philip, were regarded as natives in 1477/78, unlike Mary's husband, Maximilian of Austria, who was regarded as a new foreigner. The Burgundian dynasty was therefore assimilated and adopted in the decades following 1384. The reticence with which the 'foreigners' Philip the Bold and Maximilian were confronted, was due to their strong connections with foreign dynasties (the French and the Austrian) which threatened to absorb the Netherlands into a larger and foreign entity, thereby threatening the considerable independence which they still enjoyed. Early in the Burgundian period, any feelings of unity were purely on a regional level : people were loyal Flemings, Artesians or Brabanters. It was not until the reign of Philip the Good that a feeling of unity developed ; a sense of Burgundian nationalism. Burgundy became a collective title for all the lands controlled by the dukes, and this feeling of solidarity developed around the Duke. From 1384 onwards the Burgundian dynasty evolved from being a foreign power to an accepted national ducal line to which fealty was due if the socio-economic welfare of the Netherlands was to be preserved. The spread of the concept of a national dynasty and the acceptance of the Burgundians was above all a question of time, although the liberal attitude of the first dukes towards their new subjects made them more readily acceptable. In general, therefore, the first fifty years of Burgundian rule in Flanders passed peacefully, with no insurmountable differences occurring between sovereign and subjects.

There were nevertheless definite echoes of discontent under Philip the Bold and John the Fearless. Olivier van Dixmuide, in about 1443, adopted an anti-ducal, pro-urban stance. But Adriaan de But, whose source was Olivier van Dixmuide, has nothing at all negative to say about the first Burgundian dukes in his later writing in about 1466. Under Philip the Good there are countless chronicles portraying him in a favourable light. The *Excellente Cronike van Vlaanderen* calls him the father of the fatherland. Chastellain referred to the Flemings in 1436 as the 'subjets naturels' and states that : "leur seigneur.....ny ne vouloient cognoistre autre". The pro-dynastic sentiment of the Artesians also manifests itself in the work of Jacques du Clercq, who wrote between 1467 and 1475. Joos van Billau (†1489), a textile worker from Ghent, was equally loyal to the dukes, which is somewhat surprising for a craftsman. Moreover, descendants of the earlier ruling lineage were increasingly regarded as closer than any foreign newcomers. As the son of a Flemish countess, John the Fearless was looked upon as a 'natuerlijcke prince', as was Philip the Fair, who was played off against his father

172. Battle scene : the Battle of Westrozebeke in 1382, from the Chronical of Froissart, early fifteenth century. It was only by putting in the French royal army that Duke Philip the Bold could overcome the Flemish militia that had revolted against Count Louis of Male, Philip's father-in-law.

(Besançon, Bibliothèque Municipale, ms 865, fo 135 V°).

Maximilian, a foreigner. The same course of events followed Philip's death in 1506 : his sister Margaret of Austria was more acceptable as governess than Maximilian. Charles V was to be the last 'natuerlijcke prince' of the Netherlands, not only because of his descent but also because, like his predecessors, he was born and bred in the Netherlands.

Loyalty towards the dynasty was vigorously buttressed in crisis situations when the newly developed Burgundian unity came under threat from foreign powers such as France, England or the German Empire. The Order of the Golden Fleece was the spectacular symbol of a fully-fledged Burgundian political entity. The extent of the support offered to various members of the dynasty could nevertheless vary. Maximilian of Austria was readily accepted in 1477 during Burgundy's resistance to France. Shortly afterwards however, conflicts arose between the Austrian and his subjects, in whose eyes he would always remain an outsider. Though he had hastened to aid their own weak Duchess Mary of Burgundy, his orientation towards Europe did not win him much support as a national ruler. He was not sufficiently familiar with the customs of the Netherlands area, and had been brought up under an archaic autocratic régime. In addition he caused much resentment by surrounding himself with German councillors. Mary, on the other hand, was the perfect sovereign. She was a native, and was known as "onze natuerlicke vrouwe" a title which only emphasised the contrast between her and her husband.

Maximilian's regency, which began in 1482 after Mary's death, was subject to conditions laid down by the States : they wanted to know the aims of his foreign policy. The larger Flemish towns were so disturbed by his unremitting autocratic behaviour that they refused to recognise him as regent ; this they were legally entitled to do. Maximilian, however, preferred to enforce his laws at the point of a sword, a practice which cost him ten years of civil war. In 1488 Maximilian was even imprisoned by his own subjects for a period of three months ; the ultimate humiliation for a king of the Holy Roman Empire. Meanwhile the 'natuerlycke prince' Philip the Fair was to all intents and purposes held in captivity by the Flemings, while they allowed the six-year-old pretender to carry out quasi-legal acts of government in his own regency council, established by Maximilian himself in 1483. So the government of the Netherlands was no easy matter for the future emperor Maximilian. Maximilian's views on national and international policies differed considerably from those of his subjects. Maximilian was chiefly concerned with the interests of the Hapsburg dynasty, which he understandably promoted on the chessboard of Europe. The States General, on the other hand, and also the nobles and the towns of the Netherlands, were loyal to the idea of a Burgundian entity in the sense of the group of provinces 'on this side' which had been united under the Burgundian sceptre of Philip the Good and Charles the Bold.

Philip the Fair, on the other hand, was immediately popular in the Netherlands. Olivier de la Marche christened him croit-conseil because he chose to appoint 'native' counsellors and also appeared to follow their advice. Philip's diplomacy was more successful than Maximilian's tough methods in strengthening the central authority. Philip's policies, unlike those of his father, were based on national interests rather than on expansionist aims. For many years Maximilian had devoted his energies to regaining those territories which the Burgundians had lost : the Duchy of Burgundy, Artois and Guelders. When in 1498 Maximilian again had to crush

173. Portrait of Duke Philip the Bold (1342-1404) who acquired Flanders and Artois through his marriage in 1363 to Margaret, the only heiress of Louis of Male. This portrait clearly reveals his proverbial ostentatiousness.

(Dijon, Musée des Beaux-Arts. Panel 42 × 28 cm. Copy by a Burgundian master of a lost, late fourteenth century original from the Carthusian monastery at Champmol near Dijon).

200

Guelders' autonomy, Philip and the States did not support him. Still worse : Philip granted the king of France access through his territory so that the latter could lend military support to the duke of Guelders. Through his marriage, however, Philip the Fair was drawn into the larger policies of the international alliances at the expense of his nationalist leanings. In 1500 he unexpectedly became sole heir of the kingdoms of Aragon and Castille through his wife. Thus a personal union between the Hapsburg Netherlands and wealthy Spain came into prospect.

The dilemma which had confronted the States of Brabant a century earlier now reasserted itself much more seriously : should the States tolerate being absorbed into a larger international unity, thereby risking the loss of autonomy, or insist on being governed by a 'natuerlycke prince' ? All the dukes who had been heralded as 'national' – Philip the Good, Philip the Fair and Charles V – had become imperialists under the pressure of circumstance. Their home-lands, Burgundy, Flanders and the Netherlands, became a smaller part of their total territories, though still remaining important. Although Charles V declared before the States General at Brussels in 1520 : "que son cœur avoit toujours été par deçà", the Netherlands were for him as emperor of Germany, king of Spain and its overseas territories and king of Italy, although still a healthy and strategically interesting area, nevertheless a territory whose future was subject to the interests of his whole empire. Charles' imperial coronation at Bologna on 24th February 1530, his thirtieth birthday, can be seen as the end of the development of a 'Burgundian' state in the

174. When Charles, the later Emperor, made his Royal Entry into Bruges as Count of Flanders, he was fifteen years old (18th April 1515).

(Vienna, Österreichische Nationalbibliothek Cod. 2561, fo 7 V°).

175. Portrait of Margaret of Bavaria, wife of John the Fearless.

(Lille, Musée des Beaux-Arts. Flemish master, copy of a lost original).

Netherlands. Although Guelders was added to the territory in 1543 and in 1549 the right of succession was uniformly established in all the provinces of the Netherlands in order to maintain their unity, nevertheless the Netherlands could no longer be considered a state since the power had moved to Spain.

TERRITORIAL UNIFICATION   The establishment of a modest Burgundian territory in the Netherlands actually began in 1369 with the marriage of Philip the Bold (duke of Burgundy since 1363) and Margaret, daughter of the count of Flanders ; a marriage which ensured his succession in Flanders, Rethel and Walloon Flanders. This succession was realised in 1384, on the death of his father-in-law, with the addition of the county of Artois and Franche-Comté, which Louis de Male had inherited from his mother in 1382 along with the county of Nevers and the barony of Donzy which had belonged to both Louis and his mother. During the reign of Philip the Bold interest was expressed in the territory to the east. In 1387 Joan of Brabant handed Limburg and Overmaas, her sovereign territories, over to Philip, who had supported her in the clash between Brabant and Guelders.

The next phase of territorial expansion involved Brabant itself, and did not go unopposed by the Brabanters. Brabant had always been keen to maintain its autonomy, a desire which was formally recognised in its constitutional texts known as the Blijde Inkomsten (Royal Entries), to which each new ruler had to swear. The Blijde Inkomsten specified to what extent the sovereign's power was limited by the representation of the people. Whether or not the sovereign's subjects remained loyal, therefore depended upon whether the sovereign kept to the terms of the Blijde Inkomsten. All the officials were to be Brabanters. War could only be declared if the towns and country agreed to this. In 1404-1406, Philip the Bold's son Anthony became duke of Brabant, being succeeded by his brothers John IV and Philip of St Pol ; but the autonomy of Brabant remained as yet unthreatened. It did not appear at this stage that this was in any way a step towards the absorption of Brabant into the Burgundian territories – on the contrary : the States of Brabant had themselves chosen Anthony in preference to his elder brother John the Fearless since they believed that John would seldom be in residence in the Netherlands, and would give priority to the interests of Burgundy and France.

A totally different plan was hatched in the mind of Albert of Bavaria, a contemporary of Philip the Bold's who governed Hainault, Holland and Zeeland. He attempted to bring about a block formation whereby Brabant and Limburg would be united with the two Burgundies against the Flanders-Artois block. This arrangement was specified in the double marriage contract between the heirs of Philip the Bold and Albert of Bavaria and daughters from the other ruling dynasty. Opposition from the States of Brabant achieved a different arrangement but by about 1400 two things were certain : the various dynasties in the Netherlands were becoming more closely connected, and at the same time Burgundian influence was spreading.

The marriages in the next generation between Anthony, Duke of Brabant and the heiress of Luxembourg and Cluny and between Anthony's son John IV and the heiress of Hainault, Holland and Zeeland point to a well co-ordinated attempt to extend the Burgundian territories. No one could have foreseen that the extinction of the ruling dynasties governing all the other territories of the Netherlands (apart from Flanders and Guelders) would clear

203

the way for diplomatic and military intervention by the dukes of Burgundy.

In 1430 Brabant landed so unexpectedly in the hands of Philip the Good that it was thought that Philip of St Pol, the former duke, had been murdered. The institutions which had come into being during the period of Brabantine independence (1404-1430) continued to function after 1430. They were the Council of Brabant (for legal administration), the Chancery (for legislation) and the Accounting Office of Brussels (for finance). The format of these Brabant institutions revealed a definitive Burgundian influence, since Anthony imitated the structure of the Burgundian state – a tendency which was to make the later integration into the Burgundian régime considerably easier. Brabant nevertheless continued to resist a Burgundian take-over. From the beginning the States of Brabant decreed that Brabant would remain independent of Burgundian foreign policy and was not obliged to participate in any of the dukes' military expeditions. This was a short-lived illusion; the wars of Charles the Bold and the war between Maximilian and the King of France, Louis XI, in which Brabant participated, were clearly more in line with Burgundian ambitions than with Brabant's autonomous policy.

Philip the Good's interest in Holland and Zeeland was undoubtedly due to the wealth and prestige of these urbanised regions and their economic expansion during the fifteenth century. The imposition of Burgundian principles on these provinces was nevertheless a delicate process, both before and after the definitive personal union in 1433. These northern provinces had different forms of institutions and had developed their own traditions. In the established conflicts between the political factions of the Hoeken and the Kabeljauwen, Philip lent his support to the latter, thereby alienating the rural Hoeken as well as the less wealthy urban population and those not part of the town-guilds' organisation. Burgundian intervention in fiscal policy also constituted a break with the traditions of Holland and was thus a cause for resistance, Philip's aim being to establish a fiscal policy based on the real economic strength of the towns and villages. The division of the count's own council into a Court of Holland for jurisdiction and a Chamber for Finance, was also in the Burgundian tradition. The establishment of the States of Holland, as a representative organ separate from the count's council, was also evidence of Burgundian influence.

When it came to Guelders and Zutphen, Burgundian attempts at annexation transpired to be highly precarious. In 1471 Charles the Bold imprisoned Duke Adolf of Egmond, whom he forced to abdicate in favour of his son Arnold who was under Charles' tutelage. When Arnold died in 1473, Charles the Bold could only break the resistance of the towns and nobles by capturing them. Burgundian rule finally collapsed in 1477, and the power struggle that ensued lasted fifteen years and was finally won by Charles of Egmond, son of Adolf. The Burgundians made repeated attempts to regain the territory, but were unsuccessful. Charles of Egmond took several opportunities to extend his territory to the north, albeit only temporarily and with varying degrees of success. From 1515 he had control of Groningen and the Ommelanden, and from 1522 of Drente. Charles V had the greatest difficulty in regaining these territories after 1523. It was not until 1543 that he could claim the undisputed titles of duke of Guelders, count of Zutphen and lord of Overijssel, Drente, Groningen and the Ommelanden. Meanwhile (1528) Charles V had also gained secular control of the Oversticht area of the see of Utrecht, in response to the threat from Guelders.

176. Portrait of John the Fearless (1371-1419). His contemporaries describe him as a small, dark-haired man with blue eyes, very ambitious and heroic, but above all sharp.

(Antwerp, Royal Museum of Fine Arts. Flemish master, copy of a lost original reputedly from the first half of the fifteenth century and originating from the school of Rogier van der Weyden).

It was certainly not unusual for Guelders to seek the support of successive French kings, and this together with a powerful aristocracy and its own distinctive orientation explains the continued resistance to Burgundian penetration of Guelders, a stubbornly independent province.

It is surprising that so little of the Burgundian territory was gained directly at the expense of the kingdom of France. In addition to Charles the Bold's short-term capture of Lorraine, it was principally the regions along the banks of the Somme, Ponthieu and Picardy which were gained. Philip the Good acquired these lands peacefully according to the terms of the Treaty of Arras in 1435 and they were in effect redeemable security against his new alliance with the king of France. The Somme can be seen as the natural border, an idea which Margaret of Austria still favoured. In fact the surrendered territory extended far south of the river to include the towns of Roye and Montdidier. Small wonder then that this possession was so valuable to both parties.

Shortly after his coronation in 1463, King Louis XI paid 400,000 crowns for the repossession of the Somme region, the sum stipulated in the treaty of 1435. Charles the Bold regained the territory two years later when, as newly-appointed Lieutenant-General, he launched the war known as the 'Guerre du Bien Public' together with a number of leading crown vassals, and succeeded in putting the French in jeopardy. In 1475 Louis took advantage of Charles' military setbacks at the small Westphalian town of Neuss by taking Montdidier, Roye and Corbie and so causing unrest in Artois and Hainault. After Charles' death in 1477 the French armies took the whole area without any difficulty.

Burgundian territory was affected both in the north and the east by the French invasions of 1477. During the first two months of that year the entire Somme area, large parts of Artois and the county of Boulogne fell into the hands of the king. The towns of Aire and Le Quesnoy and the episcopal towns of Arras, Thérouanne and Cambrai were also captured. By the Peace of Arras in 1482, Maximilian was forced reluctantly to cede the whole of Artois, as well as a number of estates bordering Burgundy, as the dowry of his three-year-old daughter who was to be married off to the Dauphin. After almost fifteen years of war, Artois and Franche-Comté were recaptured by Philip the Fair in 1593 and his sister, who had been brought up for ten years at the French court, was sent back.

The home-lands – the duchy and Franche-Comté – had been completely overrun. June 1477 saw the repression at Dijon of a popular revolt against French occupation and the traitors to the Burgundian cause. The recapture of Burgundy was to remain the preoccupation of Maximilian and Charles V for decades to come. Charles V, in his Testament of Bruges which dates from 1523, mentioned Burgundy as one of his military objectives. He wished to be buried in Dijon, but added Bruges as an immediate alternative, where he could be buried next to his grandmother (Mary of Burgundy). Even at this stage, therefore, Charles would not have been totally convinced that the recapture of Burgundy was possible. Some six years later Charles definitively renounced his claim to Burgundy in the Peace of Cambrai which was drawn up at the instigation of Margaret of Austria in 1529. The Burgundian lands without Burgundy : the Netherlands had so clearly become the focal point of Burgundian interest that no one was really surprised by this.

What does all this prove ? That in many cases the integration of

177. Portrait of Mary of Burgundy's daughter, Margaret of Austria, at three years of age. This portrait was to mark the occasion of her marriage to the Dauphin according to the Peace of Arras in December 1482.

(Versailles, Museum. Anonymous Flemish master, 1483).

regions in the Netherlands into the Burgundian state was not always an easy process. It also proves that there was real resistance against absorption into the Burgundian state, and that there was a real sense of identity in many areas which for centuries had had their own ruling dynasties and institutions. New traditions and institutions were not welcome, particularly when introduced by sovereigns who would not reside permanently within the sub-regions of their states. Even under Philip the Bold and John the Fearless, the Flemings found it frustrating that their duke spent more time in Paris or Dijon, and was consequently not familiar with their needs and was not available to hear their complaints or requests. They submitted a petition to Philip himself, asking either that he should remain in Flanders or delegate his spouse or son : "auquel vos villes et subges de Flandres puissent avoir recour et ait pooir de faire adrechement de pluseurs grans fins et charges que de jour en jour nous sourviennent et aucune fois requirent hastieve expedicion". Such was the request in the file of complaints put to John the Fearless in 1405, who subsequently delegated his son to be Stadtholder of Flanders from his coming of age in 1411. This practice was taken up in the long term by the appointment of a governor to each of the territories.

THE AMBITIONS FOR A COHERENT TERRITORIAL ENTITY For years the leading authorities have spoken of a Burgundian State as denoting those regions which were united under a single authority by the dukes of Burgundy from 1369, and in particular after 1384. But it is still an open question whether these rulers consciously attempted to form a new state which was separate from and independent of the kingdom of France and the German Empire. Some centuries ago Pontus Heuterus referred to Philip the Good as the 'imperii Belgici conditor', thereby implying that the united Burgundian provinces formed an entity known as the Netherlands, which would divide into the Northern and Southern Netherlands during the sixteenth century. Henri Pirenne subscribed to this thesis, as is widely known, and saw in the Burgundian state the forerunner of the later Belgium.

In the opinion of Johan Huizinga, Philip the Good was far from being the cunning, calculating sovereign who slowly and deliberately constructed the Burgundian state. According to Huizinga, Philip simply benefitted from fortunate circumstances and coincidence and left the execution of his policies to his officials – particularly to the chancellor. Paul Bonenfant modified this view, however, by claiming that there were indications during Philip the Good's reign of the formation of an independent state next to France and Germany. Territorial expansion under the duke was one such clear indication. But Bonenfant placed this in a truer perspective by stressing how loyal Philip the Bold (as the son of the king), and John the Fearless were to the interests of the French crown. More significantly he showed how Philip the Good remained loyal to his role as leader of the Burgundians with a view to playing a dominant role in France, even after his father was murdered at Montereau (1419) by the rival faction of Armagnacs. This ambition was achieved when Philip claimed the office of Lieutenant-General of France. By showing all the evidence of Philip's ambitions towards the French court, Bonenfant is saying that Philip would not have been able to concentrate on the formation of his own state, separate from the French crown.

Was this so ? Without doubt, political opportunism *would* have enabled Philip to derive material benefit from a strong position in

France whilst at the same time forming his own separate state. The first of four works on the Burgundian dukes by Richard Vaughan, was given the sub-title *The Formation of the Burgundian State*. Vaughan is of the opinion that not just Philip the Good but also Philip the Bold before him had ambitions towards a state of his own. His view is that we have evidence of this in his various attempts to appear on the international stage as a recognisable European power in, for instance, the crusade against Islam in 1396, and in the appointment of Burgundian ambassadors more or less all over Europe. His desire for recognition is particularly evident in a document of 1398, in which Philip mentions his state as a European power clearly distinct from the French state. Philip the Bold also provided an integrated structural framework in the form of central institutions that he created : Chambers for Finance and Chambers for Jurisdiction for the northern and southern parts of the state were established at Lille and Dijon respectively. The ducal households, the Grand Council, the *Chambre aux Deniers* and the Receiver General of all finances presided over all the regions and are proof of the fact that central institutions linked all Burgundian territories. The appointment of a single chancellor was also proof of this political unification.

Was the Burgundian state merely the result of a series of chance circumstances ? It is difficult to establish exactly when coincidence was replaced by conscious calculation. It is possible that circumstances produced a clearly formulated plan, but at what point ? Had this already happened when the son of the French king inherited the county of Flanders in 1384 after the duchy of Burgundy, or when Philip the Bold seized the opportunity of giving members of his family

178. A delegation from Ghent tried in vain to reach an agreement with Count Louis of Male during the Flemish revolt, lead by Filips van Artevelde (1379-85).

(Paris, Bibliothèque Nationale. Ms fr. 2644, f° 81 V°, *Chroniques de Froissart* (15 th century).

179. Portrait, reputedly of Robert van Massemen, Flemish nobleman and army captain under Dukes John the Fearless and Philip the Good; knighted by the latter after the Battle of Melun, and died in battle.

(Lugano-Castagnola, Thyssen-Bornemisza collection. Supposedly painted no later than 1430 by the Master of Flémalle).

the duchy of Brabant? Who can say? Philip the Good's systematic intervention in the government of the ageing and childless Duchess Joan was undoubtedly calculated. The various schemes of succession drawn up in the form of marriage contracts and wills around 1400 are equally indicative of conscious planning. Their aims were in fact more limited than the results which they achieved in 1443 would suggest. Philip the Bold's intervention in Hainault, Holland and Zeeland was part of a much more resolute strategy: he intervened at the papal court to revoke the dissolution of the marriage between Jacqueline of Bavaria and John IV of Brabant; then he proceeded to capture, *manu militari*, several places in Hainault and Holland from which position he persuaded Jacqueline gradually to cede her rights of succession. The dukes used the institution of marriage as a means of bringing more territory under Burgundian rule. The purchase of the county of Namur in 1421 and the acquisition of Luxembourg between 1441 and 1443 were even less of a coincidence, and conveniently brought the prince-bishoprics of Liège and Utrecht under Burgundian control, albeit in the guise of a bishop from their own Burgundian family itself.

It should not be forgotten that this territorial expansion was realised outside the sphere of influence of the French king, and indeed mainly within the empire, and this in itself points to the conscious formation of a separate state. This extension of the original Burgundian territories was also possible because of weaknesses inherited in both the French state and the German Empire. The strength of the Burgundian state as a third power in continental Europe was therefore not a matter of coincidence or chance, but the result of skilful international politics which turned the disputes between the other great powers to its own advantage.

Both Philip the Bold and John the Fearless extended their territories at the expense of France and Germany, and at the same time profited from their position at the French court by allowing funds from the French crown to flow into their own coffers. The dukes were obliged to maintain peaceful relations with England from about 1400 onwards since many of their Flemish subjects, and later many of those in Brabant and Holland as well, had built up sound trading links with England, although such a policy was apparently in conflict with their position at the French court.

The situation can be more easily understood when one bears in mind that the dukes attempted to give equal attention to all these interests to ensure the survival of their own régime.

The Burgundian rulers were French princes (just like those of Savoy and Brittany for example), they were of French descent with duties within the kingdom, but they also sought to become independent of the French state – very often to its own detriment. It would serve no purpose to establish whether Philip the Bold and John the Fearless were French, Burgundian or Flemish rulers; they were either all three or none at all. Their role in the conflicts between the Armagnacs and the Burgundians points to French loyalties, but this is misleading: the dukes were essentially sovereigns of their own territories and strove to serve these territories – their loyalties lay there and there alone. Their relations with the kingdom of France were purely tactical and strategic.

The development of Burgundian territorial policy reached its zenith around 1430, when Brabant and Limburg became part of the Burgundian-Flemish complex after the death of Duke Anthony's second son. Meanwhile Namur had also become part of this complex. After the Treaty of Delft in 1428, Philip the Good was confident of his tutelage over and succession in Hainault and Holland-Zeeland. This shed a new light upon the whole situation and from this point onwards the dukes of Burgundy had no choice but to govern in a manner befitting the sovereign of an important power-bloc.

A similar attitude to the German Empire arose in connection with plans to transform the Burgundian territories into a kingdom. Philip the Good refused to have anything to do with this if it were to involve any kind of feudal subordination to the German Empire; and in any case Philip did not need to be crowned king in order to prove that, where political power was concerned, he stood on a par with the rulers of France, England and Germany. Philip's equality was acknowledged on several occasions by the popes. The great dukes of the West were empire builders no less than all the other kings and emperors.

AN ITINERANT COURT OR A CAPITAL? The Burgundians established central institutions in order to unify their state, and this was largely successful. Did they also think it necessary to establish a capital – a central seat of government – in their state? Philip the Bold and John the Fearless definitely did not find this necessary. At this time the duke and his chancellor travelled a great deal, spending several months in Paris and in other parts of their state. Lille was the financial, legal and political centre, but only for Flanders, Artois, Antwerp and Mechelen. Dijon was the centre for the two Burgundies and their dependencies; Brabant and Holland had their own institutions. The duke and his council continued to travel around their territory; it was not until the reign of Philip the Good that one town, Brussels, was advocated as the favoured town of residence after the castle at Coudenberg had been enlarged for the duke in 1451. Philip continued, however, to divide his time fairly equally between Lille, Arras, Bruges, Brussels and Dijon, so that even during Philip's reign there was to be no fixed centre of administration; this was not established until the reign of Charles the Bold who set up new central institutions (Parliament and Chambers for Finance) at Mechelen. Charles chose Mechelen not only because of its central location but also because it was a small independent seigniory, and rivalry between the main provinces could thus be avoided. The duke himself travelled constantly within his territory since he believed that his power would only be effective if he maintained his presence; and anyway he slept more often in tents than in palaces. The demands made by the dukes and their huge entourage wherever they were in residence, were known to be considerable, particularly their need for wood and game. The problem was alleviated if the ducal domain contained woodlands in the vicinity of the town (as was the case in Brussels) since these woodlands provided prized hunting-grounds; hunting being either a form of relaxation or a form of training for the young nobles.

Philip the Fair showed a definite preference for Mechelen as a residence for his court, and his sister Margaret of Austria even more so during her stadtholdership. Here Margaret had her palace; and Mechelen was also the seat of the high court, the Grand Council of Mechelen. After Margaret's death, Brussels became the undisputed capital and, from 1531, the seat of the Court and the Collateral Councils, then the highest organs of government. This then, heralded a new era.

180. Allegory of the four marriages of Jacoba of Bavaria, Duchess of Hainault, Holland and Zeeland. Jacoba is standing to the left with her entourage. Her father, Count Willem VI, stands to the right in the company of her successive spouses. This illustration depicts, with a fine subtle humour, the angling for profitable deals in Philip the Good's expansionist policies.

(Paris, Louvre Museum. School of the Van Eyck brothers, early fifteenth century. Drawing and aquarel on paper).

THE DREAM OF BEING KING The crowning of the Duke of Burgundy as king was first advocated in 1447. This was, remarkably, not an initiative on the part of the duke himself, but came from the German King Frederick III, and was passed on by his chancellor, Gaspard Schlick. The suggestion was in fact made with a view to securing two contracts of marriage which would be particularly advantageous to the House of Austria : the first between Albert (brother of Frederick III) and a second cousin of Philip the Good, and the second between Elizabeth of Austria (sister of King Ladislaz of Bohemia and Hungary) and the duke's only son and heir, Charles, the count of Charolais. The German chancellor had in mind that either Friesland or the illustrious duchy of Brabant would acquire the status of a kingdom ; a title which Friesland had never borne in former times. Philip, however, remained fastidious, demanding that all his territories falling within the German Empire (Hainault, Holland-Zeeland, etc.) should belong to this prospective kingdom. He would not have his proposed kingship entailed with marriage contracts and demanded that German territories such as Cleves, Jülich and Berg be included in his kingdom. Philip was moreover convinced that the Roman Catholic king was minded to lay claim to Friesland. The price proved too high for both parties and the plans were dropped in May 1448.

A similar situation arose in 1463. Philip was once again offered a crown by Emperor Frederick III in exchange for the hand of Mary (granddaughter of Philip and heiress of Burgundy) for Frederick's son Maximilian ; Frederick's intentions being to unite the prestige of Valois and the military and financial power of the Haps-

181. Detail from the fourth in the series of
Caesar tapestries. This tapestry extols the
chivalrous virtues and government attributed to Caesar, with whom Charles the Bold
gladly compared himself. The set of tapestries was reputedly intended for a throne-
room and presented to Duke Charles.

(Berne, Historisches Museum, inv. nr 6-13;
ht. 432, lg. 750 cm. Tournai workshop;
executed in wool and silk).

burgs. Pope Pius supported Frederick in this since he wanted to persuade the Duke to participate in the Crusades. Philip was also offered an imperial vicariate over the territories on the left bank of the Rhine. This plan proved fruitless ; Philip's vanity gave way to common sense.

The situation with Charles the Bold was totally different. He was also offered the crown by Emperor Frederick III and Pope Paul II in 1467 in exchange for military support against the heretic king of Bohemia. In 1469 Duke Sigismund of Austria revived the plan on the basis of a marriage between Maximilian and Mary of Burgundy. This plan was unsuccessful because the emperor was thinking in terms of promoting one of Charles' territories to a kingdom, while Charles himself had set his sights on the title of King of the Holy Roman Empire. During new negotiations at Trier in 1473, it appeared that Charles was prepared to renounce his claim to the title of Catholic King as long as Frederick III was alive and, having borne the title for a period of time would abdicate in favour of Maximilian, who would meanwhile have married Mary. It is possible that opposition from the German Electors and the schemes of the French King Louis XI frustrated not only these plans, but even the more modest plans to raise the Duke's principalities to a kingdom owing fealty to the German Empire.

Thereafter the dream of royal dignity lay dormant until some time later. In 1508 there was a concrete proposal to unite Austria and Franche-Comté into one kingdom ; a proposal which was not taken very seriously. As late as 1544 Charles V expressed a desire to establish a separate kingdom of the Netherlands in the Peace of Crespy. How real was the dream of royal dignity ? It is now clear that it was not engendered by Philip the Good, who saw it more as an opportunity for territorial expansion than as a means of bestowing a title of honour on his unified state. Charles the Bold, on the other hand, cherished ambitions to become a full king and even Holy Roman Emperor, as his physician revealed in a treatise called *De custodia principum,* which was probably intended to promote precisely this idea of royal dignity. It is known that he acknowledged Maximilian as his prospective son-in-law in an agreement with Frederick III at Trier, and assumed that a higher royal title would thus be bestowed upon the Netherlands.

182. Meeting between Emperor Frederick III and Duke Charles the Bold during a banquet at Trier in 1473. The Duke was hoping to be offered the King's crown. However, the Emperor secretly left the town early, leaving the Duke bewildered. One permanent result was the engagement of their heirs, Maximilian and Maria, whereby the Burgundian dynasty was absorbed into the Hapsburg dynasty.

(Zürich, Zentralbibliothek, ms A5 fo 121. Chronicle of the Burgundian War by Diebold Schilling (1480).

Propaganda and the legitimation of power

Power tends to be centred on a single person : the man in power presides over the office which he occupies. The ruler was the linch-pin in the medieval principalities. His power was based upon feudal rights, which were expressed most clearly in the inauguration ceremonies. On these occasions sovereign and subjects took mutual vows of loyalty which resulted in constitutional instruments known as the 'Blijde Inkomsten', or Royal Entries. There were several aspects to this ritual :

– subjects had the right to accept or reject their sovereign ; there could be several candidates for each succession, according to the rules of succession which varied greatly from region to region ; this lent real weight to the sentiments of the subjects ;

– the chosen sovereign was obliged to keep to a certain code of behaviour. If he failed to do so, his subjects were no longer obliged to co-operate. This right of resistance clearly has feudal origins ;

– the relationship between the sovereign and his subjects was personal and mutual, as it was in feudal contracts. By analogy with the feudal nobility, town communities were also bound by oath to the person of their sovereign.

Decision-making was consequently a personal matter. The subjects sought to please the duke by, for example, levying a tax and the duke in turn governed 'a nostre gré et plaisir'.

Every political occurrence involved the duke, who personally intervened in virtually all matters which concerned him, whether large or small. The duke was thus the true centre of the Burgundian régime. This personification of political power meant that subjects could more easily identify with the establishment that he embodied. They were more ready to follow a recognisable individual who possessed likeable personal qualities than to support an impersonal, alienated state system. It was therefore important for the dukes of Burgundy to be accepted by the ruling classes and, if possible, also by broad sections of the populace. They therefore surrounded their persons with extensive propaganda which was directed at the masses as well as at the élite.

183. Cornet pennon and a fragment bearing part of the motto of Duke Charles the Bold: *Je l'ay emprins*. It was plundered after the Battle of Grandson (1476).

(Berne, Historisches Museum).

INFLUENCING THE ÉLITE   The most direct way in which the duke could win the support of the more important among his subjects was to address himself personally to them, or send his highest representative.   The limited capacity of the human voice meant that any well-argued debates were restricted to halls with audiences of several dozen people – at most a couple of hundred. Large propaganda meetings were organised with a great feeling for diplomacy.   The meeting at Oudenaarde in 1390, at which French theologians and officials tried to persuade the Flemings to support the Pope of Avignon in the Great Schism, was in line with the appeal of Philip the Bold in a letter to the sovereign-bailiff of Flanders in December 1384 : "We do not wish to force any of our subjects to obey the Pope (of Avignon)".   This meeting was also in line with the placatory propaganda mission undertaken in another part of Flanders by the bishop of Thérouanne and Yolande van Bar in 1384.   John the Fearless undertook various diplomatic missions to the Flemish towns on his father's behalf in order to persuade them to provide subsidies.   In 1394 John even addressed the citizens of Ypres (who seemed somewhat unwilling to contribute to the crusade) in Flemish : "...and I even spoke to them in Flemish, as far as I was able... of the love and dedication which you [Philip the Bold] have shown them in so many different ways ; of the fact that you have

215

visited them on two or three occasions – more than any other town in your land of Flanders; of the special trust which you have in them...". Personal and even sentimental reasoning was not shunned. The direct and warm-hearted nature of the relationship between the duke and his subjects of Ypres was emphasised to the full, to ensure that they would not be mean in their response.

Philip the Good struck the same note in 1447 when he appeared in person in the *Collacie* Room of the town hall at Ghent, to lend weight to his request for the imposition of a salt tax in the presence of representatives of the wealthy burghers and the guilds. The father of Philippe de Commynes, the knight Colaert van der Clyte who was a sovereign-bailiff, read out a lengthy speech in the name of the duke, which opened as follows : "My good men and trusted friends, you know that I have lived and been brought up here in this good city of mine since my youth, for which reason I hold this city and you all in greater favour, affection and amity than any which I have visited often, for never was anything asked or petitioned of me by this my city, without my always complying gladly and affectionately and with a good heart. For this reason I have placed a singular and special trust in this my aforesaid city and in you people, that you will support me in this my necessity...".

This was followed by a lengthy review of all the wars which Philip had had to wage, which had increasingly brought him into financial straits. Existing subsidies were not sufficient, particularly since "I see and realise that my good cities, my municipalities and my country – especially my poor people in the countryside – are so drained and exhausted that they cannot go on, since they cannot properly pay the sums they still owe for the settlements and subventions which are in force in Flanders".

The proposed tax on salt would, according to the Duke, bring solace since those hardest affected by it would be foreign buyers and large-scale consumers. The duke was *personally* offended when the citizens of Ghent, and later the other three Members of Flanders, refused to listen to his friendly persuasions and arguments ; he was particularly offended by the deans of the guilds whose praises he had previously sung to secure their loyal support. All the professions of warmth and love cooled instantly and Philip so provoked the city that it rose in revolt, which he promptly punished as a lesson to others. The tendentious interpretation of his policies and of his grounds for imposing his new tax were thus little more than fancy words. Such propaganda had a very personal flavour which varied according to the ruler's needs of the time.

Charles the Bold also addressed representatives of his subjects on many occasions, but not always in such flattering terms as his ancestors. *The Excellente Cronike van Vlaanderen* reported that for two hours the Duke addressed representatives of Ghent, who had come to do penance for the rising of 1467, during which he made the characteristic remark "I love you but I will not spare you". By contrast, the speech given by Chancellor Hugonet in 1473 during a meeting of the States-General showed all the characteristics of a propagandist oration. He drew his inspiration from Roman Law which, in its Justinian form, supported an autocracy based on Christian beliefs. The argument was further embellished with quotations from the works of Latin authors and Thomas Aquinas, and also from biblical texts. He defended the monarchy by saying that it provided united leadership, unlike free societies or government by the aristocracy. His argument was supported by Aristotle's image of society as a body, with the ruler as head determining the functions of the parts ; there was thus a perfect community of interests between head and members.

The chancellor and the duke repeatedly defended themselves by referring to France : there the subjects knew no freedom and reeled under the *gabelle*, the *taille* and all manner of taxes and incessant demands for military service. Although Charles' tone was generally imperious, it was nevertheless not lacking in persuasive and personal appeal. It was in a similar vein that he addressed members of the States of Flanders in 1475 : "In defending the land of Flanders, of which he has always been particularly fond, he has spared neither his body, his weapons nor his wealth which he has spent primarily on this cause ; nor has he spared his armies and subjects. What he has done, and continues to do, in defense of this land, has been of more benefit to his Flemish subjects and their wives, children and property than to himself, for whom they have been a constant concern and worry. When they are sleeping, he is awake ; when they are sitting in the warm, he is in the cold ; when they are in their residences, he is outside in the rain and wind, and when he is suffering hardship they are eating and drinking in the comfort of their homes."

Although the already monomaniacal duke struck a completely different note from that of his predecessors, he placed just as much emphasis on the mutual personal relationship between himself and his subjects. He also referred to the vows during his 'Blijde Intrede' as "...your privileges which you say I have sworn to uphold ; this is true, but at the same time you have sworn to serve me and to be loyal and obedient servants" (1704)... ..."He [Charles] remembered the beautiful words which his subjects had spoken to him at his coronation, which they repeat whenever he enters one of his good towns of Flanders ; words with which they pledge their loyalty and obedience as good subjects..." (1475).

Charles the Bold's powerful personality elicited concessions from the deputies of the towns which his officials were often unable to achieve. The strong emotion, tinged with cursing and threats apparently caused feelings of resentment which came to a head in 1477. The customary political addresses to the various bodies representing the people nevertheless continued. These addresses always contained a justification of past policies and a call for further

184. Miniature depicting civil war in Ghent. The largest city of the Netherlands has a long history of social unrest.

(Wells-next-the-sea, Norfolk, Holkham ms 659 F).

support. The finer personal feelings towards the sovereign remained a striking feature of these samples of political propaganda.

Leading sections of the population could also be influenced by letters and charters issued by the sovereign. Philip the Good occasionally found it expedient to explain his attitude towards a crisis to those institutions whose support he wanted to retain. After the humiliating retreat of his army from the siege of Calais in 1436, he sent out no less than 718 letters to nobles and officers in Artois, Picardy, Hainault, Flanders and Brabant, and a further forty, which were written in Latin, to Italian and German rulers. In these letters he attributed the failure to the unreliability of the Ghent militia, obviously concealing his own tactical errors. He reacted similarly a year later when he failed – in an equally humiliating manner – in an attempt to suppress an uprising at Bruges by using military force. While Philip himself had the narrowest of escapes, several of his best captains paid for the miscalculation with their lives. In a letter circulated among the senior clergy, the nobility and the towns, Philip related his own version of the course of events and in doing so highlighted the dirty tricks of the citizens of Bruges. Charles the Bold applied the same method to defend himself in the clash between himself on the one hand, and his father and the influential Croy family on the other. During the civil war against Maximilian all manner of pamphlets and other propagandist literature were circulated to win support for one or other party.

On a day-to-day basis, charters usually contained a speculative introduction, which could take the form of a policy outline. The dozens of instruments issued by the ducal Chancery, which found their way to a literate and probably reasonably wealthy public each year, always contained traces of propaganda. Such passages usually alluded to general welfare, justice and the support of those in need, in short, to the image of the righteous, Christian ruler.

By its very character fifteenth century literature was a medium which only reached a small élite. Nevertheless, the dukes of Burgundy invested lavishly in this means of spreading their propaganda, thereby hoping to gain the support of the ruling classes. They engaged a number of court writers such as Georges Chastellain, Jean Wauquelin, Olivier de la Marche, Jean Molinet and many other more or less talented hack-writers. Their task was to relate, in a quasi-journalistic way, what had happened in and around the Burgundian territories. The emphasis lay on ceremonial events (pseudo-events, we should call them now) which were themselves propagandist, but were given an extra dimension when immortalised in word and picture (usually in the form of miniatures). By definition, these writers were biassed historians. In their historical and mythological writings and their statements on current political affairs they established a favourable image of the Burgundian dukes as a beloved and meritorious dynasty, and they formulated a justification for the dukes' political ambitions. When plans were hatched in 1447-48 to promote parts of Burgundian territory to a kingdom, Wauquelin conveniently translated Jacques de Guise's Annals of Hainault and Edmond de Dijnter's chronicle of the Dukes of Lorraine and Brabant, while Philip meanwhile, commissioned the writing of a *Chroniques et conquestes de Charlemaine*.

These fitted perfectly into the attempts to revive a 'national' Lorraine sentiment, by way of support for kingship under the German Empire. This feeling of Lorraine solidarity could even be described as a tradition in Brabant where the dukes had always considered themselves successors of the dukes of Lorraine. Philip the Good,

185. Several days after the devastating suppression of the insurgents at Ghent at Gavere on 23rd July, more than 2,000 Ghent citizens were forced to kneel before Duke Philip the Good in their shirts. Ghents had to pay a heavy penalty, the political power of the guilds was curtailed and the jurisdiction of the aldermen of Ghent was restricted by the Council of Flanders.

(Vienna, Österreichische Nationalbibliothek, Cod. 2583, fo 349).

219

however, being a good 'French' prince had not contemplated withdrawing his lands from the French crown, upon which they were feudally dependent. Charles the Bold who was an anti-French duke, went a step further and this political twist is reflected in the propaganda. Charles planned to establish an independent *regnum Burgundie*, a Burgundian kingdom which would include French feudal fiefs. In order to justify this, Charles discarded the idea of promoting the old Lorraine and turned his attention instead to the still older political existence of the pre-Merovingian kingdom of Burgundy, which had been dismantled by the French king.

Philip the Good's crusading plans were made more amenable to the populace by David Aubert's reviving of the earlier romance *Bauduin de Flandre* in which Baldwin IX, count of Flanders and Hainault and emperor of Constantinople 1204-05 was heralded as Philip's illustrious predecessor and mentor, thus giving the romance a topical relevance.

Pure political ambition was also cloaked in literary terms. When Philip the Good showed interest in incorporating the bishopric of Utrecht into the Burgundian state, his supporter Wolfert van Borselen quickly commissioned a French translation of Johannes van Beka's fourteenth-century Latin *Chronographia*. Beka saw the destinies of Utrecht and the county of Holland as inextricably bound together, and this fully supported Philip's plans for annexation. Philip was further inspired in his quest for kingship by the idea of reviving the ancient kingdom of Frisia, ruled by Radbod between the seventh and eighth centuries, and now within Burgundian territory; this inspiration had come from the revival of the ancient Legend of Radbod. The mythology thus involved convincing the populace that the Burgundian state was in fact the continuation of a real political entity of the past.

Finally the authors of the Burgundian court also cultivated links between the Burgundian dynasty and the rulers and heroes of ancient times, by alleging all manner of similarities. With contemporary events at the back of his mind, Jean Wauquelin idealised Alexander the Great in his *Livre des conquestes et Faits d'Alexandre le Grant* as a courtly knight, warrior and conqueror, thereby implying that the great man and his achievements were the model for the Burgundian dukes' campaigns in the East. Chastellain adorned Philip the Good with the title 'the last Alexander' and 'the second Hector' since literature concerning the legend of ancient Troy was also considered suitable material. Wauquelin, Jean Germain and Olivier de la Marche all did their best to imply in their writings that Philip the Good was descended from mythological Trojans such as Francus and Hercules.

Hercules was a central theme in the decorations at the banquet of the Pheasant at Lille in 1454, where Philip formally announced his plans for the Crusade and invited those nobles present to take the vow. A lengthy official account of this ceremony was distributed, and many artists were commissioned for the staging of this splendid propagandist spectacle. Such events, graced by the Order of the Golden Fleece, also took place at Leuven and Mons, so that the reputation of the duke as a glorious Christian sovereign might reach those areas too. To give the Order a historical foundation, Philip the Good also encouraged the revival of the mythological literature about the legend of Troy, of which the Fleece was a part : Guillaume Fillastre thus wrote a *Toison d'Or* and Michault Taillevent a *Songe de la Toison d'Or*.

The adventures of Alexander the Great were also the theme of

186. Portrait of the chronicler Enguerrand de Monstrelet (1390-1453).

(Arras, Bibliothèque Municipale, ms 266. Sketch from the *Recueil d'Arras*).

187. The chronicler Jehan Froissart (ca 1337-after 1404).

(Arras, Bibliothèque Municipale, ms 266. Sketch from the *Recueil d'Arras*).

a series of tapestries commissioned by Philip the Good; literary mythology was therefore conveniently reinforced by other forms of art. The depiction of the dukes in presentation ceremonies in the miniatures which adorned the frontispieces of so many Burgundian manuscripts, or as cup-bearers in the panels of illustrious paintings, was clearly propagandist. The purpose of the various illustrations was to record the glorious moments of a reign, such as the subjection of the rebellious town of Ghent in 1453 or the installation of the Parliament of Mechelen in 1473-4. A series of tapestries depicting the Battle of Othée (where William of Bavaria and John the Fearless defeated the citizens of Liège in 1408) hung in the ducal palace during the wedding celebrations of Charles the Bold in 1468. The duchess and other members of the dynasty appeared in countless scenes performing acts of charity, and were again intended to emphasise the goodness and Christian inspiration of the ruling house.

The very nature of these instruments of propaganda meant that they were only within the reach of a select few : namely those who attended the court and those who purchased manuscripts. Throughout their lands, the dukes made concerted efforts to forge links with the ruling classes by creating political factions which were favourably disposed towards the dukes' policies. A ducal party existed in the Netherlands from the beginning of the Burgundian period and was referred to by its contemporaries as 'le parti de monseigneur'. It was already obvious during the conflict surrounding the Great Schism that the duke was aiming to please the clergy and nobility, whose support he managed to gain by his skilful management of appointments.

He also won over the nobility by various society gambits such as service at court, banquets, tournaments and acceptance into the Order of the Golden Fleece. Supporters were, however, not only encouraged within the Netherlands. John the Fearless and Philip the Good maintained a Burgundian party in France – in Paris especially – which gave the duke an enthusiastic reception in the French capital in 1461. Between 1440 and 1448, however, René of Anjou established an anti-Burgundian party and even in the heart of the duchy of Burgundy itself, at Dijon, propagandists spread "tres malvaises paroles... contre l'oneur de mgr. de Charollois" (Charles the Bold) in 1466. These agitators were not natives of Burgundy, but members of the French lower classes who were paid to create confusion in the minds of the inhabitants. The opposite was true in Besançon where the association with Burgundy was fostered from the reign of John the Fearless onwards by a number of the duke's supporters. This party saw to it that the annexation by the occupying marshal Thibaud de Neufchâtel was achieved without too much difficulty. To ensure the success of political schemes, the dukes built up an intensive spy network in the fifteenth century. Via informers, who fed their information to the bailiffs, the duke knew precisely what the Four Members of Flanders were planning at their secret meetings, thereby always gaining a tactical advantage. But the French king, however, also bribed Burgundians to keep him informed, and sent secret agents against Charles the Bold into the northern towns.

In Holland and Zeeland there was a long tradition of party conflict between the so-called Hoeken and Kabeljauwen. The two parties dressed in the appropriate liveries and armed themselves with long knives. During the hard-fought campaign between 1425 and 1428, Philip the Good placed himself at the head of the Kabeljauw faction which drew support from the towns, particularly from traders,

221

Cy commence le liure frere Jehan hayton de lordre degle monstre conste[n]
germain du roy darmenie qui parle des merueilles &c. en proiaul mes deste

E royaume de cathay est tenu pour le plus no ble roy
aume et le plus riche qui soit ou monde et est sur le ma
gre et la mer occane. Tantes istes p[ar] le mer que len nen
puet pas bien sauoir le nombre. Les gens qui habitit
en cellui royaume sont appelle cathains. et se treuuet
entre culte mains beaux hommes et femmes selonc
leur nacion mais tous ont les yeulx moult petis. et ont poute barbe. Celles
gens ont lettres qui de beaute ressemblet a lettres latines. et parlent une
langaige qui moult est diuerse des autres langues du monde. La creance de
ceste gent est moult diuerse. Car aucuns aourent au soulail. autres a la lu

entrepreneurs and craftsmen. The Hoeken were strongly supported by the landed nobility but until 1433 they could also count on support in towns such as Dordrecht and Amsterdam, particularly from the city fathers. This form of local aristocracy was typical in the northern provinces, especially in Holland and also in Guelders, and kept the power strictly within their own circle. It was therefore relatively easy for the Burgundians to win the support of the towns.

The political factions were obviously in evidence during times of conflict. The thrusting manner of Charles the Bold, who 'had jobs for the boys' everywhere, thoroughly aggravated the tensions. After his death his supporters were made to suffer for this, and in the ensuing years relations polarised to such an extent that most of the members of the municipal magistratures in Flanders were emphatically either for or against Maximilian. In this respect Philip the Good's policy of gentle yet systematic indoctrination was the more successful.

A THEATRE STATE The methods used to influence the masses may have had technical limitations, but they were certainly not to be underestimated. The ceremonies in which the dukes presented themselves in all their splendour to the people, were an essential part of this – the staging of such spectacles became better and better during the course of the fifteenth century – high points being the funeral of Philip the Good in 1467 (according to Olivier de la Marche: "Un service et un obseque, le plus beau que je veiz oncques") and the wedding of Charles the Bold to Margaret of York at Sluis, Damme and Bruges in 1468. The whole town participated at such festivities which projected as it were an ideal view of society. The young newly-weds – the solemnization of the marriage took place at Damme – arrived in a procession at Bruges, where all the streets had been decorated. All organisations of the city life took part in the procession: the magistrature, the clergy, foreign merchants displaying their nationality, the guilds, all turned out in magnificent and colourful dress. Everyone made their contribution and had their part to play. Firework displays and the famous Gold Tree tournament organised by Anthony the 'Great Bastard' of Burgundy provided attractions lasting a whole week in the city square. Meanwhile in the ducal palace, adorned with numerous historical tapestries, gigantic banquets and dances were held.

On 5th August 1435 when diplomatic negotiations between France and England were launched at St Vaast's Abbey at Arras, Philip the Good (who along with Chancellor Rolin actively participated in the conference) promptly surrounded the discussion with a plethora of religious and courtly ritual. He requested that the Bishop of Auxerre read a bible text from Abraham to Lot, by way of a peace message: "I ask of you that there be no more conflict between us." At the same time he organised a spectacular tournament between the Spanish knight Juan de Merlo and the Burgundian lord of Charni. Despite the provision of a splendid banquet, the like of which only the Burgundians could stage, Philip was unable to reach an agreement with the English. The private Franco-Burgundian agreement which came after this (the Peace of Arras; September 1435) was announced in public at an equal show of pomp and splendour in St Vaast's Abbey, for which the Duke brought in his knights of the Golden Fleece and also ambassadors of the German Emperor, the kings of Aragon, Castille, Portugal, Denmark and representatives of the great Italian and Flemish cities. In short, the whole of the contemporary Gothic of Europe.

188. Offertory scene in which Duke John the Fearless is presented with the *Livre des Merveilles*.

(Paris, Bibliothèque Nationale, ms fr. 2810, fo 226).

Very occasionally the populace took great exception to the festivities of the Burgundian court, as was the case in September 1424 when the luxuriant festivities laid on by Philip the Good for the Duke of Bedford so incensed the people of Paris who were exhausted by the war, that they began to revolt. Philip pacified them with bread and entertainment; bread, thanks to better supplies for the town; entertainment in the churchyard of the Innocents in Paris, in the form of a morality, a *Danse Macabre*, mixing comedy and tragedy in its treatment of the fear of death. Meanwhile Philip continued with his festivities, now with more plausible pretexts such as the marriage of the nobleman Jean de la Tremoille to the Lady of Roche-Baron. In this refined environment of high society Philip sustained the image of a courtly playboy, keen on dancing, tournaments, *haute cuisine* and erotic adventures. During one of these balls held in Paris, Philip seduced the Countess of Salisbury, one of the most attractive English ladies in the Duke of Bedford's party, much to the disapproval of her husband the earl. Chastellain noted, as any good psychologist would, the ease with which Philip "par diverses villes se communi-quoit avec les bourgeois, se réclinoit en leurs maisons", and how rapidly he established a rapport "aux femmes surtout".

On the occasion of Philip the Good's first royal entry into Ghent after the revolt of 1458 the populace seemed to have forgotten all its earlier resentment, since they received the duke "As if God himself has descended from heaven". On the Kouter there was a *tableau vivant* of the Van Eyck brothers' *Adoration of the Lamb*, which with its

189. The magic of love. A bride prepares for the ritual of love.

(Leipzig, Museum der bildenden Künste. Copy of an original from the school of Jan van Eyck).

190. Erotic and suggestive drawing by a fifteenth-century anonymous Flemish master.

(From auction catalogue H.P. Krauss, The Illustrated Book, cat. nr 108 nr 33. New York).

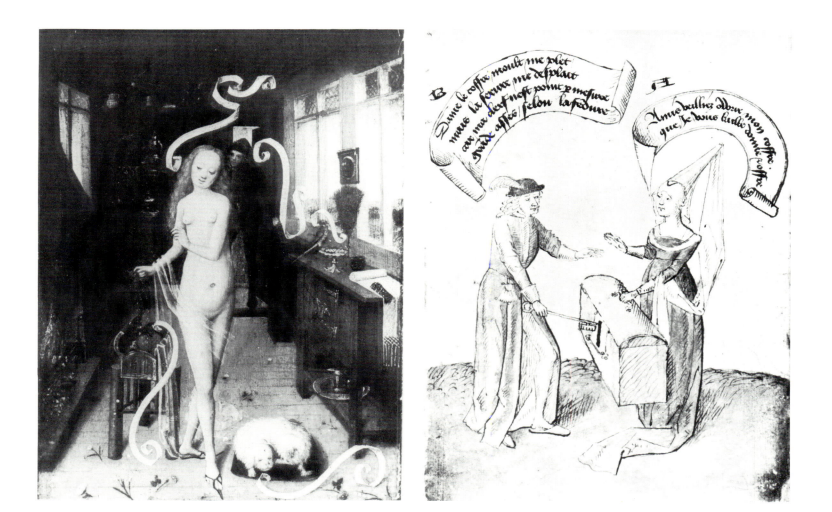

224

191. Portrait of Lysbeth van Duvenvoorde, member of one of the most important noble families in Holland.

(Amsterdam, Rijksmuseum. Master from the Netherlands, ca 1430).

reference to the Golden Fleece, was a particularly suitable theme. Ordinary processions were frequently commissioned by the secular powers throughout the Netherlands for purely political reasons. Thus in 1482 the Three Members of Flanders undertook to hold a procession in celebration of their agreement with Maximilian, and also in December of that year during a meeting of the States-General "praying to God in heaven that they might negotiate a good pact with France". In 1501 the Council of Flanders gave such an order to celebrate the marriage between Prince Charles and a French princess. In 1503 the States-General decided to do likewise to mark Philip the Fair's safe and successful journey to Spain. In 1505 the Council ordered that "the people should by conducting processions, in sermons and other ways pray for the salvation, victory and prosperity of the King [Philip the Fair] whose intention it was to defeat the Duke of Guelders on the battle-field". In all corners of the land, the population was mobilised to join such political celebrations. These manifestations were generally intended to influence the masses not just in their religious context but politically too in order to win their loyalty to those in power. In this particular case there was also a purely practical motive, namely to seduce their subjects into providing a subsidy for the war with Guelders.

The participation of all social ranks and estates was a vital part of such ceremonies. The poor also received additional distributions from the ducal alms on such occasions, and these sometimes even included wine. Everyone felt involved and identified with what was going on, and had, for a short time, direct personal contact with those in highest authority. The influence of such an event was also felt in areas far from where it actually took place, as those present took their accounts home to other towns or countries. There was consequently an extensive report of Charles' wedding celebrations in the Strasbourg Chronicle, and an English account of the proceedings was printed three times. The exuberant splendour of the Burgundian ceremonies was therefore intended to resound far beyond those present, into the entire western world.

There is thus no doubt that an active mass-media operated in the Burgundian Netherlands. Many art forms can also be interpreted in this way, especially works of architecture, sculptures and paintings exhibited in the churches. We may also be underestimating the effect of the spoken word : in a society with few written documents, reports were carried by travellers, messengers and eye-witnesses, by word of mouth. The messages given directly to the élite by the dukes and their officials eventually filtered through to the masses, albeit indirectly, simplified and possibly distorted, but nevertheless clear in essence. The effectiveness of such influence is evident from the enthusiastic reception which the people of Ghent gave their duke in 1458, and this in spite of the fact that, five years earlier, he had deeply humiliated them, put an end to their autonomy and imposed heavy financial penalties. The projected image of the sovereign thus requires further examination. There is no doubt that what actually came before the eyes of the masses was a staged spectacle ; a grand mystification of power in which the audience's role was to pay and to applaud.

THE SOVEREIGN AND HIS ILLEGITIMATE CHILDREN There are three facets to the image of the ruler : that of the fashionable nobleman ; that of the Christian sovereign and that of the charismatic, inviolable ruler. According to circumstances the emphasis between these self-conflicting facets would tend to shift.

The occurrence of illegitimate childbirth was possibly no greater in the fifteenth century than in the fourteenth and twentieth centuries, but it was of a different character ; acceptance of illegitimate children was certainly different, particularly in wealthier circles. The begetting and care of an illegitimate offspring was a relatively acceptable pattern of conduct. This was due to the example of the leading social classes, led by the dukes of Burgundy. Their performances were nevertheless very dissimilar. While Philip the Bold was content to have only two bastards, John the Fearless was the father of four. The undisputed champion is Philip the Good who left at least twenty-six illegitimate offspring and this figure could have been much higher but for the fickleness of fortune, since he kept at least thirty-three mistresses. Little is known of Charles the Bold in this connection, although he is sure to have had his flutters in Lorraine. It is striking that the first three dukes had illegitimate children in inverse proportion to the number of their legitimate offspring – Philip the Good had only one legitimate son – this could possibly be due to excessive endogamy. (See Appendix : table 3).

Michèle de France – whom Philip married at the age of thirteen – had the same great-grandfather as him. This marriage, which was childless, lasted from 1410 until 1422 and was followed by a second marriage to Bonne d'Artois which was to prove equally fruitless since Bonne died after one year of marriage. Thereafter Philip remained unmarried for some five years, much to the discomfort of his subjects, who insisted that he should set about producing heirs – giving further evidence of their strong attachment to the dynasty. Philip's only son and heir, Charles, was finally born a good three years after his marriage to Isabella of Portugal and an earlier unsuccessful pregnancy. The mother was by then, in 1433, almost thirty-seven years old and it is quite possible that in view of her age she would have been unable to conceive again. The dynastic risk implicit in such a single offspring was later to have serious consequences for the Netherlands. Philip can only be reproached for waiting too long to marry again between 1428 and 1430, and for having chosen a partner who was too old. There is no possible doubt about his own potency. Endogamy could also have played a part in this, at least in the first two marriages. Michèle was Philip's third cousin on the French side, and fourth cousin on the Bavarian side ; Bonne d'Artois was also a third cousin, and had had children in her first marriage.

The chronicler Olivier de la Marche, like many of his colleagues, was openly moved by the good duke's conduct. He called him "Un prince le plus dameret et le plus envoiseaux que l'on sceut, avoit de bastards et de bastardes une moult belle compagnie ". Nevertheless, Philip did not differ in this respect from the general pattern of the Valois dynasty. His contemporary King Charles VII was the first actually to display his concubines, with Agnes Sorel being the most illustrious example. The dukes of Burgundy did not go this far. King Louis XI was discreet with his mistresses ; indeed his entire behaviour was characteristically reticent.

It is nevertheless striking that the phenomenon of illegitimate children in the French royal houses was no longer a matter of chance after the fifteenth century, but took on a political dimension. This additional progeny after all provided the basis for an extended marriage policy whereby the links between the royal and ducal families on the one hand, and the dynasties ruling over adjacent territories on the other, could be strengthened. The conduct of the dukes was closely imitated by other sovereigns of their time : John II, Duke of Cleves, was given the nickname "kindermaeker" (childma-

192. Portrait of Duke Philip the Good (1396-1467). On coming to the throne Philip governed Burgundy, Flanders and Artois, to which he subsequently added Brabant, Limburg, Hainault, Namur, Holland, Zeeland and Luxembourg by marriages of convenience, a great deal of luck and money and a certain amount of love.

(Bruges, Groeningemuseum. Copy of an original reputedly painted by Rogier van der Weyden).

ker), as he was the father of sixty-three bastards. The higher nobility also imitated the dukes, one example being Jan van Glimes, father of forty illegitimate offspring. The upper levels of the ducal officials were equally convinced that this was how things should be done : Jean Jouard, solemn chairman of the Parliament of the County and Duchy of Burgundy had his bastard legitimated in 1459, as did Thierry Gherbode, councillor to Philip the Bold. The illegitimate offspring of the dukes were automatically given important positions – including clerical positions, after legitimation – although this was not so self-evident for the illegitimate children of nobles and burghers who often required an act of dispensation. The fact that the clergy were not to be outdone in this is discussed elsewhere. The apparent champions were John of Burgundy, Bishop of Cambrai, himself the illegitimate son of John the Fearless, who left seventeen bastards on his death in 1480, and particularly Jan van Heinsberg, Bishop of Liège (1419-1455) who left sixty-five illegitimate offspring because, according to the chronicler Jan van Stavelot "il amoit en hantoit amoureusement les desmoiselles".

What were the contemporary views on this issue ? It was, in an age of very limited methods of contraception the fatal corollary of a highly attractive, distinguished game of courtship. The 'mistresses' as far as we can tell, were not seedy whores but probably the wives of burghers, noblewomen such as Agnes de Croy, from the famous noble family, and noble demoiselles such as the Lady of Bonville and the Lady of Quiéry la Motte. Sometimes we learn how these escapades actually came about : Agnes de Croy cheerfully led Duke John astray at a party, or vice versa, since a contemporary wrote ; "qu'il l'avoit débauchée en un bal". So it was still called 'débaucher', dissoluteness in the minds of puritans and moralists. Authors such as Chastellain (and Jean Germain) publicly reproached Philip for his sensuality : "Avoit aussy en lui le vice de la chair. A souhait de ses yeux complaisoit à son cœur et au convoit de son cœur multipliait ses délits. Ce qu'il ne vouloit en venoit." The chronicler Fillastre consoled himself with the thought that the situation could have been worse, and that the sovereign had at least avoided scandal by not indulging in abduction. The loudest moan came from Jacques de Clercq : "Lors le péchié de luxure regnoit moult fort et par especial ès princes et gens mariés ; et estoit le plus gentil compaignon qui plus de femmes scavoit tromper et avoir au moment, qui plus luxurieux estoit."

Extra-marital affairs were in many ways a man's business ; a consequence of the man's initiative and not of the woman's. Such behaviour was tolerated without difficulty where the dukes were concerned but it was inconceivable for the duchess to be unfaithful since this caused progenitorial confusion.

The duchesses were apparently not so delighted by these one-sided sexual adventures and by way of sublimation sought solace in asceticism or art. After some violent domestic rows Isabella of Portugal returned to her estate of La-Motte-au-Bois, passing the time in reading and acts of charity and particularly in ascetic meditation and prayer, and her special relationship with her son Charles the Bold was some compensation for the frustration in her marriage. Margaret of York, Charles' wife, and Margaret, governess of Austria found comfort in artistic pursuits. When on the odd occasion a female ruler strayed sexually – as Jacqueline of Bavaria did – this was taken very seriously by her contemporaries.

However, the dukes' lovers also probably had little freedom of initiative in all this. They were inevitably one step below the dukes

193. Portrait of Jeanne de Presle, mistress of Philip the Good.

(Arras, Bibliothèque Municipale, ms 266. Sketch from the *Recueil d'Arras*).

194. Portrait of Catherine Thieffries, also named de la Tufferie, mistress of Philip the Good.

(Arras, Bibliothèque Municipale, ms 266. Stketch from the *Recueil d'Arras*).

195. Portrait of Anne of Burgundy (d. 1508), illegitimate daughter of Duke Philip the Good from his affair with Jacqueline van Steenberghe. In 1457 Anne married Adriaan van Borselen, and in 1470 her cousin Adolf of Cleves, Lord of Ravenstein (1425-1492).

(Arras, Bibliothèque Municipale, ms 226. Sketch from the *Recueil d'Arras*).

on the social ladder, and probably acted under pressure. There were not so many problems for unmarried girls, who could at least reckon on a show of gratitude of some sort. Even where a noblewoman or the wife of a 'valet de chambre' was involved, we may suppose that there was pressure from one side, and the hope of social promotion on the other. In the majority of cases the mothers, as well as their illegitimate offspring, were indeed taken into the ducal household after the event. Agnes de Croy, after bringing the duke's son – John, later Bishop of Cambrai – into the world, remained unmarried but was safely adopted as a maid of honour to the Duchess Isabella.

Although morally condemned by some, bastardy was at the same time a normal part of honourable high society life. The Christian puritan Jan van Stavelot openly spoke of the follies of 'his' bishop. The common law of Artois accorded all the privileges of the nobility to the illegitimate children of a noble father ("de noble génération de par père"), since they, and their own children, were recognised as nobles. In the accounts of the receiver-general of Flanders dating from 1417, an official noted a sum received for the legitimation of "Elisabet, fille naturele de honnourable homme et saige maitre David Bousse, conseiller de monseigneur et maistre de ses comptes à Lille". So one could apparently get up to much more mischief than Master Bousse before forfeiting the status of 'wise and honourable' councillor. Bastards, it is true, had to be legitimated before they could make their way in a career : as the unmarried parents of the illegitimate Niclais Scoorkinne did. After reading law at the university, Niclais became canon of St Donatus' at Bruges (1368) and a renowned clerk of the town 1379-1414. Once legitimated, it was even possible to reach the rank of bishop, as John did, the illegitimate son of John the Fearless.

Such career opportunities were apparently not widespread in Europe judging by the Czech nobleman Leo van Rosmital, who on his travels through the Netherlands in 1465-1467 was somewhat perplexed by the state of affairs there. "At the Burgundian court", he noted in his diary "there are three bastards in residence whose food is tasted beforehand, just as it is for the duke's legitimate son. Because in these parts there is no disgrace at all attached to the status of bastard, in contrast to what happens in our country [Bohemia], kings and sovereigns keep concubines in their castles". The illegitimate sons of the sovereigns did indeed climb numerous social ladders with unsullied reputations. The bastard sons of Philip the Good became bishops of Utrecht (David and Philip); dean of St Donatus' (John); abbots of Oudenburg and St Bavon's at Ghent (Rafaël de Mercatel); admiral of Flanders and Knight of the Golden Fleece (Philip) and the lord of extensive estates such as Beveren (Cornelis, the Great Bastard). Illegitimate daughters were also respectably married off to members of the Van Borselen family and to the Lords of Ravenstein and Pecquigny. Barbara van Steenburg rose to the rank of abbess of Broekburg, but most of her half sisters consolidated the duke's political relations by marriage.

Philip's most distinguished illegitimate sons were also the two eldest: Cornelis and Anthony. The first was appointed governor of Luxembourg in 1444 and enjoyed a very considerable annuity. Philip deeply mourned his loss at the battle against the citizens of Ghent at Rupelmonde in 1452; he ordered that the gateway through which the militia had left the town be bricked up, endowed requiem masses in perpetuity and had his grave sprinkled with holy water every day. Anthony later achieved high honours, as count of La Roche-en-Ardenne, and as diplomat and general to Charles the Bold. In 1464 he undertook to lead the crusade which finally got no further than Marseille. In 1468, Anthony, christened 'Le Grand Bâtard' by the chronicler Philippe de Commynes, received (along with the duke, the duchess and the widow of Philip the Good) a sixteen-year endowment of Flanders, and possibly also of other provinces. He honoured his father's memory by earning a similar reputation in the games of courtship, which gained him the reproach of the Order of the Golden Fleece to which he belonged. He also won great renown as a participant in tournaments, and it was he who staged the Golden Tree during Charles the Bold's wedding feast at Bruges in 1468. His son Philip, lord of Beveren, played a leading role on the Flemish side in the fight against Maximilian.

Like the other great men of their time, the most renowned among these illigitimate children had their portraits painted by Memlinc, Van der Weyden and Jan Gossart. To the prominent people these illegitimate offspring were status symbols with which they could impress their contemporaries, as with any *objets d'art*. That this flourished to such an extent was due to the fact that the church did not consistently disparage bastardy, and allowed matters to be put to rights by legitimation and dispensation. Even the popes, such as Innocent VIII and Alexander VI, fathered illegitimate children. The fifteenth century could then justifiably be referred to as the 'Bastard Era'. A prime example of their complete integration into society is the existence in 1403, in Brabant, of an "association familiale" of the Brabantine bastards.

Many of the dukes' various 'maîtresses' were by no means unattractive creatures, as we know from the drawings in the *Recueil d'Arras*. This gave them an advantage, as did the attraction of forbidden fruit, over the legal wives of, for example Philip the Good, whose marriages to Michèle of France and Bonne of Artois were concluded solely with a view to improving political relations with France. Affairs of the state could not apparently compensate for the affairs of the heart.

196. Seal of Anthony of Burgundy. His coat of arms is pierced by a cross-beam as a sign of his illegitimate status. The 'Great Bastard' fulfilled an important role in the Burgundian State as an army commander and prominent councillor.

(Zürich, Schweizerisches Landesmuseum. Inv. nr. dep. 400. The silver matrix, among the loot from Grandson is by a Flemish master of ca 1455 and is 5.1 cm thick).

197. *The man with the arrow*, alias Anthony of Burgundy, nick-named the 'Grand Bâtard'. From 1452, when the 'Great Bastard' Cornelis perished in the war against Ghent, he was the oldest of the dozens of illegitimate children of Philip the Good. Anthony was an exceptional knight and led the great tournament during the celebrations of the Golden Tree at Bruges in 1468 on the occasion of the marriage of his half-brother Charles the Bold to Margaret of York. After Charles' defeats in 1476 and 1477 he transferred his loyalties to the enemy French camp.

(Brussels, Royal Museum of Fine Arts. Portrait attributed to Rogier van der Weyden).

198. Seal belonging to Mary of Burgundy. (Brussels, State Archives, nr 33. 426).

THE CHRISTIAN SOVEREIGN The Burgundian dukes made full use of the image of the 'Christian Sovereign', as being protectors of religion and the church and hence of social order. In a series of Bulls issued between 1453 and 1458 by Pope Nicholas V and Pope Calixtus II, Philip the Good is given the honourable title of "Fervent athlete and intrepid champion of the Christian religion". In the opening words of an agreement of 1447, in which Nicholas V granted the duke a free hand in clerical appointments within his territories, the pope refers to him as a 'dearly beloved son', whom he looks upon as a 'righteous and catholic sovereign'.

This image was not only upheld in the sphere of high politics, the duke also showed his subjects that his day-to-day life was pious and Christian. The duke's aims were asseverated by senior members of the clergy. The court chapel had to compensate for the somewhat frivolous society-life at the court. It is nevertheless true that the way in which Philip the Good in particular played fast and loose with Christian marital ethics, conflicted with the official representation of his piety. The duke indeed received much criticism for this from the moralists within the church. One of the fiercest attacks was levelled at Philip in his own castle at Hesdin, by Jean Germain, Bishop of Chalon, whose allegorical sermon before the duke and duchess reproached the sovereign for neglecting affairs of state and for his adulterous behaviour.

The clearest examples of the intimate connection between the 'Christian sovereign' and his 'Christian people' are to be found, logically, during the Western Schism (1376-1415) when Philip the Bold, as champion of the Pope of Avignon, clashed head-on with his Flemish subjects supporting Rome. At the great propaganda meeting at Oudenaarde in January 1390, the duke's spokesman lamented "ceulz de Flandre sont singulers contre les opinions de leur seigneur souverain et naturel". And had they been better informed : "ilz croiroient volentier comme font monseigneur et madame". It is true that the latter, duke and duchess, had ulterior political motives, and in fact wanted to bring Flanders under their political control via the church. But the game was played to the bitter end – not moreover without some success. The sovereign was of course no priest ("Combien que le prince n'a point cure des ames"), yet it was his duty "de monstrer à son peuple" all that signified unity between himself and his people, in the interest of their salvation. If errors continued for too long he would be regarded as a secessionist by the people. The 1390 document ends with an unequivocal synthesis of the view of the union between sovereign and Christianity : "monseigneur est fondeur et protecteur des églises, qui tiennent leurs possessions de monseigneur et de ses prédécesseurs". In strife "Dieu n'est point servi".

The sovereign's position was stronger if his authority was linked to another firmly founded authority, the Church. It was for this reason that the duke was presented as the 'Champion of Christianity'. This Christian sovereign had to be a sort of hero, who did not hesitate to step into the breach for his religion, *e.g.* by organising crusades. The unrealised plan for the crusade against the Turks after the Oath of the Pheasant (1454) is widely known. Less well known, but equally illustrative, is Philip the Good's plan for a crusade

199. Fifteenth-century miniature depicting the sinking of a Flemish ship on a pilgrimage to Jerusalem. The souls of the drowned fly as doves towards heaven.

(Oxford, Bodleian Library, ms Douce 374, fo 40 r°).

against the Hussites in 1428/29 – which also never came about. The 1419 revolt of the Hussites against the Roman King Sigismund in Bohemia set the rest of Europe in turmoil as well. There were also related incidences of heresy in the Netherlands which were egalitarian, critical of society and thus potentially revolutionary. One well-known group consisted of those who had fled from Picardy to Prague. In 1420, in Tournai, there was a Hussite-inspired movement which had no qualms about posting up texts in which the Roman Catholic church was portrayed as the church of the antichrist.

Philip the Good was aware of this threat and in September 1427 took repressive measures against these heretics in Holland, and thereafter also in Lille and the bishoprics of Liège and Cambrai. Messengers informed him of the situation in Bohemia. Thus the idea grew that the duke should participate personally in a crusade against the Hussites. Philip, as cautious as they come, sent his ambassador Gilbert de Lannoy to Hungary and the Roman King in order to see how the land lay. From the ambassador's report, with its recommendations to the duke, we are able to discover the reasoning behind all this. The king and the German towns appeal to Philip for help, de Lannoy advises the duke to persuade the pope to give him responsiblity for this 'noble' undertaking to suppress heresy "devant tous aultres princes". This expedition was therefore a question of prestige. Europe must see how important the Grand Duc d'Occident was to the pope, and how the duke was the appropriate defender of European Catholicism. The plan was unsuccessful. Between 1427 and 1429 Philip was politically fully occupied with the conflict with Humphrey of Gloucester over the sovereignty of Holland and Zeeland. There were also tensions in the relations with King Sigismund and with France, caused by the activities of Joan of Arc, in whom the German Catholics had nevertheless placed their hopes in the struggle against the Hussites. The duke's role of 'Christian hero' was never to disappear, and was uppermost in the minds of those on the expeditions against the Turks in the Mediterranean led by the ducal councillors Thoissey and Wavrin, and also in the plans for crusades in 1454 and 1461.

THE INVIOLABLE SOVEREIGN At the above-mentioned assembly concerning the Schism in 1390, yet another political dogma was proclaimed by the officials of the duke of Burgundy, namely the unquestioned trust placed by the subjects in the sovereign's policies : "Quar le peuple est bon et obéissant à monseigneur". The interests of the sovereign, the state and the population were one and the same. When Philip the Bold dealt severely with a Flemish rebel in 1388, he justified his action in a personal note to his chancellor, whose duty it was to explain to the Flemings that the duke could not tolerate this "traison contre nous" and this "esmeuterie contre la paix faite entre ceulz de Gand" (peace treaty with Ghent in 1385) since these actions were not only directed "non pas contre nous seulement, mais contre le bien commun de tout nostre pais de Flandres". It may only be theory, but it was nevertheless a form of legitimation of ducal policy which is reflected in numerous passages from the Burgundian chronicles. Chastellain, with reference to events in 1436, describes the Flemings as "leaux subjects naturels" of Philip the Good. The author of *De Wonderlijcke Oorloghen van Keyser Maximilian* (beginning of the sixteenth century), although an outspoken monarchist, refers to subjects as those who "shall remain true Burgundians for the rest of our lives, in life or in death ; and we shall not fail the House of Burgundy, but will remain good and loyal". When Adriaan de But,

200. The Dukes Philip the Good and Charles the Bold as chief-mourners at the tomb of Emperor Maximilian of Austria in Innsbruck. The forefathers of the deceased were, according to tradition, placed around the tomb as guards of honour. Bronze statues cast by Stephen Godl from a wax model by Leonard Maght, in larger than lifesize dimensions.

(Innsbruck, Hofkirche).

monk of Ter Duinen, in his *Chronodromon*, took the side of Ghent against the duke in the conflict of 1436, he did not hesitate, nevertheless, to emphasis his loyalty to the prince : "quod non dico ... principi meo detrahendo" ("which I do not say ... in order to bring down my lord"). The duke was personally responsible for all decision-making, although the majority of decisions were taken after consultation with, and on the advice of his political councillors and officials in the first instance, the chancellor – and after taking into consideration the wishes of his most influential subjects as expressed in the peoples' parliaments, the consultative bodies of the cities, *i.e.* the Provincial States and the States-General. The final decision was nevertheless the duke's, and this was one aspect of sovereignty to which he was very attached.

The person of the duke was, in theory at least, the true centre of authority in the Burgundian state ; and on certain occasions this was also very real. Philip the Bold, for example, played an active part in discussions with his subjects concerning their petitions or other matters, or else he delegated his wife, son or high officials to do so. The correspondence which they exchanged shows a constant and deep personal concern. In his letters, Philip often gave very clear tactical guidelines for discussions with the towns, or for

235

negotiations with England relating to a trade agreement. He was personally so concerned about the limits of the public revenue, apparently so that he could cut his coat according to his cloth, that he commissioned his financial advisers in 1395 to draw up an estimate of these revenues. In 1407 John the Fearless demanded the same of his central Chamber for Finance at Dijon. According to statements from his contemporaries, Philip the Good, on the other hand, was largely unconcerned about the financial circumstances of his state. In the chronicles he appears as a *bon-vivant* who shied away from the responsibility of the routine tasks of government. Other sources show, however, that he insisted on presiding over most sittings of the court Council, and also insisted on taking all final political decisions. For routine tasks, however, he relied entirely on his officials : "ceulz qui son fait governoient, en fissent et disposassent à l'honneur de Dieu et au bien fait du peuple". But even he found it necessary to have a general account of all his revenues drawn up in 1446 ; since with the considerable increase in his territories, these had become very complicated. Financial affairs in the Burgundian state nevertheless remained extremely confused.

The criticisms levelled at the dukes of Burgundy by the chroniclers were mostly related to the more or less immoral aspects of their conduct. The legitimacy of their political power and their right to exercise that power was sacrosanct. Critical reactions thus concerned only the finishing touches of policy formulation. We see this best in the kind of mirror for princes written by Gilbert de Lannoy, ducal diplomat and adviser from 1435-1442, who wanted to present Philip the Good with an idealised image based upon his own practical experience. Together with worship of God and the importance of legal functions, de Lannoy stresses at length the importance of unimpeachable ducal officials from wealthy, established families. He

201. Whores and soldiers' wives constantly followed the army. The subjects lived in constant fear of army mobs, and not only because of their possessions.

(Brussels, Royal Library, ms 9242, fo 184. Miniature illustrating the *Invasion of the Hercinians in Gallia*).

202. Miniature depicting the murder of John the Fearless by the Armagnac clan at Montereau in 1419. 'Bourguignons' and 'Armagnacs' were involved in a bitter struggle to gain control of France. In 1407 John the Fearless had had his rival, Louis of Orleans, murdered.

(Leiden, University Library. *Chroniques de Enguerrand de Monstrelet*. Cod. Vossius, GG, F2, late fifteenth century manuscript from the Southern Netherlands).

also recommended that a permanent Grand Council be established as an advisory body. He further proposed that the sovereign must be able to live from his domains and that private and state finances should be clearly separate, and that an estimate of anticipated revenues be drawn up each year. These recommendations were, so it appears, only followed to a very limited degree.

The person of the sovereign was universally seen as inviolable. He could not be blamed for misjudgments, since these were the result of bad advice from those around him. It was for this reason that Chancellor Hugonet and the Lord of Humbercourt were brought to trial at Ghent in 1477. They were, after all, responsible for all that had gone wrong during the reign of Charles the Bold. In his first peace treaty with the king of France (Arras, 1435), Philip the Good demanded moral reparation. Even when citizens in revolt against the duke had him personally in their power, they still scrupulously

237

203. Aquarel copy of the Order of the Garter which King Edward IV of England conferred on his brother-in-law Charles the Bold on 10th January 1469 and which was handed over to Charles at Ghent on 4th February 1469.

(Basle, Historisches Museum).

respected his inviolability; Philip the Good found this at Ghent in August and September of 1436 when he was effectively held prisoner by the guilds, who had disarmed his bodyguard. The adroit duke saved himself from the situation by granting far-reaching concessions which were largely only symbolic and included an acknowledgement of tactical miscalculations and set-backs during the siege of Calais earlier that summer, and an undertaking to exonerate the Ghent militia, whom he had earlier blamed, in front of the entire western world, for this defeat. He had, however, to accept the fact that the aldermen of Ghent had banished some of his highest officials from the county, to wit, the sovereign-bailiff Colaerd van der Clyte, the captain of Sluis, Roeland van Uitkerke and the chamberlain Gillis van de Woestyne. In a less dangerous situation such as that in 1432, also in Ghent, when the guildsmen had also taken up arms and harassed several of the town magistrates – christened 'liver-eaters' – the duke could humbly beg for forgiveness.

In January 1488, Maximilian found himself in an almost identical situation in Bruges, but he reacted harshly. The citizens of Bruges suspected him of wanting to occcupy the town, whereupon they closed the gates in order to keep out his troops – while the Roman King himself was inside. Their grievances – which had already led to an uprising – were this time also directed towards the ruler; namely that he was not keeping to the terms of the peace treaty with France, and that he was sapping the wealth of the land. Nevertheless, the blame was still laid elsewhere: with the chancellor (Jean Carondelet), the treasurer (Pieter Lanchals), the receiver-general (Roland Lefevre), and the councillor Thibaut Barradot. A ransom was put on their heads and some were imprisoned in the Gravensteen at Ghent. The polarisation of relations explains why Maximilian himself was imprisoned and was subsequently forced to leave the ducal palace for a house on the market – The Cranenburg – where he daily witnessed the violation of his authority and the execution of his supporters. Despite the resentment which his subjects felt towards him and the ease with which, in such circumstances, heads rolled and punishments were dealt out, they did not dare to touch the person of their ruler – the future emperor. Maximilian's incarceration brought ever greater problems for the citizens of Bruges, who did not know how to escape the situation of stalemate. The pressure of an approaching German army and Maximilian's willingness to secure his freedom with any kind of concession, led to his liberation on sixteenth May, after three and a half months. The problem of the legitimacy of ducal conduct was particularly relevant where Maximilian was concerned. Flanders only recognised him as regent to his son, who was not yet of age, at the point of the sword. According to common law, the States of Flanders had every

204. Portrait of Baudouin de Lannoy (1388-1474) Lord of Molembaix, nick-named 'le Bègue'. He was chamberlain to Duke Philip the Good, governor of Lille in 1423 and captain of castle Mortagne in 1428. In 1431, one year after the institution of the Order of the Golden Fleece, he became a knight of the Fleece. The de Lannoy family from Hainault weilded considerable influence and two members of the family became governors of Holland between 1433 and 1462.

(Arras, Bibliothèque municipale, ms 266).

right to refuse him this recognition in that capacity, but their decision was not freely taken. The same can be said of the circumstances in which Maximilian, after months of imprisonment, abdicated from the regency : his formal oath of peace, taken upon the relics of Bruges, was taken under duress. Once outside Flanders, he refused to recognise this oath any longer and once again fought for the recognition of his government for a period of four years. Could force of arms then establish any legal recognition ? Charles the Bold's opinions concerning the sovereign's authority were very clearly formulated. Although he felt more strongly than his predecessors and successors on certain matters, their opinions did not differ greatly from his. For this reason we will again quote from his speeches.

"I am well aware that there are those among you [the Flemings] who hate me, and between you you have always obstinately resented or hated your sovereigns. If they were not strong, you despised them, but if they were so powerful that you could do nothing against them, you hated them. I would rather you hated me than despised me because I shall not be deterred either by your privileges or for any other reason ; nor will I allow anything to happen to the detriment of my highness or my estates for I am powerful enough to resist such things. ... It would then be as the pot and the glass : as soon as the glass hits the pot it breaks. Therefore, those who think in this way do not know what it is to stand in the grace of their sovereign ... Begin, then by conducting yourselves well, and so worthily as not to forfeit my favour, since you know not what you would be losing : be good subjects, and I shall be a good ruler" (1470).

"I have spared neither my body nor my wealth in defending my Flemish subjects, as a good shepherd I have devoted my soul to this end 'bonus etiam pastor animam suam ponit pro ovibus suis' [the good shepherd giveth his life for his sheep], and as yet only death have I not suffered for them ; yet they still show me ingratitude ... Since you have refused to be governed by me as children by their father, you could be disinherited as an unworthy son from his father's property. You shall then live under my authority as subjects under a lord, for as long as this pleases the Creator, because it is from Him and none other that I have my sovereignty. I shall remain sovereign for as long as it shall please Him, in spite of all those who regret this, which I do not doubt since God has given me the might and the powers which I would advise you not to challenge.

To demonstrate to you that I have the power to act as sovereign ; a power which God has entrusted to me and not to my subjects, it is sufficient to read the Book of Kings in the Bible, in which God grants in clear terms the sovereigns' authority over their subjects. I have pleaded long enough, and since I am not obeyed with prayer or entreaty, I shall then punish the disobedient in a manner which others have already experienced, and which I do not recommend since it is not good to try anything." (1475).

These central ideas can be reduced to the following. The monarchy is desired by God, to whom the sovereign owes his power. He governs according to godly principles : he provides for his subjects as a good shepherd and father, he holds them in his love and ensures justice and welfare. Worthy subjects are expected to be obedient and grateful for the favour shown to them by their sovereign. If they are disobedient, the sovereign becomes a strict ruler who commands instead of requesting, withholds his favour and punishes severely. All the dukes of Burgundy bore witness to this paternalistic conception of their role, in terms of strictness and, equally, in liberal clemency – or at least what that was assumed to be. Refusal to comply with a ducal request always meant a risk of losing the duke's favour; disturbance of the public order always constituted a direct challenge to the duke's authority which was exercised by delegates in each locality.

In 1475 Charles the Bold went as far as to represent the reluctance to offer yet more military support as lèse-majesté. A sovereign who owed his power to God and God alone was on that account inviolable, if not infallible. Direct accusations were only made against Maximilian in Flanders, apart from this the legitimacy of the sovereign was never questioned. It was for this reason that uprisings among those in authority were also always represented as crimes against the prince who then also dealt out exemplary punishment for such behaviour. The prostration of villagers around Cassel in 1431, the humiliation of Bruges in 1438 and Ghent in 1453, 1469, 1485, 1492, and 1540 (the infamous halter-bearers of Charles V), and the merciless destruction of Dinant and Liège by Charles the Bold in 1466 and 1468, all consistently follow the same line : disobedience will be punished. The prince is the personification of justice and therefore cannot accept any other views of what is right and wrong.

But there was also another aspect of paternalism : after a demonstrative humiliation the ruler would mercifully once again receive the guilty party into his favour and was prepared to allow a gradual decrease in punishment. After 1453 Philip the Good granted an extension of payment to Ghent and partial remission, and also revoked some of his repressive measures in 1458. With his spectacular punitive ceremonies in 1540, Charles V was more intent upon establishing his authority in the eyes of the world than he was upon making the people of Ghent groan under the yoke of oppression. 'Duke by the Grace of God' : like God the Father at the day of judgment, so too were the rulers enthroned : wroth with sinners, loving the righteous and piteous to all.

206. Fragment of a stained glass window bearing the emblem of the Golden Fleece and the motto of Duke Philip the Good 'Aultre nauray', from the ducal chapel at Dijon.

(Dijon, Musée des Beaux-Arts. French school, leaded glass, fifteenth century).

205. Liège and its destroyed walls after the siege of 1468. Duke Charles the Bold – with support of King Louis XI – plundered, burned and massacred the town, which had twice resisted his authority.

(Düsseldorf, Hauptstaatsarchiv. Pen drawing from Nicolaas Clopper's chronicle *Florarium temporum* of 1472).

Church and State

The church traditionally aspired to play a part in international as well as national politics. This brings to mind the heroic skirmishes for universal power between Gregory VII and the German emperors in the eleventh century, or between Boniface VIII and the French King Philip the Fair, around 1300. In the Burgundian period, however, it is true to say that it was the political world that used the church rather than the church that managed to manipulate the political circles. After 1300 a great many church dignitaries became involved in non-clerical activities and were thus eventually absorbed into lay politics in the service of this laity. The malleability of the church increased considerably through the rapid rise of the national States which benefited from a church over which they had strict control. The papacy also became the victim of the tug-of-war between these states. Before 1300 it was her charismatic approach to matters which made the international church's impact on world affairs. After 1300, however, it was this charisma itself which crumbled. A worldly-minded church took its place and such a church had no power with which to achieve its universal ambitions.

The papacy of the fourteenth century was nevertheless a state whose financial and bureaucratic organisation was exemplary. Around 1300, the papal revenues were three times those of the kingdom of France, enabling the construction of the prestigious Palais des Papes at Avignon. But that was about all. At the end of the fourteenth century the revenue of the French state was already fifteen times as great, and the Burgundian state revenue twice as great as that of the papacy. The universal support for the crusades was also on the wane. The papacy was reduced to the proportions of a state and was, just like the other states, equally vulnerable and doomed to compromises and coalitions.

PAWNS OF THE BURGUNDIAN SOVEREIGN   Just at the point when the first duke of Burgundy – Philip the Bold – made his entrance onto the political stage, the church fell prey to an internal conflict – the so-called Western Schism whereby from 1378 the Pope, resident for many years at Avignon, was challenged by a pope elected in Rome : Clement VII at Avignon, Urban VI in Rome. The sovereigns of western Europe, and in particular Philip the Bold, saw immediately that there were political gains to be made from this conflict. Since, as French prince and member of the regency council, Philip harboured ambitions of playing an active role in the French kingdom next to and in place of the weak French king, lending active support to the Pope at Avignon fitted well into his plans. Philip would have more control over the Pope at Avignon than he would have over the Pope in Rome. Philip's pro-Avignon stance became even stronger when it became clear that England supported Rome. This, however, caused problems : Philip's Flemish subjects – highly orientated towards England for economic reasons – chose to support Urban VI. Philip moved heaven and earth in an attempt to convert them to Clement; he organised a synod at Lille in 1384, arranged propaganda speeches by the best French theologians at a meeting of the Flemish clergy, nobles and towns at Oudenaarde in 1390, and appointed someone from Avignon as Bishop of Tournai (albeit in addition to an Urbanist who remained in office). This led to the 'conversion' of Walloon-Flanders (1384), Ypres (1392) and Bruges (1393). We get the distinct impression that among all this propagandist activity with its various options there was little mention of theological distinctions or even internal ecclesiastical government, and little concern for the welfare of the church. It is clear that the rulers, like the duke of Burgundy, were concerned to achieve two things, a political hold on the church and, via control of clerical institutions, better control over the whole of society. The intention was to use the solution of the church problem as a means of bringing the rebellious Flemings back into line.

After 1398 and with the same political opportunism, Philip the Bold followed the French king's lead in supporting the neutralisation of the opposing popes, and John the Fearless joined with many other rulers in supporting reunification around one pope, namely the Pisan pope. This did in fact lead to the resolution of the Schism in 1417.

When in 1431 Pope Eugène IV seemed prepared to honour Philip the Good by recognising him as an equal to the sovereigns of Europe and also by allowing him to participate in the appointment of cardinals, Philip took a pro-papal stance against the Council of Basle, which wanted to restrict papal prerogatives. Philip also remained loyal to the Pope in the Councils of Ferrara and Florence, summoned by Eugene in 1439. The result of all this was a concordat between the Pope and the Duke in 1441. The French king, in the dispute between the Pope and the prelates councils, took the side of the French clergy against the curia in the Pragmatic Sanction of Bourges, a decree issued in 1438 which curtailed papal authority over the French church and placed considerable restrictions on the appointment of French clergy to the Roman curia. Philip the Good, however, adopted a more differentiated approach in 1441. The papal-ducal concordat was based upon the conditions laid down at the Council of Basle, but nevertheless spared the Pope the dishonour of a Pragmatic Sanction by formally taking a curial line, although the relationship actually contained many anti-curial elements. In 1447 and 1463, Popes Pious II and Paul II, respectively, lent their support to Philip the Good's plans to acquire kingship, as a reward for his sympathy.

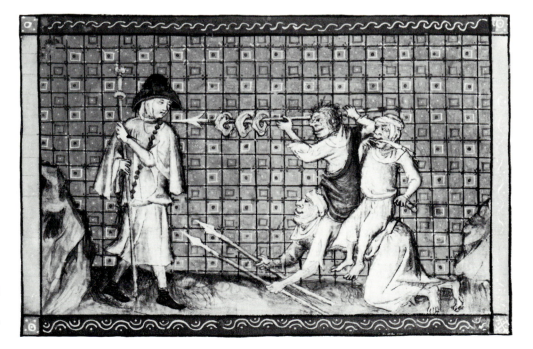

207. Pilgrim threatened by Envy, Betrayal and Destruction.

(Brussels, Royal Library, ms 10176-78, Guillaume de Deguileville, *Pèlerinages*).

The concordat (as did an earlier text in 1418) allowed the Pope to retain, in theory, his right of reservation (*i.e.* the right to make the final choice) in the appointment of bishops ; although in practice this right was only to be exercised according to the duke's recommendations. In return, the Pope often accepted payment for his services and, for example, accepted 12,000 ducats in 1439 for appointing John (natural son of John the Fearless and Agnes de Croy) bishop of Cambrai.

The dukes manipulated the church most where their own provinces were involved, namely by appointing countless bishops who were politically favourably disposed towards the Burgundian state. Philip the Good appointed no less than an estimated thirty-two confidantes and kinsmen. The peak of these appointments can be placed around 1455, when Philip's nephew Louis of Bourbon was bishop of Liège, his natural brother John was bishop of Cambrai and his illegitimate son David was bishop of Utrecht (after occupying the see of Thérouanne since 1451). The duke also appointed confidantes in Tournai, Arras, Cologne, in the Burgundian bishoprics of Besançon, Autun, Mâcon and Auxerre and as far as Lyons, Bayeux and Nevers. This policy had several goals : to place more pawns on the political chessboard (*i.e.* in the prince-bishoprics of Liège and Utrecht) ; intervention in ecclesiastical politics (by, for example, appointing at Tournai and Cambrai prelates favourably disposed towards Avignon during the Schism, who would therefore support Burgundian policies at home and abroad) ; and to reward loyal servants. In 1439 the chapter at Arras appointed (under heavy pressure from the duke) Fortgarius of Piacenza as their bishop, who up till then had been councillor, chaplain and almoner to Philip the Good. Those who had been promoted were not slow to perform services in return : Jean Chevrot (head of the ducal council who was appointed bishop of Tournai in 1436) did his utmost – naturally, in the interest of his benefactor – to increase revenues from tax levied on the churches by including properties which were hitherto untaxed, thus raising a tax on behalf of the duke. Moreover, clerical and secular offices were permanently combined : Jean Canard, chancellor to the duke from 1385,

244

was also, from 1391, bishop of Arras and from 1397 was also provost of the largest chapter in Flanders, at St Donatus' in Bruges. Jean de Thoissey, the duke's master of petitions from 1404, and later head of the ducal council, was also bishop of Auxerre (1409-1410) and Tournai (1410-1433). This trend continued into the reign of Charles V who in 1525 promoted a member of the loyal Croy family to the office of bishop of Tournai (though at too young an age, since he had to remain in Italy until 1539 to complete his studies), and three further members of the Croy family monopolised the see of Cambrai between 1502 and 1556.

The combination of the office of bishop of Tournai and the role of head of the Grand Council was a striking feature ; this happened consecutively with Jean de Thoissey (until 1433), Jean Chevrot (until 1460), Guillaume Fillastre (until 1473) and Ferry de Clugny (until 1483). This went so far that when Chevrot was dismissed in 1457 as head of the Grand Council, he also had soon after to hand over his episcopal throne to his successor. Tournai was both politically and economically important to the Burgundian Netherlands. It constituted a French enclave along the Scheldt, where it was advisable to have authority in reliable hands. This combination of offices strengthened the power of the dukes through the church structures, by *e.g.* the appointment to clerical offices which were under the authority of the bishops who were also the sovereign's right-hand men.

A similar policy of appointment was followed in the abbeys and chapters. Here, moreover, they could conveniently revive the ancient tradition which recognised the authority of the dukes as patrons of the church. This right of patronage was redefined in

209. Mary of Burgundy riding, followed by death. The tragic death of the beloved sovereign, the last branch of the Burgundian dynasty, strongly affected the popular imagination.

(Berlin, Kupferstichkabinett, ms 78 B12, fo 220 V°, miniature from the *Livre d'heures de Marie de Bourgogne*).

1441, and led to the Bull 'Fervor Purae Devotionis' (1515) in which Pope Leo X undertook not to appoint a single abbot without the consent of Charles V. It would appear from a document dating from 1522 that the emperor took this to be a plenipotentiary right of appointment, but the abbeys of Brabant nevertheless claimed that the Bull of 1515 fully maintained the clergy's canonical right of election. The dispute was to drag on until 1564. This policy of appointment can in itself be seen as part of an attempt by the dukes of Burgundy to establish a state church. It was political rather than spiritual interest which governed this policy both before and after the Western Schism. It was a question of extending their influence not only to the church as an institution, but also to the congregations who could sometimes hear political messages from the pulpit.

One particular means by which the dukes could actively intervene in church policy was the right delegated by the Pope to the Burgundian duke of distributing incomes attached to clerical offices (benefices, canonries), which the duke naturally did selectively to benefit his favourites and supporters. This right regularly affected some hundred benefices. The result of this policy was the highly unhealthy concentration of offices and income in the hands of a few political favourites. This led to increased absenteeism among those priests who could not adequately fulfil all their duties simultaneously, and a deepening rift between a clerical élite (those holding a combination of offices) and a clerical 'proletariat'. The lay-lords apparently did not object to the fact that such a policy was detrimental to the interests of pastoral care, nor that the rule that the clergy had to reside in the locality in order to receive a prebend was being ignored.

Proof of the fact that the dukes wanted to carry intervention in church policy a step further was Charles the Bold's unsuccessful attempt to bring the borders of the Burgundian state into line with those of a newly formed church province. This would reduce the influence of the king of France who, as a temporal ruler, naturally attempted to appoint his favourites to the sees which served his territories. As long as this was the case, anyone awaiting trial before a church tribunal could appeal to a higher court outside those state boundaries. A papal decree put an end to this in 1515, and this development culminated in the establishment of new bishoprics in 1559. Before this time the dukes had, however, concluded special concordats in this connection, such as the one with Utrecht in 1434.

In Brabant, the trial of Brabanters in clerical cases outside the region had already been stopped by the Imperial Bull of 1349, which is an indication of Brabant's political autonomy.

A SOURCE OF STATE REVENUE The original fiscal immunity of the clergy came to be regarded in the late Middle Ages as a somewhat out-dated privilege. It was in the reign of the Burgundian dukes, that this tradition came under attack.

In the first place the sovereign reacted against the fact that goods which came into the hands of the clergy were, from a fiscal point of view, 'defunct' and, as so-called defunct possessions or mortmain they were now immune from municipal and state taxes, and in particular from transfer tax, since the majority of these goods did not change hands again. For this reason a tax was introduced in 1389 on all new goods acquired by the church; and in 1396 a retro-active measure was added to this whereby tax was payable

210. St Margaret of Antioch (1470-1480).
(Bruges, Gruuthusemuseum).

on all mortmain, property acquired in the preceding forty years on which no transfer-tax had been paid (and had therefore not been amortised). This affected both feudal-and non-feudal lands. Philip the Good issued similar decrees for Brabant in 1446 and Holland in 1439 and 1446, with much opposition from the latter. Until 1474 the clerical institutions could withdraw from these obligations with relative ease. Charles the Bold, however, put an end to this on 10th July 1474 by demanding the registration of all goods which had not been amortised in the past sixty years; this time revenues came from virtually all the regions, apart from Luxembourg. Resistance remained nevertheless strong and the revenue was far less than had been expected. Prince Charles followed this example in 1515 and went a step further in an edict issued in 1520 by demanding that in Brabant every transfer of property to the churches be subject to his approval.

In theory clerical institutions enjoyed fiscal immunity from the secular world and various episcopal councils reinforced this privilege from 1179 onwards, although it was eventually modified in two ways. Firstly, an internal ecclesiastical tax (the so-called papal tithes) was diverted to the temporal rulers. This was raised originally for the crusades planned in the twelfth century, but this tax was in fact used for a totally different purpose and was appropriated by the laity. Numerous rulers usurped these revenues during the thirteenth and fourteenth centuries, as did the dukes of Burgundy who admittedly disguised the transfer of this revenue behind quasi-motives of supporting the church. This happened in 1441 and on three occasions in 1455-1456 on the strength of tax-lists on a sliding scale drawn up by Chevrot, bishop of Tournai, who was the chief of the duke's Grand Council. The clergy also had to make frequent contributions to the levies from the laity; on the one hand the regular reparations from the rural population, with whom the clergy were classified on the strength of their mortmain, on the other hand the clergy were forced by the dukes, after separate negotiations conducted without the Third Estate, into the payment of their own levies; although these were sometimes – for fear of resistance – discribed as loans. Sixteen such levies are known to have been made between 1394 and 1496. In Brabant, 'voluntary' subsidies were paid by the clergy from 1280 onwards, in 1356 the abbeys of Brabant undertook to pay one third of the regional levies although in practice many reductions were made; this share moreover decreased to 12 per cent in 1451 and 4 per cent in 1473.

Similar attempts by Charles V who, with a view to financing his wars, tried to force the clergy into the payment of levies, met with strong opposition from the abbeys of Brabant. The clergy's fiscal involvement in the Netherlands did not always guarantee a compatible say in politics. In Flanders the clergy (and the nobility) only participated in 255 meetings of the States (i.e. 6 per cent of the 4,055 representative sittings organised between 1385 and 1506) on the initiative and in the interest of the effective powers in the province, namely the sovereign and the cities. In Brabant, however, the connection between finance and political standing was more evident since scarcely anyone but the tax-paying abbots (the so-called twelve prelates) had seats in the States during the fifteenth century.

The attitude of the government towards the clergy as a group was therefore, as we have seen, far from generous. On an individual level the relationship was better: at this level every service was rewarded with services-in-return and promotion. Individual clerics often functioned as diplomats for the dukes, as, for example, the abbot of Affligem in 1417 and Antoine Haneron, clerk in holy orders at Mons and Bruges and councillor to Philip the Good from 1441, who negotiated with his subjects and foreign representatives, and was also guardian to Charles the Bold.

INTER-RELATIONSHIPS Were the dukes in their support of the bishops, abbeys and churches mainly concerned with displaying their piety, and with repaying their personal services – or with using the church as one of the means towards the aim of controlling society? The dukes' conduct was possibly prompted by a combination of these various motives. According to Huizinga, we should recognise a tension between mental attitudes – between pure, religious feelings and sensuous impulses. There were striking contrasts within such a figure as Philip the Good who endowed a great many foundations "for our own and our female companions' and our land's salvation", who had close dealings with visionaries and ascetics and who in 1443 postponed a campaign in order that he might first attend mass – in the middle of the night. The ducal family arranged charitable acts on all the major church festivals: on Maundy Thursday 1417, for example, for the benefit of forty-two paupers at the gates of the palace at Dijon. One aspect of these charitable donations is particularly intriguing; according to the annual accounts of the ducal alms, a sum of money was made available to the duke's confessor to be distributed as 'les aumosnes secretes du duc'. Was he then aware of the duplicity in his lifestyle? Could this have been a separate budget to salve his conscience for all sorts of misdemeanours? The prince-bishops of Liège (more prince than bishop, or so it would seem) also displayed this osmosis of worldly authority and intense devotion which is so remarkable to us, a case in point being John of Bavaria.

The dukes' faith – whether or not it had any real depth – was in any case outwardly displayed to contemporaries in religious ceremonies. It was the sovereign's duty to display the outward signs of faith. Philip the Good had a court chapel in the palace on the Koudenberg in Brussels where he frequently and ostentatiously attended mass. Blessed Coletta and also Dionysius the Carthusian were regular guests at the palace, the former even undertaking political negotiations with Savoy in Philip's name. Dionysius, who was very close to Nicholas of Cusa, was able to convince the Duke of the needs of the international church.

Equally characteristic of this image-building was the organisation of all ducal support for the poor and needy in the service of the chaplaincy – a division of the ducal chapel. The confidential servant appointed to make the allocations was usually a senior cleric who, in the eyes of the general public, had a high reputation as an actual or potential bishop or theologian, such as the theologian Jean Gerson or Fortigarius of Piacenza, bishop of Arras, who could therefore put the finishing religious touches to the sovereign's charitable acts.

The dukes and their spouses were also involved in the building of new religious foundations. These initiatives concentrated on a few selected religious orders and this was by no means coincidence; by directing their sympathies towards the orders that were fashionable at the time, the dukes ensured their popularity. Firstly, the Carthusians: with a mausoleum at Champmol, a house at Brussels (1456), and a foundation by Charles the Bold at 's Hertogenbosch in 1461, this order became more popular than the mendicant

211. Philip the Good attends a mass in his private chapel, sung by the court choir.

(Brussels, Royal Library, ms 9092 fo 9, miniature from the *Treatise on the prayer 'Pater Noster'* translated by Jean Miélot and illustrated by a pupil of Jean de Tavernier).

Dominican order due to their purer faith and their air of piety in isolation from the towns. Secondly, there was the Order of St Clare : St Coletta was supported by the dukes, and particularly by the duchesses in foundations at Hesdin (1437), Ghent (1440), Amiens (1444) and Antwerp (1453). This order also insisted on strict purity, and the restoration of the original Franciscan rule, which had fallen into abuse. There were also the strict Observants, who placed less emphasis upon material possessions – a view which was in keeping with the dukes' policy to restrict the possessions of the church. Support was given to the orders with a markedly social vocation : the Grey and Black Sisters (at Ghent, La Motte near Aire and Binche) : Franciscans and Dominicans (1459 at Brussels). Both Duchess Isabella of Portugal and Margaret of York stood as patronesses in the reformation of the monastries in the Netherlands.

There were, however, generally ulterior motives in the support given to the churches. The dukes may have established foundations and granted subsidies and support, but they quickly took these back by means of ecclesiastical taxation. Meanwhile the desired effect was achieved. The dukes granted, as Philip the Good did in 1444, exemption from tolls and mortmain levies as their predecessors in the twelfth and thirteenth centuries had done, but it was also they who were responsible for eroding the church's fiscal immunity and its right to acquire property. In 1451 the same Philip the Good set up a commission to curb, amongst other things, financial malpractice in the control of properties belonging to the religious foundations. It would seem that material concerns were paramount in relations between the church and the dukes. In 1394, during

212. A state barge with baldachin approaches the quayside during a Royal Entry.

(Brussels, Royal Library, ms 10777, fo 53 V°. Fifteenth century miniature from *La Première guerre punique*).

negotiations between the duke and clergy concerning a levy – which the duke justified by claiming that it was in the interest of the church – one of the ecclesiastical representatives archly proposed that the church should celebrate masses of the Holy Spirit during the crusade instead of paying subsidies, but this proposal was disdainfully dismissed by the duke as a joke in bad taste.

A very marked secularisation in the conduct of many of the clergy can be noticed at this time. The political appointment of clerics turned them into figures with political ambitions themselves and made them more vulnerable to political corruption, particularly in the bishoprics which were also principalities (Liège, Utrecht).

This secularisation also tainted the clerics' whole pattern of social conduct : like laymen, the clerics had realistic portraits of themselves painted by renowned artists, and purchased *objets d'art* ; like their upper-class contemporaries in the secular world they even kept mistresses and fathered illegitimate children.

By drifting into lay society, these clerics also neglected their own duties to the church : hence the widespread absenteeism among the priesthood ; hence the immoral behaviour, the pursuit of material gain, lack of respect for the rule of poverty and the materialistic application of indulgences.

But such flouting of standards also provoked equally outspoken reactions : strong moral sermons by successful preachers who spared

213. Polychrome statue of St Georges on horseback. The emblem on the breastplate and the chain of the Golden Fleece lead one to suppose that it is a portrait of Duke Philip the Fair at about eighteen years of age.

(St Joris-ten-Distel, St George's Church. Polychrome oak statue. Anonymous master from the Southern Netherlands, late fifteenth century).

214. Engraving after a drawing from the *Ehrenspiegel* by the Nuremburg financier Johann Jakob Fugger, who bought jewels from the Swiss and also this hat set with pearls and precious stones belonging to Duke Charles the Bold. These objects were plundered at Grandson after the defeat of the Burgundian army in 1476. Original hats from the Burgundian period are rare.

(Basle, Historisches Museum. Copper engraving, seventeenth century).

neither the clergy nor the laity; the advent of purging movements within the church such as the Devotio Moderna, mysticism and finally also the Reformation itself.

ITS OWN IMPACT ON SOCIETY? Despite the fact that a large part of the church became secularised during the Burgundian period, and entered the service of secular political leaders, part of the church nevertheless retained an obvious impact on lay society. With religion as a guiding principle the church continued to monopolise a large proportion of education, and greatly contributed to the organisation of social services for the sick, the elderly, orphans and other marginal groups. Clerics were also responsible for the day-to-day pastoral care which all this entailed, ministrations now carried out by doctors, social workers and psychiatrists. Sometimes it was a question of special tasks, such as burying the dead – particularly the feared victims of the plague – carried out by the Alexians and the Sisters in Black, or helping out in cases of fire and other disasters. The village priests supervised the provision, if any, of the largely inadequate poor relief through the system of parish charity (Tables of the Holy Spirit).

So it would seem that help for the needy depended upon their faith and orthodoxy, and was further conditional on conforming to acceptable social (and political) conduct. So this 'other' part of the church, which looked as yet untainted by politics, was nevertheless in reality a means of regulating society. The church's social institutions did not indeed have a completely free hand. In most towns the magistrate appointed supervisors who were responsible for controlling the material and financial aspects of hospitals, religious houses, mendicant monastries, the Beguinages and other religious social services. This control enabled the urban politicians at the same time to maintain the social order.

The Keys to Power

The internal organisation of the state and territorial expansion were closely connected. To implement an expansionist policy the government had to be able to draw upon the necessary financial and military resources in its most important regions, and this required a sound constitutional framework. On the other hand, its concentration on foreign policies forced it to make political concessions on the domestic front. These usually took the form of conditions which their subjects attached to the subsidies that were demanded. As the dukes demanded more and more resources for their foreign enterprises, they were less and less able to challenge internal power structures.

FOREIGN EXPANSION OR DOMESTIC CENTRALISATION The Burgundian period can be divided into distinct phases during which emphasis on external policy alternated with domestic reforms. The period which ran roughly from 1385 to 1435 was characterised by involvement in French politics and territorial expansion. Consequently, the popular representation at home had, so it would appear, a great deal of say in what went on, and was even granted executive powers. It is true that Philip the Bold created new centralised institutions, namely the delegations from the ducal council which specialised in legal and financial matters. After 1386 these institutions were named the Council Chamber (Chambre du Conseil) and the Chambers for Finance (Chambre des Comptes), and were located at Lille where they supervised the whole of the north; such institutions had already been in existence since 1367 for the southern provinces. This innovation was nevertheless more appearance than reality, since specialised councillors had already been carrying out the same tasks in Flanders for decades, and these people, incidentally, also became members of the new institutions. In 1407, at the instigation of the Flemings, John The Fearless moved the Council Chamber to the Dutch-speaking part of Flanders, to Ghent where the legal section of the ducal council had resided during the fourteenth century. While these institutions offered no more innovations in their aims than in their personnel they were constantly forced to bow to the large towns in their capacity as supreme court and exchequer, since these towns stubbornly defended their legal and fiscal autonomy.

A similar development took place in Brabant, though in that case upholding Brabant's autonomy. With successive personal unions with Luxembourg (under Duke Anthony), and with Hainault, Holland and Zeeland (under Duke John IV) some centralisation and shifts in the institutions was possible in these areas too. Councillors from the newly acquired provinces joined the ducal council of Brabant; this council also acquired powers in the other principalities, so that people from Brabant and Limburg were active in, for example, Holland. The Chamber for Finance at Brussels, established in 1404, controlled all the territory under the authority of Duke Anthony. In 1420 John IV gave orders for the minting of gold and silver coins for general circulation in Brabant, Hainault and Holland-Zeeland. This silver double-groat which came to be known as the 'three-lander' was the direct predecessor and source of inspiration

215. Jousting watched by the people. This aristocratic sport enjoyed a last revival – referred to by Huizinga as an Indian summer – under the Burgundians.

(Brussels, Royal Library, ms II, 158. Miniature for the month of June from the book of hours *Les Heures de Notre Dame* also known as Hennessy, early sixteenth century).

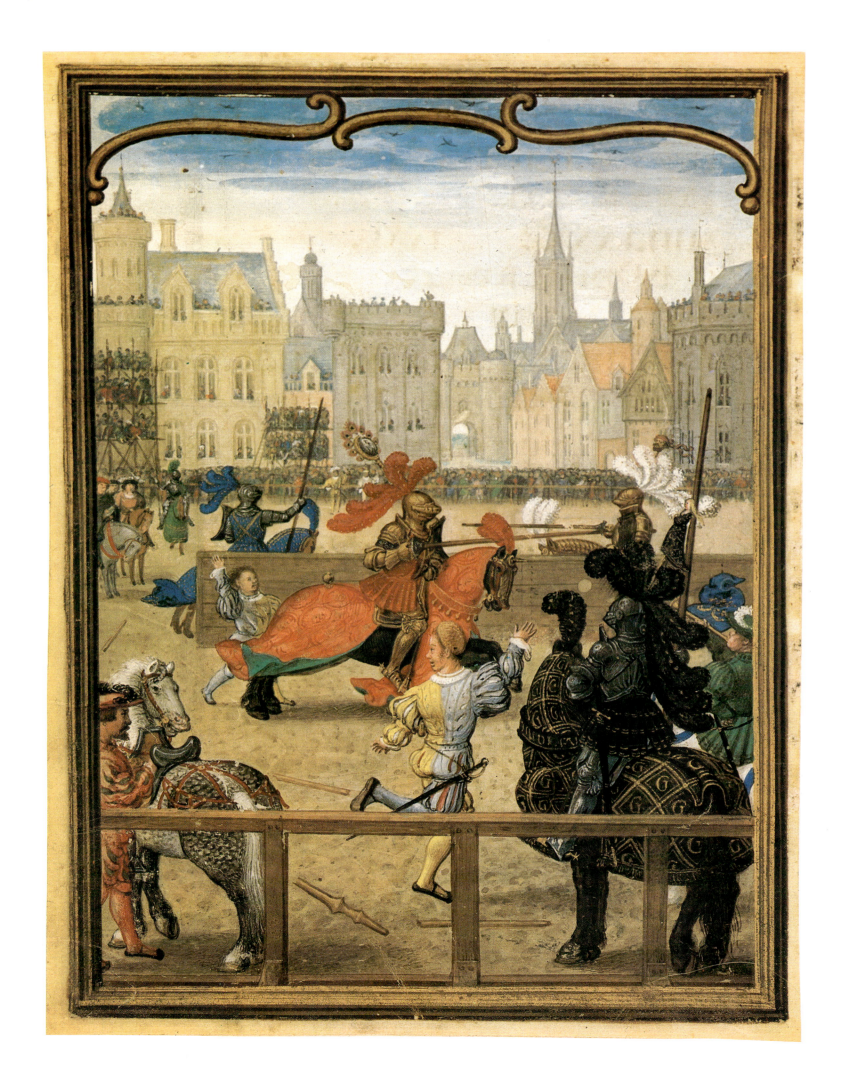

for Philip the Good's 'four-lander' of 1433. The Chancery, Council and Chambers for Finance of Holland and Zeeland remained separate from those of Brabant; Philip the Good respected the difference in regional traditions by allowing legal and financial councils to function at The Hague as well as Brussels.

Until about 1435 the internal organisation of the state was achieved in moderate and easy stages, but after this time institutionalisation became more rapid culminating in the creation in 1473 of central courts and financial administrations covering the whole of the Netherlands. The Netherlands were now at peace with France and the state of war with England, which had never assumed serious proportions, had in point of fact already been resolved in the trade treaty of 1439. The territories of Philip the Good had doubled in a short space of time forming a continuous geographical entity within the Netherlands. It was now time to bring together the various regions into a single institutional unit and to strengthen central power at the expense of local and regional autonomies. The existing government offices systematically extended their control, and new offices came into being. The most important innovation was the formation, between 1435 and 1445, of a Grand Council. This grew, in 1473, into the sedentary Parliament of Mechelen, the purpose of which, as the fully-fledged counterpart to the Parliament of Paris, was to confirm the autonomous and homogeneous status of all principalities of the Netherlands. Charles the Bold already had this in mind during his negotiations with Emperor Frederick III over a

216. Duke Philip the Good grants privileges to the citizens of Ghent. This miniature presumably represents the Duke's clemency during his visit to Ghent in 1458. Five years before, he had imposed various penalties to the city and withdrawn its privileges.

(Vienna, Österreichische Nationalbibliothek. Cod. 2583, fo 13. Miniature from the Master of the Flemish privileges, ca 1454-1467).

217. Portrait of Jacob of Savoy, count of Romont, painted in 1466 when he was sixteen. His older brother Philip was admitted to the Order of the Golden Fleece in 1473. In 1468 Jacob became army commander under Charles the Bold and also served under Maximilian, taking part in the subjugation of Flanders, 1488-1492. Maximilian's daughter Margaret, later governess, was married to Philibert, Duke of Savoy, from 1501 to 1504. The Burgundians and Hapsburgs were keen to maintain good relations with Savoy, the land between their territories and France, Germany and Italy.

(Basle, Öffentliche Kunstsammlung, Depositum der Gottfried Keller-Stiftung. Anonymous Flemish master).

kingship, and despite the failure of the discussions at Trier, he put these plans into effect immediately afterwards.

During the period in which the central government was strengthening its position, it regularly clashed with powers which had hitherto been able to go their own way, particularly the large towns. The Burgundian state system systematically took over functions which had previously been the preserve of the large towns; these were legal and fiscal functions, but the system also encroached – albeit less noticeably – on economic policy and foreign affairs. The dukes could not now avoid conflict with their most important opponents. The uprisings in Bruges (1436-1438), Ghent (1449-1453, 1467), Utrecht (1455/1456), Dinant (1466) and Liège (1465-1468), also gave the dukes an opportunity to assert their supremacy over turbulent towns and to make short work of the power which these towns exercised both within their own walls and over their extensive hinterlands.

From 1473 onwards the Netherlands became once again involved in a virtually uninterrupted series of external conflicts. Even the powerful Duke Charles the Bold was forced to make concessions in that year in order to secure the large subsidies required to finance a standing army. The towns triumphed completely after his death in 1477 and succeeded, at least on paper, in winning back a great deal of power. The war with France entered a critical phase leading to the loss of Artois and considerable damage in the surrounding regions of Hainault and Flanders. In 1482, under pressure from the States General, Maximilian was forced to agree to an unfavourable peace treaty with France.

Mary of Burgundy's untimely death in that year brought about a power struggle which considerably weakened the position of the monarchy, particularly in the duchy itself. During the following year Maximilian found himself obliged temporarily to renounce his claims to the regency of Flanders in order to deal with the uprising at Utrecht. The years of domestic wars which Maximilian waged in Flanders, Brabant and Holland, in order to maintain his authority, left him no opportunity to consider institutional expansion. The period 1473-1492 can be characterised as one in which central power crumbled, not least due to expensive wars at home and abroad.

From about 1492 the domestic situation became more peaceful after the uprisings, and after 1498 relations with France also began to return to normal. The last decade of the fifteenth century was characterised by recovery on all fronts, a return to law and order. This led logically to the reorganisation of the central institutions. In the years that followed, a series of controlling financial institutions were established and in 1504 Philip the Fair set up a supreme court under the name of the Grand Council of Mechelen, which was in fact a continuation of the Parliament of Mechelen abolished in 1477.

Maximilian's appointment as King of the Romans in 1486 had already drawn most of his attention towards German and European politics. His son Philip the Fair, brought up by nobles like Guillaume de Croy-Chièvres and Jan van Bergen and by Frans van Busleyden (a humanist from Mechelen), exercised a policy blatantly orientated towards the Netherlands, even opposing his father's international calculations. However, when in 1500 his wife Joan of Castille became the designated heiress of Spain and its possessions, his persuasions inevitably changed. Joan's brother, who had married Philip's sister Margaret in 1496 when Philip married Joan, had died by this time and his mother Isabella, Queen of Castille, died in 1504.

219. Portrait of Duke Charles the Bold in his twenty-seventh year. In contrast to the panel portraits of his father Philip the Good, of which there were many replicas, there is only one copy of this official portrait of Charles the Bold. Charles was known to be extremely conscientious and a diligent organiser, which led his contemporaries to refer to him as 'Charles le Travaillant'.

(Berlin-Dahlem, Staatliche Museen Preussischer Kulturbesitz, Gemäldegalerie. Copy from ca 1460 of an original attributed to Rogier van der Weyden).

218. Earliest known girlhood portrait of Mary of Burgundy. As the only heir to Charles the Bold she was known as Mary 'the rich'.

(Private collection. Anonymous Flemish master).

Philip's death, two months after he was recognised as king-consort by the Cortes of Castille, delayed the integration of the policies of Spain and the Netherlands, but it was still certain that this would soon come. As governess, Margaret of Austria attempted to compromise between national (which she still saw as 'Burgundian') and dynastic interests. The absorption of the Netherlands into a much larger territorial entity, that of the Hapsburg-Spanish empire, was, however, a reality that could not be ignored. Domestic objectives were increasingly modified in favour of international objectives. In 1521 the southern Netherlands were once again directly involved in a war against France; this war gave Charles V control of Douai, but his subjects had to pay for this by way of taxes which were higher than ever before. The war with Italy drew from the States the remark that they were unable to finance the emperor's conquest of both Spain and Italy.

If the government was still to obtain the necessary funds, it had to grant certain powers to the States. From 1512 the States of Flanders acquired joint authority over finances in return for the subsidies it provided for the war against Guelders. In 1524 the States of Brabant, Holland and Zeeland also followed this example. In 1519 the governess refused the request of the States of Brabant to convene the States General. The emperor had supported her in this: "We desire and ask that you do not agree to a convention of the so-called States General so that there can be neither conspiracy nor bond formed against our great majesty, nor resistance grow against our servants." A separate request for subsidies was made to each of the States; a procedure which was far more time-consuming than it would have been via the States General, as had happened for the first time in 1472 and 1473.

Summarising; the decades between 1490 and 1510 can be characterised by gradual centralisation and extension of state power while, during the two decades which followed, far-reaching concessions were once again made to the regional authorities. The war efforts of the Spanish empire were clearly to blame for this.

THE GROWTH OF BUREAUCRACY   In the late Middle Ages it could no longer be said that all the royal officials were members of the clergy; this ancient tradition was gradually disappearing. Laicisation was completed before the Burgundian period. This does not mean, however, that the dukes no longer had clerics in their employ. Philip the Bold's chief official, the chancellor Jean Canard was also a bishop, as were all those who headed the Grand Council between 1410 and 1483. Clerics were no longer appointed on the strength of their own particular merits; they were primarily agents of the sovereign.

A shift in favour of the nobles and burghers nevertheless took place in the matter of bureaucratic appointments. The weakened economic status of the nobility forced its members to turn to other activities. There were also considerable opportunities for the burghers since the increasing complexity of administration meant that the emphasis lay on educated, technocratic qualifications. However, highly educated clerics and nobles were just as successful as those from the Third Estate who had a university education.

The real primacy of the nobility is illustrated by the fact that the dukes knighted all their chancellors, who were chosen in the first place on the strength of their administrative qualities, immediately after their appointment. This remained, however, an extremely rare and prestigious event. The only exception to this rule was the last cleric to hold this office : Jean de Thois, who already held an honourable title, though his brothers and a cousin were, incidentally, knighted. In general the dukes honoured countless deserving officials, with patents of nobility for the lower classes. More than half of the twenty-seven general stewards were given titles.

The increasing importance of (technical) training of the officers was particularly evident on two fronts : jurisprudence and finance. The introduction of learned, graduate lawyers at state level began in France as well as in the Netherlands about 1300. This was connected to the formation of the modern, centralised state which had everything to gain from the revival of Roman law. This example was soon followed by the cities, and even the smaller towns had already, by the beginning of the Burgundian period, started appointing clerks known as municipal pensionaries. The legal officials in the Netherlands during the fifteenth century came principally from the law faculties of Orleans, Cologne, Bologna and Padua ; from 1425, and increasingly towards the end of the fifteenth century, they also came from the university of Leuven.

In the financial sector too, operations became increasingly sophisticated and inaccessible to non-specialists. Before the Burgundian period, during the first half of the fourteenth century, it became the tradition for the sovereigns to turn to the most astute Italian financiers, who would perform these services as private financiers, free-lance financial experts or sometimes even fully-fledged state officials. The Burgundian dukes continued this tradition. There were financiers, such as the Rapondi family of Lucca, who served the dukes on an occasional basis, but at the same time the dukes were establishing their own network of financial officials with full-time specialists in a perfectly structured hierarchy. This applied to treasurers at all levels ; from the lowliest bailiff who collected fines, to the 'receiver-general of all finances'. The financial experts also called the tune within the supervisory and managerial authorities in all the larger territories of the Burgundian state.

The increasing technocracy in the Burgundian government organisation encouraged a similar development elsewhere – both in the lower echelons of government and in the private sector. The distinct improvement in the standard of auditing in the towns was furthered by the creation of the Burgundian audit offices which demanded high standards of supervision. The transfer of their model to the accounts of the Bruges office of the German Hanse in the fifteenth century was possibly an enforced response to the increase in professionalism.

In spite of specialisation there was nevertheless a strong degree of mobility between the various sectors. In the towns there was a classical path of promotion from the less important positions, such as the treasurer of the poor-relief or assistance-clerk, to the better-paid positions of municipal pensionary or town clerk. A further possibility for the brightest bureaucrats was to move from municipal service to the centralised state services. The career of Simon van Formelis is an example of such success : between 1400 and 1440 he rose from the position of councillor to the duke of Brabant, finally becoming president of the Council Chamber of Flanders. The ability to rise within the hierarchy was undoubtedly a question of talent (such as the 'homo novus' Nicolas Rolin – chancellor to Philip the Good), but also a question of family connections and nepotism. In the Burgundian state, the involvement of competent, top civil servants in day-to-day policy-making also gave

220. Duke Philip the Good, during a session of his Grand Council. On his right his son and sole heir, Charles the Bold and Wauquelin (kneeling) ; on his left Chancellor Nicolas Rolin and Jean Chevrot, head of the Grand Council and Bishop of Tournai. This representation definitely dates from before 1457, when a crisis at the Burgundian court led to Chevrot's dismissal, the repression of Rolin and a conflict between the old duke and his dynamic son.

(Brussels, Royal Library, ms 9243, fo 1. Miniature by Willem Vrelant from the second volume of the *Chroniques de Hainault* by Jacques de Guise, translated by Wauquelin).

them real powers and a considerable say in political decision-making. From mere executives they became ambitious competitors in the political chess-game.

The great geographic, linguistic and psychological diversity within the Burgundian territories made it desirable for the officials in each principality to be trusted within and familiar with that region, and hence, consequently, influential in local politics. The extent to which top officials became 'politicised' can be seen at the end of our period, when the officials split into two groups who either supported or opposed centralisation. Among the 'centralists', some strove for centralism under the auspices of a greater Hapsburg empire, while others chose centralism within the Netherlands. In the sixteenth century professional lawyers were employed to support royal centralism against the career nobles representing traditional regionalism.

The dukes' political successes were largely the work of their competent advisers, in particular their chancellors, including such outstanding examples as Jean Canard under Philip the Bold and Nicolas Rolin under Philip the Good. Chastellain says of Rolin : "Cestui chancelier soloit tout gouverner tout seul". The influence of such officials upon the sovereign should not be underestimated. From the earlier fourteenth century, powerful figures began to criticize the sovereign, and when the latter's character was not among the strongest, they often succeeded in securing a sizeable proportion of political planning for themselves. This seems to be what happened in 1399 when Philip the Bold, during discussions with the Members of Flanders, had to postpone his decision because Chancellor Canard was not present. Philip the Good, however, wanted to be personally involved in decision-making, so that Chancellor Rolin always had to consult his superior before making a decision.

The social prestige of the officials was as high as their politics. They aimed, successfully, for the highest rungs on the social ladder. In this they succeeded as a social group by identifying themselves with and assimilating the lifestyle of the traditional – mostly noble – royal councillors and the royal courts with their typical late-medieval lifestyle ; a marvellous mixture of archaic elements, hankering for the past and the continuance of knightly and military ideals with, at the same time, concern for new social developments such as the modern, centralised state. In order to advertise their 'social success', many of these civil servants tried to gain access to the aristocracy.

The import of foreign technocrats into the Netherlands at the beginning of the Burgundian period was not only part of an attempt to increase the efficiency of the state, but was also a political act by a duke who had since 1384 been bringing confidants from the duchy of Burgundy with him to Flanders. The consequent removal of indigenous Flemish lawyers and councils met with much resentment. Files of complaint of 1405, 1417 and 1477 contain protests against this invasion. Such complaints were also made at the beginning of the sixteenth century when those who supported centralism under the Hapsburgs clashed with those who opposed it.

At the end of the fifteenth century the chronicler Petrus Impens attributed the revolt against Maximilian to his foreign councillors who had no consideration for domestic interests. In 1477, and again in the 1480s, regionalism flared up fiercely. Commynes, albeit a biassed source, records that in 1477 the people of Ghent "avoient en grant hayne les Bourguignons".

Language was also occasionally a bone of contention. Philip the Bold being a French prince, spoke no Dutch and the letters from the town of Ghent to the viscount of Rupelmonde had to be translated into French for the duke. This was hard to accept since during the reign of Philip's father-in-law, Louis de Male, Flemish had flourished as the language that was used in relations between the head of state and his subjects and also in ducal administration. In 1405 the Members of Flanders demanded that cases coming before the central ducal court be conducted in Flemish, as they had been in Louis de Male's time. Despite this, virtually all communication between the duke and his subjects was in French. Philip did, nevertheless, compromise to a certain extent. He employed Master Boudewijn van Niepe to teach his son John Flemish, while Philip himself was taught by Peter Tacquelin. This did not prove a great success, although John the Fearless retained a Flemish motto : "Ic

221. Silver pendant of a shawm player of the City of Ghent, made by the silversmith Cornelis de Bont, with a leather case by Melchior van den Abeele, 1483.

(Ghent, Bijlokemuseum).

houd" – which in its French version, "Je maintiendrai", is ironically still the national motto of the Kingdom of the Netherlands.

The issue remained a sensitive one. The privileges of 1477 stipulated more than once that civil servants should be natives of the Netherlands and must speak the national language. When, in 1482, the Flemings in their revolt against Maximilian actually acquired autonomy for a short while, they immediately restored Flemish as the language of their audit office.

Holland and Zeeland in turn began to appoint administrators who had already proved their loyalty to the Burgundian dynasty. The regional privilege of 1477 also opposed the appointment of alien councillors, whereupon Wolfert van Borselen, Lord of Veere, was appointed stadtholder. Van Borselen's predecessor had been a Fleming, Lodewijk van Gruuthuse, who succeeded Hugues de Lannoy, Guillaume de Lalaing and Jean de Lannoy – all nobles from Hainault. In 1445 Philip appointed three Flemings to the Council of Holland, one of whom – Goswijn de Wilde – even became president, an office which temporarily replaced that of stadtholder at the time. It was to last some decades before the Burgundian dynasty felt sufficiently secure to concede to the demand for native administrators.

PATRONAGE AS A SYSTEM OF GOVERNMENT All the aforementioned groups lent themselves to the same kinds of corruption and 'treason'. The basis of this was the struggle for power and material gain, the latter being greatly encouraged by the relatively low salaries paid to officials. Around 1400, a senior official working in a town received some 400 pounds parisis per year; equivalent to almost 22 shillings per day – more than double the salary of a master bricklayer or master carpenter, who pocketed 10 shillings a day during the summer months. This salary was, it is true, supplemented by allowances for travel costs, official uniforms, premiums for special achievement, and by occasional gratuities and gifts, which were really only bribes from the overlords. But the relatively low salaries also increased the temptation to practise fraud. Duke John the Fearless was twice forced to dismiss his receiver in Burgundy, Joceran Frepier, because of fraudulence: once in 1404 and again in 1413, after a reinstatement. Ducal officials allowed themselves to be bought with gold and precious stones, particularly by the town politicians who wanted to conceal their own malpractices when the town accounts came before the duke's financial inspectorate.

It is no coincidence that of the forty-seven articles contained in the privilege of Flanders in 1477, the first thirteen concern various forms of corruption in the appointment of local magistrates, and that

222. Sea-knight, misericord in St Sulpice's Church at Diest, ca 1480-1490. The chain with the half-moon pendant is an allusion to the fact that the sea-knight was looked upon as a child of the moon during his stay in the water.

a whole series of ducal officials were also reproached. These practices were certainly recognised as an improper abuse of power, but were too widespread to be effectively dealt with. Was it not, after all, the highest in the land who set the example on a grand scale ? In 1435 King Charles VII granted illicit commissions to the value of 60,000 gold saluts to a dozen or so of Philip the Good's most influential councillors in order to secure their co-operation in a peace treaty. Among the recipients were no less than four knights of the Golden Fleece, the chancellor and the duke's receiver-general. Chancellor Rolin and Antoine de Croy (to whom the duke paid the equivalent of the yearly wages of, respectively, fifty-five and sixty-six unskilled workers – namely 275 and 330 Flemish pounds) were also in league with these recipients and each received 10,000 saluts, while the others received somewhat less. This sum was equivalent to five hundred years wages of a trained building worker at Bruges (bricklayer's journeyman, carpenter, plasterer etc.). *Noblesse Oblige.*

Illicit commissions were given by the government municipal officials as well as by the town authorities to government officials. In 1530 shortly before her death, the Governess Margaret of Austria sent a memo to her nephew, the Emperor Charles, in which she advised him to make available more 'benefices' for the governor of the land, who could thereby win more support for his policies. "In the past" she wrote "it has been usual, during negotiations concerning subsidies in the Netherlands – and in Brabant and Flanders in particular – to offer benefices to the children or other relatives of the aldermen of the most important towns". She should know, and records of payment in the audit office's archives show that favours were already being extended to influential local figures at the beginning of the fifteenth century, in return for their support in negotiations concerning taxation.

The municipal authorities in turn approached the duke's officials with proposals, in the hope of gaining some benefit, such as a special tax reduction. The town accounts were full of considerations, gifts, gratuities and courtesies, all of which were intended to win support for and promote goodwill towards the duke and his administration. In the mid-fifteenth century the town of St Omer maintained particularly close relations with the previously mentioned Antoine de Croy, from whom it expected tax concessions, political advice and information, and very often help in defending its privileges against the threat of state centralisation. In return, De Croy could count on loyalty, money and gifts for himself and his protégés, and he could also count on municipal offices for his clients. When Charles the Bold dismissed the De Croy clan in 1465, the role of patron of St Omer was taken over by Anthony of Burgundy, the 'Great Bastard', and thereafter passed to his son Philip, Lord of Beveren. Philip, as governor of the town, was smothered with 'pots de vin', gold and silver, and his wife and lieutenants also enjoyed similar favours.

At Lille the situation was the same. Baudouin de Lannoy was governor there from 1485 and was also the town's patron. The town, however, expanded its network in various directions. At Charles the Bold's Entry in 1468, the town gave four hundred and twenty pounds parisis to the Great Bastard himself, one hundred and five pounds to the chancellor and eighty-four pounds to master Jean Gros, secretary to the duke. Even the chancellor's wife, mistress de Goux, was not forgotten : she was given Lille cloth worth at least one hundred and fifty pounds – at a time when a skilled worker could earn a maximum of sixty-eight pounds per year. Real wine jars were also handed out, often to the chancellor or other officials (some of whom did not want to be named), sometimes simply as commendation, sometimes in return for services rendered. The chancellor's gatekeeper and barber could also make a little on the side in return for aiding access to the chancellor. Again, ducal officials would accept bribes to pass on to friends secret documents bearing the duke's seal. Willem van Naaldwijk, receiver-general of Holland made use of the ducal seal in this way to give the banished participants in the Roterdam uprising permission to return, and also to bestow favours upon other friends. He himself received ten pounds per document for this service. Since the privileges of 1477 contained an article dealing explicitly with the remuneration of those in possession of the ducal seal for the provision of documents, this was by no means an isolated case.

There is no doubt that gifts given from those above to those below, and in all directions, were the cement of the Burgundian state. The universality of this phenomenon cannot be attributed to individual weaknesses; it was a system which had to compensate for the short-comings of the state. The weak and the threatened bought support, not from the institutions themselves, but from those employed there, who consequently built up a position of power around themselves in the form of a clan. As protective patrons placed more of their clients in various key offices, their position became stronger. All in all this system of patronage appears to have been a strong unifying force within the Burgundian state and one which brought about solidarity above the local and provincial level. After 1477, this solidarity was strong enough in Artois and Walloon-Flanders to offer resistance to the French invasion based on a feeling of Burgundian national conscience. Nevertheless, patronage indicates internal weaknesses within the institutions whose

223. Painting by Jan Coessaet of Mechelen, who in 1587 depicted a parliamentary session with its founder Duke Charles the Bold on the throne. Charles never actually attended a parliamentary sitting. To the right of Charles are Chancellor Guillaume Hugonet and the head of the Grand Council, Ferry de Clugny, Bishop of Tournai.

(Mechelen, Town hall).

duty it was to solve the problems using formal procedures. The Burgundian state appeared unable to allow its institutions to function as their objectives required.

The dukes fought in vain against this deeply rooted abuse with repeated decrees – in 1414, 1431, and 1446 and so on. In 1416, and particularly in 1457, government commissions were even set up to investigate the sources of the fortunes of ducal officials. Nevertheless, Burgundian officialdom did contain a firmly inbuilt control mechanism. From 1386, financial supervision was organised by the Chamber for Finance which had been set up at Lille, where strict experts rigourously scrutinised the affairs of all the financial officials in the Burgundian Netherlands ; these experts had at their disposal substantial records in which they could trace all past transactions, and also chancery registers recording all outgoings – a veritable data-bank for the Burgundian state. Moreover, the government commission of 1457 was not ineffectual. The six special investigating magistrates were granted exceptional powers of attorney, had access to special funds and could rely upon the total support of the ducal staff in their efforts to track down all kinds of fraud. Many penalties were dealt out and certain persons even dismissed. These reforms nevertheless turned into a political conflict between Chancellor Rolin's old power group and a triumvirate of his political opponents : Antoine de Croy, Marshal Thibaud of Neuchâtel and Bishop Guillaume Fillastre who were actually all trying to use the commission to unseat the Rolin clan from its position of power. Rolin was consequently put out of the running and his closest aide Chevrot president of the council, was dismissed in favour of Fillastre.

To serve two opposing institutions simultaneously was a more subtle method of pursuing material gain, and was practised frequently and with great cynicism during the fifteenth century. Certain town

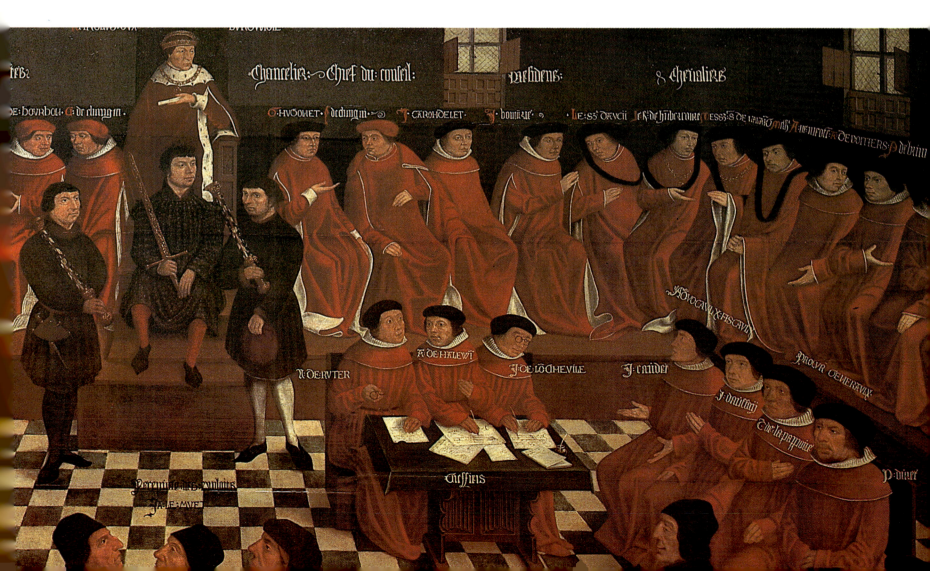

clerks were so loyal to their native towns that they willingly offered themselves as hostages in times of political strife, thereby also losing their fortunes and their lives. Many others, however, played a double game. A veritable 'trahison des clercs' was rampart in the Netherlands. Flemish town clerks performed the most confidential diplomatic services under instruction from and in the interest of their town, while at the same time receiving fees from the ducal coffers for services rendered to the duke – presumably for passing on that same confidential information. There were also double-dealers among those who served the duke himself. During the 1450s the Croy family carried out important duties at the court of Philip the Good but also received gifts and payment from lucrative offices, held in the opposing political camp of Louis XI, the king of France. The Croys had known Louis since he was Dauphin in exile in the Netherlands. The two parties were in league with each other, which greatly angered the chronicle-writer Chastellain, who described the Croy brothers and the Dauphin as : "trois testes en un sac toujours ensemble". Duplicity was certainly recognised for what it was by contemporaries, witness one record : "Croy, on peut mal servir deux maistres à gré." This attitude was nevertheless quite usual. For that matter the dukes were no better. To support the central state they thought it was necessary to have loyal and obedient officials and to strive for docility among their clientèle which transcended the particularism of the provinces. Money, honour, titles and power were their bait.

224. Wars posed a threat to the lives and possessions of all subjects. Soldiers happily drag away all the loot from the town, which they subsequently burn down on their return. The Northern and Southern Netherlands were affected by the Hundred Years War during the first half of the fifteenth century.

(Paris, Bibliothèque Nationale, ms fr. 2644. Miniature from the *Chronique* of Froissart).

225. Diplomats negotiating, from *Traité contre les prétentions des Anglais à la couronne de France – La vraie Chronique d'Ecosse*. As kinsmen – sometimes rivals – of the King of France and rulers of those regions of the Netherlands particularly dependent upon the good trading relations with England, the Dukes of Burgundy were obliged to steer a delicate middle course during the Hundred Years War. Duke Philip the Good resolutely supported the English between 1419 and 1435.

(Brussels, Royal Library, ms 9469-70, fo 1 r°. Miniature by a Flemish master, possibly Willem Vrelant).

THE SCALES TIP On several occasions during the fourteenth century the counts of Flanders were forced to flee their territories when their subjects rose in revolt. They only succeeded in regaining their power with the help of France. As late as 1467 Prince-Bishop Louis of Bourbon fled from Liège and it was the external power of Burgundy which restored order. By contrast Philip the Good and his successors actually used their lands as a means of conquering other territories or keeping them under control. In 1421 Philip requested a subsidy from Flanders for the purchase of Namur and Béthune, and in 1425 for his campaign in Holland. Although this request was denied, Brabant and Flanders still paid their dues in the form of currency devaluations. Philip was able to repress the revolts in Bruges and Ghent since he could rely on other regions for his income, and these territories even supplied him with extra troops and money. Legitimism towards the prince always operated against the insurgents who now saw themselves confronted with an overwhelming supremacy.

Territorial expansion finally tipped the scales of power in the prince's favour. In the first place this was a question of scale: since the mid-fourteenth century the populations of the largest cities in the Netherlands, Ghent and Bruges, were on the decrease. On the other hand, the duke's resources increased considerably. At the same time, the greater diversity of their sources of power offered them greater security. Against the prince's aggrandisement, pockets of frequently envious subjects remained which could be isolated and rendered ineffectual. Communal awareness and community of interests were conspicuous by their absence, though there was an exception in the formal declarations of unity and mutual assistance between the territories of the Netherlands in 1488 and 1509 ; but even these remained platonic. When, in February 1488, a strong delegation from Ghent arrived to decide upon the fate of the imprisoned Maximilian, the citizens of Bruges did not even dare to allow their armed allies within the city walls. Generally speaking, local and regional solidarity remained intact to the advantage of the amused third party, who exploited their mutual disagreements.

The cities were themselves often unable to solve material conflicts by compromise. The weaker party consequently turned to the duke, who welcomed the opportunity to increase his influence. In conflicts

227. Medieval cannons with opening breeches in a fifteenth-century illustration of an event from antiquity; the landing of Alexander the Great in Scythia. The three-masted ship is defended from the large castles and masts with bows and firearms. Duke Charles the Bold was keen to learn about the great war heroes of antiquity and the early Middle Ages.

(Paris, Bibliothèque Nationale, ms fr. 6440, fo 173. Miniature from the *Histoire d'Alexandre* by Vasco de Lucena).

226. Hallucinatory impression of an army retreating from a burning town at night. Detail from the right-hand panel of Hieronymus Bosch's *Garden of Delights*, a striking recreation of the horrors of war. The most dramatic examples were the destruction, on Duke Charles the Bold's order, of Dinant and Liège in 1466 and 1468.

(Madrid, Prado).

Es choses dist le
barbarin. A sen
contre se roy sui
respondi quil vse
roit de seur conseil et de soy eur.
Car il sieuuroit son eur ouquel
il se fioit et se conseil quilz sui
donnoient a scauoir quil ne
feist riens soubdainement. Et
ayant enuoie sesdits legat

mist es bateaulz son ost. Sur
les vraces logea ceulx qui estoiet
conuers de sais et de targes puis
ses fist mettre a genoulx affin
de estre plus seurs contre le trait
des sayettes. Apres lesquelz es
toient ceulx qui trayoient dau
tre habillemens de guerre ad
uironnez de front et a dextre se
de gens tous en armes. Les

228. Duke Charles the Bold began his second siege of Nancy on 22nd October 1476, he died there on 5th January 1497. He had perceived Alsace and Lorraine as the links between his 'lands hither' (the Netherlands) and his 'lands thither' (the Burgundian principalities). Philip the Good and Charles the Bold had also previously attempted to acquire the County of Champagne as an interim territory. Nancy would become the capital of such a great Middle Kingdom, comparable with the ninth century Lothar.

(Nancy, Musée Historique Lorrain. Wood carving from the *Liber Nanceidos*, Saint-Nicholas-de-Pont, 1518).

between large and small towns the duke lent his support to the latter since they counterbalanced the great powers and this also enhanced his status as the supreme jurisdiction. It was not until the latter part of the sixteenth century that the subjects had organisd themselves on a national scale to provide an adequate response to the reinforced powers of the state. The consciousness of large groups develops slowly, which is always an advantage to well organised minority groups.

The various bodies representing the subjects to the ruler developed in two ways. Firstly, the economic interests of the townsmen caused the spontaneous emergence of representative courts in the urbanised regions. It was the largest towns which provided the spokesman on these occasions often representig the country against the monarch or foreign authorities. In fact each participant in such negotiations, represented his own town and it was only against others (the prince, foreign authorities or traders, the noble lords, small towns or the rural areas) that the large towns formed a united block. As a rule they were only concerned with the particular needs of their own town, and this jeopardised the growth of solidarity among the subjects whose monarch was constantly extending his power over other territories.

The second route towards popular representation was via the sovereign's exceptional convocation of the Three Estates (of the clergy, nobility, commoners) of each province. It is remarkable that, apart from Brabant and Hainault where this form of representation had existed since the fourteenth century due to dynastic problems, the first meetings of the Three Estates were held just as the dukes of Burgundy came to power. This was in 1384 in Flanders, at Namur in 1430, and in 1428 in Holland at the Treaty of Delft. French influence definitely played a part in this. These representative meetings took place almost exclusively at the behest of the monarch. They took place with increasing frequency during the fifteenth and sixteenth centuries – possibly to counterbalance the

229. *L'accident.* A poem written by the chronicler Olivier de la Marche shortly after the Burgundian wars of Charles the Bold, relates the story of an idealised Burgundian knight who has to do battle with a rough Swiss soldier whose strength is almost bestial and who knows nothing of the real art of war. In 1476 the troops of Charles the Bold were soundly defeated twice by the Swiss infantries, despite the fact that the former carried the most modern arms.

(Olivier de la Marche, *Le Chevalier Délibéré*, late fifteenth century).

230. Illustrations of the Battle of Grandson in 1476, in which the best equipped army of its time was defeated by the Swiss militia. Charles the Bold in gilded armour, took an active part in the battle.

(Lucerne, Zentralbibliothek. *Amtlicher Luzerner Chronik* (1513), fo 99 v° and 100 r° by Diebold II Schilling).

autonomous assemblies of the large towns but they were seldom able to exercise a permanent influence on the government.

On both sides – the urban league and the meetings of the States – intermediary organisations grew up between the seigniories of the dukes of Burgundy. Towns of Holland-Zeeland, Brabant and Flanders, and sometimes also Hainault, met to discuss typical economic issues such as monetary problems, textile trade and fishing. The dukes also summoned the States of the various provinces to discuss their common interests. Thus, in 1437, representatives of the States of Brabant, Flanders, Hainault, Holland, Zeeland, Namur and Mechelen met to discuss monetary problems at the behest and in the presence of the duke's councillors. All the 'landen van herwaarts over' (the territories on this side) were thus united, as they were able to be at this level on four further occasions before 1464. This procedure gradually became a matter of course and from 1472 to 1523 the majority of requests for subsidies were made at such gatherings. In 1464, as a result of a dispute with his son about the succession, Philip the Good convened a solemn meeting at Bruges of what was to be known in the sixteenth century as the States-General of the Netherlands. There had never been any effective co-operation with the States meetings in the duchy of Burgundy, which again goes to show the separate identities in the traditional complexity of the Netherlands. During the constitutional crises of 1477 and 1488 the States-General played an important part in the confrontation between the sovereign and *all* his subjects in the Netherlands, although it was then especially obvious that the particularism of the large towns and their regions was much stronger than the sense of common identity. In fact it was not until the revolt

271

against Philip II that opposition grew on a truly national scale in the Netherlands. The fact that this was lacking at an earlier stage meant that centralisation of power could be far more easily maintained.

THE MONARCH'S MILITARY ADVANTAGE   The citizen militia which had made a great impression on the battlefields between 1302 and 1383 had become, tactically speaking, worthless by the fifteenth century. Their lack of discipline made them more of a hindrance than a help in the ducal campaigns of 1411 and 1436. Also, technical improvements in weaponry and strategy meant that a degree of training and discipline was indispensable to the troops.

For this reason, the towns seemed far less able than the monarch to make efficient use of firearms ; most of the fighting men from the towns were mere artisans dressed up for battle, whose heightened political awareness ill suited them for discipline and obedience. The town walls, built to withstand battering rams, were shot to pieces by the artillery, which developed rapidly during the fifteenth century, but was, however, as yet unsuitable for employment on the battlefield. The firearms of this period were still large, unwieldy and immobile and it was thus the besieger who derived the benefit from their use. Charles the Bold proved as much at Dinant in 1466. However, in 1476 by contrast, he was made to realise what little use artillery was against the well-trained Swiss infantry.

231. Swiss soldiers celebrate their victory with Burgundian soldiers' girls. Drawing from the *Amtlicher Berner Chronik*, vol. III (1483) by Diebold I Schilling who, being Swiss, witnessed the battles against the Burgundians at Grandson and Murten in 1476.

(Berne, Bürgerbibliothek, Ms Hist. Helvetiae 1, 3).

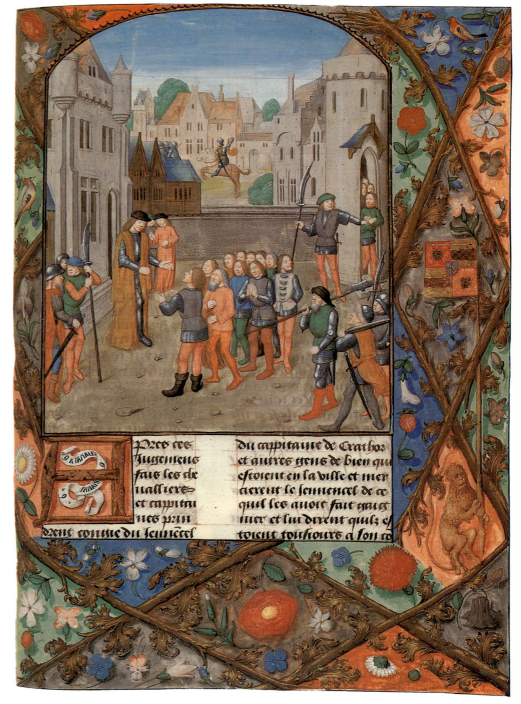

In dealing with a rebellious town, the dukes would exploit its political isolation, maintaining an economic blockade to starve it out. While access routes were cut off, troops plundered the surrounding countryside, which had to supply their provisioning. The most important weapons at the disposal of the townspeople, their overwhelming numbers and their fanatical fighting spirit, no longer appeared adequate in the fifteenth century. The sovereigns were still then able to mobilise thousands of fighting men due to the rise of the professional soldier. Charles the Bold recruited entire companies from Italy, England (particularly archers) and Germany. Motivation on the side of the towns weakened, as the reason for fighting became less clear to them; it was, after all no longer a question of defending the independence of the fatherland. The division, even among the guilds between those supporting the status quo and those stubbornly clinging to their urban autonomy also scarcely contributed to good morale.

Even in the traditional fighting techniques of their armies of foot-soldiers which had taken the world aback in 1302, the townsmen lost out to the professional monarchic armies. In 1471 Charles the Bold established a standing army, composed of 5,000 volunteers. By 1473 their number had increased to 8,400, half of this number were mounted archers and heavily armoured soldiers : among the infantry the 'pikemen' were the largest group, armed with lances several metres long. Considerable training was required in the use of these corps, but they were extremely effective. When they advanced as a broad phalanx, in closed formation, no cavalry could stand up to them. The undisciplined town militias with their short staves were a complete write-off when they became involved with a modern army in an ordered battle. Bloodbaths like the one at Gavere in 1453 were mainly due to this although here there was also characteristically panic in the ranks of the Ghent army when one of their gunners let a spark ignite a sack of gunpowder.

MORE MONEY The establishment of a standing army greatly increased the tax burden, so that Flanders' annual taxation from 1472 to 1482 was three times greater than in the preceding fifteen years. It is true that this army was not intended only for use abroad, but was equally available against domestic insurgence. It was undoubtedly a tangible enhancement of the monarch's power.

Naturally, the expansion of the civil service and of a less formal network of clients, also made great demands upon the state budget. This entire apparatus in its turn improved the efficiency of tax enforcement. There was nevertheless something amiss in the civil service since corruption took place on a large scale. These civil servants consequently became less effective – at the expense of the common people, who, after all, paid their salaries *and* extra allowances, but still, with all this, had no real legal security.

The maintenance of an extensive army and body of civil servants was seemingly beyond the means of the state, since the payment of salaries was repeatedly suspended. The widespread mortgaging, leasing and sale of government offices points to the same problem. Employers were seemingly so hard up for means of payment that they would relinquish a large part of their revenues in exchange for an immediately available 'lump sum'. A system in which the state, in the longer term only received a fraction of the revenues paid by its subjects meant that a group of civil servants increased their wealth at the expense of the state as well as its subjects. A second effect of corruption in government offices is no less serious : it was not the most competent who were in office, but those willing to pay the most for the privilege – a downward spiral which also encouraged nepotism. An alderman of Eekloo thus complained in 1425 that "the bailiff is so incompetent that he is not familiar with the laws, privileges and decrees of the town, and never will be, and he is thus even unable to pass sound judgement on the facts brought before him".

Around 1400 the practice of leasing was widespread, particularly the leasing of lower offices such as receiver of the ducal domain, and also occasionally of other offices. Where legal offices were concerned, it was customary for a large sum of money to be lent to the duke when the appointment was made. From 1440, Philip the Good introduced the system of leasing for these functions, after which time

233. Tapestry illustrating the Royal Entry of Duke Philip the Fair into Brabant in 1494. On this occasion he had to swear allegiance to the 'Blijde Incomst' of Brabant which omitted a number of concessions which his mother had been forced to grant in 1477.

(Amsterdam, Rijksmuseum. Early sixteenth-century tapestry from a Brussels workshop).

the practice spread like wildfire. The government's reasoning was that the leasing of offices raised more revenue than straightforward appointments. Around the middle of the century the duke's revenues from legal offices amounted to only one fifth of the sums raised around 1400. The real explanation for this decrease is embezzlement by civil servants. Searches reveal that legal officers received more income than they declared in their accounts, and once again, the corruption was so widespread that it could not be brought under control. The great inquiry into financial misappropriations among civil servants in 1457 was abruptly brought to a halt when both the States of Brabant and the States of Flanders offered the duke a subsidy to terminate the investigation. The local authorities were apparently willing to go to considerable lengths to avoid having their coffers inspected too closely.

The bailiff of Ypres from 1420 to 1441 whose large-scale misappropriations were discovered, justifiably defended himself by claiming that he was forced to go into debt in order to raise the sum required to buy himself into office, and he therefore had to recoup his losses while in office. It is obvious that the whole administrative apparatus lacked the constraints necessary for imposing proper working methods. The system continued to deteriorate : leasing became commonplace in all areas and was extended to almost every legal office ; by 1495 only the four highest offices in Flanders had been spared. It was in this year that Philip the Fair decreed that all legal offices in Hainault and Namur should be leased out.

Despite the fact that the tax burden on the populace increased with each passing decade, the revenue accruing to the state was certainly not proportional to these increases. Is it not surprising that the most powerful western empire found it so difficult to force Guelders to submit to its authority ? Every government, and that of the young Charles V most of all, regularly found itself in dire financial straits whenever it launched a military campaign. On various occasions operations had to be interrupted at a crucial point due to a shortage of money. The suppression of domestic revolts sometimes took years. The revenues from the ducal domain, comprising his lands, tolls, and income from fines, rents and the like amounted to the equivalent of 150,000 pounds parisis for the county of Flanders in 1443. The grants paid by the subjects, which the government had to negotiate each year at the States assemblies, brought in some 127,000 pounds per year. Thus almost half of the revenue accruing to the duke was controlled by the subjects. When certain aspects of his policy did not meet with their approval, they resolutely denied their further grants. They were particularly reticent when the money was intended for military campaigns abroad.

It is easy to understand why the dukes attempted to increase the revenues from their domains, since these came in regularly and did not create any political problems. The towns were against this, partly because new tolls could possibly be detrimental to trade but largely because the automatic way in which they would be collected would virtually eliminate the towns' political influence. Other European rulers derived the majority of their incomes from indirect taxes : wool-export in England, salt tax in France and customs duties in Genoa. Philip the Good first tried this at Gravelines, with a toll on all wool imported from the English outpost of Calais. The Members of Flanders opposed this so strongly that they offered an even larger subsidy in return for the abolition of this toll (1440). The subsidy flowed into the state coffers, but the toll was not abolished until 1477. In 1447 Philip wanted to introduce a tax on the sale of salt – an indispensable preservative – throughout the Netherlands. The opposition from Ghent and the other Members of Flanders forced him to relinquish his plans but this incident gave rise to the great conflict between the duke and the powerful town on the Lys. The Great Privileges of 1477, moreover, dealt at length with the opposition to the various levies which had also been introduced by Charles the Bold without the approval of the people's representatives.

The government consequently still found it necessary to approach the representative bodies with 'aids'. Between 1472 and 1523 the States-General was the institution to approach, but after this time the government was too afraid of mass opposition, while hoping to

234. Coin commemorating the marriage of Maximilian of Austria and Duchess Mary of Burgundy, designed by the Italian artist Candida.

(Brussels, Royal Library, Coin Collection).

235. Bust portrait of Emperor Maximilian of Austria, heralded on his marriage to Mary of Burgundy in 1477 as the saviour of the Burgundian territories. After some years, however, there were mounting conflicts with his subjects.

(Vienna, Kunsthistorisches Museum, Gemäldesammlung. Attributed to Bernard Striegel, ca 1510).

236. Portrait of Duchess Mary of Burgundy, alluding to her favourite pastime, falconry. Her death resulting from such a hunt made a deep impression on her contemporaries.

(Gaasbeek, Kasteelmuseum. Anonymous Flemish master, ca 1520).

gain more by negotiating separately with the various provincial States. This process was, however, very time-consuming and involved many political concessions and constant individual favours for the most influential negotiating partners. Of course humbler mortals soon cottoned on too to the way business was done. The town administrators, 'les mengeurs des bonnes villes' as Charles the Bold plainly referred to them, were consequently called to account during every people's revolt and dozens of them were subjected to the ultimate sanction of kangaroo courts.

A GIANT WITH CLAY FEET? Finally, in summarizing the strengths and weaknesses of the Burgundian state, we shall consider whether throughout its one and a half centuries it acquired, according to the criteria of the time, a solid structure. First the weaknesses. The Achilles tendon of the Burgundian state was without doubt the corruption which, in various forms, became the normal method of government at all levels. As a result, the state was unable to achieve many of its established objectives and lost internal credibility. A further consequence was that, although the populace was crippled by ever-increasing taxes, the state repeatedly suffered acute shortages and thus failed to meet external obligations as well as its obligations to its own servants. The senior peers and officials increasingly financed the execution of their plans themselves. The regions were

277

never completely integrated and the resistance to 'alien' administrators (from outside the region) was legion. The large cities in particular, which tended to dominate an entire region, greatly hindered the penetration of Burgundian central authority. There were daily clashes between the courts of law which questioned each others' powers, and between the representative bodies which would not yield an inch to governmental institutions. From time to time, however, these conflicts led to larger or smaller uprisings which the rulers often found difficult to suppress. Once things had got thus far demonstrative reprisals were taken against the cities who were in any case roughly treated in their political, legal and economic privileges. It remains to be seen whether the smaller towns and rural areas proved to be better off under the centralizing bureaucrats than they had been under the cities.

Immediately after the unification of the key areas of the Netherlands, several decrees on legislation were issued, which were enforceable in all the regions. In 1433 this concerned the introduction of a new, common currency, and in 1434 the regulation of the international cloth trade. These measures were discussed at the emergent consultations between the representative bodies of the regions. Nevertheless central legislation remained limited during the following decades, and only concerned international trade, coinage and public order. The majority of legislation continued to be introduced at the level of the separate principalities, even on major issues. Thus, in 1459 and 1461 separate but analogous decrees were issued in Brabant, Flanders and Holland concerning public order and poor-relief, but it was impossible to come to a general agreement on the grain trade. The central government thus showed little initiative in arriving at general legislation for the Netherlands. The particular rights of the regions and towns still offered stubborn resistance. The county of Hainault, for example, where local common law was rationalised and sanctioned by the sovereign in 1484, remained an exception. This co-ordination did not take place in the other provinces until after 1530, and was still strongly resisted.

The dynasty was strong until 1477, and thereafter weakened. Dynastic convergence, which, from a personal union of several principalities, led to a world empire, was an essential factor in the extension of the monarchy in the Netherlands. Equally certain is the fact that the Burgundians benefited from the dynastic good fortune that each successor appeared to be sufficiently capable of more or less carrying out the tasks of government – including procreation. France and Spain, whose kings were of a weak constitution or died at an early age, could not count themselves so lucky. Nevertheless we must not forget that Philip the Good and Charles the Bold both played a dangerous game, since both brought only one heir into the world, although their talents in this field were proven beyond doubt.

After Mary of Burgundy's succession, there was an almost constant stream of circumstances less favourable to sovereignty. Mary was young, inexperienced and not very active. Her spouse Maximilian did not adapt himself well to his new circumstances. Mary's premature death caused a thorny problem where the regency was concerned, which arose again after the premature death of her son in 1506. Absence in Spain was the problem from 1500 onwards, since the king still wanted to have a say in northern affairs.

That brings us to the remaining strengths of the Burgundian state. One essential factor is that the territories of the Netherlands did not assume a passive role in the unification under the duke, for

237. Portrait of Duke Philip the Fair, at approximately twenty-two years of age, when his son was born, Charles of Luxembourg, later Emperor Charles V.

(Amsterdam, Rijksmuseum. Anonymous master, ca 1500-1503).

278

238. Bust of the future Emperor Charles V during his youth. This bust, which expresses Charles' physiognomy particularly well, is one of the best portraits of him as a young man. Like his father he was declared of age when he was fifteen, and was charged with the government of the Netherlands.

(Bruges, Gruuthusemuseum. Terracotta and wood, polychrome; height 51 cm, ca 1515-1520, by Konrad Meyt).

they had developed dynastic, economic and cultural links long before this unification took place. The wealth of the Netherlands, which was remarkable by European standards, was without doubt the foundation of Burgundian power. There were various means towards integration : the successful creation of a myth around the person of the duke was a means of propaganda whereby sentimental links were forged between the state and the various sections of the population. Another means of integration was the creation of an extensive system of patronage which linked the influential persons of different standing in all the territories to the person of the duke or, by delegation, to his favourites. This relationship based on trust, mutual help and support, given substantial remuneration, could be described as quasi-feudal, particularly since traditional chivalry was revived at the Burgundian court. The stability of the regime was furthered by the practice of dukes negotiating, regularly, willingly or unwillingly, with representative bodies. In this way the complaints and problems of the people – or at least their spokesmen – quickly reached the government which, in co-operation with the local governments, could find an acceptable solution. States

Assemblies were held several times each year, with representatives from the clergy, the nobility and the towns (and also, in Flanders, from the rural districts), usually in the presence of top government officials, if not of the duke or members of his family. In the urban regions, several times each year, the large towns assembled to discuss all aspects of policy with each other, with the government and with foreign governments and representative bodies. On such occasions, however superficial this may have been as far as the government was concerned, information was exchanged which enhanced the prestige of authority.

Last but not least, the power of the Burgundian state developed thanks to the deeply-rooted particularism of its subjects. This apparent contradiction is easily explained. Since there was not a single trade guild, town or territory which would grant its neighbours the smallest concession, the government could strengthen its own position as mediator and arbitrator when conflicts arose, thereby also supporting the weaker party and ousting the stronger. The legal apparatus, a learned system soundly based on Roman law, together with the army, both supplied the force necessary to break the strongest resistance.

In 1530 the 'Burgundian' state in the Netherlands was far from centralised. The hesitant progress of the reforms, and the succession of precipitous innovation followed by retraction (before and after 1477) account for the eventually deeply-rooted stability of the regime. The regime weathered the shock of 1477, not without making readjustments but without any fundamental challenge to the Burgundian state, which had taken root so deeply that even the loss of the Burgundian homeland did not alter the situation.

239. Charles the Bold surprises a miniaturist or calligrapher in his workshop. This is clearly a tribute to the Duke's patronage.

(Brussels, Royal Library, Ms 8 fo 7. Miniature by Loyset Liedet from the *Histoire de Charles Martel*, 1470).

6

Burgundian Culture

A Hive of creativity

ART FOR EUROPE   The artistic production in the Netherlands during the Burgundian period undoubtedly reverberated throughout the rest of Europe.   The painters and sculptors gave such original expression to the spirit of the age in their work, which was so universally accessible, that it was admired, extolled and sold throughout Europe, from Iceland and Estonia to southern Italy and Portugal.   It was an art which was respected and diligently reproduced by artists elsewhere in Europe.

From about the second quarter of the fifteenth century, a wealth of creative talent converged on one or two centres, mostly situated in or around Flanders (Bruges, Ghent, Tournai) and in Brabant (Brussels, Leuven).   This would certainly not have happened, or not to the same extent, had there not been a sound cultural environment and strong interest in the arts in these areas.   There was a sense of the monumental and of form in the tombs and sculptures – work on St Gudule's at Brussels and St Rombaut's at Mechelen had begun as early as the first half of the thirteenth century – and the sturdy warriors on the bell tower of Ghent date from the fourteenth century.   Long before 1420 the Flemish rulers, burghers and clerics resided in palaces, hospitals and houses adorned with colourful frescoes such as those which have been preserved in the Bijloke refectory in Ghent and St Brice in Tournai. Hubert and Jan van Eyck would possibly never have come to Flanders if Melchior Broederlam had not been active there before them, and had it not been necessary to adorn the beautiful but rather sparse St John's church in Ghent with something like the *Adoration of the Lamb* retable.   It is of course no coincidence that artistic circles should flock to Bruges, Brussels, Flanders and Brabant. In the fourteenth century, long before Holland, these were among the most highly urbanised, highly industrialised and most commercially active parts of Europe. Bruges was a world market and centre of international banking.   There there was money, a demand for good investments, social prestige and vanity, so that the burghers and foreign merchants at Bruges rivaled one another in the ownership of *objets d'art*.   The presence of the Burgundian dynasty was also a stimulating factor ; it gave a European dimension to the Netherlands on a political level since the dukes were closely acquainted with all the great political figures of their time.   Thus Philip the Good presented King Alfonso of Aragon with a world map, produced by the court painter Jan van Eyck.   The dukes fostered contacts with the kings of France, England and Portugal and also with the popes and the German emperors. This international dimension was beneficial to centres such as Dijon and Beaune, but in particular also the towns of the Netherlands. It is even less of a coincidence that the so-called 'Flemish School' flourished during the second and third quarters of the fifteenth century, just at a time which is recognised, according to many indicators, as the economic boom of 1440-1470.   The doubling of the volume of trade in the Netherlands between 1400 and 1475 naturally had positive repercussions in the artistic sector, since financial reserves were released for investment.   For dukes and businessmen, art was a fitting society or business gift.   The production of works of art was

240. View of town and countryside. Detail from the central panel of the Columba altarpiece, the *Homage of the Kings,* attributed to Rogier van der Weyden.

(Munich, Alte Pinakothek).

a luxury industry comparable to the luxury textile industries of Ypres, Ghent and Leiden. The tableaux from Brabant were real merchandise and the works of Memlinc were already distributed over a large part of Europe in the fifteenth century.

Although the painters, musicians and poets of the Netherlands each had their own individual style, and there were distinct regional contrasts between the schools of Bruges, Leuven and Tournai, 'Flemish Art' from van Eyck to Bosch had a certain unity and homogeneity whose elements will be criticised in more detail.

And in spite of the European response to this 'Flemish Art', it nevertheless retained a form and content which was manifestly associated with the Netherlands. The clearly recognisable Flemish and Brabantine church towers and townscapes which form the back-ground of many of the paintings were undoubtedly intended to forge a link, for those commissioning the works, between the panel itself on the one hand and on the other the parish, the actual church building where it was to hang and the person of the donor.

PAINTING : INTERNATIONAL GOTHIC IN THE SHADOW OF FRANCE Until around 1350, painting in the Netherlands was overshadowed by artistic achievements abroad, principally in France. In the second half of the fourteenth century, however, the tide turned. Painters such as Melchior Broederlam, André Beauneveu, Jan Maelwael and Hennequin of Bruges were names to conjure with and enjoyed such international fame that many of them received commissions from the French king, the Count of Flanders, the dukes of Burgundy and the Duke of Berry. Stylistically, they followed the then international gothic movement, which placed emphasis on gently flowing lines ; the movement created a furore in Germany, where it was known as the 'weicher Stil'. But we cannot deny the individual

personality of these painters in the Netherlands. The 'weicher Stil' had its counterpart in sculpture particularly, but also pictorially in the very realistic, graphically accurate and far from pallid rendering of bodies and garments. They also brought their own emotion and pathos to human suffering. In many respects, therefore, they broke away from their models.

With an eye to their patronage, they were, however, most strongly oriented towards their French contemporaries. This also explains Beauneveu's and Broederlam's easy conquest of Philip the Bold, the Burgundian duke with French leanings. Hence the three brothers Maelwael, called Van Limburg, were likewise welcomed by his nephew, the duke of Berry. Around 1400, then, Flemish painting was flourishing – albeit in the shadow of France – although its successes were achieved essentially outside the Netherlands, probably under French impulse. The ars nova of Van Eyck was a complete innovation, quite distinct from that of about 1400 and with different characteristics. The earlier painters' naturalism and the exuberance with which they depicted commonplace details were the only characteristics shared by Van Eyck. It was in the miniatures of the brothers Van Limburg themselves that we find the first Van Eyck landscapes. The Ars Nova takes wing.

A much more profound and original revival was accomplished by the Van Eycks, Van der Weyden, and many others. At the time there were attempts to link this 'ars nova' to technical innovations, such as Van Eyck's introduction of oil-paints to replace the earlier frescoes and tempera works (*i.e.* water-colour with eggwhite and lime on wood surfaces). In actual fact, Broederlam was already using oil-paints in 1395 and the technique is certainly older still. The Van Eyck brothers were, however, responsible for advancing the technique. But we do not need these details to recognise that a profound change was taking place between 1420 and 1430. Despite the

241. The so-called *Calvary of the curriers* with St Catherine and St Barbara.

(Bruges, St Saviour's Cathedral. Anonymous Bruges master, ca 1390-1400).

284

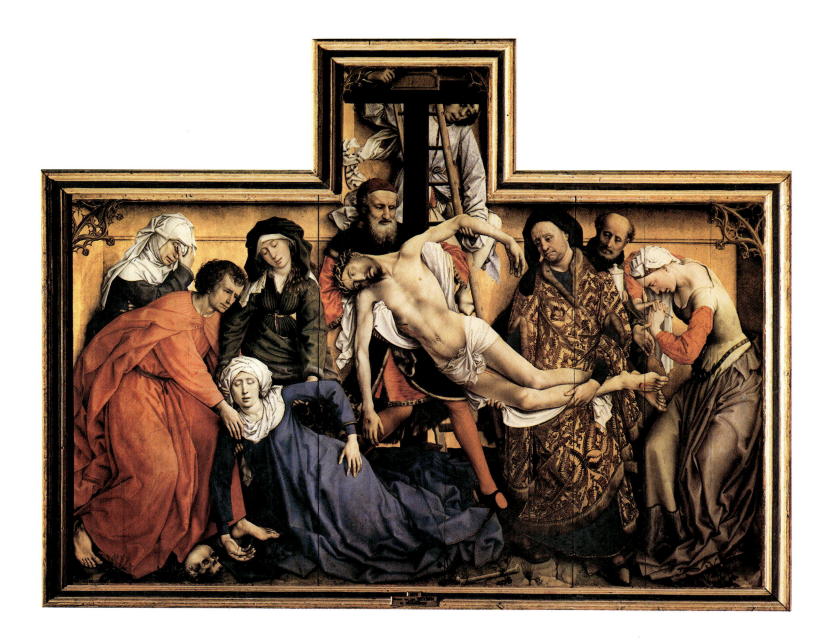

242. The *Deposition from the cross*, attributed to Rogier van der Weyden, 1435. The powers of expression, composition and colouring in this painting make it one of the high points of the Flemish primitives.

(Madrid, Prado).

collective name of the 'Flemish Primitives' – which is in any case a somewhat inadequate label – various schools can be distinguished within the group (Bruges, Tournai, etc.) which were associated with local traditions but differed above all in both their styles and their objectives. The lines branch out from a naturalistic representation with a strongly emphasised underlying symbolism (Van Eyck) to the expression of deeper, mainly religious feelings and the expression of the individual's specific character (Van der Weyden) and its ascetic and meditative facets (Bouts, Van der Goes), and finally to the representation of the fantastic and the visionary (Bosch). This third approach is to a certain extent a synthesis of the previous approaches, since it seeks out the international man via the realism and symbolism of Van Eyck, but also via Van der Weyden's character analysis. In other words we find, simultaneously or in succession, perfect observers (Van Eyck), rational architects of religious compositions and analysts of character (Van der Weyden) to passionate analysts of what lies under the surface (Van der Goes) and engaged observers of the human condition (Bosch) whereby one artist stands in the midst of day-to-day realities and reproduces them as clearly as possible, while another penetrates the underlying and subjective realities.

243. *The Birth of Christ* by Geertgen tot Sint-Jans, (ca 1490).

(London, National Gallery).

MASTERPIECES The *Adoration of the Lamb* of 1432 by the Van Eycks was a singularly moving example of the naturalism mentioned above. After the death of Hubert (1426), whose role and worth should not be underestimated, Jan completed the retable and ably carried the style further until he died in 1441. What so overwhelms both ourselves and their contemporary, Facius, historiographer to the king of Aragon around 1450, is the remarkably realistic rendering of, on the one hand, the figures, and, on the other, the faithful depiction of objects, interiors and landscapes. The realism on each of these levels, however, varies greatly.

The representation of people was achieved with such photographic precision that, on the basis of his work, our own medical specialists can diagnose skin disorders in those portrayed (*e.g.* Canon van der Paele), and for this reason one of them even christened Van Eyck with the somewhat pompous epithet of dermatologist. Many buildings were also realistically depicted : the background of the

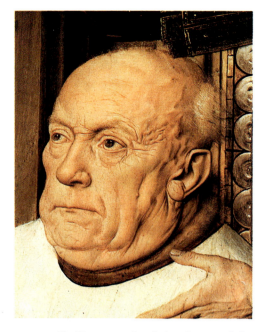

244. Life-like portrait of the donor of the painting, canon Joris van der Paele, by Jan van Eyck, to mark the foundation of a chaplaincy at the Church of St Donatus in Bruges.

(Bruges, Gruuthusemusem. Detail from the *Madonna and canon Joris van der Paele*, 1436).

245. *The Last Judgment,* early copy of an original by Hieronymus Bosch. Bosch is one of the most outstanding early Dutch painters. He created a totally original, fantastic world of forms, thereby producing a high pictorial quality and constantly captivating the viewer with his remarkable creations.

(Munich, Alte Pinakothek).

Adoration of the Lamb gives us a fine insight into fifteenth century interiors, buildings, streets and market places ; but it is difficult to link them with monuments preserved today.

Finally, the landscape is not a true representation of an actual site, although it is composed of realistic elements. In the central panel of the *Adoration of the Lamb* a new ficticious composition is introduced in which most of the people and objects depicted have a deeper symbolic meaning. The seemingly real meadow is a reference to what Van Eyck believes to be a heavenly reality. At first sight, the *Adoration of the Lamb* is simply an impressive representation of the All Saints Day liturgy, but the fact that all the Saints with the name John were placed in the foreground, and this in the church of the Ghent parish of St John, in a town whose patron saint was John, is an emphatic allusion which must have appealed strongly to contemporaries in Ghent. The appearence of St Joseph – with the same name as the patron, Joos Vijd – was also allegorical. But the retable contains much more symbolism. It is no coincidence that the Mystic Lamb assumes such a central position in this panel which was completed in 1432 ; the Lamb of God is, after all, the symbol of Christ but it is also perfectly applicable to the Order of the Golden Fleece, established by Philip the Good in 1430 ; the symbol of the order was a golden ram's fleece and alludes to the legend of Jason, but has little to do with christianity. Were the people of Ghent looking to flatter Philip the Good with this allusion ? Moreover, when he held an Entry in Ghent in 1458, the Duke was received with a three-storey scaffold containing a tableau vivant of the Lamb of God, with Christ on his throne at the top.

Many other paintings by Van Eyck are distinguished by similar symbolic allusions. In the portrait of Arnolfini (possibly Michele) and his spouse, the realistic details (an apple on the window-sill) must not blind us to the fact that the scene is loaded with symbolism and allusions to the morganatic nature of Arnolfini's marriage. This is

subtly achieved : Jan van Eyck has depicted himself as one of the witnesses at the ceremony, albeit through the small mirror on the wall.

Van Eyck's landscapes were also revolutionary by comparison with what went before. In these landscapes, space is suggested atmospherically through the workings of light and shadow, and is so subtle that even the play of the wind in the foliage seems real to the viewer. This new vision of plein-airisme even induced Van Eyck to paint panels in which the landscape featured very strongly, one example being Falconry.

Rogier van der Weyden (c. 1399-1464) used a completely different approach which also distinguishes the Tournai school including Robert Campin, Rogier's teacher, who was supposedly responsible for some of the works attributed to the so-called Master of Flémalle. The *Last Judgement* from the Hôtel-Dieu, Beaune, which can with reasonable certainty be attributed to Roger, shows the salient features of the school – masterly composition. The central figure of Christ as judge, next to the chosen few and the doomed, the depiction of hell and paradise, remained a classic composition after Rogier's time which many other painters – among them Memlinc and even Bosch – imitated whenever they depicted this theme. Another departure from the naturalists such as the Van Eycks is his much more intense and emotional use of Christian iconography, so that figures are approached more from within, thus achieving a portrayal of their actual personalities. In this internalisation he introduced yet another trend.

In the second generation, dating from the latter half of the fifteenth century, the problem of space was dealt with rather differently. Both Hugo Van der Goes (d. 1482) from Ghent, and Dirk Bouts (1415/20-1475), a Haarlemmer active in Leuven, in respectively the *Birth of Christ* (1476) and the *Last Supper* (1464-1467), struggled with the van Eyck tradition of suggesting space by shadowing and with Van der Weyden's sharp delineation, by experimenting with new lighting effects, and especially with a better logical integration of people, buildings and landscapes. While Bouts' appeal lies in his dreamlike facial features, Van der Goes holds our attention with his striking depiction of the moods of his figures. This psychologist, himself tormented by fits of depression, probed much more deeply into the psyche, where there was room for asceticism and religious depth – but also for panic and rational doubt.

Hieronymus Bosch (c. 1450-1516) probed deeper still, though he started out from the traditional form. His *Last Judgement* had the same tryptich form as Van der Weyden's. His landscapes can be as real as Van Eyck's. But he does not stop there. Bosch fills the space between these real elements with strange creatures. Peculiar animals climb out of a cliff as if from a haunted castle. The most surprising combinations of commonplace things take on hallucinatory form, just as they would in the mind of a child. There is a constant fusion of reality with the unreality of dreams. It has been pointed out, and rightly so, that Bosch was not the gadabout heretic which he was once made out to be, but that his roots were firmly in the Christian environment of the Illustrious Fraternity of Our Lady at 's Hertogenbosch, of which he was a member and for whom he worked. Countless details can be traced back to biblical texts. His work, in many respects, also represents well-known folk tales, which were critical of society but had been commonplace for some time. Bosch's work was partly a contemporary record of the folklore of his day. But there is more to him than that. He also used themes

246. *Portrait of a young woman,* attributed to Rogier van der Weyden.

(Washington, National Gallery of Art, Andrew W. Mellon Collection).

250. *Woman kneeling.* Ink on drawing paper, from the school of Hugo van der Goes in Ghent, ca 1490-1500.

(New York, The Pierpont Morgan Library).

251. *Portrait of a young man* by Dirk Bouts or one of his school, (1462-1470).

(Northampton, Mass., Smith College Museum of Art. Silver needle on paper).

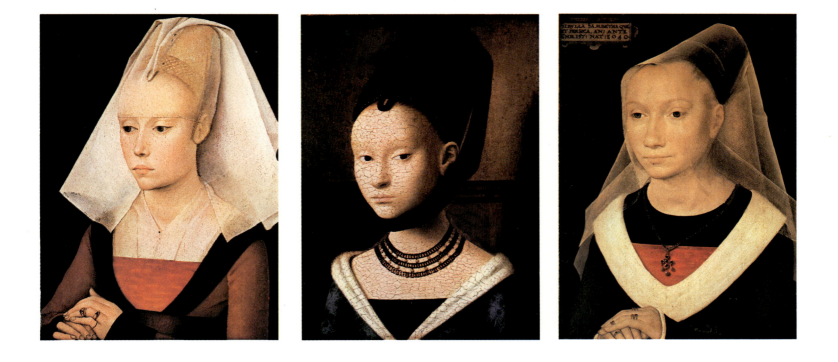

247. *Portrait of a woman,* attributed to Rogier van der Weyden.

(London, National Gallery).

248. *Portrait of a young girl* by Petrus Christus, ca 1465-1470.

(Berlin-Dahlem, Staatliche Museen Preussischer Kulturbesitz, Gemäldegalerie).

249. *Portrait of a woman* by Hans Memlinc. The sixteenth-century inscription identifies this woman as Sibylle of Persia.

(Bruges, St John's Hospital, Memling Museum).

from times gone by, but only occasionally. He usually filled his canvasses with the most individual forms. Take, for example, the *Ship of Fools,* a wondrous company in a small boat steered with a ladle, possibly sailing to the Land of Fools as in Sebastian Brant's *Narrenschiff,* a book which appeared almost simultaneously in 1494 ; or was it a carnival scene as in The Blue Barge, a tale that was creating a furore in the Netherlands at that time ? A Franciscan and a nun making music attempt, without using their hands, to reach a cake hanging above them. Satire on a thousand and one situations ; social criticism ; criticism of the clergy, great men, nobles and snobs. The *Garden of Delights* is even more typical. The side panels depict the creation of Eve and paradise, and hell. The central panel is a vast landscape filled with an unbelievable number of nude figures, eroticism setting the tone. This vision has been seen by some as a salute to a nudist sect (Adamites) while others saw it as a depiction of the primeval age in which there was no personal property, or even as a warning against earthly love – since hell threatens from the right-hand panel. On the other hand, many painters in the fifteenth century began to use nude figures prominently in their works.

The work of Bosch is thus open to many interpretations. In any case he gives a dramatic representation of the many tensions in society, and of the fears, obsessions and frustrations of the individual. Miraculous natural occurences were not yet looked upon rationally in Bosch's time, the illiterate masses were the easy prey of religion and superstition, and the many simplistic vulnerable people frantically sought for explanations for inexplicable natural disorders, famine, plague and poverty. In the panel depicting hell, sinners at an inn-table are served by a female devil, acting the whore, which is probably a lampoon of dypsomania and lascivious pub-crawlers. Though it all seems demonic and visionary, in fact it consists of very rational constructions and many of the details have a logical explanation with particular allusions. It was during Bosch's lifetime that 's Hertogenbosch, where Hieronymus lived, introduced a wider range of social provisions than anywhere else, to care for all conceivable types of marginal groups from poor pupils to lepers,

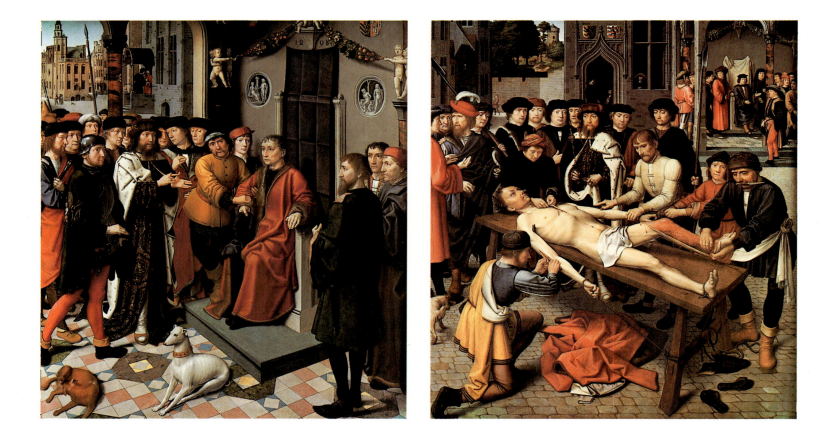

for the elderly, the sick and artisans in need. Bosch was even connected to one of these institutions : the Illustrious Fraternity of Our Lady. He observed human suffering and humanitarian sympathy, but also human baseness and pettiness with a particular critical eye.

CENTRES OF PRODUCTION The centre of art in the first half of the fifteenth century was Tournai, at least until 1440 ; Campin trained Rogier van der Weyden there, who then went to Brussels where he achieved great success. Bruges was a second art centre, with Van Eyck in its first generation. Petrus Christus, (1419-1472/73), Jan van Eyck's only real apprentice, continued his work as a celebrated portrait-painter. He forms the chronological link with Hans Memlinc (1430-1494), though he in fact followed Van der Weyden's technique of composition at Bruges ; this can be seen in the splendid composition of the triptych depicting the mystical marriage of St Catherine, which also depicts the martyrdom of St John the Baptist, St John on Patmos and countless apocalyptic visions. The background contains still more : the feast of Herod (left-hand panel), a view of Bruges and a great deal more. There is no question of confusion, everything harmonises perfectly. In particular Memlinc's portraits idealise – with Van Eyck's precision – a tranquil piety. A third generation was also native to Bruges, the central figure of which was Gerard David (c. 1460-1523). We here return to earth again after Memlinc's meditation. In the Cambyses diptych (1498) we see real people again : worthy judges, cruel executioners with knives between their teeth, this time placed in a realistic setting with a recognisable Poortersloge and the former St John's church. In David's *Baptism of Christ* the grand composition reminds us of Rogier and the accurate detail in the landscape of the central panel of the

252. *The Arrest of Sisamnes, the unjust judge,* after Gerard David's *The Judgment of Cambyses* (1489). Judgment scenes such as this were hung by the towns in their courtrooms. They originate from a period of governmental changes which were accompanied by many political executions.

(Bruges, Groeningemuseum).

253. *The torture of unjust Sisamnes,* involving flaying alive. This work by Gerard David formed a diptych with the *Arrest of Sisamnes the unjust judge,* and was hung in the aldermen's residence.

(Bruges, Groeningemuseum, 1498).

Adoration of the Lamb. The new element in David's work is the evidence of a transition from late Gothic to Renaissance. Renaissance architecture can already be seen in the side panel of the *Baptism of Christ,* showing the second husband of the patron, Magdalena Cordier. So art flourished at Bruges throughout the century 1420-1520. Ghent, too, should not be forgotten, where the *Adoration of the Lamb* was completed in 1432 ; where Van der Goes (Ghent-born) had his studio and where Joos van Wassenhove (Justus of Ghent) belonged to the painters' guild from 1464 and painted a Calvary triptych for St Bavon's. Justus is particularly important because, during his long stay in Italy, he was able to marry the essence of the Flemish school with the artistic climate of Italy, without the former losing its identity.

In Brabant, Leuven flourished from about 1450 until well into the sixteenth century, thanks to Dirk Bouts and his sons. Antwerp came to the fore somewhat later, with its economic boom : in the second half of the fifteenth century, the number of members in the Antwerp painters' guild rose from thirty-five to two hundred and twelve. Quentin Metsys (1465-1530) continued to use classical themes and in his adherence to the Italian Renaissance, is far removed from the piety of Memlinc. Joachim Patenier continued the landscape tradition but at the same time introduced the setting in which Brueghel would place his figures. Albert van Ouwater and Geertgen tot St Jans were active in Haarlem in the second half of the fifteenth century. Geertgen adhered closely to the tranquil world of Memlinc, and Dirk Bouts was possibly also from this school. Utrecht, home of the miniaturist Willem Vrelant, must also have been a centre of some importance. We can safely say that there were fewer artists in the northern Netherlands, and that their originality and lustre could not compete with that of the south, whither the best of them migrated.

256. Celebration at the court of Philip the Good after a falconry expedition, on the eve of his marriage to Isabella of Portugal in January 1430. The upper section of the painting possibly contains an allusion to the revolt of the farmers in the Kassel region during the same period, which was put down by force of arms in 1431.

(Versailles, Museum. Sixteenth-century copy of a lost original of the Van Eyck school).

257. St Catherine. Alabaster statue by André Beauneveu, of ca 1374-1386.

(Kortrijk, Church of Our Lady, height: 185 cm).

SCULPTURE Sculpture, in Klaas Sluter's work, introduced the Ars Nova earlier than painting. The southern sculptors who preceded Klaas worked, from 1350, mainly at the court of King Charles V of France (André Beauneveu and Hennequin of Liège) and the court of the Duke of Berry at Mehun (the same Beauneveu and Jean de Cambrai). This was therefore in the French style, which had in fact been diligently copied from the twelfth century onwards as a so-called international style. The transformation came with Klaas Sluter (d. 1405/06) who moved from Haarlem to Brussels. Between 1379 and 1385 he became involved with a group of non-conformists who wanted to break away from the contemporary tradition of the studios in Brabant and Liège with its mannerism, strong French influence and the inextricable link between painting and monument. Jacob de Baerze (from Dendermonde) created two altars in this style around 1390 for Duke Philip the Bold : these were intended for the Carthusian abbey at Champmol near Dijon. It was for this same abbey that Sluter and a number of Brabanters received a commission in 1385 from the same duke. This was where the transformation in Sluter and his contemporaries became fully evident. The figures in the famous Well of Mozes at Champmol did indeed assume a character of their own, having been freed from monumental tradition. The linear form of previous years was replaced by shapeliness and a lyrical realism, to be seen in the work of Van Eyck. The artificial smile of the past died on the lips and the stereotyped face was replaced by the personal expression of a living individual. The body was no longer concealed in pleated garments, but became a living figure whose natural form was freely depicted. Sculpture had closed the gap. After Sluter's death, the mausoleum of Philip the Bold and Margaret de Male in Champmol, with its portal sculpture and realistic mourners, was completed by his nephew Klaas van der Werve.

This first triumph of sulpture left traces in Burgundy in particular, although it was not much in evidence in the Netherlands during the first half of the fifteenth century, except for the tomb of Louis de Male at Lille, adorned with family portraits which were possibly the work of Jan Van Eyck. This prototype was also copied for the tomb of Isabella of Bourbon. The flourishing art round Liège during the fourteenth century did not last. It is probable that much of the perishable woodcarvings and vulnerable soft stone statues have been lost, or were destroyed in the sixteenth century. The more sturdy monumental tombs in St Bavon's abbey at Ghent, and those of Adornes of 1472 in the Jerusalem Church at Bruges and the castle chapel at Antoing, have been preserved. However, the work of the Sluter school was not really continued, apart perhaps from the prophets in the entrance-hall to the Town Hall at Bruges, the apostles in the church at Halle (*c.* 1410) and the work, at Diest, of Sulpicius of Diest.

The second impulse did not come until the end of the fifteenth century – again in Brabant, but particularly at Brussels where Jan Borreman and his son Pasquier raised the art of wooden retables to a high European level with, among others, the retable of St George (1493) and the retables of Our Lady and St John in St Peter's church at Leuven. Borreman also worked at Zoutleeuw and Bruges, from 1495-1502, on the mausoleum of Mary of Burgundy. This follows the line of naturalism in the pictorial tradition since c. 1420-1430, and Sluter's expressionism, albeit in a more restrained form. Borreman is, however, only one supreme master amongst a plethora of lesser gods who remained largely anonymous in their fields. They

258. The Moses Well by Klaas Sluter, ca 1385-1404, was intended to decorate the spring in the Carthusian monastery at Champmol near Dijon, showing the prophets Moses, Isaiah, Jeremiah, Daniel and Zachariah. These prophets are not ethereal, mannerist creations but powerful, true-to-life characters with the emphasis on monumental form.

achieved a highly technical mass production which was protected by the hallmark of the guild and found an easy market throughout Europe. Borreman's works are known in Sweden, but many other anonymous retables from Brabant are to be found throughout Scandinavia, in the Hanse towns, the Baltic ports as far as Finland and Reval in Estonia, as well as in France and southern Europe. In addition to Brabant there was also a flourishing school of sculpture in Utrecht, due to the work on the local cathedral, whose work was exported far less because of the small scale of production. Adriaan van Wesel was master of a workshop there, in the tradition of Sluter, between 1470 and 1500.

THE BUILDING FEVER OF THE BRABANTINE HIGH-GOTHIC From the fourteenth to the sixteenth century, a veritable building fever swept the Netherlands, and Brabant in particular. This was not only a question of new buildings, but in many cases also the conversion or extension of churches, town halls and houses which were too small or considered to be too modest. But just as happened with the town walls of the time, the future expansion had been overestimated and new buildings were oversized. Architectural ambitions were often too grandiose for the technical and financial resources of the time; and, in particular, spires and vaulting remained unfinished in the centuries which followed. Architecture exhibited a greater uniformity and stylistic unity than the art and sculpture of the time, and

259. Carthusian monk with breviary. Figure from the funeral procession around the tomb of Duke John the Fearless (d. 1419), by Klaas Sluter.

(Dijon, Musée des Beaux-Arts).

260. Mourning figure sculptured by Klaas van der Werve, part of the tomb of Duke John the Fearless (d. 1419).

(Dijon, Musée des Beaux-Arts).

261. Statue retable from Mechelen, ca 1500, with painted side panels.

(Antwerp, Museum Mayer van den Bergh).

the originality of the town halls thus overwhelmed the cathedrals inspired by the French style. This was clearly to be expected in this part of Europe where the towns were so politically and culturally dominant. The clerk to the Cardinal of Aragon, A. de Beatis, also saw this when he visited the lands of the Netherlands in 1517/1518 and praised the aldermen's house at Leuven as the most beautiful in the world.

During the long thriving period outlined above, two phases can be distinguished during which unbridled activity, creativity and an urge for renewal were particularly evident : the second half of the fourteenth century with Jan van Osy and his pupils, and the decades before and after 1500 with the Keldermans family.

Jan van Osy, who originated from Hainault or northern France, joined the builders of St Rombaut's in Mechelen at a time when the French Gothic cathedral was the unchallenged norm in Brabant (St Gudule's church at Brussels of 1226, and the church of Our Lady at Diest of 1423), the Netherlands, and the whole of Europe.

St Rombaut's was still an imitation of Amiens, with its ground plan showing a choir and apse and seven identical radial chapels ; a structure which remained a model in centuries to come. Osy and his school were able to break through this imitation mentality, and create a Brabantine High Gothic which had a character of its own. The French model was notably adapted to the new prototype in the church of Our Lady at Tienen, where Osy had worked since 1358 and where he could express himself more freely than in Mechelen. This building is remarkable for its unusually rich decoration, with paintings in the porches above which there was an open ambulatory, a characteristic which was to become a feature of secular architecture such as that of the town hall in Brussels. This harmony is, moreover, no coincidence. It was Jacob van Tienen (or Gobbertingen), a colleague of Osy's on the sacred prototype of Our Lady in Tienen, whose left-hand wing of the town hall at Brussels became the prototype of the High-Gothic civic architecture of Brabant.

From then onwards we see a single, inextricable network of master-builders who within the fraternity of their craft, passed among themselves the secrets and techniques of their profession, and also its stylistic creativity, as they moved around from one building site to another. From 1383, Jacob van Tienen became master-builder at St Gudule's and the town hall at Brussels, and also became involved with the Church of our Lady at Antwerp ; he consequently resigned from Tienen in 1396, but was promptly succeeded by Botso van Raatshoven, and by Sulpicius of Vorst in 1418. Sulpicius was another of Osy's pupils who, after Tienen, created another masterpiece in church gothic, in St Peter's at Leuven (1427-1439). At Brussels, Jacob van Tienen was assisted by Jan van Ruisbroek, who worked on the tower of the town hall in 1449, and also on the ducal palace (1433-1436). While Sulpicius of Vorst was working on St Peter's church, yet another of Osy's pupils was building the famous town hall, also in Leuven, as well as the Sacrament tower in St Peter's (1450). Other disciples of Osy carried his style outside Brabant itself, first to its borders at 's Hertogenbosch where Willem van Kessel worked on the cathedral from 1390 to 1410 and thereafter

262. Tombstone of Anselmus Adornes and Margaret van der Banck in the private Jerusalem Church of the Bruges-based Adornes family from Genoa. Anselmus had travelled to the Holy Land in 1470 and brought back relics for 'his' Church of the Holy Sepulchre. In 1470 he was the successful negotiator of Mary Stuart's return to Scotland. In 1472 he was appointed by king James III as consul of the Scottish nation in the states of the duke of Burgundy. Anselmus was a knight and burgomaster of Bruges, 1475-1476.

263. The Church of Our Lady in Antwerp, ca 1507-1514. Ink drawing from the collection in the possession of Albrecht Dürer.

(Vienna, Graphische Sammlung Albertina. Anonymous master from the southern Netherlands).

264. The Sacrament tower in St Leonard's Church at Zoutleeuw.

265. View of the Church of St Gudule, now St Michael's Church at Brussels, second half of the fifteenth century.

266. Leuven Town hall by Matthijs de Layens, built between 1448 and 1468.

on St Lambert's at Liège (1400-1425). Jan Spijsken, initially a freemason of the Brussels guild, introduced the Brabantine style to Hainault, with his striking St Waudru's church at Mons (1450).

Finally, the Brabantine style was also brought into Holland, one example being the town hall in Gouda, dating from about 1450. The end of Brabantine High Gothic is largely attributable to the Keldermans dynasty. The joint efforts of Rombaut II Keldermans and Domien de Waghemaker in particular produced glorious monuments such as the new exchange at Antwerp (1527-1530), now no longer in existence, and the town hall at Ghent (1518-1533). The long period of inactivity at Ghent thereafter is proof of the fact that the late Gothic style had had its day and that taste was now moving towards the new forms of the Italian Renaissance, to which Rombaut had already occasionally alluded in his later works. The Keldermans dynasty can possibly be traced back to Jan van Mandale, named Kelderken, a member of the Brussels guild of stonemasons from 1377-1385. Jan II (d. 1445) worked on the church of St Gomarus at Lier and was the municipal master-builder of Leuven and Mechelen, as well as working in Leiden. His son Andries (d. 1480) followed in his father's footsteps at Mechelen where he continued the completion of St Rombaut's and also built a copy of it in St Lieven's at Zierikzee. Antoon I (1450-1512) designed the gables of the town hall at Middelburg. Antoon II (d. 1515) was master of the Bakers' Hall in the Market Place at Brussels, and Rombaut II (1460-1531) was master of the Marquis's court at Bergen-op-Zoom and St Rombaut's at Mechelen, in addition to the accomplishments already mentioned. Apart from the Keldermans, the Brussels architect Hendrik van Pede was so renowned that Oudenaarde town hall was dedicated to him in 1527. This town hall, along with those of Leuven and Brussels, was one of the most perfect treasures of late Gothic architecture.

THE EUROPEAN SUCCESS OF THE 'FLEMISH' POLYPHONISTS Music in the Netherlands, like the fine arts, was discredited from the twelfth century to the end of the fourteenth century, and was often second-rate and eclipsed by French music. This reached its zenith towards the end of the twelfth century in the Notre Dame school with Leoninus and Perotinus Magnus, and polyphonic music continued to be the preserve of the French in the fourteenth century, with Guillaume de Machaut. It was isorhythmic, in other words, certain rhythmic patterns were repeated in another tempo, quite separate from the melody. This music showed distinct mannerist features, harmonising remarkably with what can be observed in the sculpture of its time. At around 1430, simultaneously with the revival in painting and somewhat later than the revival in sculpture, there was a similar regeneration in music when a number of talented composers emerged in the Netherlands, who created a new and individual style which differed from the French and European norm ; a style with which they won the hearts of audiences far beyond their own borders. Contemporaries even spoke of 'Flemish' composers to distinguish this group, although some of them came from Liège and other parts of the Burgundian Netherlands.

The founder of this new movement was Guillaume Dufay(1400-1474). But his anti-mannerist polyphony did not spring from nowhere ; there is evidence of English influence and Italian inspiration, both of which acted upon the underlying French style, as in the Italianate Johannes Ciconia (d. 1411) from Liège. Nevertheless the change heralded by Dufay was both fundamental and original. He began with work in the isorhythmic tradition but in his more personal compositions – secular as well as sacred – he chose

267. Musicians on the steps of a palace or church. Flemish miniature, ca 1497, from a breviary presented to Isabella of Castile by Francis de Rojas. Her son Philip the Fair became King of Castile after her death in 1504.

(London, British Museum, Ms add. nr. 18851, fo 184 V°).

268. Miniature illustrating Martin the Franc's well-known work, *Le champion des dames,* in which he refers to Dufay's originality of style in religious music and Binchois' in secular music.

(Paris, Bibliothèque Nationale, Ms fr. 12476, fo 98).

300

a polyphony which reached a distinct counterpoint between the Gregorian theme and a second, new melody. Polyphonic music in the Netherlands was generally choral, particularly in sacred works : the music was composed for the human voice, and instruments, when used, simply provided an accompaniment. Different voices followed their own melodic and rhythmic line.

The chapel of the dukes of Burgundy, and later of governess Margaret of Austria, was a cultural centre of international importance and influence. The musicians, who were at this time both composers and performers, can be distinguished in successive generations. The first generation included Dufay and Binchois (*c.* 1400-1480). The second, Busnois (appointed by Charles the Bold in 1467) and Ockeghem. The latter was born between 1420 and 1425 at Dendermonde, but from 1448 until his death in 1497, he worked almost exclusively at the French court. His impact was so great that his influence can be seen in numerous composers of following generations. This was the most productive period for the musicians in the Netherlands: apart from the ten or so 'great names' such as Josquin des Prés (1440-1521), Jacob Obrecht (from Bergen-op-Zoom), Alexander Ackerman (Agricola), Pierre de la Rue, Heinrich Isaac etc., there were any number of others including the English instrumentalist Robert Merton.

The Burgundian court chapel of around 1500 consisted of a 'grande chapelle' of a dozen or so boys. In addition there were twelve trumpets and other wind instruments, and a tambourine. Particular attention was paid to the organ. Margaret of Austria was taught to play several instruments by Gommaar Nepotis (Neefs), himself an organist. His successor, Hendrik Bredemers (d. 1522) was initially the organist in the church of Our Lady in Antwerp but, at the request of Philip the Fair, accepted the position of Master of the Royal Music to Prince Charles and Princess Eleonora. In addition, the cathedrals and city churches also maintained choirs employing countless musicians. The court of Philip the Fair and Margaret of Austria was, moreover, an active centre for the production of music manuscripts. No less than fifty beautiful illuminated manuscripts are extant, each one of which is

269. An aubade under a young lady's barred window. Ink drawing and aquarel by the Master of Wavrin, ca 1465.

(Brussels, Royal Library. Print Collection, nrs. 9632-33, *L'histoire du chevalier Paris*, fo 1).

a unique example. Particularly interesting is the 'Basses Danses', dating from about 1500, on black parchment with silver notes on gold staves. Their present state indicates that they were used intensively.

The new movement in the Netherlands was immediately successful in Europe. The new technique was seen as a fitting accompaniment for the liturgy, and it was thought that the composers of the Netherlands were probably the best able to lend stature to the new innovation. Dufay was consequently lured to Italy at a very early age, where he served the Malatesta family of Rimini and the pope. Dufay's reputation is evident from the fact that he was commissioned to compose festal music reflecting the proportions of the cathedral at Florence to mark the consecration of this new building in 1438. And he maintained close relations with the Medici : he sent them musical scores and singers for their choir whom he had trained himself. All this appealed greatly to Pietro di Cosimo and his son Lorenzo (the Magnificent) who, when he was eighteen, sent 'Master Guillaume' a love-poem, asking him to set the text to music.

Meanwhile Dufay was in residence at the French royal court where his contemporary, Ockeghem, worked for the rest of his life in the service of the Kings Charles VII, Louis XI and Charles VIII. Jacob Obrecht and Brumel composed at the royal court in Ferrara, Josquin des Prés composed for the Sforza's in Milan, Ferrara, Florence and Paris and at the papal court ; Isaac composed in Florence, Vienna and Innsbruck ; Mouton, Compère and De Vitis composed for the court chapel of the French king, and Adriaan Willaert became Master of the Choristers of St Mark's in Venice in 1527.

There was considerable mobility among the singers from the Netherlands and Italy. One of these was Jacques (Jachetto) de Marville, a member of the choirs of Alfonso (d. 1458) and Ferdinand (d. 1494) – both kings of Naples – and that of the pope. In 1466 Jacques wrote to Lorenzo de Medici as he understood that Lorenzo wanted to revive the St John's choir in Florence. Jacques offered his good services although he was already being "well paid and well treated" by Cardinal Davietto. A short time later his advice was indeed sought, whereupon he recommended four singers as yet unheard of in Florence. As tenor he took Jean de Bourgogne, who had a "grand high and low voice ; soft and very suitable", then three very high voices with a rich, soft tone : the first being master Jacob Francere, whose voice Marville described as the most beautiful imaginable ; the second, Jacob van Nieuwpoort 'Flamingho' had a pure, high voice ; the third, Jenino van Brabant, also had a beautiful high voice. Jacques de Marville himself sang with them as a counter-tenor. Within a month they had been joined by a baritone singer, Bartholomew, and were able to sing in four parts and once established in Florence they searched for a bass voice in France. The Medici choir was thus composed of three singers from the Netherlands, two from France, one from Burgundy and an Italian. Other musicians also performed at the Florentine court, including, as we know from the correspondence, pupils of Guillaume Dufay.

In 1486, the same Lorenzo il Magnifico once again engaged two singers from the Netherlands, one of whom, François Millet, was already in the service of the duke of Milan, and the other, a priest called Willem van Steynsel was in the service of the pope. Both saw themselves in a position to make demands, since in earlier employment they were "sent from shop to shop, from person to person and from house to house for our clothes as well as our salaries, which is not fitting for honourable men who have served in the choirs of kings and other sovereigns."

This polyphony in the Netherlands definitely pointed ahead to the Renaissance which is scarcely surprising in view of the many connections with Italy between the fourteenth and sixteenth centuries, from Ciconia to Willaert. The Rennaissance aspect lay essentially in the attempt to bring together the various parts of a musical score, whether a mass or a secular work, to form a coherent entity, rather than a collection of individual parts. This was done by repeating the same theme as a sort of refrain in the introduction to each section or by inserting repeated passages in the text. The 'unitary' masses of Dufay and Obrecht thus became well-structured entities, integrated compositions, in the same way that Van der Weyden made the architectonic aspect the central feature of his art at this time. Gradually, harmony too claimed more and more attention, particularly among those who had discovered at first hand the emotional force of expression in Italy.

There were three main genres within polyphony : 1. The cyclical mass which brought together the five separate parts by means of a *cantus firmus*, a well-known popular tune. 2. The *motet* which made more liberal use of sacred or secular texts in Latin and French. 3. The secular *chanson* akin to dance music, often with amorous, rustic and even burlesque texts (though Flemish songs are extremely rare).

Sacred music usually contained elements of folk music. A large number of masses were composed around the popular theme of *L'homme armé* but in many other instances where this must have been the case, it is difficult to trace the original melody from the paraphrase. The *chanson* also contained folk elements, in addition to refined, romantically inspired poetry. The tambourine, the lute and the shawm provided the accompaniment for dance music.

If the performance of music is compared to the other art forms in the Netherlands, then particularly in the generation of 1480 to

1520, it is remarkable how many musicians found their way to the royal courts of France, Spain, Italy and Germany. There were apparently not enough opportunities for the number of highly talented musicians in the Netherlands, but in addition, they were so highly respected in other countries that they were offered attractive positions abroad. The performance of music was still, nevertheless, restricted essentially to the courts and large churches, since only they had the means to employ a sufficiently large number of singers, instrumentalists and composers.

The cathedral schools of Arras, Tournai and Liège played an important part in the training of the singers from the Netherlands. They combined the high technical ability of the performing singers with a renewal of form and style. Because of their reputation, these schools attracted far more talent than was demanded in the Netherlands. Their performances after all demanded of the musicians a perfect blend of vocal quality, singing techniques and style. The demand for such singing came from the courts of the temporal and spiritual potentates in southern Europe. There were too few opportunities in the Netherlands. According to their financial circumstances, the towns restricted themselves to a few instrumentalists, usually horn players and trumpeters. However, although one or other of the guilds or wealthy burghers would occasionally commission an altarpiece, painting, sculpture or tapestry, and the surge in monumental building provided work for architects and sculptors, they could not allow themselves the luxury of a music ensemble. At most they would employ a few 'jongleurs' and 'tambourins' at their festivities, but these

272. Moresca performed by male and female actors.

(Brussels, Royal Library. Ms 9632-33, fo 168. Ink drawing and aquarel from the *Histoire du Chevalier Paris*, produced in the studio of the Master of Wavrin, 1469).

Pour ce que toute
creature de raison a-
ble entendement de-
sire et appete sauoir.
z oyr choses nouuelles pour la recreation et esiopssement de son co-
raige. z ossy que eus ou record des
choses aduenues anchiennement
z mesmes des haultes et nobles
proesses et emprises des nobles
hommes proeces et euiertes des
haultes et nobles procreations et
sirenes. tous preudommes ay ans
sentendement esleuet en honneur
quant ilz teilz fais oent recorder sen
esiouent z esmeuuent en plus grant

perfection de baleur z de proesse.
Est il que a ceste instance moy non
digne. poure de sens. et menre a len-
tendement. debille et soible de ceste
haulte matere mettre a effect. Se
non que il me fust comande come
il est de par mon tresredoubte z tres
puissant seigneur. monsieur philippe
par la grasse de dieu. Duc de Bourtongne. de lottringhe. de brabant et
de lembourg. Conte de flandres. dar-
tois. de bourtongne. palatin de hay-
nau. de hollande. de zelande et de
namur. marquis du saint empire.
Seigneur de frize. de salins z de ma-
lines. me suy determines z disposes

273. Jean Wauquelin presents his *Chroniques de Hainault* to Duke Philip the Good in 1448, in the presence of the young Charles the Bold, Chancellor Nicolas Rolin, Jean Chevrot, (Chief of the Grand Council) and a number of knights of the Golden Fleece.

(Brussels, Royal Library. Ms 9242; miniature by a Flemish master, possibly Rogier van der Weyden, ca 1446).

274. Unloading a ship, ca 1460, after Jan de Tavernier of Audenarde, miniature from *Les Chroniques et Conquêtes de Charlemagne*.

(Brussels, Royal Library. Ms 9068, fo 100 V°).

players often had to travel round to make their living. These musicians were technically at a much lower level than those attached to choirs. So the fact that the Netherlands produced an exceptional number of talented musicians, meant that they were generally forced to make a living abroad due to the limited demand for musicians at home. This accounts for the remarkable diffusion in this art form, as compared with painting, where only a few second-rate artists emigrated, or the best ones spent only a period of time abroad. So whatever their field, it was the artists from the Netherlands who set the tone technically and stylistically in Europe.

MINIATURES, TAPESTRY AND JEWELRY   It is not surprising that the art of miniature painting, in illuminations, flourished during the Burgundian period. This was the result of the first duke's passion for collecting books, which as a French prince he had inherited from his native country, that found a wealthy potential in pictorial artists in the Netherlands. However, the actual principal of illuminating literary and scientific texts was certainly borrowed from the French tradition by the artists of the Low Countries. Like the French kings at the turn of the thirteenth century, the Duke of Berry, uncle of Philip the Bold, was also an ardent connoisseur of beautiful manuscripts. This interest drew artists away from the Netherlands and one of the greatest achievements in this field, namely the *Tres riches heures du Duc de Berry* came with the delicate brushwork of the brothers Paul and Jan Manuel, or Maelwael, better known as the Van

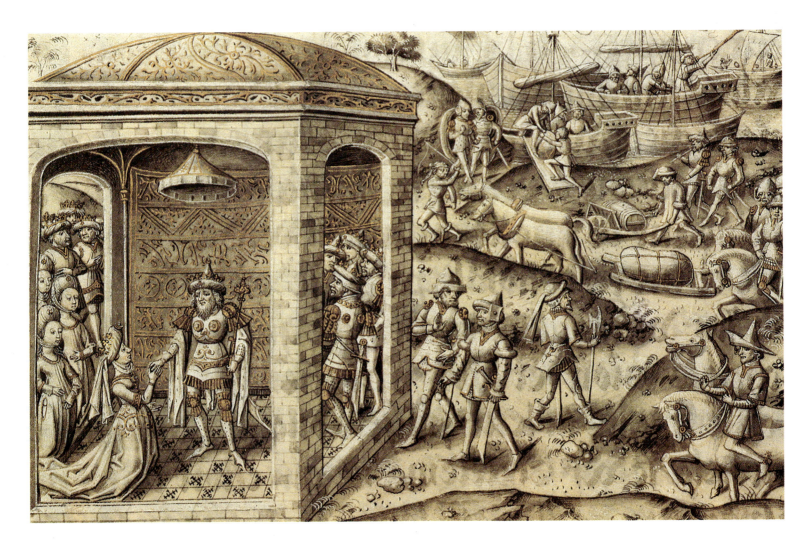

Limburg brothers, who were resident in France. They worked according to French taste in the classical international style which was also coming into painting at that time. The workshop of the dukes of Guelders also worked in the French tradition and an anonymous artist produced a comparable breviary for the duchess around 1415. It is significant that it was still Paris where John the Fearless in about 1410 commissioned his breviary to be illuminated with miniatures, but it was nevertheless completed a couple of years later at Bruges. The break-through in the Netherlands was also encouraged by Philip the Good, whose passion for illustrated books was even greater than that of his predecessors. The first blossoming of Burgundian miniature art came between 1440 and 1480; this time in local Burgundian workshops. The originality of this form of art equalled that of the contemporary 'Flemish' school of painting; here too, the emphasis lay on realistic detail and the perfect mastery of techniques. Nevertheless, the personality of the miniaturists introduced a broad spectrum of variations in style. There were those who came close to being 'great' artists, such as the sensitive Jan de Tavernier from Oudenaarde who produced colourful initial miniatures and picturesque ornamental borders full of acanthus, vine leaves and strawberries in David Aubert's *Chronique et conquête de Charlemagne* (1460), as well as sober grisailles with delicate drawings. There were also those like Willem Vrelant of Utrecht, active in Bruges, who illustrated the second part of Jean Wauquelin's translation of Jacques de Guise's *Annales Hannoniae* in 1449.

Others, such as Simon Marmion are close to Memlinc by virtue of their refined temperament. There were also the spontaneous improvisations of, for instance, the fluent Dreux Jean and in particular the so-called Master of Wavrin, whose telling pencil drawings, highlighted with colour washes, graphically depict daily scenes in their essence. These artists give an exact representation of the rich culture of the Burgundian courts of their time. When the Bruges miniaturist Loyset Liédet, who was very productive in his time, was commissioned by Charles the Bold between 1465 and 1472 to illustrate an *Histoire de Charles Martel*, his singularly colourful miniatures scarcely sported one genuine Frankish major domo. What it did contain was a pageant of courtly nobles, totally indifferent to the glaring anachronism, with their familiar pointed shoes and courtly fifteenth-century damsels with their appropriate frivolous pointed coifs, who were lampooned by the puritanical moralists of the time. Although he had come over from Paris where he had worked for the French king, Philippe de Mazerolles (d. 1479) was equally inclined towards the Flemish school and he was consequently accepted without any difficulty into the milieu of Charles the Bold's court workshop. He was so perfectly integrated that he was the most prominent forerunner of the Ghent-Bruges school of 1480 onwards.

This renewal in miniature art was also taking place at the same time in the northern Netherlands where the master of Catherine of Cleves' Book of the Hours also produced miniatures worthy of the paintings of the great realist artists. Although the North lapsed into a dull lethargy at the end of the fifteenth century, Ars Nova flourished once again in Flanders from 1480 thanks to the so-called Ghent-Bruges school with its leading figures like Simon Bening in Bruges, who possibly also created the unique *Book of Hours of Hennesy* in which he raised the miniature from its place of subservience to the content and transformed it into an art-form in its own right. Alexander Bening, a member of Simon's family, and the master of Mary of

275. Detail from a cope of the Order of the Golden Fleece.

(Vienna, Kunsthistorisches Museum).

276. Dalmatic of the Order of the Golden Fleece, a beautiful piece of lapis-lazuli embroidery.

(Vienna, Kunsthistorisches Museum).

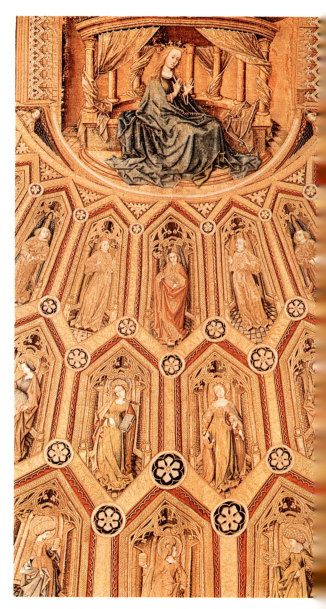

Burgundy who depicted the presentation of a Boëthius manuscript to Margaret of York, worked in the same atelier (1476). The most superb artists were perhaps the anonymous authors of two breviaries, the *Breviarium Grimani* and the *Breviarium* in the Antwerp museum Mayer van den Bergh, from the beginning of the sixteenth century.

The links between painting and miniatures are many and varied. The relationship is so close that it is not surprising that the beautifully constructed presentation to Duke Philip the Good (1448) by Wauquelin, who translated Jacques de Guise's Hainault Annals, was attributed to the compositional talent of Rogier van der Weyden. This miniature, perhaps the best known in the Burgundian period, has in its unique composition all the magnificence and brilliant colours of the panels by the great masters. Nor is it surprising that people thought of Gerard David when they saw the two anonymous miniatures with the preaching of John and the Baptism of Christ. Generally speaking, miniature art developed along the same lines as painting : the *Breviarium Grimani* was illuminated with what were definitely miniature paintings. Occasionally the reverse was true. In the background of a painting by the anonymous master of St Gudule of about 1475, one sees between the pillars, behind the Madonna and donors, a harbour view with

a city gate and mannered figures which could easily have been taken from a miniature by Philippe de Mazerolles, and with his composition.

The art in tapestry has already been referred to from time to time. It flourished essentially at Brussels, Tournai and Arras, but there were also growing tapestry-weavers guilds in other towns. The tapestries often depicted themes from mythology (The Golden Fleece) or antiquity (The Caesar tapestries from Tournai). Between 1472 and 1476 Pasquier Grenier of Tournai produced no less than ten tapestries for the town of Bruges showing the history of Troy. Around 1500, the workshop of Peter van Aalst was working on designs created by Quinten Metsijs. In addition to the tapestries, embroidered copes and chasubles were also a speciality of the Netherlands. Their originality came from the famed lapis lazuli stitching – a technique whereby two gold threads were attached with coloured silks at irregular intervals, thereby creating a subtle play between light and shade.

Glass painters were active in Bruges from about 1386. This flourished to such an extent in the second half of the fifteenth century that in Bruges alone eighty members of the St Lucas guild could be identified as glaziers.

Goldsmithery also flourished at Bruges. Antoine de Croy had his chain of the Golden Fleece made by Jean Puetin. The goldsmith Lodewijk van Berchem working for Charles the Bold at Bruges, devised a new technique for the splitting and polishing of precious stones, bevelling the faces in order to gain an optimal intensity of light. One of the most famous gold statuettes is the reliquary which Charles the Bold commissioned from Gérard Loyet, a Lille goldsmith, in 1466/1467. The Duke later donated this piece, as a sort of expiation for the scandal of his bloody razing of the town of Liège in 1468, to St Lambert's Cathedral in that city, where it was deposited in 1471. The links between the various art forms is illustrated particularly well here : a similar representation of St George, who accompanies the kneeling duke on the reliquary of Liège, can be found on Van Eyck's panel for Canon van der Paele of 1436 and also in a miniature by Philippe de Mazerolles contained in a 1466 prayer book.

The gold chalices, enamelled spoons, lecterns, window panes, waffle-irons, chasubles, decorated helmets and weapons, and in particular the quantities of jewelry which were produced throughout the fifteenth century for the dukes and the public who imitated them, are too numerous to mention in detail.

A FUNCTIONAL LITERATURE The literature of the Burgundian period was even more functional than the art-forms already discussed. This does not mean, however, that there was no room for fictional works which merely provided amusement, or a chance to escape from the environment and an era which could be less than pleasant and livable, enabling the reader to relieve some of his personal tensions. The poetry and drama of the fifteenth century rhetoricians were partly didactic and moralising, but they were also intended for pure entertainment. Just as the nineteenth century reader found a temporary relief from his social discontent and his dingy housing in the penny dreadfuls of his day, so the fifteenth century townsman could let up in the many performances of plays, both farcical and romantic. In the farces and interludes he could chuckle at the angry wives who were chastised because they wanted to wear the trousers or, in the farce of Playerwater at the poor man who was sent out by his apparently sick wife to fetch curative water

278. Reliquary, presented by Charles the Bold to St Lambert's Cathedral in Liège (1468-1471) as a gesture after the destruction of the town. The duke is shown kneeling with St George standing behind him.

(Liège, Treasury of St Paul's Cathedral: Gerard Loyet of Lille, chased gold and enamel).

277. A two-part miniature showing, above, the so-called philosophers Timeo and Placides in conversation and, below, the *Livre des secrets aux Philosophes* being presented to Duke Philip the Good. The margin shows the duke's coat of arms surrounded by the chain of the Order of the Golden Fleece.

(Brussels, Royal Library. Ms 11.107, fo. 1. Flemish miniature, ca 1450).

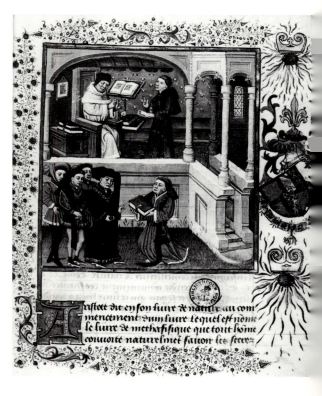

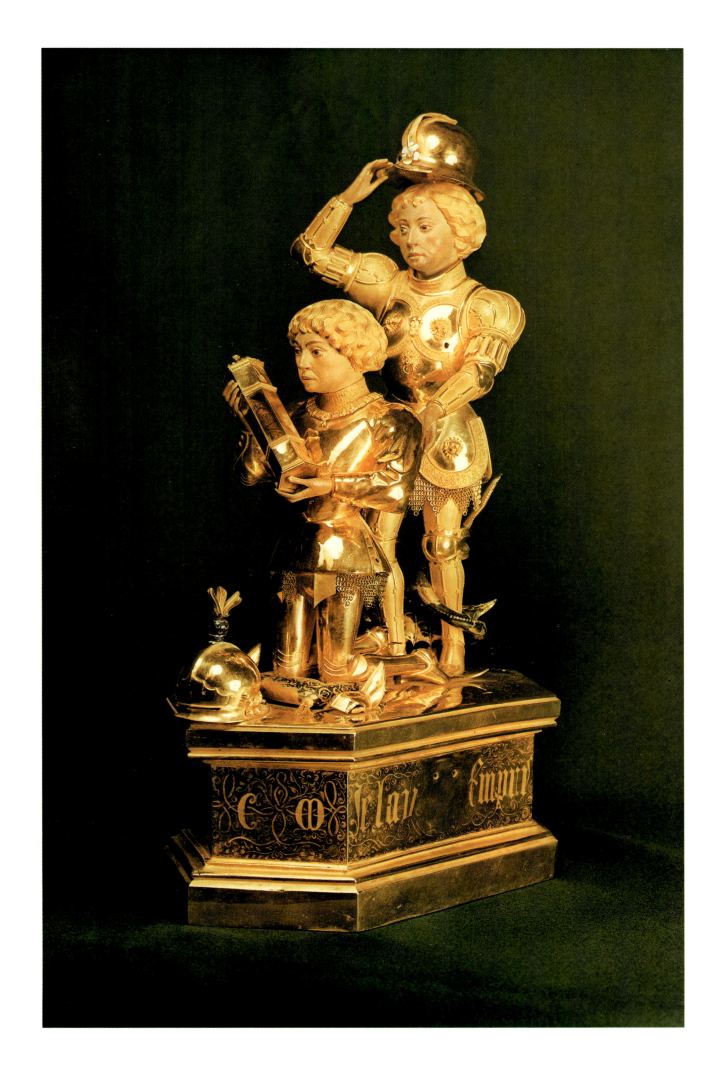

and, in his absence, proceeded to indulge in a lusty romp with the local pastor. The themes of the *Decameron* and the *Cent Nouvelles nouvelles* were also very much alive in Dutch popular literature. The Dutch burgher was moved by, and could easily recognise himself in the romantic play *Mirror of loves*, written by the Brussels rhetorician Colijn van Rijssele, which was a striking precursor of nineteenth century bourgeois drama.

Even high society, right up to the Burgundian court, had similar requirements. Philip the Good probably found relief for his own tensions and frustrations by reading *Cent Nouvelles nouvelles* – probably written for him – which was an imitation of Boccaccio's *Decameron*, whose works first graced the ducal library at the end of the fourteenth century.

Much of the literature of the Burgundian Netherlands emanated from the municipal literary guilds which originated in the southern Netherlands in the fourteenth century and took a definite form in the fifteenth century as the Chambers of Rhetoric, comparable to other artistic guilds. These chambers were also commissioned by the towns to add lustre to their festivals. In 1474, Colin Caillieu was elected city poet of Brussels from such a background. In the French-speaking towns the authors of the 'Confréries' produced satirical poetry and drama, as well as mystery plays and, particularly at Arras, the famous passion plays. The Chambers of Rhetoric in the Dutch-speaking centres, particularly from the time of Philip the Good, also produced highly creditable literature, including not only literary masterpieces such as *Everyman* and *Mary of Nijmegen*, but also works so critical of contemporary society that the dukes tried to impose some control on the Chambers at the end of the fifteenth century.

The work of the rhetoricians was virtually the only alternative to the literature of the Burgundian court which was dictated entirely by the government. Court writers and historians such as Georges Chastellain, Olivier de la Marche, Jean de Wavrin and Jean Molinet have already been discussed at length with regards to ducal propaganda. They tirelessly extolled their employers and were the mainstay of the committed historiography of the Burgundian period. There were also the routine professional translators and editors of earlier works which would enhance the image of the Burgundians : Jean Wauquelin worked on Jacques de Guise's history of Hainault, David Aubert on the fortunes of Charles Martel and Charlemagne and Jean Mansel with his history of the world from the beginning to 1400, so-called *Fleur des histoires*.

There was also a profusion of works based on contemporary themes, such as Jean Petit's *Justification du duc de Bourgogne* (ca 1408) which attempted to gloss over Louis d'Orleans' murder by Duke John the Fearless, and pamphlets such as the pro-French *Prétentions anglaises à la couronne de France* (ca 1410) or the *Epistre lamentable* by Philippe de Mézières which, after the defeat of the Franco-Burgundian army by the Turks in 1396, contained a call for another holy war. The French literature of the poet Eustache Deschamps and of Christine de Pisan, whose *Débat des deux amants* (ca 1400) was written in imitation of the sayings of Guillaume de Machaut, was very popular in Burgundian high society and much of Christine's poetry was set to music by Gilles Binchois.

Much of the literature, whether it originated in the towns or the court, did however contain a common element : it propagated a courtly, chivalrous mentality, one and the same Christianity and faith, one and the same glorification of the Burgundian court.

Investment in art

The term 'investment' is a dangerous one to apply to the commissioning of works of art in the Middle Ages. Works of art were seldom resold, although they were reproduced many times over. People did not invest in art, in the true economic sense, as they did in property and land, although these *objets d'art* were passionately sought after. Traders in art even appeared in the mid-fifteenth century, so even at this stage a Memlinc was a marketable commodity. However, the intrinsic value of, for example, a painting, was far from obvious, whereas it was possible to speculate on the value of tapestries or jewelry. The production of other art forms was governed by aesthetic motives, piety and the pursuit of status.

The reigns of successive members of the Burgundian dynasty were characterised by the promotion of many forms of élitist culture. The purely aesthetic passion for art, and in particular for illustrated books was hereditary, being derived from the royal bibliophiles in France from Charles V onwards, and should certainly not be underestimated. The fact that the dukes' promotion of culture was directed almost exclusively to image building, is also significant. The example they set was followed by the upper classes who were thus able to raise themselves to a higher status. Art is, after all, an ostentatious expenditure which, apart from its aesthetic enjoyment, also brings social prestige and, moreover, conveys a message.

279. The Portugese writer Vasco de Lucena presents his translation of *Les Faiz du Grant Alexandre* to Duke Charles the Bold. The miniatures from this manuscript are of great value for the study of the furniture, vessels and costumes of the second half of the fifteenth century. The manuscript dates from 1468-1470.

(Paris, Bibliothèque Nationale. Ms fr. nr. 22.457, fo 1).

313

280. *Carola in the garden.* Three musicians play a dance performed by eight nobles.

(Paris, Bibliothèque de l'Arsenal. Ms fr. nr. 19153, fo 7. Flemish miniature attributed to the Master of Juvenal des Ursins, from the *Roman de la Rose*).

THE MAINSTAYS OF COURT CULTURE Even before his arrival in the Netherlands in 1384, the first Burgundian, Philip the Bold, had taken to employing artists as part of his retinue of servants for a yearly salary known as a 'pension'. This was a tradition peculiar to the French royal house, from which Philip was directly descended, and was also peculiar to Philip's father-in-law, the count of Flanders. Philip took on the Flemish painter Melchior Broederlam, who had been in Louis de Male's service since 1381. As Philip's 'Valet de Chambre', Broederlam worked on the retable of Champmol, the duke's future mausoleum near Dijon. Prior to this, Jan Maelwael had been engaged as an artist, Jacob de Baerze from Dendermonde as a wood-carver whose particular task was the wood retables, and most notably the celebrated Klaas Sluter from Haarlem and his nephew Klaas van der Werve, who worked for the duke at Dijon from 1385 to 1439. These northerners overshadowed the group of French artists centred round the famous Jean de Marville, who had been in permanent service with Philip since 1372. Philip being a bibliophile, also employed celebrated miniaturists at his court, such as the Maelwael brothers, Paul and Jannequin (who can perhaps be identified with the Van Limburg brothers) who produced an illustrated bible for him in 1402. The succeeding dukes maintained this tradition, particularly Philip the Good – being the connoisseur of illustrated books that he was – who engaged the talented miniature-painter Dreux Jean on a permanent basis in 1439, and Jean Hennecart in 1454. His most prestigious courtier was, however, Jan van Eyck, official court artist from 1425 until his death in 1441, who was pampered in many ways, being the only royal servant allowed to retain his full salary at a time when everyone had to forfeit part of their income for reasons of economy. Nor did his position in court prevent him from accepting private commissions. In 1432 he received no salary since he was about to complete the *Adoration of the Lamb,* the cost of which was to be met by a Ghent burgher. Charles the Bold kept on his father's artists and in 1470 Jean Hennecart illustrated a *Livre de l'instruction du jeune prince* according to his instructions. Charles employed experienced copyist-calligraphers such as David Aubert and brought Philippe de Mazerolles, the celebrated painter and miniaturist, over from France to work for him. After Philip the Good, artists were also employed in two other fields. Jan van Ruisbroek who, along with other commissions, was also the architect of the ducal palace at Brussels from 1433 to 1436, was taken into the duke's service as master-builder from 1459 to 1483 for the restoration of his castles and other residences. This office was retained until 1516, when, on Rombout II Kelderman's appointment, it was changed to Chief Architect of the Netherlands.

Philip the Good was also responsible for the famous Burgundian court choir, with which Gilles Binchois was certainly connected, and Guillaume Dufay less directly although he did hold the prestigious title of 'cantor illustrissimus domini ducis Burgondiae'. Charles the Bold continued this tradition too, and appointed Antoine Busnois master of the choristers, as Philip the Good subsequently did with Pierre de la Rue.

The selection of these artists was often a question of chance. Jacob de Baerze was taken into service for Champmol after Philip the Bold had noticed his retable in the Bijloke at Ghent on a journey through Flanders in 1389/1390. Other artists had first made their names in the service of other sovereigns: Melchior Broederlam under Louis de Male, Jan van Eyck in the Hague under John of Bavaria, count of Holland.

The demand for works of art, however, exceeded what could be produced by those in permanent service, and it was for this reason that the dukes also placed many orders elsewhere. Rogier van der Weyden was commissioned by Philip the Good to enamel coats of arms. Between 1454 and 1460, Jan de Tavernier from Oudenaarde, who was a member of the Tournai guild, illustrated manuscripts (of Jean Miélot) with amongst other things, a ducal portrait. Magnificent festivals like the one at Bruges in 1468 in celebration of Charles the Bold's third marriage, involved a great deal of contracted work which was carried out by Jacques Daret (a painter from Tournai), Vrancke van der Stockt from Brussels and others. The famous reliquary in St Lambert's at Liège was a commission given by Charles in 1466/1467 to Gérard Loyet, a goldsmith in Lille. Even Hieronymus Bosch produced a triptych for Philip the Fair in 1504, using his familiar theme of the Last Judgement.

The painters, musicians and other artists in the duke's employ belonged to a structure referred to as the ducal 'hotel', within which all officials responsible for duties of the household were placed in a strict hierarchy. The duke's musicians such as the cantors, together with the chaplains and almoners, belonged to the top section of this 'hotel'; the so-called 'chapel'. The painters and sculptors, under the title of 'valet de chambre' belonged to another section, the chamber, supervised by the chamberlain and a 'grand maistre d'hôtel' (Lord high chamberlain). Charles the Bold employed some forty 'valets', from painters to barbers and cobblers and others responsible for various practical tasks. It was thus a question of a title, to which honour and a fixed income were attached, but definitely not a top position. Only work by a Van Eyck received exceptional treatment and remuneration. The other lesser artists – even a not insignificant man such as Broederlam – had to concern themselves with painting coats of arms and standards, like the average artisan. In 1394 Colaert van Laon was responsible for freshening up a host of standards intended for the crusade against the Turks. Pierre Coustain (d. 1484) produced up to 2,000 blazons in a single year and painted, amongst other things, Charles the Bold's arms which were placed in the church of Our Lady in Bruges during the chapter-meeting of the Golden Fleece, and is still kept there today. Nor did a certain Hugo van der Goes refuse a commission offered in 1467 to paint a number of coats of arms for the city of Ghent. The gap between art and artistic crafts was, at that time, not so great as in later years.

The odd exception, like Jan van Eyck, and Peter Paul Rubens later, was also given diplomatic tasks to perform in addition to his artistic work. He went on secret missions between 1426 and 1428 as the duke's confidant, and during his trip to the Iberian peninsula in 1429, his brief included the painting of a portrait of Isabella, the Portugese Princess and prospective bride of Philip the Good, to prepare him for a – possibly unpleasant – surprise.

THE MOTIVES BEHIND DUCAL PATRONAGE The main reason for patronage was the social prestige which it brought through the show of wealth and splendour. The élites were dazzled by the duke's displays of splendid paintings, statues and tapestries ; and festivities were held at the castle of Hesdin with this in mind.

This first motive was very often coloured by religious feelings, by the patron's concern for his own salvation. Works of art, like a concrete prayer, were thus seen as a redemption for earthly sins. A fine example of this second concern is Isabella of Portugal's votive plaque at Basle which depicts the patroness and members of her family.

A third motive was the duke's preoccupation with his image as sovereign, and the legitimation of the Burgundian unitary state. Piety often had a political flavour. The mausoleum at Champmol, begun in the Carthusian monastery near Dijon in August 1383, while Philip the Bold was still alive, was intended to immortalise his glory, and is a splendid illustration of these mixed motives. The duke and the duchess are omnipresent : immortalised as recumbent on their tomb and also as statues in the church doorway where their connection with the faith is immediately established since they are shown kneeling around a Madonna and child and are accompanied by St John the Baptist and St Catharine respectively. Religion is depicted in a more intense form in Moses' well with its impressive prophets crowned with a crucifix.

The connection with society and social prestige was also not forgotten. The ambulatory around the tomb at Champmol contains the representation of a funeral procession of mourners, prelates, knights and officials. Charles the Bold established a similar link between religion and the state when, after 1468, he gave a reliquary to the devasted town of Liège ; the reliquary shows the duke holding the shrine in the keeping of St George. The link between church and state was also symbolised in the staged performance of the so-called 'tableaux vivants'.

The chapter on propaganda has already indicated the extent to which works of art were used to endorse the sovereign's point of view. This was also possible in aggresive treatises such as Jean Petit's pamphlet which defended Duke John after the murder of the

281. Votive plaque from the mid-fifteenth century, given by Isabella of Portugal to the Carthusian monastry in Basle.

(Basle, Historisches Museum. Anonymous Flemish master after 1466 (?); bronze plate, text in marble).

leader of the Armagnacs. But the art of endorsement also worked in a more subtle way, in, for example, the introduction of the Order of the Golden Fleece via literature and tapestries featuring the figure of Jason. The duke's subjects played the same game. The town and Franc de Bruges presented Charles the Bold with a number of tapestries depicting the Trojan War, which had been made by Pasquier Grenier between 1472 and 1476. The remarkable thing about this is that the scenes did not come directly from the Iliad, but from a fifteenth century French translation of Guido de Columna's version of the story of Troy of 1287. There were no less than three copies of this in Philip the Good's library. When Philip's thoughts turned to the crusades, he promptly had a *Directorium ad passagium faciendum* (Directions for crossing the Sea) translated in 1455. And as proof of the heights to which the dynasty aspired, tapestries depicting the Coronation of Clovis were commissioned for the wedding of Charles the Bold and Margaret of York, and another series of tapestries featured Philip of Macedon and Alexander the Great, no less.

The dynasty was further reinforced by heightening its appeal in the idealisation of its knighthoods. Religion was a means of legitimation, but so was 'pagan' history. The glory of distant ancestors constantly reflected the glory of the dynasty. In 1476 a tomb was built in St Michael's Abbey at Antwerp at the request of Mary of Burgundy; the tomb was for her mother Isabella of Bourbon, second wife of Charles the Bold. The tomb was surrounded by a funeral procession with members of Isabella's family, carved in stone, forming a guard of honour : Duke Philip the Good, Countess Jacqueline of Bavaria, Duke John IV of Brabant, William IV of Bavaria, and many other members of the dynasty. Even these figures were imitations of the bronze statuettes from the mausoleum of Louis de Male (d. 1384). In the same way the tomb of Emperor Maximilian

282. Series of ten mourners who, as her kin, formed the guard of honour around the tomb of Isabella of Bourbon. There is some disagreement as to the identity of some of the figures. A total of twenty-four can be seen.

(Amsterdam, Rijksmuseum. Bronze statuettes made by the Brussels bronze-caster Jacob de Gérines).

283. Tomb of Isabella of Bourbon, cousin and second wife of Charles the Bold. Mary of Burgundy commissioned a tomb for her mother who died young, to be built in St Michael's Abbey in Antwerp. The monument, completed in 1476, was originally surrounded by statuettes of mourning relatives.

(Antwerp, Cathedral. Anonymous Flemish master).

at Innsbruck is also surrounded by life-size figures of all his Burgundian ancestry.

Legitimation reached down to the smallest and most commonplace of everyday objects. The mourning hood of the Golden Fleece belonging to Charles the Bold, seized by the Swiss at the battle of Murten, boasted not only the emblems of the Order itself, but also Charles' coat of arms, and those of Zeeland and Franche-Comté. Philip the Bold's coat of arms, in stained glass, adorns the monastery at Champmol, while Philip the Good's occurs on the table-clock and knives. 'Je l'ay emprins' – the motto of Charles the Bold, glistens on the shields of his soldiers, as does the pre-eminently Burgundian symbol, the St Andrew's cross. The symbolism contain-

ed in the offertory scenes of many manuscripts was clearly for the benefit of the dukes.

It is important not to forget that personal relaxation and the simple need for self-assurance were also among the many reasons for patronage. John the Fearless read Boccaccio, and Philip the Good *Cent Nouvelles nouvelles* by way of diversion. Philip the Good, however, was not only keen on erotica; he was a great music-lover and played the harp. Music for music's sake, therefore, and not simply as an obligatory part of religious ritual in the ducal chapel.

Few palaces were built in the Netherlands under the dukes; there was Coudenburg in Brussels and a few others, but little now remains of these. In any event they were no match for the feverish building in the towns, whose citizens built cathedrals, parish churches, town halls and guildhalls one after the other. Ducal patronage generally favoured court recitals, richly illustrated manuscripts, paintings, tapestries, silver and statuettes. In other words, anything which could be transported easily. The Alexander tapestries hung first on the walls of the palace at Bruges for Charles the Bold's wedding feast in 1468, the following year at Brussels to overawe the citizens of Ghent who had come to pay homage to the duke, and then at Trier in 1473 in the hall where Charles was to receive the German Emperor, impressing him in passing with this image of an illustrious predecessor.

The Burgundian court, in fact, hardly had a permanent base. The dukes spent their lives and reigns travelling. The only resting place was the grave and it was for this reason that, as at Champmol, their monuments were both imposing and permanent.

THE PATRONS OF THE TRIPTYCH : INVESTMENT IN PRESTIGE

From time to time, the same artists who worked for the dukes also produced works for the clergy, for nobles and court officials, and for burghers and foreign businessmen. Jan van Eyck was court painter to Philip the Good although he also produced the *Adoration of the Lamb* for Joos Vijd, a Ghent burgher, a panel for Chancellor Rolin and a Madonna for the Bruges canon Joris van der Paele; he was commissioned by Albergati, the papal legate, while the latter was travelling through Flanders; King Alfonso of Aragon bought his St George through a dealer and, in particular, his works were bought by Italian bankers and merchants in Bruges. Roger van der Weyden worked for the town of Brussels, for the Burgundian court, for Philippe de Croy and Anthony of Burgundy, for Chancellor Rolin, the archers of Leuven and the Este family at Ferrara.

But what was the real reason for all this? The purchase of a work of art was a sign of high social standing, and followed the tradition of the much-admired dukes. Buying a work of art was both a prestigious expenditure and an investment which seemed sensible for other than economic reasons.

Religious works of art, intended to enhance acts of worship, also express the desire for a magic, triumphal link with the supernatural. Having one's own portrait painted with family and friend in a religious context was intended to make this link as visible as possible. The art-historian Wackernagel has shown that this deeper meaning is connected to the custom of placing votive wax statuettes before altars.

Whose are the many famous and lesser known faces which stare out at us from countless side-panels (and sometimes even the central panel) of illustrious and less renowned triptychs from the Burgundian Netherlands, faces showing eminence and devotion such as befits

285. Detail from a 'millefleur' – tapestry bearing the coat of arms of Duke Charles the Bold, completed in Brussels in 1466 by Jan de Haze. This beautiful tapestry was part of the war spoils at Grandson.

(Berne, Historisches Museum. Wool, silk, gold and silver thread).

284. Mourning cope of the Order of the Golden Fleece, from the third quarter of the fifteenth century, bearing the arms of Duke Charles the Bold, with that of Zeeland on the bottom-left, and that of Franche-Comté bottom-right. This cope was looted by the Swiss after the Battle of Murten in 1476.

(Canton de Fribourg, Musée Gruérien de Bulle).

286. Early sixteenth-century tapestry from Tournai, reputedly representing *Le jeu à la main chaude.*

(London, Victoria and Albert Museum).

322

287. Chancellor Rolin, senior official, served Duke Philip the Good for fourty years. He came from a modest background, but had become extremely wealthy by the end of his career through countless gratuities from the Duke and many others. The duke often referred to him as 'father' because of his wise counsel and the fact that Rolin was twenty-three years his senior.

(Paris, Louvre Museum. Detail from the *Madonna with Chancellor Rolin* by Jan van Eyck, 1425).

288. Portrait of Francesco d'Este (ca 1403-1475 [?]), illegitimate son of Leonello d'Este, Marquis of Ferrara. In 1444 he was sent to the court of Burgundy where he was brought up with the young Charles the Bold. He spent most of his life in the Netherlands and acted as Burgundian ambassador on missions to Italy.

(New York, The Metropolitan Museum of Art. Attributed to Rogier van der Weyden, ca 1460).

those posing next to the Madonna, the Mystic Lamb, or St George? They are the faces of the many pious and/or vain, god-fearing donors who, for their own salvation or social prestige, were the small-scale patrons of artists, modelling themselves on the great dukes, and certainly deliberately imitating them to a certain extent.

THE CLERGY AND ART That the allure of patronage rubbed off onto the bishops of the Burgundian Netherlands is hardly surprising, since some of them were also princes (in Utrecht and Liège) like the dukes, with whom they were in many cases on familiar terms and whose mental outlook they often shared. It is highly probable that David of Burgundy, illegitimate son of Philip the Good and bishop of Utrecht (1456-1496) was depicted as a donor in a triptich by the master of Delft (Rijksmuseum, Amsterdam). John of Bavaria, bishop-elect of Liège, employed minstrels and other artists at his court. Rafaël de Mercatel, however, offers the clearest example of the imitation of ducal patronage. Rafaël was abbot of St Peter's in Ghent, and thereafter of St Bavon's abbey, and was also a natural son of Philip the Good. Like his father, he was an ardent collector of manuscripts most of which have been preserved at Ghent, and was thus a patron of the Ghent-Bruges school of miniatures at the

end of the fifteenth century. It is easy to deduce from this that the commissioning of works of art was only possible for the richest of the clerics during the fifteenth century. In a third prominent abbey, namely Ten Duinen, and the distinguished chapter of St Donatus at Bruges, patronage was equally prestigious. In about 1472, Jan Crabbe, abbot of Ten Duinen, bought a triptych from Hans Memlinc, and Hugo van der Goes also painted the *Death of Mary* for this abbey. The same applies to Brabant and Artois : Hieronymus Bosch worked intensively for the wealthy church of St John at 's Hertogenbosch and Jean de Clerq, abbot of the equally wealthy abbey of St Vaast at Arras commissioned the Tournai painter Robert Campin to produce a polyptych and designs for wall-hangings.

However, we must not assume that the senior clerics monopolised the commission of quality works of art. The artistic activity around St John's hospital at Bruges provides the best evidence to the contrary. Memlinc's grandiose *Shrine of St Ursula* of 1489 was donated to the institution by two nuns, Jossine van Dudzele and Anna van den Moortele who were also depicted as if they were sovereigns or abbesses.

Local art around St John's church in Ghent (later St Bavon's cathedral) was largely promoted by an artistically motivated parish priest, Jan van Impe, who was pastor there from 1421 to 1440 and was possibly the person who encouraged the wealthy burgher Joos

On the previous pages

289-290. The shrine of St Ursula was donated by two sisters from St John's Hospital in Bruges : Jossine van Dudzele and Anna van den Moortele, immortalised in 1489 by Hans Memlinc on one of the side-panels.

(Bruges, St John's Hospital, Memling Museum).

291. Hugo van der Goes, centre-panel of the Monforte altar-piece, showing the adoration of the Kings.

(Berlin-Dahlem, Staatliche Museen Preussischer Kulturbesitz, Gemäldegalerie).

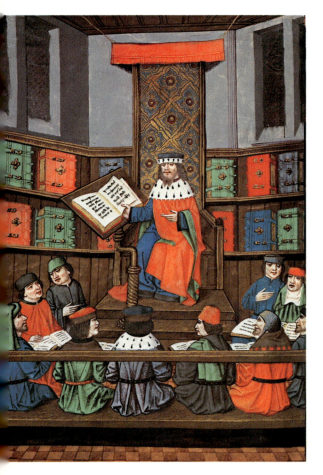

292. A university professor lectures 'ex cathedra' in a library. In 1425, during the reign of Duke John IV, a university was founded at Leuven, destined to restore new life to the town after the decline of its textile industry.

(Ghent, University Library, Ms 10 fo 37 V°. Miniature from the *Rhetorica Vetus I* from the Library of Rafael de Mercatellis; ca 1482-1487).

Vijd to commission the *Adoration of the Lamb* retable (1432). He must also have been thrilled by the calligraphic activities, from 1429 onwards, of the Hieronymites in the nearby Nedershelde Street. This learned promotion of the book in this part of the town is reflected in the depiction of so many manuscripts in the *Adoration of the Lamb,* and in the rich collection of seventy volumes presented to the Ten Hoye beguinage in Ghent in 1468 by the widow of Simon Borluut, who was related to the wife of Joos Vijd.

These last examples and certainly in St John's parish in Ghent, definitely show the sincere piety and, most of all, religious zeal and faithful emulation of a dynamic and unsung cleric as the very impulse for the promotion of art, art as a medium of devotion and evangelism. This naturally develops into a more triumphal form of religious sponsorship, with the emphasis on the splendour of church or hospital buildings, and on local pride. This art naturally confronted the faithful with God, the Madonna and numerous saints, together with the traditional iconographic assemblage of the prophets, taking them from the birth of Christ to, in particular, the Last Judgement in the many versions which encouraged deep contemplation and self-examination. However, direct associations with local saints, local clergy, the local parish and hospital, and the evocation of chauvinism, pride and sentimental bonds were never forgotten. It was done with discreet touches such as the suggestion of the Bruges crane site between the pillars in the background of the St John altarpiece by Memlinc, and the depiction of the measuring of wine to be reserved for the brothers of St John's hospital which commissioned the work, and the panel showing canon Van der Paele also boasts the local saint Donatus.

However, the *Adoration of the Lamb* sheds a whole new light on patronage and the commissioning of works of art. Joos Vijd and his wife, Elizabeth Borluut, were undoubtedly inspired by piety. Yet here, and surely frequently elsewhere though we may note know it or cannot prove it, this pious motivation had another side to it. Several years before the *Adoration of the Lamb* was commissioned, Vijd's father, one of Philip the Bold's officials, was accused of corruption. The theme of the righteous judges was then possibly an attempt to make a statement about the rectitude of the father's actions. Or are we to regard this Van Eyck retable as a means of redeeming the dishonour which the family had suffered? – art as a means of effacing moral guilt. As we have seen, Charles the Bold behaved in this way after his brutal devastation of Liège in 1468. This brings us to the more secular motives prompting the bishops to emulate the patronage of the dukes. But even patrons of this sort, such as De Mercatel, the worldly abbot of Ghent, did not turn to the muses solely for reasons of vanity or snobbery. Among the clergy of the fifteenth century, there was clearly a scholarly thirst for knowledge not unlike Humanism in Italy. The abbot of Ten Duinen had a copy made of the *Facta* by the early Valerius Maximus. This was, however, not just a platonic possession. When a short time later, Gerard David was commissioned to paint the well-known story of the *Verdict of Cambyses* for the town of Bruges, he did not base his work upon Herodotus' record of this Persian tale, but upon a variant of this, or possibly another copy of this widely-known work by Valerius Maximus.

According to an inventory dating from about 1417, the library of the chapter of St Donatus in Bruges contained a fairly modern collection of scientific text-books. The classification of the books according to university faculties, and the division into a lending library and a reference library – where books were chained for protection – make this comparable to a university library. It is not surprising then, that Petrus Militis, who established the library at St Donatus, had obtained a university degree in Paris ; so too had Niclais Scoorkinne, a canon from Bruges. And the famous theologian Jean Gerson, chancellor of the university of Paris, was also deacon of St Donatus' for fifteen years, and although this did not mean that he stayed in Bruges for long, his intellectual influence can by no means be discounted. By the end of the fifteenth century, in 1497 in fact, the cathedral chapter library at Tournai was equally impressive. Apart from a section devoted to Aristotle it contained many notable works from the classics, by Strabo the geographer, Valerius Maximus, Boëthius and Terence, as well as works by the early humanists such as Petrarch, Boccaccio and, in the Tournai tradition, many medical treatises. Mercatel at Ghent boasted, in addition to theological treatises, atlasses, works on Arabian astrology and the classics such as Cicero and Virgil. It is thus clear that the humanism which was flourishing in Italy at the end of the fifteenth century was echoed simultaneously in the North.

ART FOR NOBLEMEN, SENIOR OFFICIALS AND BURGHERS It is only to be expected that the interests of the nobles and senior figures in the Burgundian administration should have been very similar. In many respects these two groups were like identical twins since they cherished the same ambitions and experienced the same impulses as members of Burgundian high society.

In 1413 Jan de Visch, lord of Axel, presented his daughter, who was entering the convent at Broekburg, with a painting by Hubert van Eyck. Petrus Christus did work for the count of Etampes, and Roger van der Weyden worked for the nobleman Philippe de Croy. This is all a question of social prestige, but like the clergy, the nobility were also intellectually motivated as well. In 1492 Lodewijk van Gruuthuse had Boëthius' *De Consolatione Philosphiae* translated for himself and also commissioned a copy of Jean Froissart's chronicle, doubtless as a tonic of élitist aristocratic class-conscientiousness which Froissart had interpreted so well. A literal imitation of the duke can be seen where Jacob van Lichtervelde, sovereign-bailiff and lord of Koolskamp, had himself immortalised in a monumental tomb with mourners – just like the one at Champmol.

The same phenomenon is evident among officials as among the clergy. Art commissions were as much the concern of the lower ranks as they were of the upper echelons. In 1443 chancellor Rolin, the son of a burgher from Autun, founded a social institution at Beaune called the Hôtel-Dieu. This was undoubtedly a socially motivated act of piety but was conceivably also a means whereby he could spend his wealth, accumulated in government service, wisely and honourably, at the same time immortalising his own glory and that of his family. Shortly after canon Van der Paele had himself painted by Jan van Eyck in his *Adoration of the Madonna*, chancellor Rolin wished to see himself immortalised in the same position by the same artist. This was apparently how things were among the élite in the Netherlands. Even more typical is the fact that Rolin commissioned Van der Weyden to produce a *Last Judgement* for the altar in the hospital of his Hôtel-Dieu at Beaune, to be placed in such a position that the sick could, and must look up at the painting – face to face with the theme of death but also with the image of the late lamented donor and benefactor. Finally, we have another instance of idolatry, in the figure of St Anthony, honoured by the royal house

293. Portrait of Lodewijk van Gruuthuse, also known as Van Brugge (1422-1492). Lodewijk was knighted after the Battle of Gavere in 1453 and became a knight of the Golden Fleece in 1461. In this capacity he received King Edward IV of England who landed in 1470 in Texel as an exile and remained in Gruuthuse Palace at Bruges until spring, 1471. For these good services, Lodewijk was honoured with the title of Count of Winchester.

(Bruges, Groeningemuseum. Attributed to Lieven van Laethem, ca 1475).

294. Portrait of Jean III Gros (1483-1484), member of one of the greatest families of officials of Burgundian origin. In about 1450 he was already secretary to Philip the Good and he subsequently held various high financial offices during the reign of Charles the Bold. After Charles' death in 1477 he was taken prisoner, but released on Duchess Mary's intervention and appointed Treasurer of the Order of the Golden Fleece.

(Chicago, Art Institute. Attributed to Rogier van der Weyden. One panel of the diptych, *Holy Virgin and Child*).

295. Portrait of Jean Carondelet II, member of a Burgundian family of officials, chancellor under Archduke Maximilian : previously councillor and master of petitions at the court of Charles the Bold, and councillor in the Parliament of Mechelen.

(Besançon, Musée de Besançon, Jean Gossart, first half of the sixteenth century.)

ever since Philip the Bold had been born on his Saint's day, who was portrayed on one of the thirty-one tapestries hung between the beds of Rolin's paupers' dormitory.

However, one did not need to have Rolin's wealth before commissioning masterpieces. Jean Gros and Jean Carondelet, senior officials, had their portraits painted by Rogier van der Weyden, and Jean Gossart. Even junior ducal lawyers and financial officials took themselves off to renowned artists. Hippolythe de Berthoz, a Burgundian official in the Netherlands, commissioned a triptych by Dirk Bouts showing the martyrdom of St Hyppolytus, when he was just an ordinary petitions registrar to Charles the Bold on a moderate income. Berthoz was in a position to do this long before he became a treasurer in 1477, subsequently becoming master of the Chambre aux Deniers before moving to master of the government Chambers for Finance (Chambre des comptes) at Lille in 1490.

Municipal officials were also in a position to commission masterpieces. Around 1502, Jean des Trompes bought the unique *Baptism of Christ* by Gerard David, and had his first and second wives depicted on the side-panels. At this time he was town councillor pensionary of Bruges, after holding the less prestigious office of bailiff of Ostend in 1498/1499. He did not become an important political figure until he was burgomaster and alderman of the town (1507-1512), and he did not begin to ascend the administrative ladder until 1509-1512, when he became receiver-general of the extraordinary revenues of Flanders.

The large, wealthy towns, particularly those in Brabant, frequently called in the service of artists, just as royalty did, often, but not always, the more famous ones. Rogier van der Weyden, having come from Tournai, was the town painter of Brussels from 1435 to 1464. This did not prevent Rogier from continuing to carry out other work, and he was also active in Italy. Vrancke van der Stockt, an epigone of Rogier but by no means outstanding, also received many municipal commissions in the latter half of the fifteenth century. Leuven commissioned Dirk Bouts, who painted two allergories of justice around 1468. The town of Mechelen similarly employed municipal

master-builders from the Keldermans family. In Brabant, countless commissions followed one another in quick succession, unlike Flanders where the town magistrates seem to have preferred more limited short-term commissions. In 1379 Bruges commissioned Jean de Valenciennes to beautify the newly completed town hall by decorating the corbels with the Celtic tale of Tristan and Isolde and also with bibical themes ; and between 1488 and 1498 the town commissioned various works by Gerard David to hang in the aldermen's hall including the apposite diptych of the verdict of the judge Cambyses around the perjured judge Sisamnes. Ghent for its part gave city commissions to Hubert van Eyck and Hugo van der Goes.

From a social point of view, it is the commissions of individual burghers which are more interesting. Their reasons for having themselves depicted as donors on the side-panels of the diptychs or triptychs were probably the same as those of the previous categories : social prestige, piety and legitimation of the office they held. Here too purchases were made by established figures as well as up-and-coming successful burghers. One such established figure was Willem Moreel, alderman and burgomaster of Bruges between 1472 and 1483, who commissioned a triptych of St Christopher by Memlinc in 1484, not forgetting to feature his wife Barbara van Vlaenderberghe and her eleven daughters on the left hand side-panel, and himself and his five sons on the right hand panel. There is no doubt as to his devotion, since the triptych was made to be hung above the altar of St James's church in Bruges. His flair for talent was equally clear : by 1478 he had already had further portraits painted of himself and his spouse, possibly as side-panels for another triptych (now in the Museum of Fine Arts in Brussels). The young Maarten van Nieuwenhove, who was still only twenty-three years old, also commissioned a work by Memlinc in 1485 : the diptych of Our Lady with child. This was commissioned five years before Van Nieuwenhove became alderman of Bruges, and ten years before he became burgomaster. This too became a pious donation – this time to St Julian's hospital. Around 1490, Jean du Celier, a member of the grocers' guild at Bruges, commissioned a diptych by Memlinc showing the marriage of St Catharine ; and so the list could be extended with countless examples.

Nor should we overlook the social institutions. Around 1506 the brewer's guild of Leuven donated a retable by Jan Borreman to St Peter's church in Leuven, and Dirk Bouts' renowned *Last Supper* was donated to the same church by the Brotherhood of the Holy Sacrament between 1464-1467. Most of what hangs in the churches came from lay foundations and other such corporations. Sometimes the social institution founded its own adornment. In 1475, the wealthy Illustrious Brotherhood of Our Lady of 's Hertogenbosch could afford to pay from its own coffers for the oak statuettes on its Lady Chapel altar, which were carved by Adriaan van Wesel, and the wing shutters to be painted by Hieronymus Bosch. This retable, along with many others, is an example of the remarkable osmosis between the religious and the profane elements of artistic activity in the towns. The theme is religious – here concerning Christmas music – the motif is devotional – an altar in the chapel. The figures depicted are, however, far from pious and unwordly. On the contrary, they are an assemblage of hard and brutal, alongside gentle and refined people straight from the lives of Brabant society. The sculptor Adriaan van Wesel also introduced a secular tone and atmosphere into his work for the less devout milieu of the court of

296. *The Last Judgment,* (1443) possibly painted by Rogier van der Weyden and commissioned by Chancellor Rolin to hang in the great ward in the hospital founded by Rolin in Beaune. At the great festivals, the patient's eyes looked towards the inner panels. Otherwise the altarpanels remained closed, and the patients looked upon their benefactors, depicted as donors on the outer-panels.

(Beaune, Hôtel-Dieu).

bishop David of Burgundy at Utrecht. As we have seen, Brabantine retables were shipped from Antwerp, destined for the churches from the Baltic to the tip of the Iberian peninsula. Thus many anonymous works of art from the Netherlands found their way throughout Europe.

Well-known works were also sold by famous masters, particularly to the many bankers and merchants who were temporary residents of Bruges. Let us just consider the Italian families. Tommaso Portinari, representative of the Medici of Florence will never be forgotten, thanks to Hans Memlinc's portrait of Portinari and his wife. He also commissioned the so-called *Portinari triptych* by Hugo van der Goes, which depicted the adoration of the shepherds and also the founders. From 1480 to 1497 Portinari lived in Bruges, in the so-called hotel Bladelin in Naalden Street, which was built by Pieter Bladelin in 1440 and had housed the Medici bank – of which Portinari had been governor – from 1466 to 1480, and which he subsequently extended at his own expense. The interior is a marvellous reflection of the integration of autochthonous and foreign elements, which must have made those many Italians feel very much at home in Bruges. Bladelin's decor was Burgundian : the coats of arms of Philip the Good and Isabella of Portugal on two beam-heads and the flintstones of the Golden Fleece on three corbels. Two Renaissance plaques hung in the Italian-style inner court, with the portraits of Lorenzo de Medici and his wife, the owners of the bank, on the occasion of their marriage in 1469. The Arnolfinis of Lucca were another well-known family ; Van Eyck's portrait of Michele is set in a Bruges interior with which the commissioner of the work was well familiar.

However, transactions were not always successful. The ship carrying the altarpiece by Memlinc, which was commissioned by Jacopo Tani from Florence and was to be transported by sea to his home town, was captured by a merchant from Danzig ; and Tani's commission can still be seen in the church of Our Lady in Danzig.

297. *The Worship of the Shepherds,* ca 1476, painted by Hugo van der Goes under commission from Tomassino Portinari, agent of the Medici bank in Bruges, who was at that time councillor to Duke Charles the Bold.

(Florence, Gallerie degli Uffizi).

332

An economic product
and a business concern

ART AS A PROFESSION The artists of the fifteenth century generally enjoyed a twofold status : on the one hand they were servants of the prince, on the other they were 'independent' professional craftsmen. In both capacities they were then part of a structure which was well established long before 1400. It is not clear, and would anyway be difficult to prove, whether any of the artists working in the Netherlands were entirely freelance and independant of these structures.

The court artists, as one would expect, worked in the various ducal residences. According to the court accounts, the painter Beaumez worked for several months in the castles of Germolles and Argilly (in Burgundy) and also in the residence at Dijon. Similarly, Beauneveu was resident for some time in the duke of Berry's castle at Mehun-sur-Yèvre. From 1381 to 1409, Melchior Broederlam was court painter to Louis de Male and Philip the Bold and was therefore resident at their court, though that was a somethat variable situation. There was, after all, no true Burgundian capital : Melchior worked for three years in the Hesdin castle in Artois ; in 1389 and 1399 he worked at Dijon colouring the statues by Jacob de Baerze in Champmol and in 1390 and 1395 he worked in Paris. Remarkably, he still spent most of his time in his birthplace Ypres, and ensured the continued existence of his workshop by taking on several pupils. A 'vagrant' existence, but nevertheless one which, thanks to a fixed annual salary, afforded considerable social security.

The remaining artists worked in the craft-trade sector, more specifically in two clearly distinguishable organisations. In certain towns – and in Brussels already in the thirteenth century – bricklayers, stonemasons and sculptors (who were collectively known as 'stone chippers') voluntarily grouped together to form a guild similar to the German 'Bauhütte' and the 'loges' of French cathedrals. Their aim was to buy and store materials collectively, to exchange information and techniques and to protect the social interests of the group. In other towns throughout the fourteenth century, these St Luke's guilds developed along the lines of the other craft guilds. In Bruges and Ghent, Antwerp and Leuven, and many other centres, they brought together those employed in creative art, whether it was painting, building, sculpting and printing, or poetry and the illumination of manuscripts. It was often a fusion, around one artistic field, of small groups already in existence. So the artist was equated socially with the tradesmen who worked with his hands, without necessarily using any original creativity. What we now call an architect was then simply a glorified stonemason who showed more intelligence than his professional colleagues. It would appear, apart from the renowned figures who were much in demand, that creative work was not much more lucrative than simple production work. A distinction was made between art and trade only in exceptional cases.

An artist, like any tradesman, began his career with an apprenticeship with a more or less reputable – but in any case established – master. In 1387, the regulations of the painters' guild in Brussels stipulated that an apprentice had to remain under the same master

298-302. Putative self-portraits :
Jan van Eyck as *The Man with the Turban.*
(London, National Gallery).

Rogier van der Weyden, detail from the third in the Herkenbald series of tapestries, woven to the painter's design.
(Berne, Historisches Museum).

Gerard David.   Detail from the *Adoration of the Kings.*
(Brussels, Royal Museum of Fine Arts).

Dirk Bouts as landlord of the inn where the Last Supper is taking place.
(Leuven, St Peter's Church.   Centre panel of the triptych *The Last Supper*).

Hans Memlinc : detail from the central section of the *Mystical Marriage of St Catherine.*
(Bruges, St John's Hospital, Memling Museum).

334

for four years, in an attempt to eliminate mutual inequality among the masters. Nevertheless, qualitative differences still exercised considerable influence. Between 1454 and 1530, sixty-one per cent of the master painters in Bruges had no apprentices at all, while five per cent of the masters took thirty-six per cent of the apprentices under their wing. The meritorious Jacques Daret began his career in Robert Campin's workshop in Tournai, where he stayed from 1418 to 1426. From 1432, after a second period of training, or at any rate residence in Aachen, Daret became master of the artists' guild of Tournai in his own right. Some transferred their activities from one town to another, such as Joos van Wassenhove, master first in Antwerp in 1460, then in Ghent in 1464. Others began as masters but then found that the position of official town painter offered better social standing. Rogier van der Weyden moved from Tournai to Brussels for this reason and was even prepared to translate his family name, which was originally French (De la Pasture). The sculptor Adriaan van Wesel was a member and deacon of the painters' guild in Utrecht from 1477 to 1481, but in 1379 Klaas Sluter, as one would expect, joined the alternative guild of the stone-chippers which already existed there, remaining a member until 1385. The figures for enrolment into the painters' guild illustrate exactly the economic pull of a town. Between 1460 and 1500 an average of nine apprentices joined these guilds in Antwerp each year but this figure increased to around twenty after 1505. The number of masterships increased proportionately to an average of fifteen or so per year. In Bruges, however, the number of new masterships stagnated at around less than ten per year, and this figure decreased still further after 1510. The mastership of one particular town did not prevent its holder from achieving unlimited success elsewhere; in this respect it differed fundamentally from the other trade guilds. In 1445 the regulations of the painters' guild in Bruges even allowed for exemption for those in the duke's employ. The difference in quality between the various artists was the deciding factor here. Van Wesel worked in Delft and 's Hertogenbosch as welle as in Utrecht; Daret worked not only in his native town of Tournai, but also in Bruges and Lille; Van der Goes was active both in Ghent and Bruges. There was absolutely no limit to the national and international mobility of the famous names.

Many of them had what can be referred to as a studio-workshop. This was certainly so for Jan van Eyck at Bruges in 1430 and later. Vrancke van der Stockt (1424-1495) took over his father's workshop in Brussels in 1444. Sculptors also organised themselves in this way: Jan Borreman was connected with workshops in Leuven, Diest and Brussels. Tapestry-weavers had the workshop of Pasquier Grenier (d. 1493) at Tournai, and that of Pierre Foré at Arras from 1395. The clearest connection of all, however, was between the miniaturists and their scriptoria: in Brussels they could choose between Willem Vrelant's (between 1454 and 1482), Loyset Liédet's (from 1468) and Alexander Bening's (from 1487). Alexander Bening had previously had studio-workshops in Ghent and Antwerp.

These workshops did not, however, produce only for the local populace. Marmion did a prayer-book for Maria of Burgundy and left Valenciennes to decorate the banquet of the Pheasant for the duke. Jan Borreman, and his son in particular, produced dozens of retables for the Baltic countries. In 1464, the tapestry-weaver Grenier was working for Philip the Good, and in 1402 Foré was working for Toussaint Prier, court chaplain to the duke. Liédet illuminated manuscripts belonging to the lord of Gruuthuse and also

303. A Flemish artist at work in his studio, echoing the tale of Zeuxis. According to Cicero, Zeuxis had to paint a portrait of Helen, the most beautiful woman in the world. Zeuxis, who required a model, was first presented with handsome young boys, then young girls. Eventually he chose five of the most beautiful girls, and attempted to combine the best physical features of each in his portrait.

(Ghent, University Library, Ms 10 fo 69 V°).

for the duke, and Alexander Bening did likewise for both the duke himself and Philip of Cleves. Around 1400, Robert Campin's painters' workshop in Tournai must have been something of a capitalistic enterprise which produced many works of art with the help of associates, including such talented figures as Rogier van der Weyden and Jacques Daret. There were, here and there, instances of division of labour. In 1517 a contract stipulated that Master Albert Cornelis would undertake to paint a triptych, but only the most important parts and the nude figures. Memlinc also had a similar group of journeymen under his wing in Brussels.

Contemporary miniatures give us a fairly good idea of what such a studio-workshop would have looked like. An illustration in a manuscript by Cicero from the collection of abbot Rafaël de Mercatel (mentioned above), shows the Greek painter Zeuxis with a number of models, one of whom he must select in order to depict the ideal woman. In fact, the miniaturist is showing us an artist's studio of the late fifteenth century : the artist making a sketch of a 'living model' onto a canvas, assisted by a young boy, with a large assortment of paint dishes arranged on flat tables. There were also many illustrations of the interior of the miniaturist's studio, the most picturesque of these were by Liédet, who painted Charles the Bold paying an unexpected visit to his calligrapher and miniaturist in his workplace – a joke which Philip the Good also played on his copyist David Aubert. Jean de Tavernier immortalised the court writer Jean Miellot in the process of inscribing a beautifully prepared sheet of lined parchment with elegant Burgundian bastard letters on the sloping top of his writing-desk, surrounded by completed manuscripts strewn everywhere amongst all manner of writing materials : ink-pots, pens, parchments, compasses and rulers.

A builder's workshop was very different to these peaceful copying rooms, which were reminiscent of monks' cells, and which continued the tradition of the abbey scriptoria. In Jan Van Eyck's remarkable picture of a builders' workshop in all its aspects in the background of his composition of St Barbara, we are brought face to face with the rough world of the sturdy masterbuilders and stonemasons who defied wind and weather as well as vertigo high up on the cathedral walls, whilst decorating them with the freakish heads of their gargoyles. The many workplaces which remained for several decades in the fourteenth and fifteenth centuries round the building sites in Brabant, Flanders, Liège, Holland and Hainault, were power-houses of effervescent creativity where experiences, new techniques and stylistic innovations were freely exchanged. However, the copyright of such innovations was jealously disputed and then there were undisputable signs of cultism.

The building site around Our Lady of Poel at Tienen is a good example. Jan van Osy, the great architect of the Ars Nova movement, worked there and travelled up and down from Mechelen where he was working on St Rombaut's : when Osy became too busy, he sent instructions to Hendrik and Jacob van Gobbertingen (or van Tienen) who immediately took over for him at Tienen while the great master, at the insistance of the aldermen of Tienen, just rode backwards and forwards. By the time Jacob took over at Tienen, he was already well-known in Brussels where he was asked to work on St Gudule's and the town hall, at the same time advising on the church of Our Lady in Antwerp. Jacob became so busy that Botso van Raatshoven took over from him at Tienen ; however, Botso's untimely death in 1404 meant that Jacob himself took over again until 1418 when a new master-builder, Sulpicius of Vorst, engaged by Jacob himself, definitively ensured the succession. These architects were therefore travelling consultants who worked between the towns, like a certain Willem van Kessel travelling between 's Hertogenbosch, Leiden and Liège. All this travelling, consultation and advising not only promoted these people to stardom, but also led to industrial-artistic espionage, as we can see from an argument at Diest in 1397 between the town and its master-builder Hendrik van Tienen, who, it was alleged, had been bribed to show the plans of St Sulpice at Diest to another architect. Suspicion fell upon Willem van Kessel whose design for the cathedral at 's Hertogenbosch bore considerable stylistic resemblance to the church at Diest. Willem van Kessel and Hendrik van Tienen were both pupils of Osy, and had been freemen

304.   Dirk Bouts : *St Christopher,* right-hand panel of the triptych the *Adoration of the Three Kings.*

(Munich, Alte Pinakothek).

of a guild and colleagues together. So it need not be true that the stylistic similarity in plans indicated corruption. However, material gain must have become very important to these 'stars'.

During the fifteenth century the number of practising artisans increased considerably. There were one hundred and fourteen tapestry-weavers at Bruges compared to fifty-six in the previous century, and in the second half of the fifteenth century there were at least seventy-nine glass-painters there. In 1459 there were some thirty-six gold and silver smiths at Brussels. The number of tapestry-weavers at Tournai increased from forty in the second half of the fourteenth century to one hundred and twenty in the first half of the fifteenth century and two hundred and forty in the second half. Artisans were quite highly placed in the social order. The title 'valet de chambre' was an honourable one and brought royal protection, despite the fact that artisans never held high positions within the court hierarchy. The title of 'Master', however, was a more usual professional epithet, and implied only that the holder was highly respected within a particular field. In Jan van Eyck's portrait of his wife, painted in 1439 at the zenith of his fame, her appearance indicates that she must have belonged to and been accepted by the upper classes of Bruges. In Leuven, Dirk Bouts, an immigrant from Haarlem, married the widow of a Leuven burgomaster.

305. *The Mystical Marriage of St Catherine,* in which we can probably see Duchess Mary of Burgundy (left) and Margaret of York (right).

(Bruges, St John's Hospital, Memling Museum. Hans Memlinc, 1479, fragment from the centre-panel of the triptych).

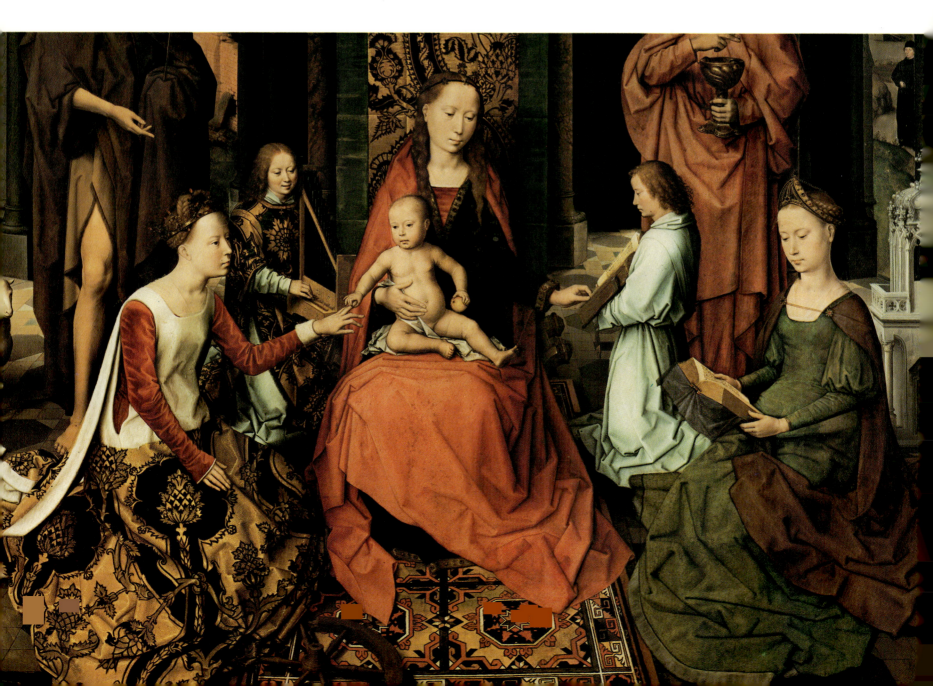

306. Benefactress (Isabella of Portugal ?) with St Elizabeth.

(Bruges, Groeningemuseum. Petrus Christus ; 1472-1473).

THE PRICE OF ART   Were the earnings of these artists in proportion to their status and fame ? Jan van Eyck received a yearly stipend of 100 pounds Parisis from Philip the Good and even before 1433 this had been increased to 360 pounds in addition to travel costs, a house and a servant and, of course, earnings from separate external commissions. We are quite well informed about the stipends of the artists in Philip the Bold's service ; a top figure such as Sluter earned a daily wage of eight French groats, the equivalent of twenty-eight Flemish groats, therefore four and a half times the wage of a skilled worker in Flanders.

There was a definitive hierarchy among the artists. Sluter received double the wage of less highly renowned sculptors such as Pierre Beauneveu and Jan Prindale, who received four French groats. An average stonemason received two French groats or seven Flemish groats. In general it can be stated that painters were more highly prized than sculptors. Melchior Broederlam received 800 French francs for colouring and gilding the statues for which Jacob de Baerze had only received 400 francs. These 800 francs are equivalent to three years and four months salary for Sluter.

The extra commissions outside salaried work were financially very important. As court painter to Louis de Male in 1382, Jan van der Asselt received groats to the value of twenty pounds per year, but a single painting for a church in Ghent earned him eighty-six pounds – the equivalent of four of his yearly salaries.

An artist's career did not usually bring great wealth. In 1389, the sculptor-artist Jean de Marville left, according to the sale of his effects, 332 francs – the equivalent of one year and four and a half months of Sluter's salary. On his death, Rogier van der Weyden owned a house and a piece of ground in Brussels and had made loans to various institutions. Van der Weyden's successor, Vrancke van der Stockt, the official city painter of Brussels, owned a house there, was drawing rents on other real estate and had land out in the country. Around 1458, on his arrival at Valenciennes, Simon Marmion bought a very modest house but gradually acquired so much property that a large part of the town was referred to as the 'grand héritage de Simon Marmion' long after his death. Pasquier Grenier from Tournai left a considerable amount of real estate and also financed the redecoration of the church of St Quentin. These artists thus had the status of successful master craftsmen in whatever field, but seldom had more than this. The only exception to this was Dirk Bouts, who had married into wealth and owned a spacious residence in Leuven itself and much property in the surrounding area.

Insufficient systematic research had been carried out to be able to pass proper judgement on the selling price of works of art. The prices vary enormously according to the format, nature and theme of the work, and also according to the artist's reputation. Dirk Bouts received 500 gold pieces for two paintings of the town hall in Leuven ; this is the equivalent of over eighty-three pounds and the annual stipend of a Leuven professor. At Arras Philip the Good paid Jean de Bailleul 360 pounds for designing the Gideon tapestries, and 11,000 pounds for making them. Between 1472 and 1476, the town of Bruges paid no less than 800 pounds of groats for a series of twelve tapestries showing scenes from the Trojan war by the famous tapestry merchant Pasquier Grenier of Tournai (only one of which has survived, and is to be found in New York's Metropolitan Museum). This means that each tapestry cost on an average sixty-six and a half pounds, or ten times the yearly wages of a skilled worker at that time. This, however, was a masterpiece. In 1499 Tom-

339

maso Portinari sold a reliquary in the shape of a florentine lily, and decorated with precious stones, to the Frescobaldi in Bruges. There it fetched the vast sum of 9,000 ducats, the equivalent of a master-craftsman salary for 200 years. There were, however, other marketable tapestries in circulation, such as that from the household effects of the Ghent magistrate Jan van Melle, which raised the sum of 5,834 pence in groats or, in other words three and a half times the annual wage or one-third the value of a luxury piece from Bruges. One of Van Melle's tapestries was sold for 200 pence – a sum which a skilled worker would earn in thirty-three days. Although we cannot derive the nature and appearance of this piece from the inventory, there is still reason to suspect that it was a simple run-of-the-mill craft product. This proves two things : the very gradual changeover from purely market-orientated products to works of art, and the suspicion that the prices for actual creative art were at a really prohibitive level – even for skilled workers.

The nobleman Jan van Gistel paid Jan de Meyere, a stonemason from Ghent, twenty-four pounds of groats (three and a half yearly salaries or two and a half times less than the expensive tapestry) for a tomb with eight mourners for the church in Zoutdorpe ; at this time a normal headstone cost only seven and a half pounds. Although a work of art such as the *Adoration of the Lamb* must have cost

307. Philip the Good kneeling before St Andrew, the patron saint of the Burgundian dynasty.

(Brussels, Royal Library, Ms 9511, fo 389 Ro. Miniature from the *Breviary of Philip the Good*; Flemish master ca 1455).

308. Guillaume Fillastre, as Chancellor of the Order of the Golden Fleece, presents *Le second livre de la Toison d'Or* to Duke Charles the Bold. Fillastre was the head of the Grand Council (1457-1473) and bishop of Tournai, one of the most important officials of the Burgundian State.

(Brussels, Royal Library, Ms 9028, fo 4, ca 1470-1480).

the Vijd family a great deal, we have no means of finding exactly how much. We know only that in 1424-1425, the town of Ghent paid the same Hubert van Eyck six shillings in groats (twelve days' wages for a skilled worker) for two copies of a retable, the normal price for such a work at this time.

We know more about the prices of manuscripts. In Lille in 1462, a normal clerk received thirty-two pence in groats (five and a half daily wages) for a banale quire without any illumination ; a quire consisted of four double leaves measuring 20 x 30 cm., with twenty-seven lines on each page ; each page therefore cost two pence. This is a good price, bearing in mind that another somewhat sloppier copyist only received one penny for ten pages ; in other words, he had to produce three and a half pages in order to earn one penny – and this included paper and binding. In 1469, a more competent clerk and calligrapher, Nicolaas Spierinc, received from the Duke twice as much as a normal clerk or four pence for each unilluminated page. Spierinc received 1,800 pence in groats (300 days' average pay) for a manuscript of some 200 pages, illuminated with sixteen large and eighty-eight small vignettes and thirteen initials ; this price was inclusive of the actual writing of the manuscript and the parchment. In order to make even an attempt at such calculations, it is necessary to know that a scribe could produce no more than approximately three to four pages a day. Spierinc, therefore, probably earned sixteen pence in groats daily. The miniaturist Dreux Jean was earning a similar salary in 1454 ; since 1448 this 'illuminator' had been earning twelve groats per day in the duke's service. The exact share of each of these artists is difficult to estimate since they often worked in a collective workshop and even sent manuscripts from town to town for completion. Simon Marmion worked for four years on the *Grandes Chroniques de France*. Tapestry patterns could be made in four to six months, but further working took many years.

We can, therefore, safely assume that small works of art were within the reach of moderately wealthy burghers, while the work of the renowned masters – panels or, in particular, luxury tapestries – were an élite art for an élite public. It is impossible to calculate how much a cathedral such as St Rombaut's at Mechelen or St Gudule's at Brussels, on which work was carried out from the first half of the thirteenth century into the sixteenth, must have cost. The building alone of the Carthusian monastery and church at Champmol between 1383 and 1388 cost Tours 75,000 pounds on behalf of the duke – excluding later sculpture-work by Sluter and Van der Werve. This sum equals the average annual income of the dukes in the duchy of Burgundy, or 148 man-years of a daily wage-earner.

As the fifteenth century advanced, the demand for manuscripts grew partly because of the passion for collecting and partly because of literary and scientific interest in their contents. This public pressure was clearly a stimulating factor which encouraged the search for quicker and cheaper ways to reproduce texts and illustrations. Experiments consequently began in wood-block printing, initially only for individual prints, but thereafter for series of related illustrations and texts. It was a system whereby drawings and texts were cut into wooden blocks, as a sort of wood-carving. The oldest known example of this proto-typography in the Netherlands dates from about 1470 but it is possible that unpreserved examples date back to the mid-fifteenth century. At approximately the same time, around 1450, Johann Gutenberg and Dirk Coster of Haarlem sought a method of printing whereby individual letters were used, and which developed into the full art of printing, which began in

309. Illustration with accompanying Dutch text from one of the oldest xylographic prints. The illustration deals with the temptations of a brother from the *Exercitium super Pater Noster*, ca 1420-1430.

(Paris, Bibliothèque Nationale, xylo. 31).

the Netherlands in about 1473. Block-printing was also used in the new typography for illustrations. From this point of breakthrough onwards, the illuminated manuscript only survived by virtue of the fact that it was a luxury product, destined for the same élite market which could previously also afford such things.

A reproduction process was also devised for paintings in the fifteenth century; a process which was the forerunner of modern reproduction. In this, the so-called tracing method was used. This involved transferring the outline of the characters onto another surface by pricking. The dozen or so copies of the portrait of Philip the Good were produced in this way, from the original attributed to Rogier Van der Weyden, and others. This may have been a sort of official portrait which the Duke intended to hang simultaneously in many locations throughout his principalities as an instrument of propaganda and an attempt to popularise the personage of the duke among the general public.

The creation and in particular the performance of music – two activities which go largely hand in hand – were much more expensive matters, particularly where groups of court musicians were concerned. Paintings, tapestries and statues were commissioned from artists who worked as independent tradesmen. For musical performances, however, a uniform company was necessary which, in addition, was also required to remain available to perform at the stipulated times (such as official and religious ceremonies). Musicians from the Netherlands travelled from one court to another, continually searching for a stimulating environment and a favourable income. Florence seems to have had the greatest powers of attraction, but nevertheless Jacques de Marville insisted on a pre-arranged sum, confirmed in black and white, of six ducats per month for himself and each of his fellows, and twelve ducats for the journey from Rome. Apart from the fact that we are concerned here with a monthly wage, while craftsmen were still paid daily rates, this income was not even particularly high, being half as much again as the salary of a master-builder in Bruges.

In 1486 priest Willem van Steynsel declared that he wanted to go to Florence because, he wrote ".. in order to become better by it we are always prepared to serve Your Highness (Lorenzo il Magnifico), on the condition that we know for what salary and for which benefices; now, in the papal state, I enjoy forty ducats per year and in addition ten sacks of spelt, six capons and a pig of one hundred heavy pounds". He asks Lorenzo to reveal exactly how much he is to be given, in secret without the knowledge of his present 'patron'. From these figures it is apparent that the difference between the income of a performing musician and that of a qualified tradesman was limited. In 1486 forty ducats were worth some 3,200 Flemish groats; at this time a master craftsman earned 3,050 groats a year in Bruges. A singing priest, however, also enjoyed many benefits in kind. Guillaume Dufay apparently found it less troublesome to ensure his income; for certain services rendered at the 'Court of Rome', the factor of the Medici bank there served him "bien grandement et traittié bien gracieusement". There was therefore a definite element of competition between the musicians for the best places and between the rulers for the best musicians. The price of art was thus a matter for serious negotiation.

ART AS AN EXPORT Paintings, statues, miniatures and tapestries were produced by artists in the Netherlands for their own people, but even more for the many residences belonging to the dukes, their

310. Willem Moreel and Barbara van Vlaenderberghe, shown as donors together with their many children on the side-panels of the *Moreel Triptych*. Willem Moreel was burgomaster of Bruges, 1478-1479 and 1482-1483.

(Bruges, Groeningemuseum, Hans Memlinc).

311. Stained glass window, 1475-1476, showing the donor, Vilain van Immerseel; designed by Rombout Keldermans, from St Gommarus' Church at Lier.

families and their officials, also in Burgundy and France, and finally for many foreign sovereigns, lords and burghers. In 1482, sixteen Flemish tapestries hung in the Medici villa at Careggi, ten of these had a religious theme and the remaining six were based on secular themes. One of these was Rogier van der Weyden's *Interment*, which still hangs in the Uffizi. When the Italian princess Bona of the Sforza family married King Sigismund I of Poland, her dowry included eight Flemish tapestries. In 1526 she imported a further sixteen tapestries from Antwerp for Wawel castle in Cracow, and no less than thirty-two from Bruges in 1523. She was imitated by the bishop of Cracow and had an even greater influence on King Sigismund Augustus who, between 1548 and 1553, commissioned the famous collection of one hundred and forty tapestries which were based on the designs of Michiel Coxcie, a tapestry artist from Mechelen, still to be seen today

343

in Wawel castle. The 'Arrazzi' in Italy were in such demand during the first half of the fifteenth century that all the important towns looked for Flemish tapestry-weavers.

The English nobleman Sir Donne commissioned Memlinc to paint his portrait at Bruges, as did Portinari, a Florentine merchant, and the Hanseatic Greverade from Lübeck. His colleague from Lucca, the textile merchant Arnolfini, had his portrait painted by Jan van Eyck. The works of art were normally shipped to their distant destinations ; to the Baltic as well as to Italy (in this case via the port of Naples). By far the most significant exports of Brabantine art were the wood retables from Brussels, Mechelen, Leuven and Antwerp which were exported, along with the less significant works through the port of Antwerp. These works are to be found not only in Zoutleeuw, Leuven and St Joris-Weert, but also upon many

312. Hans Memlinc, *The Seven Joys of Mary.* This work shows the refined and dream-like nature of the painter.

(Munich, Alte Pinakothek).

altars in Scandinavia, the Mediterranean countries, England, France
and Germany.

As well as this material export, there was also 'intellectual' export
from the Netherlands : an outflow of style and ideas and an
emigration of highly talented people. This 'brain-drain' occured
visibly, but also in ways which were less obvious and could not be
traced. Art historians point out the similarity between Brabantine
gothic and the choir-stalls at Albi, the west-front of the cathedral
at Aix-en-Provence, and the Beau Pilier at Amiens, but we do not
know by which means this influence travelled. Sluter's influence is
evident in many French statues in Toulouse and Cluny, in Spain
(Tordesillas) and on the Puerta del Mar in Majorca. In certain
instances we can point to a definite harmony between certain
artists. Sluter's pupils took his style to Lyon (Willem Smout),

345

Geneva (Jan van Prindale) and Pamplona in Spain, where Jean Lomme lived from 1411 and built a tomb for the King of Navarre in the cathedral. Another Flemish painter and sculptor, Juan de Flandres (d. 1519) worked for Isabella the Catholic in Spain, the grandmother of Emperor Charles V. Thereafter he was active in Salamanca, where he carved the St Michael retable, and he also carved the main altar of the cathedral in Palencia. Jan van der Eycken, pupil of Jan van Ruisbroek and master-builder in Brussels, brought Brabantine gothic to Spain and around 1450 he was working under the name Hannequin de Bruselos, or de Egas, or even Egas Cueman, on the tower, the baptistry and the chapel of Alvaro de Luna in the cathedral at Toledo where, in 1458, he was solemnly appointed senior master-builder. Van der Eycken's influence was particularly great and led to the development of a Spanish national variant of Brabantine gothic, under the impulse of the architect Juan Guas (Jan Was). This can be seen at Toledo in the monastery of San Juan de los Reyes which was commissioned by the catholic kings between 1476 and 1495. In the 1520s Lodewijk van Bodegem, master-builder from Brussels, took the Brabantine style into France, namely to the famous church of Brou (near Bourg-en-Bresse) which was built at the request of Margaret of Austria.

The influence of the Flemish school of painting also spread to many regions. Van Eyck's fame was so widespread that many painters, such as Colantonio, court painter to King René of Anjou in southern Italy, explicity imitated his style. The German Konrad Laib even took the Flemish master's motto, 'Als ich chun'. Louis Dalmau was possibly a pupil of Van Eyck's at the insistance of his patron, the king of Aragon – a notorious admirer of Van Eyck – since his style is apparent in his work The *Madonna of the Councilors of Barcelona* (1443-1445), in which the angels are an obvious imitation of the singing angels in the *Adoration of the Lamb.* Van Eyck clearly also influenced Antonello of Messina, just as Hugo van der Goes influenced the so-called Maître des Moulins. Painters from the Netherlands thus established a definitive or permanent presence abroad. From 1399, Jacques Coene lived in Milan and contributed greatly to the introduction in Italy of painting techniques from the Netherlands. Other masters only stayed in Italy for short periods, when they were specifically requested to do so by the various ducal houses. In 1454-1455 Hendrik Vulcop was court painter to Queen Mary of Anjou and to Charles, Duke of Berry. Frederigo de Montefeltro, the renowned Renaissance ruler whose palace at Urbino became a centre of sciences and arts, deliberately recruited a court painter from the Netherlands. He found that no-one in Italy had mastered the art of oil-painting so well. Joos van Wassenhove consequently came from Rome into his service in 1473. It is certainly true that Italian painting was still heavily restricted by the tradition of the fresco during the fifteenth century. The sharper observation of detail, the true-to-life portrait, realistic surroundings and the rich nuances of colour which the Netherlandish masters managed to achieve on their canvasses, did indeed make a deep impression. During the second half of the century, Italian painting was visibly subject to their influence.

Equally important is the spread of this influence to England. Fifteen or so jewellers and a glazier emigrated there from the Netherlands between 1435 and 1467. These figures are not insignificant bearing in mind that this art was hitherto unknown in the island, and the consequences were of fundamental importance, as in 1476, when William Caxton brought over the first printing-press from Brussels. Many English brick castles were built by the

313. Polychrome statuette, representing Our Lady, ca 1479, sculpted by Joos Beyaert. (Zoutleeuw, St Leonard's Church).

315. *St Servatius.* Polychrome statuette from the Master of St Barbara of Pellenberg, Leuven, ca 1479.

(Pellenberg, St Peter's Church).

314. *St Joseph and child.* Polychrome statuette, ca 1497, by Joos Beyaert.

(Zoutleeuw, St Leonard's Church).

316. *St Stephen.* Hendrik Roesen sculpted this statuette at Leuven, ca 1500.

(Korbeek-Dijle, St Bartolomew's Church).

Flemings. The renowned 'English' gardens were possibly laid out by gardeners from the Netherlands. Painters from the Netherlands also worked temporarily in England, one such example being Hans Corvus from Brussels who emigrated around 1528, and another, Michiel Sittow, who painted King Henry VII's portrait around 1505.

ARTISTIC FLOURISH AND ECONOMIC PROSPERITY   Art is of course not simply an economic product created in response to the material needs and calculations of the artist, nor are works of art commissioned and bought simply for materialistic ends. Equally important are such factors as the fundamental need for artistic and intellectual expression, and the expression of emotions and faith and refinement and the enjoyment of beauty. The works of art already discussed, commissioned by burghers, merchants and clerics, were not bought to smarten their own homes, but rather to be placed in churches and hospitals – a gesture with ulterior religious and ethical motives.

It was, nevertheless, no coincidence that creativity in the Burgundian period was so predominantly concentrated within the large towns, and in the wealthiest regions, Flanders and Brabant. This economic primacy affected artistic activity in two directions : artists were attracted to the most favourable areas, thus draining the other regions. During the first boom in the fine arts in the Netherlands, the duchy of Burgundy and Dijon were the focal points. This focus was almost exclusively within the ducal court. French artists around Jean de Marville, who had come from the service of the French king Charles V, were replaced for the building of Champmol by the Haarlem-born Klaas Sluter, who was working in Brabant, and his Brabantine pupils. In the middle of the century, the court painters and sculptors were also more active in Brabant and Flanders, as the focal point of the ducal court shifted to the North, particularly under Philip the Good. By 1400, artistic production was also intensive in the field of building, while painters and miniaturists' studios reached the zenith of their fame between 1420 and 1450, with a further peak between 1480 and 1520. This was due largely to the domestic market, but also to the presence of foreign merchants, and the excellent outlets through the ports of Bruges and Antwerp.

The corrollary was that less favourably situated regions lost their talent to the focal areas. The existence of talent clearly has nothing to do with economic welfare. However, many promising young artists were indeed attracted from elsewhere by inspiring masters and the opportunity for advancement which Flanders and Brabant offered due to the presence of a sound, widespread patronage and a purchasing public which was prepared to invest. Talent was thus attracted to the 'creative centres', which meant that talents were exploited more than anywhere else through training in art schools and through offers and contacts. Jan van Eyck emigrated from Maaseik (in the prince-bishopric of Liège) first to Holland (The Hague) and then finally to Ghent and Bruges. As far as Holland was concerned Klaas Sluter and Dirk Bouts came from Haarlem, and Gerard David came from Oudewater. The miniaturist Willem Vrelant came from Utrecht to the famous miniaturist centre of Bruges where he died in 1481-1482, and Jan Maelwael, Philip the Bold's court painter came from Zutphen. Hainault, Artois and Picardy not only gave their grain reserves to the more northerly provinces, but also miniaturists : Loyset Liédet came from Hesdin in Artois to Bruges, while Simon Marmion emigrated from Amiens to studios in Valenciennes and Tournai. Master-painters were also attracted from much greater distances : Hans Memlinc came to Bruges in 1485 from

317. Detail of the tomb of Duchess Mary of Burgundy. A comparison of the bronze face with the recently found skull, led to the supposition that while designing it the artist must have had access to the death mask.

(Bruges, Church of Our Lady. The figure was cast by Renier van Thienen to Jan Borreman's model. There are no mourners).

Seligenstad, where he was born, and Michael Sittow, who was born in 1469 in Reval (Estonia) later worked under Memlinc in Bruges for fifteen years before becoming court painter to Isabella the Catholic (grandmother of Charles V) from 1492 to 1504 and painter at the court of Margaret of Austria in Mechelen in 1515-1516. This is not surprising considering the intensive trading contacts between Flanders and the Baltic, but it does say something about the cultural relations. The result of these numerous migrations was that the so-called 'Flemish School' was composed mainly of non-Flemish artists, although this foreign talent only came to Flanders because it offered a fertile artistic soil which was promoted by Melchior Broederlam at Ypres and Hugo van der Goes at Ghent, both Flemings. It would appear that the number of migrations was determined by the fact that certain centres had become saturated with artistic talent and, consequently, attractive new opportunities were sought elsewhere. This could explain Rogier van der Weyden's move from Tournai to Brussels at a time when Robert Campin (d. 1444) was continuing to exploit a flourishing workshop in Tournai.

There are further indications that artists reacted sensitively to economic fluctuations. In 1515 Gerard David left Bruges, where he had achieved so much, to become a member of the painters' guild in Antwerp, although he was in Brussels when he died in 1523, providing a somewhat symbolic example of the link between art and commerce. Bruges' achievement in 1480 was still possible because the city was then still economically viable. But Antwerp was also coming to the fore in the arts, coinciding with its marked demographic and economic growth, and this new trend was sealed and exemplified by Quinten Metsijs. We might wonder why Holland, which had become urbanised to the same extent as Flanders by around 1500, was not experiencing a similar cultural expansion. It possessed enough creative talents, although many of these continued to move southwards throughout the fifteenth cen-

318. Detail from the tomb of Duke Charles the Bold, dated 1559. Charles the Bold, who died at Nancy and whose body, half-eaten by wolves, was identified by his court jester, was first buried at Nancy. Not until the reign of Philip II was he buried in a tomb at Bruges, placed next to that of his daughter Mary of Burgundy. It is not known whether his remains ever reached Bruges. Recent excavations yielded no trace.

(Bruges, Church of Our Lady. Chased and gilded bronze tomb by Jacob Jonghelinck, 1559).

tury. This leeway in Holland can only be explained by the fact that, prior to 1500, the northern towns were too small to support the wide range of specialised artistic and intellectual activities, something which the much larger towns of Flanders and Brabant and the seats of bishopries like Tournai, Arras and Liège could do without any difficulty. Artistic development – even in the South – followed a short way behind economic expansion. We must also remember that the considerable stimulus provided by the Burgundian court was only felt in the South. In short, the most talented artists from the northern towns moved to the South, and those who were left were of an inferior quality. For this reason it is difficult to promote the figure of Geertgen tot Sint-Jans to a Haarlem school in the latter half of the fifteenth century.

There was also some creative artistic activity round the ecclesiastical court of Utrecht, including Jacob of Utrecht (c. 1480-1530), who left a triptych in the tradition of the great examples of the South. A much more striking symptom of the staggered development between North and South which was shown in demography, social relations (workers in the North became aware of their situation later than those in the South), and the expansion of trade and industry, is apparent in literature. The art of the rhetoricians flourished at its height in Flanders and Brabant at the end of the fourteenth century and was a dominant art from for the rest of the century from 1430 onwards, whereas this same process did not begin in Holland and Zeeland until the end of the fifteenth century.

THE INDIVIDUALITY OF 'FLEMISH ART' Despite all the variants, the art of the Netherlands in the fifteenth century shares one characteristic common to all art forms, namely that of late gothic, which was shared by all the masters from Flanders, Brabant, Hainault, Holland and Utrecht. Individual signatures were more highly rated in sculpture and music, in paintings and miniatures, and they had

349

sufficient personality to be universally recognised as such – even by fifteenth-century contemporaries.

Bartholomeus Facius, Italian historiographer to King Alfonso of Aragon in the mid-fifteenth century points, on the basis of the Lomellino triptych, to realism and the technique of chiaroscuro as fundamental characteristics of Van Eyck's work which differed from Italian norms; the same characteristics which have also been distinguished by twentieth-century art historians.

Art in the Netherlands was simultaneously linked with the central state and the individual towns, albeit in a differentiated manner. Due to its peripatetic existance, the Burgundian court particularly patronised the more portable art forms: tapestries, which did indeed accompany the dukes as they moved from residence to residence and were even hung in the banqueting halls as temporary decoration, jewelry, illuminated manuscripts and music. The principal monumental works of art which the dukes commissioned were their tombs. This was by far the most important way in which they could immortalise their own personality and that of their dynasty. Monumental art – cathedrals, town halls, large statues, large retables – were more a matter for the wealthy burghers of the large towns, where there was a real concrete need for such art as a function of the growth and ambitions of these centres.

In this world of princely patrons and wealthy merchants, was there still room for free and independent artistic creativity? Few examples of such work have been preserved. In 1439, Jan van Eyck painted a portrait of his wife, but we cannot be sure that even this hung in his home any considerable time since we know that at one time it belonged to the chapel of painters and saddlers in Bruges. Understandably, few of these works of art have survived, since they did not belong to valuable collections. But was there any need for this kind of private art at this time? One gets the impression that Hieronymus Bosch often painted uncommisioned works, purely for the enjoyment of being able freely to perceive and depict the world in his own way. We do not know who commissioned many of his works, but that does not mean to say that they did not exist.

Art, religion and the masses

In all cultures, art and religion are closely connected, with the former serving the latter. In the Burgundian Netherlands too, religion provided a framework, a theme and a purpose for artistic expression. This is hardly surprising since Christianity was the natural, all-embracing philosophy of life. Religion provided the current patterns, motifs and explanations for all social behaviour and penetrated all aspects of daily life, the beggar's as much as the duke's.

Religious art, being destined for the eyes of the masses, achieved a far greater social penetration than élitist or court art. The fact that most artists worked for both these markets, helped to bridge the gap which could be drawn between the two. Churches were the imposing bearers of the religious message, represented in a universal language of symbols which the illiterate could also understand. Much has been written about the upward movement of gothic church architecture and the feverish competition between the towns to acquire the highest spire. The steeple of St Rombauts in Mechelen

319. The Italian couple Claudio Villa and Gentine Solaro as donors of a Passion retable.

(Brussels, Royal Museum of Art and History. Brussels studio, oak, polychrome, ca 1460-1470).

351

had to be more than one hundred metres high, so the church of Our Lady in Antwerp must then have two such steeples, and even higher... The imposing character of these largest buildings was not only designed for the burghers themselves but was at the same time also intended to enhance the prestige of the entire town community in the eyes of the outside world.

The church porches showed biblical scenes ; inside the colourful stained-glass windows glowed with other elements of the same message. Evidence of this are the windows given to the basilica of Our Lady at Halle by Count Wiliam IV of Hainault, Holland and Zeeland, which include Christ giving the blessing, St George and the dragon and St Martin. Further magnificient examples are the five or so stained-glass windows in the church of St Gomarus at Lier with the crowning of Mary in glowing colours. The art of glazing had been developed on the grand scale in the Netherlands ; such work was usually commissioned by institutions, and for no less than the whole parochial community.

In the fifteenth century, chapels and their acts of workship became more widespread. Here too, works of art helped to broadcast the religious message. In the church of St Sulpice at Diest, stained-glass renderings of the patron saints of the guilds placed under a traditional baldachin are still to be found, having been there since about 1500. In St John's church at 's Hertogenbosch the guilds dedicated twenty-two altars to their saints, altars which were similarly decorated with paintings and carvings.

Secular buildings also carried the religious message. In 1449, the local authorities of Leuven decided to decorate the front of the town hall with two hundred and thirty carvings which were to be designed by two clerics. The magistrature treated the interior likewise, and Dirk Bouts created his Judgement of the Emperor Otto under the censorship of the church. The most prominent artists thus helped to popularise the religious message and their work was consequently partly aimed at and accessible to the masses. In addition, there were other forms of popular culture which conveyed the message more directly and involved more active participation, such as the performances of the Passion plays which initially took place at the church door, or of the Epiphany or, as in Antwerp around 1400, the *Legend of St Barbara* and the *Play of Our Lady*. In addition to the great political events, there were also the numerous festivals of the church calendar, the usual holy days of course but also the festivals of the local saints and patrons of the guilds, fraternities, professions and not least of the chambers of rhetoric themselves. Such occasions were celebrated with processions, church services, performances and music.

These church festivals were of tremendous significance. The entire community became involved in these massive manifestations, and could identify with the values which they represented : religion, the town, the guild. Here the townsman found the meaning of his life expressed. Participation in the ritual gave each individual the feeling that he or she was part of something more exalted. Communal singing and processing along a familiar route towards a climax followed by secular celebrations, gradually created a sense of euphoria. This resulted more than once in wantonness as it did during the Entry of Duke Charles the Bold into Ghent in 1467. This occured just after those who had participated in the three-day procession to St Lievens-Houtem had returned to the town, when spirits would usually run high. Torchlight at an evening Entry, such as Margaret of Austria's into Ghent in 1500 and 1508 and also her father Maximilian's and her nephew Charles', lent something extra to an already impressive fairy-tale atmosphere.

All manner of companies – musicians as well as actors – performed on such occasions. They enjoyed the support of the municipal government and also the fraternities and other organisations. Their performances undoubtedly originated from church festivals. During the course of the fifteenth and sixteenth centuries the chambers of rhetoric spread from South-West Flanders. One hundred and thirty such chambers definitely existed up to about 1550. Approximately half this number were based in Flanders, thirty-one in Brabant and eighteen in the northern Netherlands, where considerable expansion of the chambers continued during the second half of the sixteenth century. By that time, however, the chambers of rhetoric were already involved in religious disputes, whereby their freedom of expression became restricted. There were numerous companies in the large towns – Ypres topped the league with six, but they were also to be found in many villages, particularly in Brabant and Flanders. The rhetoricians undoubtedly reached a wide audience and were rooted in the tradition of broad sections of the population. In towns where more than one chamber was active, a certain degree of social differentiation was apparent : the Peony Chamber at Mechelen, the Marigold Chamber at Antwerp and the Fiery Thorn Chamber at 's Hertogenbosch were élitist, while the Iris

320. '*Every Fool his Bauble*'. The man is holding a stone in his right hand which, according to medieval superstition, sent madness to the brain.

(Diest, St Sulpice's Church. Misericord dated 1480-1490).

353

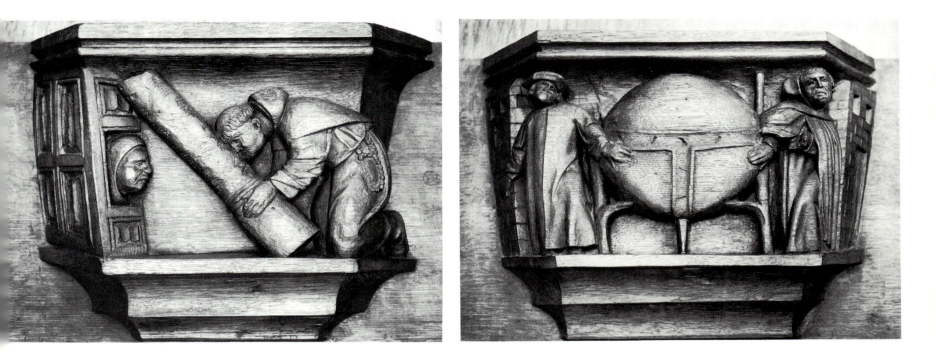

322. *The Pillar-Biter.* Misericord in St Catherine's Church at Hoogstraten.

323. Monks and rhetoricians turn the world upside-down. Misericord in the St Catherine's Church in Hoogstraten. Such works express much of the contemporary world view, not without a certain anti-clericalism.

321. *Sciapode*, a fabulous little man referred to in medieval encyclopaedias as a native of the desert who held his gigantic foot above his head to shield him from the sun. Misericord in St Sulpice's Church at Diest, ca 1480-1490, carved by Jan Borreman or Michiel de Bruyn.

Chamber at Mechelen and the Olive Branch Chamber at Antwerp were composed mainly of tradesmen. As organisations, they had many characteristics in common with the guilds : a dean and a council governed the members who placed themselves under the protection of a patron saint or honoured a religious mystery. They carried a guild banner, adorned with a coat of arms which was carried in procession as a blazon. In addition, each chamber was distinguished by a name and a motto. The specific personalities within the guilds were the 'Prince', a patron to whom all poetry was dedicated and a 'Producer' who directed the performances of plays and also, for payment and sometimes for an annual salary, wrote most of the pieces without however revealing himself as an individual author ; finally, the chambers of rhetoric had their jester or 'fool' who amused the audience with comical anecdotes and mimicry.

The chambers competed with each other in the tradition of the older archers' guilds which like the chambers still exist today as organisations for popular extertainment. The most important of these competitions were the Brabantine national tournaments which consisted of a series of seven competitions whereby the winner received a silver plate (the jewel, or *juweel*) and was at the same time obliged to organise the second competition and donate two prizes. The winner of the last competition could therefore expect to take home seven silver plates. The earliest known tournaments were held in 1411 at Leuven and in 1413 at Mechelen. by the crossbow guilds. The Brabantine rhetoricians organised one vast tournament which began in 1515 at Mechelen and did not end until 1561 in Antwerp with an unparalleled apotheosis.

There were also tournaments in which chambers from all areas could participate. The whole town population became involved in such events : the town magistrature made grants and invited the guilds to supply or contribute towards the cost of supernumeraries, horses, carts and accompanists. The entire population lived for the grand festival which reinforced the town's identity within the broader framework of the principality, or the Netherlands as a whole. Although the language barrier still affected the rhetoricians, participants in the archers' festivals came from all regions : in 1404, not only guilds from Hainault and Artois were invited to Mechelen, but also Parisian guilds.

The jesters deserve special mention because although they were originally the prerogative of courtiers they were more in evidence among the townsmen during the Burgundian period. The function of the fool – who figures in innumerable paintings and sculptures – was to express social criticism in a jovial and humorous manner. Just as satirical representations of social situations, and the clergy in particular, were to be found in the choir-stalls of many Brabantine and Flemish churches, so the fool's performance was also an outlet for social criticism. One common procedure was a reversal of roles whereby a person from the lower social ranks was suddenly made a high dignitary such as a bishop. The election of a fool's bishop (c.p. the Boy Bishop in England) assinine bishop (c.p. festum asinorum) took place at the end of the year in many towns. The chosen person wearing ass's ears and an odd disguise, led a parody of religious and other rituals and situations. These events led to a breach of the regulated norms and codes of behaviour, as also happened at carnival celebrations.

Around the feast of Shrove Tuesday, companies of jesters joined forces, carrying as their ironical motto the world upside down. Examples of this are the fifteenth century poem about the Guild of the Blue Barge (c.p. the German Narrenschiff) which enjoyed widespread fame, and the probably later text of About the Long Cart. In both examples people from all walks of life whose behaviour does not conform to the bourgeois ideal were summoned to join a merry company which was carried off to the fringe of society by the transport referred to. Leaving the Barge, (or cart), forfeiting membership of the guild – i.e. in the parody, returning to normal society – is only possible when wisdom has triumphed over idiocy, when one weds or becomes wealthy. Hence a bourgeois satire of the loss of values among the nobility and the clergy and at the same time an equally undisguised criticism of the work-shy, those who do not know how to handle money sensibly, and unmarried or unhappily married women. Hieronymus Bosch quite clearly adopted this popular literature, e.g. in his Ship of Fools and his Haycart , as many wood-carvers also did on a smaller scale. Bosch was a member of the Fraternity of Our Lady, which in its turn sponsored the chamber of rhetoric The Companions of the Passion. There must have been much contact between the artists and the men of letters on a personal as well as at an institutional level ; so that we may assume a common source for their inspiration.

Annual carnival processions provided further red-letter days in the calendar. Originally only accompanied by musicians, they gradually expanded to include apostles and prophets. In the fifteenth century they extended their repertoires with 'tableaux vivants', depicting scenes from the Old and New Testament. Carts were sometimes used, giving their name to the plays. The Play of Our Lady was a standard performance. From about 1450 the giant figure of St Christopher was gradually surrounded by other giants, in the first place Goliath of course, and later by figures from the sagas like the Antwerp Antigon, the horse Beiaard and the Four Sons of Aymon. In 1534 at Bergen-op-Zoom the Blue Barge was even taken around, manned by sword-dancers and fools.

In all these festivities it was the chambers of rhetoric that played the leading role. On every public occasion the municipal governments invited members of the chambers to perform tableaux for

324. *The Ship of Fools,* or the *Blue Barge,* by Hieronymus Bosch, in which all social values, including the social hierarchy, are reversed; as such the scene is related to carnival celebrations and the literary treatment of this theme.

(Paris, Louvre Museum, ca 1500).

356

payment and to add splendour to the parades. Originally, these citizens too, were chiefly motivated by religious inspiration, as we see in the mystery plays like the *Seven Joys of Mary* performed annually at Brussels from the mid-fifteenth century up to the Revolt. The miracle-plays such as *Mary of Nijmegen* were written in the same spirit. Gradually another genre emerged, the morality, of which the Dutch *Everyman* is a fine example. In these plays personifications of various vices appear in the allegories, endowing plays with comical satire usually expressed in a racy, not to say bawdy language.

One morality play which was particularly suited to the bourgeois milieu was the previously mentioned *Mirror of Love* by Colijn van Rijssele. This bourgeois play stages the social problems of the townspeople, and is in its form a typical product of the chambers of rhetoric. It concerns the sad story of a young man from a wealthy family who falls in love with a seamstress of lower social rank. He is sent to another town in the hope that he will forget his beloved, but this does not happen. Through a woeful series of misunderstandings, all sorts of suspicions mount up between the two lovers. Although his parents are finally reconciled to his love, they cannot bring her to the bedside of their dying son. Both young people die of grief. Colijn van Rijssele undoubtedly found his inspiration in the tale of Floris and Blancheflour, but by placing his characters in the town of Middelburg in Zeeland, in the context of a real social problem, his play must have made a deep impression on the contemporary audience. In this drama we can recognise elements of social mobility and the tensions between the various classes trying to establish their own distinctiveness as discussed in the previous chapter. Equally remarkable is the sentimentality of the play : although the love was initially neither recognised nor accepted by the parents, the play is primarily concerned with the highy individual feelings of this love between two young people who are confronted with class differences and conventions. This theme became popular again in nineteenth century plays and novels when similar circumstances led to the same literary reflection, that love is no longer confined exclusively to the nobility, but is also part of bourgeois life. Such refined feelings of love could only develop if there was room for them in the material world : free time, an independent livelihood and the opportunity to live in smaller family units. There was no place for intimacy within families spread over three of four generations. This was the prevailing situation in rural areas. The *Mirror of Love* shows that the middle classes were concerned with introducing a new dimension in personal relationships.

As pure entertainment, and entirely free of religious considerations, the abatement (*esbatement*) or interlude was a lampooning satire of concrete daily situations which developed from the farce. This genre, referred to by the rhetoricians as 'farcical', rendered marital storms, sex, excessive eating and drinking and quarrels. The fact that an *esbatement* was an essential requirement at the Brabantine national tournament shows how representative this form of entertainment was of the prevailing sense of values.

A great deal of the rhetoricians lyrical poetry was also profane, rendering the conventions of courtly love poetry 'int amoureuze' at a bourgeois level. Many of the themes were indeed borrowed from the chivalrous tradition. At a time when knighthood no longer fulfilled a useful social function it remained as a literary ideal for the middle classes. The culture of the nobility was thus reduced to a source of inspiration for the Third Estate.

Because of this, and particularly as a result of the various forms of satire, devotional literature tended to decline. As Johan Huizinga put it : "The rhetoricians released the bourgeois festival from the ecclesiastical mould and enhanced it with an atmosphere of its own. Until the fifteenth century only the court was able to adorn a purely secular festival with a wealth of art in order to give it a splendour of its own." It would seem, however, that secularisation took place on an even broader front. In the genres and themes found in popular literature, secular problems gradually thrust religious considerations into the background, and elsewhere they survived only as a formal introduction to secular messages. In 1525, satire was already being directed at socio-political problems arising from the Peace of Madrid. The characters 'Willing Labour' and 'Trading People' bemoan the endless wars which plagued their regions, but are interrupted by 'Consoling Comfort' who brings news of peace.

Profane figures also find their way into the processions, which were originally purely ecclesiastical festivals. The epics of chivalry became popular literature, providing at the same time exemplary models. Entirely secular and sometimes political ceremonies make an equal appeal to the imagination of the masses and in doing so also convey messages other than those which are purely Christian. Even in refined élitist art materialism asserts itself, and religious motivation yields some of its abstraction to a wealth of superb detail. Attention was paid just as much to the rich hues of garments and precious stones as to precision in the backgrounds. Donors had themselves portrayed in the foreground with increasing arrogance and the portrait as such also gained ground. All pretence of religious inspiration was abandoned in paintings of money-changers depicted on their premises with all their appurtinances, since the Church, after all, condemned trading in money.

325. Marinus van Reymerswaele, *The Tax-Collectors*, 1542. This exchequer is depicted with a sharp irony. Both van Reymerswaele's style and his themes were influenced by Quinten Metsijs.

(Munich, Alte Pinakothek).

This theme, introduced by Quinten Metsijs, recurs frequently in the sixteenth century when tax-collectors and lawyers had their portraits painted in their offices. This is therefore not simply a question of changing style. During the Burgundian period, the pilgrimages imposed as a punishment by the municipal authorities gradually disappeared throughout the Netherlands. Pilgrimages were no longer taken seriously by the masses and direct social sanctions were preferred. Social relations thus became secularised and this gradually came to dominate all aspects Burgundian culture.

So in some respects the 'Burgundian' period shows an evolution towards the secularisation of art. Firstly, profane subjects come to challenge the primacy of the religious themes : the portrait became an aim in itself, and scenes from ancient history, legends and folklore became much more numerous. Secondly, there was also a shift of emphasis in those works which were clearly inspired by the Christian religion, from the spiritual to the secular. In painting this can be seen in the increasingly realistic representation of details and backgrounds, even where there is no symbolic relevance, and in the introduction of profane elements in the foreground. This shift is clearly evident in the treatment, by successive generations, of the Last Judgement. The attention of the artist focusses more and more on the precise and realistic rendering of the physical properties of the damned. In addition, the infernal monsters, fires and tortures are represented with such force that they emit a profoundly dramatic power.

There is yet another respect in which Burgundian art was steadily secularised. The patrons and 'consumers' of art were increasingly to be found among the laity, burghers and even tradesmen. Hence the hypothesis that this wider evidence recognised its own visions, interests and fears in the artistic production which it evoked and valued. There is, then a connection between the public becoming more bourgeois and the representations becoming more functional. So the emphasis on individual emotions and dramatic tensions can also be attributed to the existential problems of the Burgundian period. The parody of the social hierarchy which Hieronymus Bosch shows in his *Haycart* had its roots, as did his representation of hell, in the doubts, uncertainties, fears and rancours of his own society. Day-to-day survival in the Burgundian era, the fear of sickness, mutilation and death, the fear of epidemics and war all provided a source of inspiration for artistic creativity.

326. This gilded silver coronet, set with pearls and precious stones, was worn by Margaret of York during her wedding ceremony at Bruges in 1468. This is denoted by the initials C(harles) and M(argaret). In 1474 the duchess gave this beautiful personal artefact to the statue of Mary in the Cathedral at Aachen, where it can still be seen today. During the reign of Charles the Bold, Bruges was an important jewellery centre and was renowned for the cutting and polishing of precious stones.

(Aachen, Cathedral Treasury. Anonymous master).

7

The Golden Age

In many respects the Netherlands showed a remarkable development in the period covered by this book, the period from about 1380 to 1530. A process of state formation began in an area which, although economically speaking highly integrated, was still composed of politically independent regions. This process was promoted by a desire for the political unification of these provinces, separate from their great neighbours France and Germany, both of which could originally exert their weight on much of the Netherlands. International political relations – namely the weakness of the German Empire and the Hundred Years War between England and France – certainly favoured the unification of the small but wealthy principalities of the Netherlands. A further contributory factor, alongside the economic ties between the provinces, was the fact that certain regions had shared a common ruler for some time. The continuity of the dynasty of the dukes of Burgundy, which lasted almost a century, and the political competence shown by all these dukes, ensured that any opportunity of extending their influence was exploited to the full.

Although the heartland Burgundy remained in the hands of the French King from 1477, the sense of 'Burgundian' identity staunchly persisted in the Netherlands. As recently as 1548, Charles V still referred to the whole group of territories as the 'Burgundian complex' and in 1544 still toyed with the idea of creating an independent kingdom and saw to it in 1549 that the ducal rights of inheritance were made uniform in order that the principalities should forever remain united.

The process of forming a great political unit in a strategically-placed part of Europe is in itself interesting despite the fact that its borders are no longer visible on present-day maps, and that the Burgundian Netherlands, as we have treated them, never existed as such. Tactical military factors saved the northern Netherlands from the grip of the Spanish Hapsburg monarchy in the second half of the sixteenth century, though the same revolt was put down in the South. In the period 1659-1678 France seized Artois and southern Flanders for good, thereby reducing the area of the Seventeen Provinces still further.

Nevertheless, real characteristics of the Burgundian State continued to exist. In the North, regional representative power-structures developed, the States and States-General which were supported largely by the bourgeois élite. The provincial States continued to function in the South, albeit with curtailed powers since the central government had emerged from the struggle considerably stronger than before. While both the centrifugal and centripetal tendencies held each other in equilibrium with varying success during the Burgundian period, after this time one tendency triumphed in the North and the other in the South. This split was not so much

327. John, Duke of Berry, competed with his brother, Duke Philip the Bold, for the service of foreign and native artists, among them the miniaturists from the southern Netherlands, the Van Limburg brothers. Here he is depicted dining at his magnificent court. The brothers of the weak-minded Charles VI jointly undertook the political government of France.

(Chantilly, Musée Condé. Ms T 284 ca 1415. Miniature 'month of January' from *Les Très Riches Heures de Jean Duc de Berry*).

362

328. Calvary retable from 1392-1399 sculpted by Jacob de Baerze and coloured by Melchior Broederlam. It has two painted side-panels, the right-hand panel is shown here. This retable was taken from Termonde to Duke Philip the Bold in Dijon on ox-carts.

(Dijon, Museum of Fine Arts).

caused by internal differences, but mainly by the strategic disadvantage encountered by the Spanish armies in the low-lying river areas of Holland and Guelders. If present-day political structures and relations reflect the Burgundian state in any way at all, then this is not so much due to national frontiers as to the contrast between the centralised, rather authoritarian South with its élitist patronage and the anti-centralist, individualist North, characterised by its civic loyalty.

The split in the government was accompanied by a shift in the economic focus. This lay indisputably in Flanders and Brabant until well into the sixteenth century. The suppression which followed the uprising against Philip II fell hard on the towns in the South, both economically and demographically. Many tens of thousands of people – often including the most dynamic elements of the population – emigrated to Holland and contributed in no small measure to a new 'Golden Age'. It is interesting that the most successful centres in the world economy were always towns which enjoyed a more or less autonomous status. The citizens of the city-states, the Hanse towns and the imperial towns of southern Germany, like the burghers of the towns of Flanders and Brabant were able to serve their own interests on a regional as well as on an international level virtually without state intervention. The municipal élites controlled their surroundings in order to ensure their immediate provisioning. They also governed the longer-distance trading routes as private facilities, though usually with regional co-operation.

A centralised state authority appears to be incompatible with the vested interests of the wholesalers and entrepreneurs. Although the shifting of the economic focus from Flanders to Brabant, and thereafter to Holland, was undoubtedly largely due to fluctuations in the structure of the international economy, (fluctuating demands and shifting routes), the progress in the form of government must not be ignored. Increasing fiscal pressure and the state restrictions placed on particularistic commercial jurisdiction, the abolition of municipal privileges in general, the equalising – for dynastic purposes – of competing centres within the same territorial area, all these factors damaged the commercial capitalism in the towns.

329. *The departure* from the *Histoire de Hélayne*. This miniature reflects the refined court culture of the Burgundian period.

(Brussels, Royal Library. Ms 9967, fo 39).

The vehemence of the confrontations between the two power-poles can be attributed to the opposing interests of the large commercial and industrial towns on the one hand, and the interests of the centralised government on the other. The advanced state of development and the size of the Flemish towns meant that the heaviest conflicts took place there. But also smaller towns which enjoyed a tradition of legal, political and economic autonomy, such as Liège, Dinant or Dordrecht and Leiden, soon came into conflict with the ruler. The towns in the most important regions constituted such concentrations of power that any attempt at centralising the government was inevitably an assault on the walls of these small city-states.

The Netherlands as a whole were, with their average of one townsman to every three inhabitants, the most urbanised area in Europe apart from North Italy. The consequences of this extended beyond the field of politics, and it can be safely said that the economic order of the entire Netherlands was devised as a function of this urban aspect. The regions which remained predominantly agricultural functioned as supply areas for the urbanised centres. Agricultural production in these areas was stimulated by demand from neighbouring countries and the towns expanded into transit markets. The municipal élites nevertheless continued to control the whole economy, no matter how significant the agrarian population was numerically and functionally. It was the towns which were the most dynamic elements within the societies of pre-industrial Europe, and this was due to the 'segregation' of the burgher from the nobleman or farmer. The urban environment embodied a marked degree of human interaction accompanied by a high level of demand, and this promoted inventiveness. The 'Burgundian' culture in the Netherlands is therefore essentially an urban culture. The towns were, after all, teeming with ambitious politicians and officials, smart business-men and highly-qualified tradesmen, all of whom expressed a particular philosophy. It is for this reason that the heyday of all artistic activities in the Netherlands was so closely linked to the wealth

330. Parody of riding tournaments or jousting as a form of popular entertainment. Misericord from the choir stalls of St Catherine's Church in Hoogstraten.

331. Hugo van der Goes, *The Birth of Christ*, central panel from the Portinari altarpiece. (Florence, Uffizi Gallery).

of the Flemish and Brabantine towns, probably more so than to the court milieux. While a few artists were in the permanent employ of the dukes, dozens of others swarmed to the towns from the surrounding areas. Here they would be able to find inspiration and a large clientele of burghers, and also trades-guilds and other organisations. These individuals and groups affirmed their status by commissioning works from the same artists that worked for their sovereign and the nobility. Those who could not afford to do this would look for copyists and imitators who could impress the superficial observer. The tendency to invest in art remained very strong even during periods of economic recession in areas which had previously flourished, such as Bruges after 1480 ; it even increased, relatively speaking, since there were fewer opportunities for spending money and wealth was concentrated into fewer hands. This lively environment stimulated and had a regenerating effet upon the artists themselves. New techniques and conceptions spread much more rapidly in Bruges and Brussels than anywhere North of the Alps. In

332. The quartering of a convicted person was exceptional but carried out for high treason. This is a justice retable depicting the martyrdom of St Hippolyte. This work, dating from the 1580's, possibly alludes to the outbreaks of civil war in the Netherlands at that time.

(Bruges, St Saviour's Cathedral. Dirk Bouts, centre panel of a triptych).

368

333. A noble wedding procession.
(Venice, National Marciana Library, *Breviarium Grimani*, fo 4 V°).

some fields, such as music and the craft of the gold and silversmiths, these large towns even produced more artistic and intellectual talent than they could employ. In highly urbanised areas the average level of schooling was much higher than that outside these areas, and consequently countless numbers of people with such an education went into the world to find employment suited to their capabilities. In Italy the new Renaissance style was gaining ground.

Various musicians and painters sought their inspiration in Italy, and even in the ducal court there was growing interest in the revival of classical themes. Nevertheless, the uniform late Gothic style remained more or less intact. The church of St James (first decades of the sixteenth century) and the new exchange at Antwerp (1531), the fine town hall of Oudenaarde (1527-1530) and the design for the palace of the Grand Council at Mechelen are all in the late Gothic style. The changing style can, however, be clearly seen in the work of an artist such as Quinten Metsijs (d. 1530), while the interior of the Registry of the Franc de Bruges (1528-1531) is entirely in the Renaissance style. It is no coincidence that Bruges led the field in this respect, while the established style remained in fashion longer in less central places.

The fascinating thing about this turning-point in art – it should really be referred to as a gradual transition between about 1520 and 1550 – is that is coincides with decisive reorientations in other areas. Governess Margaret of Austria's death in 1530 heralded the beginning of profound political and institutional reforms. It was just at this time that the favourable economic cycle was interrupted by a rapid succession of crises which ended in the price revolution which was a consequence of the import of American silver.

We can also trace connections between other aspects of the social dynamic. Close connections can thus be established between the developments in the standard of living and the fluctuating size of the population. In addition, the major political trends revealed cyclical tendencies, being alternately geared predominantly towards expansion, then towards internal consolidation and institutionalisation. Both trends are intermeshed : an expansionist policy tends towards a heavily increasing fiscal burden and towards inflation (usually currency devaluation), trading relations are then threatened by retaliatory blockading which in turn threatens employment. All these factors lead to a reduction in the standard of living and possibly also in the population of certain areas. If this evolution persists it comes to the point where it reaches its limits as material and human resources are exhausted, if not prevented by rational intervention at an earlier stage. If, for example, the population is drastically reduced by hunger crises and epidemics, then circumstances for those surviving are more favourable, enabling them to begin a new phase of expansion. This indeed happened, from about 1440 to 1473 and from about 1490 to 1520, coinciding with periods of external peace and the strengthening of domestic authority. Each empire which has reached the limits of expansion tends towards internal consolidation and the extension of its administration. Stable internal and external relations contribute to an increasing trade volume, and therefore also rising employment – which would be rising anyway due to a growing domestic demand (we are, after all, assuming a period of demographic growth) – the state administration aims at a stable currency and a tolerable fiscal burden. A policy geared towards internal consolidation thus leads, generally speaking, to an improvement in the standard of living and consequently to a further increase in population. However, as soon as a second generation comes along, there is a danger that this trend will operate in reverse :

a population which is too large in relation to the productive capacity leads to falling wage levels and inflation, which in turn means that the standard of living and the population decline, largely due to serious mortality rates. This double cycle within the social dynamic was so deeply rooted during the Burgundian period (see diagrams in the Appendix) that the century and a half which we have considered here as a whole can be divided into cycles which determined the life of the entire community in its most fundamental aspects. Through these trends ran a general movement towards more bourgeois social relationships. Huizinga rightly sees the revival of the courtly chivalrous ideal as a last intense expression of the forms and values of a class in decline. 'Courtly' behaviour was replaced by a more urbane behaviour, which became the model. 'Civilitas' or 'civilité' was better suited to the daily needs of an urban environment than was the nostalgia for a past glory.

It was not only the nobility which lost its identity, but also the clergy. Secular values penetrated the church at all levels, which was less and less able to improve its ethos effectively. On the contrary, even where religious symbolism was retained, it was emaciated by a deeply-rooted materialism. The few reactions which led to a deepening of religious experience were isolated exceptions. The penetration of bourgeois social attitudes coincided with the growing predominence of profane themes and realistic imagery in art. The 'Burgundian culture' cannot therefore be viewed as a static entity. Originally developing from the Burgundian court – with a strong French influence – it spread amongst broader social circles, which gradually set the tone with their own philosophy and symbolism.

The greatness of Burgundian culture can thus only be understood in the light of its combination of the French courtly tradition with the burghers' power in the southern Netherlands. The patronage which stimulated refined artistic expression was of French origin. The urbanised regions were typified by their dynamic, their intellectual and social openness, their contact with all parts of the known world, and their wealth. This combination produced the uniqueness of the Burgundian culture : a broad distribution of fine, valuable products in which religious and chivalrous elements gradually give way to profane urbane realism. This signals the beginning of the Renaissance.

In 1530 Erasmus wrote a book of etiquette which was widely distributed and was an excellent example of the townspeople's struggle to establish their own code of behaviour. It was a matter of regulating a person's physical needs so as not to harm others. Erasmus qualifies various forms of undesirable behaviour on the one hand as 'courteous' and on the other hand as 'churlish' or 'beastly'. The new bourgeois values developed between these two extremes. Much attention was paid to table etiquette which epitomises social differentiation in its essence.

"Before attending the table one should, if necessary relieve oneself. After which the trouser belt should be replaced slightly loosened, since this can no longer be done in a decent manner once seated at the table.

"One must ensure that one has washed before taking a seat at the table, and finger-nails must be trimmed to ensure that nothing unclean becomes lodged underneath. Both hands should be placed upon the table and one should not trouble one's neighbours with elbows or feet. Do not wobble upon your chair as if you need to break wind. Sit upright without gazing conspicuously round at others, particularly those at other tables.

334. Jacob van Utrecht, *The Birth of Christ* (1513) alluding to St Bernard who, as a child, asked at which hour the infant Jesus was born.

"Many handle their dishes as soon as they are sat down. They have the manners of wolves. To put one's finger in the sauce is coarse. Take what you will with a knife and fork, and do not search around the dish, but take the piece which lies closest to you. Take with a scoop what cannot be taken with the fingers. If a serviette is given, lay it to your left with the bread and place the knife on the right. Eat with two or three fingers, but not the whole hand. Do not break bread, as the courtiers do, but cut it with the knife. It is not proper to lick greasy fingers or wipe them on your clothes."

We find in Erasmus not just a prototype of bourgeois culture in the Burgundian Netherlands, but also the transition to a new period. At that point the curtains fell on the most glorious phase of a past shared by all the Netherlands.

335. Miniature illustrating the customs of the Romans at the table. This was usually represented by the medieval artist according to his own experiences.

(Paris, Bibliothèque Nationale. Ms 6185 fo. 51).

Appendices

Calendar

<table>
<tr><td>

THE ROYAL SOVEREIGNTY

1369 19th June: Marriage of Margaret of Male, heiress to the countries of Flanders, Artois, Rethel, Nevers and Franche-Comté, to Philip the Bold, Duke of Burgundy.

</td><td>

POLITICAL SOCIAL AND ECONOMIC EVENTS

1379-85 The Ghent War: uprising which during some periods extends throughout the whole of Flanders, against Count Louis of Male and later against his son-in-law Philip the Bold.

1379 1st December: An agreement is reached, through the mediation of Philip the Bold, son-in-law and possible successor to the Count, that makes provision for a body formed by the towns which will control the dealings of the Count and his officials. Nevertheless, the disagreement flares up once again and the Count forbids foreigners to trade within the county. A new agreement, reached on 11th November 1380, brings no solution.

</td></tr>
</table>

1380-88 Minority of King Charles VI of France; from 5th August 1392 his mental deficiency becomes apparent. Philip the Bold, Duke of Burgundy, plays a principal part on the Regency Council as the son of King John II the Good from 1380 to 1388, and after 1392.

1382 2nd May: The Ghent militia, led by Philip of Artevelde, leaves for Bruges and defeats the troops of the Count, who flee to French Flanders.

1382 27th November: Through Philip the Bold's influence, the royal French army was mobilised to suppress the insurgence in Flanders; it triumphed at Westrozebeke, but the uprising had still not been brought to an end.

1384 30th January: Through the death of her father Margaret of Male effectively became Countess of her patrimonial lands and through her husband Philip the Bold of the Burgundian dynasty belonging to the French royal house of Valois, acquired Burgundian territories to add to those of Flanders, Artois, Antwerp and Mechelen.

1384 May and July: Traders from Castille and Portugal receive new articles of association in Bruges.

1384 18th November: Jan Bouchier, envoy to the English King was taken on by insurgent Ghent as governor of Flanders.

1385 12th April: Double marriage (a) between Margaret, daughter of Philip the Bold and Margaret of Male, to William of Bavaria, nephew of the Count and son of Albert of Bavaria, governor of Holland-Zeeland and Hainault and Count of these lands from 1404 to 1417 and (b) between Margaret of Bavaria, daughter of Albert, to John the Fearless, the oldest son of Philip the Bold and Margaret of Male. Because the Bavarian house was without issue, Philip the Good was able to acquire Hainault, Holland and Zeeland.

1385 December: The traders of La Rochelle and Saint Jean d'Angely acquire new privileges in Bruges.

1385 18th December: Duke Philip the Bold, through the peace of Tournai succeeds in persuading Ghent to surrender its alliance with England on the condition that it retains all its privileges and gains amnesty and freedom of trade.

1386 15th February: A Council Chamber and an Audit Office for Flanders and Artois are set up in Lille. In 1405 the Council Chamber was moved to Audenaarde at the insistence of the Flemings, and again to Ghent in 1407.

1386 11th July: The powers of the Audit Office at Dijon are extended to the counties of Burgundy, Nevers and Champagne.

1387 15/24th February: Duchess Joanna of Brabant offers Philip the Bold the usufruct of her Duchy of Limburg. In 1396 she also transfers the rule of the Duchy to him.

1387 15th January: Philip the Bold grands to Flanders freedom of trade with all nations apart from England – which is involved in the Hundred Years War with France.

1387 June: Trading privileges granted to Scottish merchants.

1388 2nd March: Louis de la Tremoille appointed Bishop of Tournai.

1388-92 The German Hanse boycotts trade with Flanders; the Hanse moves its base from Bruges to Dordrecht. Relations are restored on 12th May 1392; on 21st December the staple returns to Bruges.

374

1389   14th November: John of Bavaria elected Bishop of Liège, appointment followed on March 3rd 1390.

1389   22nd December: Andreas of Luxembourg appointed Bishop of Cambrai.

1390   28th September: Duchess Joanna of Brabant secretly offers her Duchy to her niece Margaret of Male and Margaret's spouse Philip the Bold, on condition that she retains the usufruct and continues to rule there.

1392   6th September: Jean Canard appointed Bishop of Arras.

1396   19th June: Joanna of Brabant transfers her rights over the Duchy of Limburg to Philip the Bold and Margaret of Male.

1396   30th June: Birth of Philip, son of John the Fearless.

1397   19th March: Pierre d'Ailly appointed Bishop of Cambrai.

1402   21st February: Marriage of Anthony, second son of Philip the Bold to Joanna of St Pol. He receives the County of Rethel from his parents.

1404   27th April: Death of Duke Philip the Bold; though his spouse Margaret of Male formally continues to rule in Flanders, the succession passes to her oldest son John the Fearless, who is also Duke of Burgundy.

1404   7th May: Duchess Joanna of Brabant transfers her authority to her niece Margaret of Male, who, on the 19th May, appoints her younger son Anthony to be governor.

1404   2nd September: Anthony of Burgundy becomes Duke of Burgundy, with his mother as Duchess.

1405   21st March: Death of Margaret of Male; her oldest son John the Fearless succeeds her in the Counties of Franche-Comté, Flanders and Artois and the seigniory of Mechelen; her second son, Anthony, becomes Duke of Brabant and Limburg, including Antwerp.

1406   1st December: Death of Joanna of Brabant, bringing the domestic dynasty to a close.

1409   16th July: Second marriage of Duke Anthony of Brabant to Elisabeth of Görlitz.

1396   6th March: France and England draw up a 28 year truce, in view of the Crusade against the Turks. John the Fearless, hereditary prince is the leader of the Burgundian participants. John is taken prisoner during the battle of Nicopolis, which underlines the failure of the mission, and is not released until 1398 for a large ransom.

1398   July: The traders of Genoa return to Brussels.

1400-01   Widespread epidemics of the plague.

1404   1st July: Audit Office set up in Brussels for Brabant and Limburg, later also controlling Luxembourg.

1406   April: Proposals for a Council Chamber for Brabant to be based at Vilvoorde.

1406   26th September: The towns and nobility of the Prince-Bishopric of Liège force the Bishop-Elect John of Bavaria from the throne and choose a new, native Bishop-Elect, Dirk van Perwez, who is recognised by the Pope of Avignon, the Emperor and the Orléans faction within the Royal Council.

1406   19th December: Royal Entry of Anthony of Burgundy as Duke of Brabant.

1407   Anglo-Flemish trade agreement ending years of trading restrictions, and allowing free passage of goods, with the exception of English cloth.

1407   23rd November: Murder of Louis of Orléans, brother of King Charles VI, by the accompliciés of his nephew John the Fearless; they are rivals at the French Court but also in Luxembourg, which Louis has held in trust since 1402.

1408   23rd September: The army of John of Bavaria, Bishop-Elect of Liège, supported by his brother William (Count of Hainault) and his brother-in-law John the Fearless, Duke of Burgundy, defeats the troops of rebellious Liège at Othée.

1408   24th October: Verdict on Liège rebels at Lille: 500 hostages, a heavy fine and withdrawal of municipal and official privileges.

1410 17th September: Jean de Thoisy appointed Bishop of Tournai.

1411 August: Philip, Count of Charolais, son of Duke John the Fearless, appointed ruler in Flanders.

1412 7th January: Elisabeth of Görlitz and her spouse Anthony, Duke of Brabant, become joint-regents of the Duchy of Limburg (entailed).

1412 5th July: Jan van Gavere appointed Bishop of Cambrai.

1415 25th October: Death of Duke Anthony of Brabant and Limburg; succeeded by John IV, elder son from his first marriage.

1416 9th April: Louis of Luxembourg inaugurated Bishop of Thérouanne.

1417 31st May: Jacoba of Bavaria, granddaughter of Philip the Bold and Margaret of Male, becomes Countess of Hainault, Holland and Zeeland.

1417 September: Jacoba's uncle John of Bavaria Bishop-elect of Liège challenges her position in Holland and is acclaimed ruler on 10th November.

1418 8th March, 18th April: Jacoba of Bavaria marries John IV, Duke of Brabant and Limburg, her great-nephew.

1418 22nd March: Roman Catholic King Sigismond grants Hainault, Holland and Zeeland to John of Bavaria.

1418 22nd May: John of Bavaria resigns the bishopric of Liège.

1418 30th May: Jan van Wallenrode appointed Bishop of Liège; he dies on 28th May 1419.

1419 13th February: Jacoba of Bavaria, Countess of Holland etc. ceded South Holland to her uncle John of Bavaria.

1419 May: John of Bavaria marries Elisabeth of Görlitz who holds the Duchy of Luxembourg in trust from the Emperor.

1419 16th June: Jan van Heinsberg elected Bishop of Liège; his appointment followed on 20th September.

1419 10th September: Murder of John the Fearless by the ritual faction at the French court, the Armagnacs. His son Philip (the Good) succeeds him.

1420 21st April: After Jacoba had left him, John IV pledges Holland to John of Bavaria.

1411 Duke John the Fearless brings Flemish militia into his power struggle in France.

1412-14 Duke Anthony of Brabant conducts field campaigns in Luxembourg by way of reinforcement of his rights.

1415 King Henry V of England resumes the Hundred Years War. Duke Anthony of Brabant dies at the Battle of Agincourt (25th October).

1416 Duke John the Fearless demands governorship of Brabant, since the heir John IV has not yet come of age. The States of Brabant buy off his demand and set up a local regency council.

1417 26th March: The verdict of Lille (24th October 1408) is declared invalid by the German Emperor Sigismund. Prince-Bishop Elect John of Bavaria is obliged under pressure to make concessions to the trade guilds of Liège.

1417 23rd September: Bishop-Elect John of Bavaria renounces the Prince-Bishopric of Liège.

1417 The Duchy of Limburg is mortgaged to meet a financial crisis until 1429, as is the County of Dalhem in 1418 (until 1421).

1417 In exchange for a subsidy, Duke John the Fearless accepts a dossier of complaints from the Four Members of Flanders concerning trade, the law, the currency and the administration.

1418 In June, John of Bavaria takes Dordrecht and Den Briel; John IV of Brabant (as husband of Jacoba of Bavaria) abandons the struggle in February/April 1420, but Jacoba herself and the States of Brabant continue to fight.

1419-20 Treaty of Troy (21st March 1420) after the murder of Duke John the Fearless (10th September 1419) Burgundy turns against France and strikes up an alliance with England, Philip the Good recognises Henry VI, King of England, as King of France. Henry rules Southern France as far as the Loire.

1420 John IV introduces gold and silver coins common to Brabant, Holland and Hainault, the 'direlander'.

1420 October: The towns and nobility of Brabant rise against Duke John IV, whom they suspect of mismanagement; he flees and the States of Brabant appoint his brother Philip of St Pol Governor.

1420 31st December: Count John III of Namur is forced to pay heavy compensation to Dinant and Liège; he sells his County to Duke Philip the Good because of financial problems.

1421 19th February: Jacoba of Bavaria terminates her marriage to John IV.

1421 Philip the Good purchases the rights to the County of Namur, and acquires the investiture on 8th June; Count John III retains lifelong usufruct.

1422 August/October: Jacoba of Bavaria marries Humphrey, Duke of Gloucester; this marriage is declared invalid by the Pope on 13th February 1425.

1424 30 November: Marriage of Philip the Good to Bonne of Artois (d. 17 September 1425)

1425 6th January: Death of John of Bavaria. Philip the Good exercised his rights and imprisons Jacoba (1st June). Her previous (and, according to papal pronouncement, legitimate) spouse John IV, Duke of Brabant and Limburg, as heir, takes possession of Hainault.

1425 19th July: John IV, as John of Bavaria's heir, confers upon Philip the Good the rule over Holland and Zeeland for twelve years. Jacoba, having escaped from imprisonment, takes up arms in Holland (31st August).

1426 27th February: The Pope declares Jacoba of Bavaria's separation from her husband John to be unlawful.

1427 17th April: Death of John IV, Duke of Brabant and Limburg; succeeded by his younger brother Philip of St Pol.

1427 23rd June: Duke Philip the Good, without Jacoba's consent, declares himself her governor and heir in Hainault.

1428 9th January: Jacoba's marriage to John IV is canonically recognised, while her marriage to Humphrey is invalidated. In that same year Humphrey marries an Englishwoman.

1428 3rd July: In the 'Conciliation of Delft', Jacoba recognises Philip the Good as Governor and successor in Hainault. She may now only marry with the consent of her mother (Margaret, daughter of Philip the Bold), of Philip the Good and of the States of her three lands.

1429 1st March: On the death of Count John III of Namur, Philip the Good can fully exercise the rights which he purchased in 1421.

1430 7th January: Marriage of Philip the Good to Isabella, daughter of the King of Portugal.

1430 4th August: The younger branch of the House of Burgundy dies out due to the death of Philip of St Pol, Duke of Brabant and Limburg, and both of these Duchies fall to Philip the Good.

1421 11th February: The trade guilds become involved in municipal government in Brussels.

1421 4th May: John IV, Duke of Brabant, grants the privilege of the Regent: recognition of the subjects' rights to resist should their rights or privileges be in any way infringed.

1421 July: John IV of Brabant takes Brussels with the support of nobles from Overmaas, where a popular uprising breaks out.

1422 12th may: New Regime: the Duke of Brabant is granted a regency Council, responsible to the States. This is withdrawn in 1430.

1423 The Pope, in accordance with the Council of Basle, nominates Zweder van Culemborg Bishop of Utrecht, under pressure from Duke Philip the Good, however, he eventually appoints Rudolf van Diepholt, who is supported by Cleves.

1424-25 Humphrey, Duke of Gloucester, effectively becomes Lord of Hainault.

1425 February-June: Duke John IV recaptures Hainault with the support of the States of Brabant. The Hoek party in Holland support Jacoba of Bavaria.

1425 19 July: John IV, as heir to John of Bavaria, grants Philip the Good sovereignty over Holland and Zeeland for twelve years. Jacqueline escapes from imprisonment and takes up arms in Holland (31 August).

1427 23rd May: The Royal Entry of Philip of St Pol as Duke of Brabant establishes the Council Chamber in Brabant.

1428 September: Towns in Brabant, Holland, Zeeland and Liège boycott the import of English cloth.

1429 5th February-15th December 1431: War between Burgundy and Liège brought about by the transfer of villages and reinforcements to the County of Namur. The stakes: competition of Dinant and Bouvignes in the copper industry. Liège is forced to pay war contribution; much destruction takes place in this region.

1429-31 Farmers rise against the tax levies in the region of Kassel.

1429-33 Balance of payments problems between England and Flanders result from Philip the Good's currency devaluations and Englands subsequent reprisals.

1430 7th January: Duke Philip the Good institutes the Order of the Golden Fleece on the occasion of his marriage and the considerable expansion of his territories. The Order brings together the highest nobles from all his lands.

1430 The Duke of Bedford grants his brother-in-law Philip the Good Champagne and Brie. Philip, however, cannot exercice any effective authority in these territories.

1432 25th November: After the secret marriage – contrary to the 'Conciliation of Delft' – of Jacoba of Bavaria to Frank van Borselen, Philip the Good imprisons the latter.

1433 12th April: Jacoba cedes Hainault, Holland and Zeeland to Philip the Good in exchange for the release of Frank van Borselen.

1433 10th November: Birth of Charles, Count of Charolais, son of Philip the Good.

1434 1st March: Official marriage of Jacoba to Frank van Borselen; they enjoy the title of Count and Countess of Oosterbant, and Frank becomes a member of the Order of the Golden Fleece.

1434 22nd April: Jean de Harcourt appointed Bishop of Tournai.

1435 21st September: King Charles VII of France, by the Treaty of Arras cedes to Philip the Good the Counties of Auxerre, Macon and Boulogne, and gives Ponthieu and Picardy in surety.

1436 5th November: Jean Chevrot appointed Bishop of Tournai.

1430 5th October: Royal Entry of Philip the Good as Duke of Brabant: the autonomy of the Duchy would be safeguarded, Brabant would not be involved in a war against Liège or in the Franco-English war, the Council of Brabant would be retained with its own Chancellor, the Council of six high nobles would be amalgamated into the Duke's general Court Council.

1432 August: Disruption of trade with England leads to uprising in Ghent.

1432 A Council Chamber for Holland and Zeeland is set up at the Hague, comprising indigenous nobles and mainly Flemish legal figures. The Stadholder is chairman.

1430-35 Privateer's war between Holland and the Wendish towns.

1433 12th October: Monetary unification in the Netherlands with the issue of new strong, gold and silver coins: the 'Ryder', and the 'Vierlander'.

1434 The import of English cotton is prohibited in all principalities in the Netherlands; this ban is repeated in 1436, 1477 and 1464.

1434 Appointment of a Procurator-General to represent the King on the Council of Brabant; this constituted a reinforcement of royal control of the law.

1435 Revolt in Antwerp over the introduction of a ducal toll at Kallo.

1435-38 Truce between Holland and the Hansa; it was not to be renewed.

1435 21st September: Treaty of Arras between Burgundy and France.
King Charles VII succeeds in weaning Duke Philip the Good from his alliance with England, under great pressure (and among other things, large sums of money) on the Ducal Council and by means of far-reaching concessions. The King promises reparation for the murder of the Duke John the Fearless, relieves the Duke of his responsabilities as the King's Vassal and cedes Boulogne and Picardy. Philip, on the other hand, relinquishes his claims to Champagne, Brie and Tournai.

1434-35 Gradual identification of a legal section within the Duke's Grand Council.

1436 June: The Hansa leaves Bruges (until 1438), under suspicion of pro-Anglo persuasion, in the wake of the murder of a number of Hansa merchants at Sluis.

1436 June-July: Philip the Good besieges the English staplesite at Calais, with the support of Flemish militia; the expedition, however, becomes a fiasco due to tactical errors and counter-offensives.

1436 July : On their return the professional tradesmen of Bruges make demands concerning the subjection of Sluis and the Franc de Bruges; the result is uproar.

1436 3rd September: Ghent is also in uproar as a result of the unemployment and shortages caused by the wars with England and the Hansa, the two most important trading partners who make peace with each other; Duke Philip the Good pacifies the people of Ghent with rapid concessions.

1436-39 Serious food-shortage throughout the Netherlands, followed by a serious epidemic of the plague.

1438 March: After starving the town of Bruges, the uproar there is oppressed by a heavy financial penalty, restriction of the extra-municipal authority and revision of official privileges.

1456   7th April: Louis of Bourbon appointed Bishop of Liège.

1456   (Prior to) 1st September: Hendrik of Lorraine appointed bishop of Thérouanne.

1457   13th February: Birth of Maria, sole heir of Charles of Charolais.

1460   1st September: Guillaume Fillastre appointed Bishop of Tournai.

1463   20th August: King Louis XI buys back Picardy according to the Treaty of Arras of 1435.

1465   27th April: Philip the Good renounces his rulership and appoints his son Charles 'the Bold' Stadholder-General in all territories.

1465   5th October: Charles the Bold regains Picardy and acquires the County of Guines as well.

1465   22nd December: Philip the Good – in fact Charles the Bold – is recognised by the States of the Prince-Bishopric of Liège as hereditary temporal ruler as a sanction imposed on them for their coalition with the king of France against Burgundy.

1456   Philip the Good marches through Guelders with his army to confront Deventer.

1456   6th August: David of Burgundy consolidates the Statutes and Privileges of Utrecht.

1456   Summer: The Dauphin flees to the court of the Duke of Burgundy, where he resides until his coronation in 1461.

1457   Conflict between, on the one hand, the hereditary Prince Charles of Charolais, and on the other, his father Philip the Good and the Croy family. Charles retreats to Gorinchem (Holland) between 1458 and 1464. At the Court of Burgundy, an administrative investigation reveals large-scale corruption. Chancellor Rolin's power is taken away and the head of the Grand Council, Bishop of Tournai Jean Chevrot, is dismissed. The Croy and de Lannoy families dominate the Burgundian Court and maintain good relations with the Dauphin, who in 1461 becomes King Louis XI.

1459   In a conflict between the city of Brussels and the ducal legal officer, the 'Amman', the Duke declares the privilege of the Regent (1421) invalid.

1461   22nd July: Louis XI becomes King of France.

1463   20th August: Louis XI buys back the towns along the Somme, ceded at the Treaty of Arras (1435). Philip the Good uses the money from the sale for his crusade plans.

1463   The towns of Gelderland or Guelders (see 1465) form an alliance agaÏnts Duke Arnold on the grounds of his mismanagement.

1464   9th January: After some chaos from an earlier convocation, called by Charles of Charolais at Antwerp, Philip the Good summons the States of all his other territories to Bruges. This is usually seen as the first formal gathering of what was later to become the States-General.

1464   April-May: Anthony, illegitimate son of Philip the Good, assumes the leadership of dozens of crusaders journeying from Ghent to Marseilles.

1465   9th January: Duke Arnold of Guelders is taken prisoner by his son Adolf and forced to abdicate.

1465   22nd April: Mark of Baden is heralded as regent in Liège with the support of King Louis XI, taking advantage of Bishop Louis of Bourbon's prolonged absence.
Louis and the new regent agree to launch simultaneous attacks on Hainault and Brabant.

1465   5th October: The peace of Conflans, extorted from Louis XI by Charles the Bold after the Guerre Bien Public, brings the towns of the Somme back into the possession of the Burgundians, while the King is forced to cede his protégés in Liège.

1465   22nd December: Under the pressure of Charles' army, the States of the Prince-Bishopric of Liège recognise him as hereditary sovereign and they grant him war reparations and an annual income.

1466   23rd March: Thirteen towns of Liège unite against Charles' authority; after his offensive, Dinant is destroyed on 25th August because the Duke had been ridiculed there. On 16th September Louis of Bourbon is again recognised as sovereign and Charles as sovereign-ruler.

1466   23rd October: Friendship and trade between Burgundy and England.

1467 15th June: Death of Philip the Good; Charles the Bold succeeds him.

1468 3rd July: Marriage of Charles the Bold to Margaret of York, sister of king Edward IV of England.

1471 February: Adolf of Egmond, Duke of Guelders, imprisoned by Charles the Bold for his alliance with France, and forced to abdicate in favour of his father (who had abdicated in 1465).

1471 1st December: Charles the Bold accepts from Arnold of Egmond, Duke of Guelders, the governorship of the Duchy of Guelders and the County of Zutphen.

1472 30th December: Charles the Bold accepts Guelders and Zutphen as surety and is recognised as heir, to the exclusion of Adolf of Egmond.

1473 23rd February: On the death of Adolf of Egmond, Charles the Bold becomes Duke of Guelders and Count of Zutphen, and after a military campaign, he was acclaimed as such in August 1473.

1473 8th October: Ferry de Clugny appointed Bishop of Tournai.

1473 15th October: After attempts to acquire rights in Alsace, (which bore fruit between 1469 and 1474), Charles the Bold obtained from Duke René II of Lorraine the right to base garrisons there.

1467 July: Royal Entry of Charles the Bold is accompanied by riots in Ghent, Mechelen and Lier.

1467 23rd July: Liège recognises the Count of Nevers as Duke of Lorraine.

1467 17th September: The Bishop's residence, Huy, captured by rebels.

1467 28th October: Charles' army defeats the Liège army at Brustem.

1467 27th November: Liège declared an open town, Liège Pedestal is taken to Bruges, the Prince-Bishopric is broken up, war compensation.

1468 14th October: Treaty of Péronne: restriction of the authority of the Parliament of Paris in Crown-Flanders and Artois; should the treaty be violated by the French King, Charles the Bold would no longer be answerable to him, nor would Charles' lands be answerable to the Parliament of Paris. Charles forces Louis XI, on account of his complicity, to join the disciplinary campaign against Liège, which had risen again on 9th September.

1468 29th-30th October: '600 Franchimontois' unsuccessfully attack the camp of the Burgundian army; Liège is taken, plundered, massacred, burned and its walls destroyed (3rd November). Tongres also plundered. Guy de Brimeu, Lord of Humbercourt, remains as Lieutenant-General after the event.

1469 Charles the Bold makes an example of Ghent by bringing down its municipal government as punishment for the riots which broke out there during his Royal Entry. Abolition of the privilege of King Philip the Fair dating from 1301, which controlled the appointment of aldermen.

1470-72 War against France, with privateering at sea; the towns of the Somme are the stake.

1470 3rd October: King Edward IV of England, brother-in-law of Charles the Bold, flees to Holland, having been forced from the throne. He remains in exile in Bruges until April 1477.

1471 27th June: The towns of Guelders unite against Charles the Bold after the imprisonment of Duke Adolf.

1471 July: For the first time Duke Charles the Bold makes a request to all the territories of the Netherlands together, united in the States-General for a subsidy. The subsidy is required to establish a permanent army, the ordinance troops.

1473 May: For the first time the States-General agree to a communal subsidy, according to a code of distribution between the principalities, the army of ordinance troops is increased.

1473 30th September-25th November: Discussions at trier between Emperor Frederic III and Duke Charles concerning the establishment of a kingdom, the conferral of the kingship upon the Duke, and the bethrothal of his only daughter, Mary of Burgundy.

1473 December: Decrees of Thionville, on the strength of which Charles proceeds with the centralisation of institutions and affirms the independence of territories. The Grand Council, as the supreme legal body, is raised to a parliament whose seat is in Mechelen. Here, central Audit Offices are set up for the receipt of levies and domain revenue, these offices replace those of Lille, Brussels and The Hague, and the Financial commissioners. Moreover, Mechelen, a centrally-located and independent seigniory is chosen as a base because of its proximity to Flanders where the oldest Audit Office, that of Lille, was situated.

1474 Treaty of Utrecht between Holland and the German Hanse, which releases Holland and Zeeland from the staple constraint at Bruges.

1474 Upper-Alsace, held in trust by Duke Charles, conquered by a coalition of towns from Switzerland, Alsace and Tyrol.

1474 25th July: The Treaty of London whereby Lorraine, England and Burgundy form a coalition against France; Edward IV is to become King of France, and Charles the Bold granted sovereignty over the French dependencies and Picardy, and also Tournai, Nevers, Rethel and Champagne.

1474 30th July-12th June 1475: Duke Charles unsuccessfully besieges the town of Neuss in Westphalia, in the interest of the Bishop of Cologne.

1474 The new property acquired by the Church over the past sixty years is taxed by the state ('amortised') at a rate of five per cent for each twenty year period of ownership. The clergy strongly oppose this.

1475 May-November: Battle of Lorraine, conquest of Nancy 30th November.

1476 5th October: Duke René recaptures Nancy.

1476 During his attempts to recapture Upper-Alsace and Lorraine, Duke Charles is confronted with strong resistance from the Swiss militia, at whose hands Charles suffers heavy defeat at Grandson (2nd March) and Murten (22nd June). He dies during the Siege of Nancy (5th January 1477).

1477 5th January: Charles the Stout perishes in a renewed attempt to capture Nancy. His death causes a power-vacuum in which the peripheral areas of the Burgundian territories are lost. Louis XI of France conquers the Duchy of Burgundy permanently and, Picardy and large parts of Artois temporarily. Adolf of Egmond is once again recognised as Duke of Guelders and the governorship of Liège is resolved. Charles' only daughter Maria is recognised as successor to the home-territories. In Luxembourg a number of nobles supported another pretender, King Ladislaz of Bohemia, which delayed Maria's recognition there until 7th October 1480.

1477 The elimination of the Duke and his army brings great pressure to bear on the Burgundian State, both from within and from without. Mary of Burgundy is forced by the States-General, the States and the independent lands, into making far-reaching concessions. The general Grand Privilege (11th February) abolishes the central institutions of Mechelen and acknowledges liberties and rights hitherto systematically suppressed by the Dukes. Regional privileges granted to Flanders (11th February), Holland (14th March), Brabant and Namur (29th May). The first municipal charter was that of Ghent (31st January). There is unrest in the important towns, leading to the dismissal of the municipal authorities engaged under Duke Charles.

1477 21st April: Marriage (by proxy) of Maria of Burgundy to Archduke Maximilian of Austria, son of Emperor Frederic III.

1477 27th June: Adolf of Egmond, Duke of Guelders, dies in battle against France; his sister who was acting as trustee on his behalf, continues this until 25th November 1479.

1477-79 The French advance against Artois and southern Hainault and Flanders is relieved on 7th August 1479 in the Battle of Guinegate.

1477 19th August: Solemnisation of the marriage between Maria and Maximilian.

1478 22nd June: Birth of Philip the Fair, heir to Maria and Maximilian.

1479 Catherine of Egmond renounces the trusteeship of Guelders in favour of Maria of Burgundy; the power-struggle was not settled until September 1487.

1480 17th June: Henri de Berghes appointed Bishop of Cambrai.

1481 20th January: John of Montfoort captures Leiden with a number of anti-Burgundian Hoek partisans and makes a bid for power in Utrecht and Amersfoort; he is afforded future support by Hoekers in Holland and Geulres. Engelbrecht of Cleves is appointed governor of the Sticht. Bishop David seeks support from Archduke Maximilian.

1482 27th March: Death of Maria of Burgundy. Her spouse Maximilian is, with the exception of Flanders, recognised as guardian and governor acting on behalf of their son Philip the Fair.

1482 16th October: Jan van Hornes elected Bishop of Liège; his appointment followed on 17th December 1483.

1482 23rd December: Maximilian concludes the Peace of Arras with King Louis XI under heavy pressure from the States-General. His sister Margaret of Austria is married off to the Dauphin and immediately moves to the French court. By way of a dowry she takes with her Artois, Franche-Comté, Mâcon, Auxerre, Salins, Bar and Noyers. The powers of jurisdiction over Crown-Flanders are restored to Parliament of Paris.

1482 23rd December: Under severe pressure from the States General, Maximilian signs the Peace of Atrecht with King Louis XI. His sister, Margaret of Austria, is married to the dauphin and immediately moved to the French court, taking with her her dowry: Artois, Franche-Comté, Mâcon, Auxerre, Salins, Bar, Noyers. The Parisian parliament's jurisdiction over Crown Flanders is restored.

1483   5th June: The installation, by agreement between Maximilian and the Members of Flanders, of a regency council in the County, for the duration of Maximilian's absence from the Southern Netherlands. The Council was composed of three 'men of noble blood', knights of the Order of the Golden Fleece (Adolf of Ravenstein, Philip of Beveren and Louis of Gruuthuse) and three representatives of the Members of Flanders. Maximilian revoked the Council in October, although it nevertheless continued to function.

1483   15th October: Jean Monissart appointed Bishop of Tournai.

1485   16th May: Antoine de Croy appointed Bishop of Thérouanne.

1485   28th June: After eight months of war Maximilian gains control of the County of Flanders and allows himself to be acclaimed as guardian and governor.

1486   16th February: Maximilian elected Roman Catholic King.

1488   3rd February: Maximilian imprisoned at Bruges after an attempt to put down a renewed uprising. He was released on 16th May having surrendered his governor-ship over Flanders, whereupon a regency council was recognised, whose members were 'men of noble blood', consisting of Maria and representatives of the States.

1488   9th June: After Maximilian's revocation of the agreement of 16th May, Philip of Cleves places himself at the head of the Regency Council in Flanders as surety.

1483   9th January: With the support of the States of Brabant, Maximilian defeats Guillaume de la Mark, who had proclaimed himself ruler of the Prince-Bishopric of Liège.

1483   10th January: In Flanders the Members recognise Philip the Fair as their hereditary prince. King Louis XI supports this action.

1483   May: Bishop David of Utrecht imprisoned.

1483   July-August: Maximilian besieges the town of Utrecht, which capitulates on 31st August: he takes the title of temporal sovereign.

1483   30th August: Death of King Louis XI; Charles VIII is now 13 years old. Maximilian rejects the Peace of Arras.

1484   May: Adolf of Cleves and Philip of Burgundy withdraw from the Regency Council of Flanders, which has meanwhile been convened by Maximilian.

1484   October: France lends military support (until February 1485) to the Three Members of Flanders in their struggle against Maximilian's authority.

1485   28th June: Flanders now also recognises Maximilian backed by the superior forces of the German mercenaries.

1485   22nd July: Ghent is once again suppressed as a special case and loses its privileges after riots against German soldiers.

1485   July: Jan van Hornes, Bishop of Liège, finds it necessary to enlist Maximilian's support as temporal sovereign.

1486-87   Franco-Burgundian war over Artois.

1487   November: The resistance to Maximilian in Ghent flares up again.

1488   3rd February: An attempt to have the German troops capture Bruges leads to uproar, and Maximilian himself is taken prisoner.

1488   14th March: Evrard de la Mark assumes power in Liège with the support of France.

1488   16th May: Maximilian released on the condition that he recognises a Regency Council in Flanders; Philip of Cleves stands as surety that this will be done. Maximilian betrays his promise quickly, whereupon Philip of Cleves places himself at the head of the resistance, which he leads from Sluis. The sea trade of Bruges is consequently blockaded for several years to come.

1488   Hoek exiles leave Sluis for Rotterdam, Woerden and Geertruidenberg; Rotterdam capitulates (24th June).

1488   September: Brussels and Leuven and their territories join Philip of Cleves.

1489   February: Maximilian leaves for Germany and appoints Albert of Saxony Stadholder-General.

1489   14th February: Agreement on military and commercial co-operation between Maximilian and England.

1489   22nd July: Maximilian and Charles VIII reach a truce through mediation by the Pope (at Frankfurt).

1489   14th August: Stadholder Albert of Saxony subdues southern Brabant.

1489   26th November: Maximilian's tutelage over Liège is restored.

1489   29th November: Bruges taken (Peace of Damme).

1491 19th August: Antionetto Pallavicini appointed Bishop of Tournai.

1492 March: Karel van Egmond, son of Egmond, heralded as Duke in Guelders.

1492 29th July: After a war of reprisal lasting two years, Flanders is once again subjected to Maximilian as guardian and governor.

1493 23rd May: King Charles VIII sends back Margaret of Austria, who, according to the Treaty of Arras of 1482 was resident at the French court as his intended wife, and also surrenders her dowry consisting of the Counties of Artois and Franche-Comté.

1493 August: Philip the Fair proclaimed of age, so that he can succeed his mother in the Netherlands and Franche-Comté.

1495 5th November: Philip the Fair marries Joanna of Aragon and Castille by proxy; the marriage was solemnised on 28th October 1496. At the same time, Philip's sister Margaret marries Joanna's brother Juan, who died in 1500.

1496 3rd February: Philip of Luxembourg elected Bishop of Thérouanne; his appointment followed on 12th November 1498.

1496 11th August: Frederik of Baden appointed Bishop of Utrecht.

1497 20th December: Peter Quicke appointed Bishop of Tournai.

1500 24th February: Birth of Charles, son of Philip the Fair and Joanna of Castille, and christened as the Duke of Luxembourg.

1500 20th July: By a series of deaths, in particular that of her brother Juan, Joanna becomes heiress to Spain and the Spanish colonies.

1503 1st February: Jacques de Croy appointed Bishop of Cambrai.

1505 11th January: Joanna becomes Queen of Castille after the death of her mother.

1505 30th December: Evrard de la Mark elected Bishop of Liège, his appointment followed on 25th February 1506.

1506 9th March: Charles de Hautbois appointed Bishop of Tournai.

1506 15th July: Philip the Fair recognised as King-Consort of Castille.

1506 26th September: Philip the Fair dies in Spain. His father Maximilian is formally recognised as guardian to the infant Charles of Luxembourg.

1507 18th March: Margaret of Austria, Duchess of Savoy is appointed governess in the Netherlands by her father Maximilian, she settles in Mechelen.

1508 10th February: Maximilian elected Holy Roman Emperor.

1490 December: Maximilian marries Anna of Brittany by proxy; on 6th December 1491 after an invasion by a French army, she marries King Charles VIII.

1490 2nd November: Robert de la Mark heralded at Liège as captain and ruler.

1491 Summer-May 1492: Revolt of the farmers and towns in North Holland, spreading to Haarlem and Leiden: the Bread and Cheese uprising is suppressed by Albert of Saxony.

1492 5th May: Jan van Hornes restored to office of Bishop of Liège with a guarantee of neutrality between France an Hapsburg.

1492 29th July: Ghent capitulates (Peace of Cadzand), with fines and loss of municipal autonomy.

1492 12th October: Philip of Cleves also abandons his resistance.

1493 23rd May: Peace of Senlis: Margaret of Austria returns to the Netherlands, Maximilian conquers Artois, Noyers, Charolais and Franche-Comté, but not Mâcon, Auxerre and Bar.

1493 October: Engelbrecht of Nassau becomes Stadholder-General.

1496 Resumption of trading relations with England and issue of a strong currency which should remain stable.

1498 Philip the Fair abandons his attempts to conquer Burgundy and renounces his claims to Guelders.

1501-03 Philip the Fair travels to Spain.

1504 Establishment of the Grand Council of Mechelen as the continuation of Parliament from 1473-1477.

384

		1512	Emperor Maximilian unites the Netherlands and Franche-Comté separate territory, to offer greater resistance to the Turks.
1513	8th June: Louis Guillard appointed Bishop of Tournai.		
1515	5th January: Charles of Luxembourg comes of age and is proclaimed ruler in the Netherlands.		
1516	23rd January: On the death of his grandfather Ferdinand of Aragon, Charles becomes governor of Spain, Naples and the remaining possessions, in the name of his mentally-deficient mother. On 14th March he is proclaimed King of Spain.		
1516	15th August: Guillaume de Croy appointed Bishop of Cambrai.		
1517	18th March: Philip of Burgundy appointed Bishop of Utrecht.	1517	Charles V leaves for Spain.
1518	5th February: Charles recognised as King of Spain.		
1518	24th July: Margaret of Austria named Governess-General for a second time.		
1519	12th January: Through the death of his grandfather Maximilian, Charles inherits the Hapsburg lands: Austria and its dependencies.		
1519	28th June: Charles elected Holy Roman Emperor (Charles V).		
1519	17th August: Robert de Croy appointed Bishop of Cambrai.		
1520	23rd October: Karel crowned Emperor at Aachen.	1520-June1522	Charles V resident in the Netherlands and Germany.
1521	29th October: John of Lorraine appointed Bishop of Thérouanne.	1521-26	Resumption of the war between the Hapsburg Empire and France.
1521	3rd Decembre: Charles V wins Tournai from the French.	1521	December: Tournai conquered by France, Crown-Flanders released from the jurisdiction of Parliament of Paris. Bishop Everard de la Mark recognises the Hapsburg protectorate.
1522	30th January/7th February: Charles V cedes his rights to the Hapsburg possessions to his brother Ferdinand.		
1523	August: The Groningen Ommelanden recognise Charles V as their overlord.		
1524	6th May: Hendrik of Bavaria elected Bishop of Utrecht.		
1524	December: Friesland recognises Charles V as overlord. Karel van Egmond, however, quickly regains his influence in Groningen and Friesland.		
1525	29th March: Charles de Croy appointed Bishop of Tournai.	1525	Unrest in Antwerp, 'sHertogenbosch and Utrecht.
1526	10th March: Karel marries Isabella, daughter of the King of Portugal.	1526	January: Charles V holds King François I prisoner and forces him into the Treaty of Madrid in which he cedes his feudal rights over Flanders and Artois, abdicates from Tournai and undertakes to yield the Duchy of Burgundy.
1528	21st March: Overijssel recognises Charles V as overlord.	1528	Unrest in Utrecht, Brussels and Groningen.
1528	3rd October: Charles of Egmond accepts Charles V's feudal rights over Guelders and Zutphen, and assumes from him hereditary control of Drenthe, Groningen and the Ommelanden; he renounces his rights over the other areas which had belonged to his territories.		
1528	21st October: Charles V acquires temporal power in the diocese of Utrecht.		
1530	24th February: the Pope crowns Charles V (who, two days previously, had been proclaimed King of Italy) Emperor at Bologna.		

1530 1st December: Death of Governess Margaret of Austria. She is succeeded by Emperor Charles' sister, Maria of Hungary.

1536 10th December: Charles of Egmond cedes his rights over Drenthe, Groningen and the Ommelanden to Charles V.

1543 7th September: William of Julich, Duke of Guelders and Count of Zutphen, cedes his rights to Charles V.

1548 The 'Bourgondische Kreits' is laid down in terms of laws (protection) and duties (contributions) in the context of the German Empire. It no longer includes the Duchy of Burgundy, conquered by France in 1477. Four further Burgundian territories are named in addition to those in the Netherlands: on the one hand Lorraine, Franche-Comté, Charolais and Salins, on the other: the Duchies of Brabant, Limburg, Luxembourg and Guelders, the Counties of Flanders, Artois, Hainault, Holland, Zeeland, Namur and Zutphen, the Seigniories of Friesland, Groningen, Drenthe, Overijssel, Utrecht, Valkenburg, Dalhem, Mechelen, Maastricht and Tournai.

1549 The 'Pragmatic Sanction' standardises hereditary rights in all the lands of the Netherlands, in order to keep them inextricably bound together. In this year Charles' heir Philip II is acclaimed under this title in the Netherlands.

1529 6th August: Peace of Cambrai between France, the Hapsburg-Burgundian lands and England (signed by Margaret of Austria and Louis of Savoy): Charles V cedes the Duchy of Burgundy but retains Charolais for the remainder of his life; François I retains his feudal rights over Crown-Flanders, Artois and Tournai, but withdraws his support from Guelders and Liège; the trading agreement with England is renewed.

1530 Death of Margaret of Austria.

Genealogical Tables

Table 1 :   REIGNING SOVEREIGNS OF THE HAPSBURG-BURGUNDIAN DYNASTY

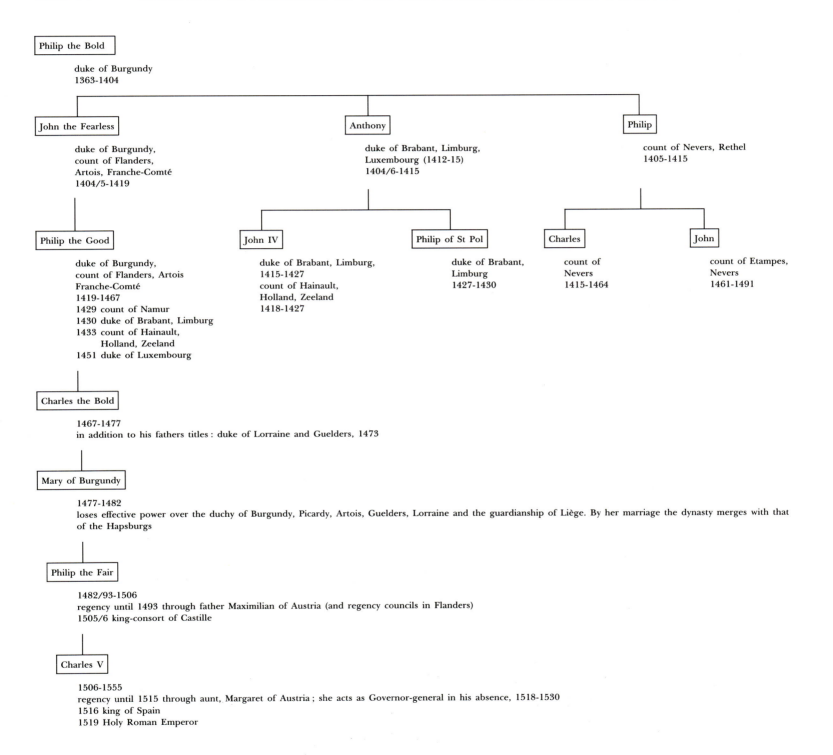

Philip the Bold

duke of Burgundy
1363-1404

John the Fearless

duke of Burgundy,
count of Flanders,
Artois, Franche-Comté
1404/5-1419

Anthony

duke of Brabant, Limburg,
Luxembourg (1412-15)
1404/6-1415

Philip

count of Nevers, Rethel
1405-1415

Philip the Good

duke of Burgundy,
count of Flanders, Artois
Franche-Comté
1419-1467
1429 count of Namur
1430 duke of Brabant, Limburg
1433 count of Hainault,
     Holland, Zeeland
1451 duke of Luxembourg

John IV

duke of Brabant, Limburg,
1415-1427
count of Hainault,
Holland, Zeeland
1418-1427

Philip of St Pol

duke of Brabant,
Limburg
1427-1430

Charles

count of
Nevers
1415-1464

John

count of Etampes,
Nevers
1461-1491

Charles the Bold

1467-1477
in addition to his fathers titles : duke of Lorraine and Guelders, 1473

Mary of Burgundy

1477-1482
loses effective power over the duchy of Burgundy, Picardy, Artois, Guelders, Lorraine and the guardianship of Liège. By her marriage the dynasty merges with that
of the Hapsburgs

Philip the Fair

1482/93-1506
regency until 1493 through father Maximilian of Austria (and regency councils in Flanders)
1505/6 king-consort of Castille

Charles V

1506-1555
regency until 1515 through aunt, Margaret of Austria ; she acts as Governor-general in his absence, 1518-1530
1516 king of Spain
1519 Holy Roman Emperor

Table 2 : THE MERGING OF THE ROYAL DYNASTIES IN THE NETHERLANDS

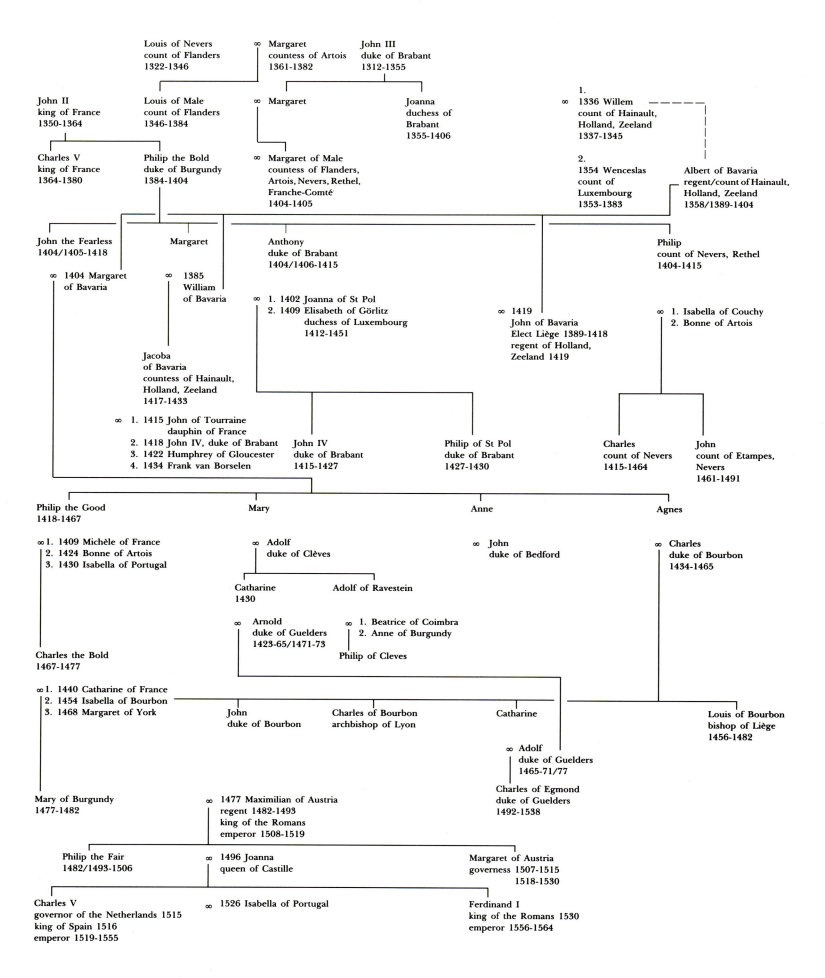

388

PHILIP THE BOLD (1342-1404)

1. Henry du Risoir (°c. 1360-December 1409) son of Mary of Auberchicourt (Artois), wife of Risoir de Bermissart († 31st October 1461).
2. Jehan, son of Aleydis of Dijon († September 1385)

JOHN THE FEARLESS (1371-1419)

1. John of Burgundy, Bishop of Cambrai († 14th April 1479), son of Agnes de Croy, attached to the court of duchess Isabella of Portugal.
2. Guy of Burgundy († 1436), son of Margaret van Borsselen († 1420).
3. Anthony of Burgundy, son of Margaret van Borsselen († 1420).
4. Philipotte, daughter of Margaret van Borsselen.

PHILIP THE GOOD (1396-1497)

1. Corneille of Burgundy, lord of Beveren, called the Great Bastard, son of Catharina Schaers.
2. Anthony of Burgundy, son of Joanna of Presles.
3. Mary of Burgundy († 1462), daughter of Joanna (or Coletta) Chastellain, known as van Bosquiel († 1462).
4. Baudouin of Burgundy, named de Lille, son of Cathérine Theiffries.
5. Philip of Burgundy (died as a child).
6. David of Burgundy, Bishop of Utrecht (°1427 – † 16th April 1496), son of Joanna (or Coletta) Chastellain († 1462).
7. Philip of Burgundy, admiral of Flanders, bishop of Utrecht (° 1464 – † April 1524).
8. Rafaël of Burgundy, known as de Mercatel, abbot of St Bavon's Abbey in Ghent (°29th September 1463 – † 3rd August 1508), son of Belleval, wife of Bonville.
9. John of Burgundy, dean of Aire and St Donatian in Bruges. (°1458 – † 25th January 1499), son of Maria Scupeline.
10. Ann of Burgundy, wife of Adolf of Cleves, lord of Ravenstein († 17th January 1508), daughter of Jacoba van Steenberghe.
11. Cornelia of Burgundy, wife of Adrien de Toulongeon.
12. Mary (of Marion) of Burgundy, daughter of Celia, nun.
13. Cathérine of Burgundy († 1523), daughter of Celia, wife of Colard de Harlay.
14. Magdalen of Burgundy, wife of Cournon, baron of Alès, councillor to the duke of Bourbon.
15. Margaret of Burgundy, daughter of Isabelle de la Vigne.
16. Mary of Burgundy, nun.
17. Cathérine of Burgundy, abbess of the Galilea monastery at Ghent († after 1515).
18. Cathérine of Burgundy, nun.
19. Jossine of Burgundy.
20. Yolende of Burgundy, wife of Jean d'Ailly, lord of Recquigny († 3rd November 1470).
21. Jerome of Burgundy.
22. Baudouin of Burgundy.
23. Arthur of Burgundy (died as a child).
24. Andrew of Burgundy.
25. Antony of Burgundy (died in childhood), son of Joanna of Mairesse.
26. Josse-Antoine of Burgundy, son of Joanna of Mairesse.

CHARLES THE BOLD (1433-1477)

1. John of Burgundy.
2. Pierson of Burgundy.

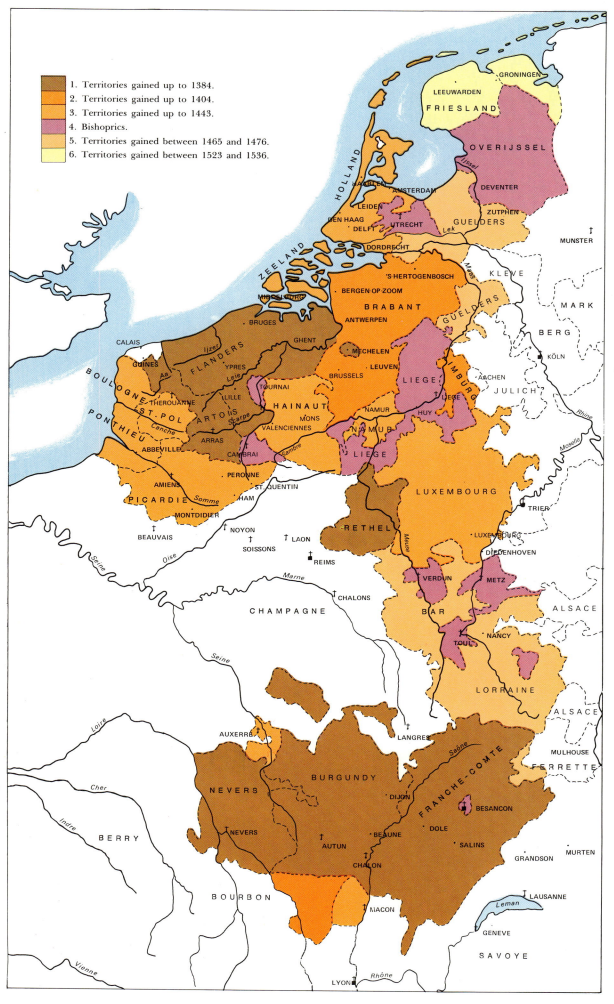

THE PRINCIPALITIES
WHICH HAVE BELONGED
TO THE
BURGUNDIAN-HAPSBURG
DYNASTY

1. Territories gained up to 1384.
2. Territories gained up to 1404.
3. Territories gained up to 1443.
4. Bishoprics.
5. Territories gained between 1465 and 1476.
6. Territories gained between 1523 and 1536.

LIST OF THE PRINCIPALITIES, WITH DATES
OF ABSORPTION AND/OR LOSS BY
THE BURGUNDIAN-HAPSBURG DYNASTY

1363	complete rule	Holland-Zeeland	1418/1428/1433
<u>1390</u>	shared rule	Namur	1421/1429
→	end of rule	Boulogne	1435 → 1477
1390/1404	phases in	Ponthieu	1435 → 1477
	acquisition of power	Auxerre	1435 → 1477
		Mâcon	1435 → 1477
Burgundy	1363 → 1477	Picardy	1435 → 1463 – 1465 → 1477
Flanders	1384	Luxembourg	1441/1443
Artois	1384 → 1477/1482 – 1493	Guines	1465 → 1477
Nevers	1384	Liège	1465/1468 → 1477
Rethel	1384	Upper-Alsace, Ferrette	1469 → 1477
Franche-Comté	1384 → 1477 – 1493	Guelders	1471/1473 → 1477 – 1481 → 1492 – 1528/1543
Mechelen	1384	Lorraine	1473/1475 → 1476
Salins	1384 → 1477 – 1493	Utrecht	1483/1528
Limburg	1387/1396	Tournai	1521
Brabant	1390/1404	Friesland	1523/1524/1536
Charolais	1390 → 1477 – 1493	Groningen	
St. Pol	1415 – 1430	& Ommelanden	1523/1528/1536
Hainault	1418/1427/1433	Overijssel	1528/1536

MAP B.

POPULATION DENSITY
AND URBANISATION
IN THE NETHERLANDS
AT THE END
OF THE FIFTEENTH CENTURY

I.   Friesland
II.   Overijssel
III.   Guelders
IV.   Utrecht
V.   Holland
VI.   Zeeland
VII.   Brabant
VIII. Flanders
IX.   Walloon-Flanders
X.   Artois
XI.   Picardy
XII.   Hainault
XIII. Namur
XIV. Liège
XV.   Limburg (Duchy)
XVI. Luxembourg.

Outside the principalities :
Tournai, Mechelen, Maastricht.

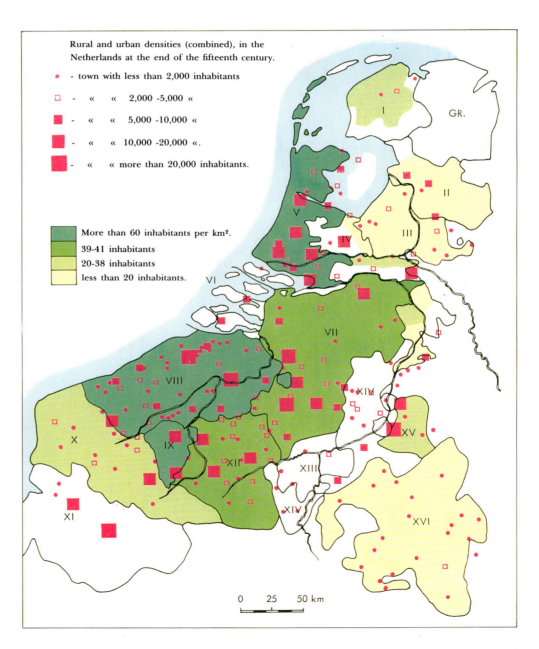

Rural and urban densities (combined), in the Netherlands at the end of the fifteenth century.

- town with less than 2,000 inhabitants
- « « 2,000 -5,000 «
- « « 5,000 -10,000 «
- « « 10,000 -20,000 «.
- « « more than 20,000 inhabitants.

More than 60 inhabitants per km².
39-41 inhabitants
20-38 inhabitants
less than 20 inhabitants.

0   25   50 km

Socio Economic Data

Table 4 : POPULATION OF THE NETHERLANDS
IN THE FOURTH QUARTER
OF THE FIFTEENTH CENTURY

Region	Urban Population %	Rural Population %	Total inhabitants	Regional % age total of Netherlands
Artois	22	78	180 300	7.0
Boulonnais	14	86	31 500	1.2
Brabant	31	69	413 200	16.1
Culemborg	100	0	1 500	0.05
Flanders	36	64	660 700	25.8
Friesland	22	78	70 500	2.7
Guelders	44	56	98 000	3.8
Hainault	30	70	209 100	8.1
Holland	45	55	268 200	10.5
Limburg (Duchy)	7	93	16 400	0.6
Liège	29	71	139 900	5.4
Luxembourg	15	85	67 900	2.6
Maastricht	100	0	12 000	0.5
Mechelen	100	0	ca 15 000	0.6
Namur	28	72	17 900	0.7
Overijssel	48	52	52 700	2.0
Picardy	21	79	188 600	7.4
Tournai	100	0	ca 20 000	0.8
Utrecht & Eemland	76	24	15 900	0.6
Walloon-Flanders	?	?	?	?
Zeeland	?	?	10 800	0.4
Total	34	66	2 563 500	99.75

Diagram one: PROFESSIONAL STRUCTURES IN THE LARGER FLEMISH TOWNS

These diagrams - because of inconsistencies in the basic information, refer in the case of Bruges, to the whole of the active population, excluding the freemen, that is: all tradesmen; for Ghent and Ypres, figures for the whole known population are given.

BRUGES (1379-1380)
A. Textiles
D. Food
E. Clothing
F. Building
G. Luxury goods
H. Brokers
I. Furnishing
J. Trade
K. Transport
L. Health

GHENT (1356-1358)
A. Textiles
B. Small trades
C. Freemen

YPRES (1431)
A. Textiles
B. Small trades & freemen

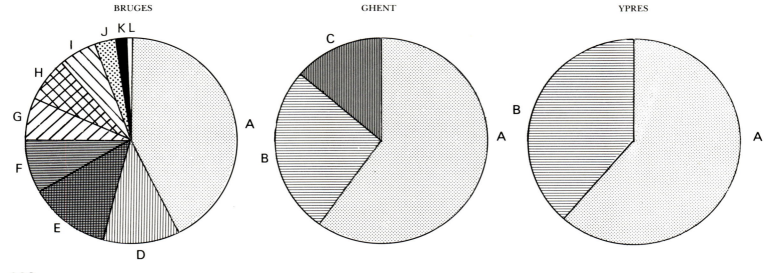

BRUGES   GHENT   YPRES

392

Diagram two

NOMINAL WAGES OF THE MASTER MASON
AND APPRENTICE AT BRUGES,
expressed in Flemish groats (according to Sosson).

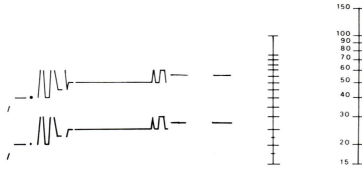

Diagram three

REAL WAGE OF A MASTER CARPENTER
IN BRUGES,
expressed in litres of rye (Sosson).

Diagram four

PRICE OF A 'HOET' OF RYE (166-172 litres)
AT BRUGES,
expressed in Flemish groats.
Thick line = running average (Verhulst).

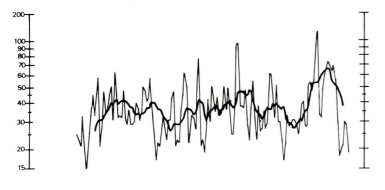

Diagram five

PRICE OF A 'HOET' OF WHEAT AT BRUGES
expressed in Flemish groats.
Thick line = running average (Verhulst).

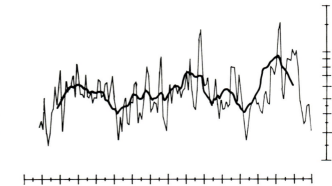

Diagram six

PRICE OF A 'WAGE' OF BUTTER (83.5 kg.)
AT BRUGES,
expressed in Flemish groats.
Thick line = running average (Verhulst).

Diagram seven

PRICE OF A 'WAGE' OF CHEESE (60.6 kg.)
AT BRUGES,
expressed in Flemish groats.
Thick line = running average (Verhulst).

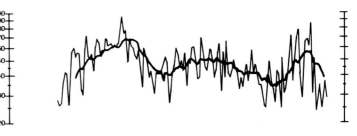

393

Currencies

Since the thirteenth century, Europe had a double currency standard, a gold standard and a silver standard. Relative values fluctuated in response to varying factors in supply and demand. Gold pieces were so valuable that they rarely came into intensive circulation. They were essentially used in international commercial and political relations, large enterprises, transactions and investment. In the fifteenth century a florin (the classic Florentine gold piece) could be earned by a bricklayer's journeyman in ten to twelve days; it was the equivalent of about 59 pounds of butter, about 94 pounds of salted meat, 320-410 smoked herrings or 750-825 eggs. Gold pieces were clearly not intended for this purpose. There were various silver coins for this purpose, of which those with the lowest value contained virtually no precious metal.

The right to mint a coin belonged to the prince. The fragmentation of power also resulted therefore in a variety of currencies. The area of circulation of a silver coin was much more limited than that of gold pieces which were accepted throughout Europe and also outside it. The value of a coin was determined by the amount of precious metal which it contained, as well as the degree of trust placed in the currency on the grounds of economic strength and the political stability in the country of issue.

The intensive, widespread trading relations of the Netherlands meant that almost all European gold coins were in circulation there. The most important of these were the Italian: the florin of Florence, the Genoese genovino and the Venetian ducat. Around 1500, the weight and content of these coins was the same as it had been when they were first issued, respectively, in 1252 (the first two) and 1284, and this naturally enhanced their stable value. Many English, French amd Rhineland coins were in circulation in addition to these. Hungarian ducats enjoyed a wide circulation as early as the beginning of the fourteenth century, thanks to the region's goldmines. The coinage issues in the Netherlands were mostly imitations of foreign coins circulating there. By offering a slightly more favourable exchange rate than the foreign rate, the rulers could attract the bullion to their workshops and consequently make considerable short-term profits.

The silver coins were also imitations of foreign examples, namely those of France and Italy. In addition to the basic coinage, the 'penning' or penny (*denarius, denier*), a heavier piece worth twelve pence was also minted: the groat (*grosso, gros*). The Flemish groat was the basis of the whole currency system in the Burgundian Netherlands. The values of the Brabantine, Artesian and Holland groats was derived from the value of the Flemish. From the unification of the currency (1433-1435) this ratio was as follows:

1 Flemish groat =
1½ Brabantine groats =
6 Artesian and Holland groats =
12 Hainault groats =
12 Pence Parisis = 1 Shilling Parisis.

This last coin was originally Parisian and struck out a course of its own from the thirteenth century onwards. This is also true of the French coin issued at Tours, the penny or groat *tournois*. The pound Tournois (= 240 pence Tournois) was worth 32-36 Flemish groats during the reign of Philip the Good.

Monetary units were based on the penny, and though no coins existed, these values served as multiples in book-keeping.
12 pence = 1 shilling
20 shillings = 1 pound
1 pound = 240 pence.

This universal system was used in Great Britain until 1973. In the Burgundian Netherlands the following pound systems, based on a real penny were used:
Flemish groat pound (=240 groats)
Pound Parisis (1/12 of the Flemish pound, thus 20 Flemish groats)
Pound of 40 Flemish groats

From about 1440 the Rhineland guilder (a gold piece) was worth 40 groats. The *stuiver* or *patard* (= 2 Flemish groats) was the most used silver coin from 1433 onwards, with a value of 1/20 of the guilder and was thus the equivalent of a shilling in that particular pound system. This system was used in most of the accounts of the Burgundian administration.

In addition to this, each region retained its own sterling system according to the Flemish exchange rates quoted above. The latter was standard for the entire Netherlands. Subdivisions of the stuiver (*patard*) were as follows:
1 stuiver = 2 (pence) groats
1 groat = 3 sterling (*esterlin*)
= 12 pence Parisis
= 24 mites

Gold pieces were not given a denomination of value, since this fluctuated. They were named after the effigy. The most important gold coins of the Burgundian Netherlands are described below.

Name	Year of issue	Weight (grammes)	Content %	Exchange Rate 1496 (Flemish groats)
BURGUNDIAN				
rijder/cavalier	1433	3,626	992,2	79
leeuw/lion	1454	4,257	958,3	92
St Andrew's guilder	1466	3,399	791,7	61
reaal	1487	14,834	991,7	367
Philip guilder	1496	3,300	666,7	50
FRENCH				
franc	1423	3,059	1000,0	68
salut	1433	3,496	1000,0	76
écu	1474	3,399	963,5	71
ENGLISH				
noble	1412	6,998	994,8	153
angel	1465	5,184	994,8	116
rose noble	1465	7,776	994,8	173
ITALIAN				
florin	1252	3,536	1000,0	79
genovino	1252	3,560	1000,0	79
ducat	1284	3,559	1000,0	79
IMPERIAL				
Rhenish guilder	1385		999	
" "	1419		790	33
" "	1490	3,278	770,8	58
Liège Peter guilder	1456-1482	3,496	680,6	51

VALUE OF THE GOLD VENETIAN (•) AND HUNGARIAN (o) DUCATS
expressed in Flemish groats, silver currency, 1370-1500
(from Spufford).

MINTING OF GOLD IN ENGLAND (□) AND THE NETHERLANDS (■)
expressed in mares of Troyes
(= 244.753 grammes of pure gold)
(From Munro).

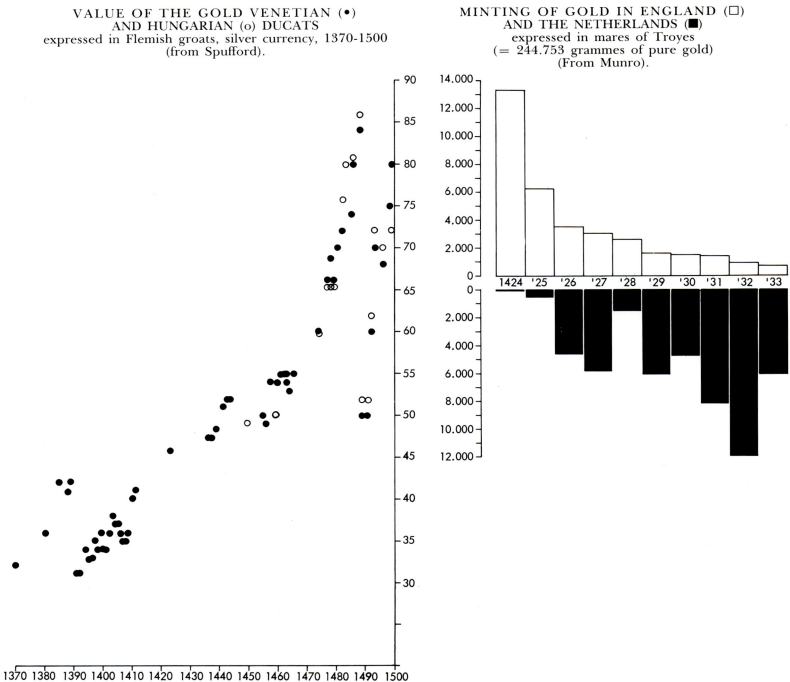

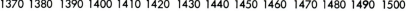

Selective Bibliography

GENERAL WORKS

An extensive bibliography is contained in the standard general reference work : *Algemene Geschiedenis der Nederlanden,* vols 4 and 5, Haarlem, 1980.

Important monographs on the four leading dukes of Burgundy have been published recently ; they are primarily concerned with the political history and are based on a thorough study of sources and secondary literature. The author has also written two shorter surveys :

R. VAUGHAN, *The Valois dukes of Burgundy,* Hull, 1965.

R. VAUGHAN, *Valois Burgundy,* London, 1975.

R. VAUGHAN, *Philip the Bold : The Formation of the Burgundian State,* London 1962.

R. VAUGHAN, *John the Fearless : The Growth of Burgundian Power,* London, 1966.

R. VAUGHAN, *Philip the Good : The Apogee of the Burgundian State,* London, 1970.

R. VAUGHAN, *Charles the Bold : The last Valois Duke of Burgundy,* London, 1973.

J. Huizinga's *Herfsttij der Middeleeuwen,* Haarlem, 1919, is still a classic of fine scholarship.
The Dutch-language area of the southern Netherlands is specifically covered in the most recent survey : W. Blockmans, *De ontwikkeling van een verstedelijkte samenleving,* in E. WITTE (ed.), *Geschiedenis van Vlaanderen,* Brussels, 1983, 45-103.

Chapter 1. THE ECOLOGICAL SITUATION

W.P. BLOCKMANS, G. PIETERS, W. PREVENIER, R. VAN SCHAIK, *Tussen crisis en welvaart, sociale veranderingen 1300-1500,* in : Algemene Geschiedenis der Nederlanden, 4, 1980, 42-60.

M.-A. ARNOULD, *Les dénombrements de foyers dans le comté de Hainaut (XIVᵉ-XVIᵉ siècles),* Brussels, 1956.

W. PREVENIER, *La démographie des villes du comté de Flandre aux XIVᵉ et XVᵉ siècles. Etat de la question. Essai d'interprétation,* in : Revue du Nord, 65, 1983.

Chapter 2. THE DAILY BREAD

B.H. SLICHER VAN BATH, *Een samenleving onder spanning. Geschiedenis van het platteland in Overijssel,* Assen, 1957.

G. SIVÉRY, *Structures agraires et vie rurale dans le hainaut à la fin du moyen âge,* 2 dln., Rijsel, 1977.

M.-J. TTIS-DIEUAIDE, *La formation des prix céréaliers en Brabant et en Flandre au XVᵉ siècle,* Brussels, 1975.

R. VAN SCHAIK, *Prijs- en levensmiddelenpolitiek in de Noordelijke Nederlanden van de 14ᵉ tot de 17ᵉ eeuw ; bronnen en problemen,* in : Tijdschrift voor Geschiedenis, 91, 1978, 214-255.

Chapter 3. URBAN ECONOMIES

W. JAPPE ALBERTS and H.P.H. JANSEN, *Welvaart in wording. Sociaal-economische geschiedenis van Nederland van de vroegste tijden tot bet einde van de middeleeuwen,* The Hague, 1964.

R. VAN UYTVEN, *Sociaal-economische evoluties in de Nederlanden vóór de Revoluties (veertiende-zestiende eeuw),* in : Bijdragen en Mededelingen betreffende de geschiedenis der Nederlanden, 87, 1972, 60-93.

J. MUNRO, *Industrial protectionism in medieval Flanders : urban or national ?* in : H.A. Miskimin e.a. (eds.), The medieval city, Yale, 1977, 229-267.

J.H. MUNRO, *Wool, Cloth and Gold. The struggle for Bullion in Anglo-Burgundian Trade 1340-1478,* Brussels-Toronto, 1973.

R. VAN UYTVEN, *La draperie brabançonne et malinoise du XIIᵉ au XVIIᵉ siècle : grandeur ephémère et décadence,* in : Produzione, commercio e consumo dei panni di lana, Florence, 1976, 85-97.

A. VERHULST, *La laine indigène dans les anciens Pays-Bas,* in : Revue Historique, 258, 1972, 281-322.

G. GAIER, *L'Industrie et le Commerce des Armes dans les Anciennes Principautés belges du XIIIᵉ à la fin du XVᵉ siècle,* Paris, 1973.

E. SABBE, *De Belgische vlasnijverheid,* Brugge, 1943.

W. PREVENIER, *Les perturbations dans les relations commerciales anglo-flamandes entre 1379 et 1407. Causes de désaccord et raisons d'une réconciliation,* in : Economies et Sociétés du Moyen Age. Mélanges E. Perroy, Paris 1973, 477-497.

M.R. THIELEMANS, *Bourgogne et Angleterre. Relations politiques et économiques entre les Pays-Bas bourguignons et l'Angleterre, 1435-1467,* Brussels, 1966.

W. BRULEZ, *Bruges and Antwerp in the 15th and 16th centuries : an antihesis ?* in : Acta Historiae neerlandicae, 6 1973, 1-26.

H. VAN DER WEE, *The Growth of the Antwerp Market and the European Economy (fourteenth-sixteenth centuries),* 3 volumes, Leuven-Gembloers, 1963.

O. MUS, *De Brugse compagnie Despars op het einde van de 15de eeuw,* in : Handelingen van het Genootschap, gesticht onder de benaming Société d'Emulation te Brugge, 101, 1964, 5-118.

G. ASAERT, *De Antwerpse scheepvaart in de XVᵉ eeuw (1394-1480),* Brussels 1973.

R. VAN UYTVEN, *Politiek en economie : de crisis der late XVᵉ eeuw in de Nederlanden,* in : Belgisch Tijdschrift voor Filologie en Geschiedenis, 53, 1975, 1097-1149.

R. VAN UYTVEN, *Stadsfinanciën en stadsekonomie te Leuven (van de XIIᵉ tot het einde der XVIᵉ eeuw),* Brussels, 1961.

R. DE ROOVER, *The Bruges money market around 1400,* Brussels, 1968.

R. DE ROOVER, *Oprichting en liquidatie van het Brugse filiaal van het bankiershuis der medici,* in : Mededelingen van de Koninklijke Vlaamse Academie voor Wetenschappen, Letteren en Schone Kunsten van België. Klasse der Letteren 15, 1953, afl. 7.

P. SPUFFORD, *Monetary Problems and Policies in the Burgundian Netherlands 1433-1496,* Leiden, 1970.

Chapter 4. SOCIAL STATUS AND CLASS

W. PARAVICINI, *Expansion et intégration. La noblesse des Pays-Bas à la cour de Philippe de Bon,* in : Bijdragen en Mededelingen betreffende de Geschiedenis der Nederlanden, 95, 1980, 298-314.

J.-P. SOSSON, *Les travaux publics de la ville de Bruges XIVᵉ-XVᵉ siècles. Les matériaux. Les hommes,* Brussels 1977.

E. SCHOLLIERS, *Loonarbeid en honger. De levensstandaard in de XVᵉ en XVIᵉ eeuw te Antwerpen,* Antwerp, 1960.

E. SCHOLLIERS, *De materiële verschijningsvorm van de armoede voor de industriële revolutie. Omvang, evolutie en oorzaken,* in : Tijdschrift voor Geschiedenis, 88, 1975, 451-467.

W.P. BLOCKMANS and W. PREVENIER, *Poverty in Flanders and Brabant from the fourteenth to the mid-sixteenth century : sources and problems*, in : Acta Historiae Neerlandicae, 10, 1978, 20-57.

R. VAN UYTVEN, *La Flandre et le Brabant, "Terres de promission" sous les ducs de Bourgogne ?*, in : Revue du Nord, 43, 1961, 281-317.

Chapter 5. THE STATE AND SOCIETY

Y. LACAZE, *Philippe le Bon et les terres d'Empire*, in : Annales de Bourgogne, XXXVI, 1964, 81-121.

Y. LACAZE, *Le rôle des traditions dans la genèse d'un sentiment national au XVe siècle : la Bourgogne de Philippe le Bon*, in : Bibliothèque de l'Ecole des Chartes, CXXIX, 1971, 303-385.

J. LEJEUNE, *Liège et son pays. Naissance d'une patrie (XIIIe-XIVe siècles)*, Liège, 1948.

Cinq-centième anniversaire de la bataille de Nancy (1477), Nancy, 1979.

W. BLOCKMANS, *Autocratie ou polyarchie ? La lutte pour le pouvoir politique en Flandre, d'après des documents inédits, 1482-1492*, in : Bulletin Commission royale d'Histoire, 140, 1974, 257-368.

R. WELLENS, *La révolte brugeoise de 1488*, in : Handelingen Genootschap "Société d'Emulation" Brugge, CII, 1965, 5-52.

J.M. CAUCHIES, *La législation princière pour le comté de Hainaut. Ducs de Bourgogne et premiers Habsbourg (1427-1506)*, Brussels, 1982.

J. BARTIER, *Légistes et gens de finances au XVe siècle : les conseillers des ducs de Bourgogne Philippe le Bon et Charles le Téméraire*, Brussels, 1955.

W. PREVENIER, *Officials in Town and Countryside in the Low Countries. Social and Professional Developments from the Fourteenth to the sixteenth centuries*, in : Acta Historiae Neerlandiae, VII, 1974, 1-17.

R. BERGER, *Nicolas Rolin. Kanzler der Zeitenwende im Burgundisch-Französischer Konflikt, 1422-1461*, Freiburg, 1971.

W. PARAVICINI, *Guy de Brimeu...*, Bonn, 1975.

J. VAN ROMPAEY, *De Grote Raad van de Hertogen van Bourgondië en het Parlement van Mechelen*, Brussels, 1973.

P. COCKSHAW, *Le personnel de la chancellerie de Bourgogne-Flandre sous les ducs de Bourgogne de la maison de Valois (1384-1477)*, Kortrijk, 1982.

T.S. JANSMA, *Raad en Rekenkamer in Holland en Zeeland Tijdens Hertog Philips van Bourgondië*, Utrecht, 1952.

J. VAN ROMPAEY, *Het grafelijk baljuwsambt in Vlaanderen tijdens de Bourgondische periode*, Brussels, 1967.

A.G. JONGKEES, *Staat en Kerk in Holland en Zeeland onder de Bourgondische hertogen 1425-1477*, Groningen-Batavia, 1942.

C.A. VAN KALVEEN, *Het bestuur van bisschop en Staten in het Nedersticht, Oversticht en Drenthe 1482-1520*, Groningen, 1974.

J. STERK, *Philips van Bourgondië (1465-1524), bisschop van Utrecht, als protagonist van de renaissance*, Zutphen, 1980.

R. VAN UYTVEN, *Wereldlijke Overbeid en reguliere Geestelijkheid in Brabant tijdens de Late Middeleeuwen*, in : Bronnen voor de religieuze Geschiedenis van België, Middeleeuwen en Moderne Tijden, Leuven, 1968 (Bibliothèque de la Revue d'Histoire Eccl. Fasc. 47).

G. GAIER, *Art et organisation militaires dans la principauté de Liège et le comté de Looz au moyen âge*, Brussels, 1968.

M.-A. ARNOULD, *Une estimation des revenus et des dépenses de Philippe de Bon en 1445*, in : Recherches sur l'histoire des finances publiques en Belgique. Acta Historica Bruxellensia 3, 1973, 131-219.

E. VAN CAUWENBERGH, *Het vorstelijk domein en de overheidsfinanciën in de Nederlanden (15de-16de eeuw)*, Brussels, 1982.

C. DICKSTEIN-BERNARD, *La gestion financière d'une capitale à ses débuts. Bruxelles 1334-1467*, Annales cercle archéologique Bruxelles, 1977.

A. UYTTEBROUCK, *Le gouvernement du duché de Brabant au bas moyen-âge*, Brussels, 1975.

R. WELLENS, *Les Etats généraux des Pays-Bas des origines à la fin du règne de Philippe le Beau (1464-1506)*, Heule, 1974.

W.P. BLOCKMANS, *De volksvertegenwoordiging in Vlaanderen in de overgang van middeleeuwen naar nieuwe tijden (1384-1506)*, Brussels, 1978.

W. PREVENIER, *De Leden en de Staten van Vlaanderen (1384-1405)*, Brussels 1961.

W.P. BLOCKMANS, (ed.), *De algemene en gewestelijke privilegiën van Maria van Bourgondië van 1477*, Kortrijk, 1984.

Chapter 6. THE "BURGUNDIAN" CULTURE

O. CARTELLIERI, *Am Hofe der Herzöge von Burgund. Kulturhistorische Bilder*, Basle, 1926.

G. DOGAER EN M. DEBAE, *De librije van Filips de Gœde*, Tentoonstellingscatalogus, Brussels, 1967.

De eeuw der Vlaamse Primitieven. Tentoonstellingscatalogus, Brugge, 1960.

Flanders in the fifteenth century : art and civilisation. Catalogue, Detroit, 1960.

Anonieme Vlaamse Primitieven. Tentoonstellingscatalogus, Brugge, 1969.

Liège et Bourgogne. Exposition, Liège, 1968.

Karel de Stoute. Tentoonstellingscatalogus, Brussels, 1977.

Margaretha van Oostenrijk. Tentoonstellingscatalogus, Mechelen, 1980, en handelingen Kon. Kring Oudheidk., letteren en kunst v. Mechelen, 84, 1980, 38-102.

Corpus van de Vlaamse primitieven, Brussels, 1951...

E. PANOFSKY, *Early Netherlandish Painting. Its origin and character*, Cambridge Mass., 1953, 2 vol.

M.-J. FRIEDLÄNDER, *Ealy Netherlandish Painting*, Leiden, 1967-1976.

E. DHANENS, *Hubert en Jan van Eyck*, Antwerp, 1980.

G. DOGAER, *The Flemish miniature-painting in the 15th and 16th centuries*, Amsterdam, 1983.

Index

400

PHOTOGRAPHIC ACKNOWLEDGMENTS

AACHEN, Domschatzkammer 326 ; – Ann Münchow 326 ; AMSTERDAM, Rijksmuseum 1, 15, 112, 141, 153, 191, 233, 237, 282 ; ANTWERP, Archives de la ville 3 ; – C.A.P. 118 ; – Cathédrale 283 ; – Musée Mayer van den Bergh 14, 31, 32, 33, 34, 35, 36, 37, 53, 56, 168, 261 ; – Musée Royal des Beaux-Arts 59, 106, 125, 143, 176 ; – Photogravure De Schutter 19, 87, 102, 104, 108, 167, 283 ; ARRAS, Bibliothèque municipale 105, 186, 187, 193, 194, 195, 200 ; BASEL, Historisches Museum 203, 214, 281 ; – Offentliche Kunstsammlung 217 ; BERGEN-OP-ZOOM, Gemeentemuseum 139 ; BERLIN, Bildarchiv Preussischer Kulturbesitz 18, 23, 119, 129, 140, 204, 219, 248, 255, 291, 334 ; – Kupferstichkabinett 151, 209 ; BERN, Bürgerbibliothek 231 ; – Historisches Museum 137, 181, 299 ; BESANÇON, Bibliothèque municipale 172 ; – J. De Grivel 172, 296 ; – Musée d'histoire 296 ; BOSTON, Museum of Fine Arts 24, 60 ; BRUGES, Archives de la ville 4, 7, 8, 84 ; – Bibliothèque de la ville 163, 164 ; – Cathédrale Saint-Sauveur 120, 138, 241, 332 ; – Collection J. Taelman 94 A-B-C-D ; – Église Notre-Dame 318 ; – Groeningemuseum 122, 192, 244, 252, 253, 254, 293, 298, 306, 310 ; – Gruuthusemuseum 58, 62, 116, 149, 160, 210, 238 ; – Hôtel de ville 25 ; – Hôpital Saint-Jean 73, 249, 289, 290, 303, 306 ; – Hugo Maertens 4, 7, 8, 25, 73, 84, 86, 122, 147, 148, 157, 241, 249, 262, 289, 290, 302, 305, 310 ; – Société archéologique 94 E-F-G-H-I-K-L ; – Société européenne de numismatique 94 J ; BRUSSELS, A.C.L., 43, 45, 46, 55, 65, 128, 170, 213, 301, 311 ; – Archives générales du Royaume 9, 117, 198 ; – Bibliothèque Royale frontispice, 5, 6, 13, 22, 26, 88, 89, 95, 98, 110, 124, 127, 142, 155, 201, 207, 212, 215, 220, 225, 232, 234, 239, 269, 273, 274, 277, 307, 308, 329 ; – Musées royaux d'Art et d'Histoire 319 ; – Musées royaux des Beaux-Arts 197, 300 ; – Nels-Thill 257, 302 ; – J.-J. Rousseau 107 ; CHANTILLY, Musée Condé 208, 272, 327 ; CHICAGO, The Art Institute 294 ; CLEVELAND (OHIO), The Cleveland Museum of Art 77 ; COLOGNE, Historisches Archiv 83 ; KOPENHAGEN, Rigsarkivet 150 ; KORTRIJK, Eglise Notre-Dame 257 ; DETROIT, The Detroit Institute of Arts 159 ; DIJON, Fasquel 131, 258, 296 ; – Musée des Beaux-Arts 101, 167, 173, 183, 206, 259, 260, 328 ; DUSSELDORF, Hauptstaatsarchiv 205 ; EDINBURG, National Gallery of Scotland 85 ; ENSCHEDE, Rijksmuseum Twenthe 132 ; FLORENCE, Photo Scala 67, 297, 330 ; FURNES, Hôtel de ville 147, 148 ; GAASBEEK, Château-Musée 236 ; GHENT, Kathedraal 86, 91, 133, 145, 169 ; – Universiteitsbibliotheek 111, 161, 162, 292, 303 ; – L. De Rammelaere 11, 51, 93, 221 ; – Musée de la Byloke 11, 51, 93, 130, 221 ; – Studio Claerhout 130 ; GRUYERES, Musée Gruérien de Bulle 284 ; HAMBURG, Stabi 166 ; HASSELT Photo team 264 ; – 'S-HERTOGENBOSCH, Noordbrabants Museum 79 ; KASTERLEE, De Vroente 120, 154, 222, 320, 321, 322, 323 ; LEIDEN, Bibliothèque universitaire 202 ; LEIPZIG, Museum der Bildenden Künste 189 ; LONDON, British Museum 61, 75, 268 ; – The National Gallery 16, 74, 80, 109, 144, 243, 247, 298 ; – Victoria and Albert Museum (Crown copyright) 121, 286 ; – The Wallace Collection (reproduced by permission of the Trustees) 29 ; LEUVEN, Musées de la ville 27, 313, 314, 315, 316 ; – Photo Oosterlynck 266 ; LUGANO, Collection Thyssen-Bornemisza 179 ; LIEGE, Cathédrale Saint-Paul, 278 ; – Musée d'Art religieux et d'Art mosan, jacquette, 2, 49, 72 ; – Photo Mascart, jacquette, 2 ; – Université, Bibliothèque centrale 39, 40, 41, 42, 57, 70, 126 ; LILLE, Musée des Beaux-Arts 175 ; LUZERN, Zentralbibliothek 230 ; MADRID, Museo del Prado 48, 99, 226, 242 ; – Biblioteca Nacional 30 ; MALIBU, Hôtel de ville 223 ; MELBOURNE, National Gallery of Victoria 50 ; MINNEAPOLIS, The Minneapolis Institue of Arts 20 ; MUNICH, Alte Pinakothek 240, 245, 270, 304, 312, 325 ; – Bayerische Staatsbibliothek 12 ; NANCY, Musée historique lorrain 228 ; LA NEUVILLE, Musée 69 ; NEW YORK, The Metropolitan Museum of Art 21, 54, 71, 81, 90, 97, 288 ; – The Pierpont Morgan Library 250 ; NIMEGUE, Musée de la Commanderie de Saint-Jean 66 ; NORTHAMPTON (Mass.) Smith College Museum of Art, 251 ; OXFORD, Bodleian Library 199 ; PARIS, Bibliothèque Nationale 47, 100, 115, 178, 188, 224, 227, 267, 271, 279, 280, 309, 335 ; – Giraudon 105, 186, 187, 193, 194, 195, 200, 208, 272, 327 ; – R. Liot 156 ; – Musée du Louvre (Cliché Musées Nationaux) 64, 78, 92, 113, 180, 265, 287, 324 ; ROTTERDAM, Musée Boymans-van Beuningen 28, 63 ; SAINT-GERMAIN-EN-LAYE, Musée municipal 156 ; SCHONEWERD, Bally-Schumuseum 134, 135, 136 ; STRASBOURG, Musée des Beaux-Arts 146 ; TORUN, Archives de la ville 82 ; UTRECHT, Centraal Museum 68 ; VENICE, Biblioteca Nazionale Marciana 38, 152, 159, 333 ; – Photo Toso 38, 152, 159, 329 ; VERSAILLES, Musée (Cliché Musées Nationaux) 117, 256 ; VIENNA, Bildarchiv der Österreichische Nationalbibliothek 10, 17, 123, 171, 174, 185, 216, 263 ; – Kunsthistorisches Museum 76, 235, 275, 276 ; – Photo Meyer 76, 235, 275, 276 ; WASHINGTON, National Gallery of Art 246 ; WELLS-NEXT-THE-SEA, Norfolk, Holkham Estate Office 184 ; ZURICH, Schweizerisches Landesmuseum 196 ; – Zentralbibliothek 182.

Contents

Composed and printed by Maury Imprimeur S.A. at Malesherbes (France).
Binding by Boekbinderij Brandt at Weesp (The Netherlands).
Design by Louis Van den Eede.